The Self-Defense Forces
and
Postwar Politics in Japan

JAPAN LIBRARY

The Self-Defense Forces
and
Postwar Politics in Japan

Sado Akihiro

Translated by
Noda Makito

Japan Publishing Industry Foundation for Culture

The Self-Defense Forces and Postwar Politics in Japan
Sado Akihiro. Translated by Noda Makito.

Published by
Japan Publishing Industry Foundation for Culture (JPIC)
3-12-3 Kanda-Jinbocho, Chiyoda-ku, Tokyo 101-0051, Japan

First edition: March 2017

Originally published in Japanese language as *Sengo seiji to Jieitai* by Yoshikawa Kobunkan
Co., Ltd, in 2006. A completely new and original postscript was added by the author in
2017 to be included in the English version.

English publishing rights arranged with Yoshikawa Kobunkan Co., Ltd.

Jacket and cover design by Niizuma Hisanori
Front and cover photo:
JSDF members dispatched to Iraq in 2004 © Yomiuri Shimbun/Aflo

As this book is published primarily to be donated to overseas universities, research institutions, public libraries and other organizations, commercial publication rights are
available. For all enquiries regarding those rights, please contact the publisher of the
English edition at the following address: japanlibrary@jpic.or.jp

Printed in Japan
ISBN 978-4-916055-74-3
http://www.jpic.or.jp/japanlibrary/

Contents

Translator's Note to Readers

Initially, "National Defense Plan Outline" was used as the formal translation of "Boei Keikaku no Taiko"; later the government adopted "National Defense Plan Guidelines" as the official translation. Similarly, the translation of "Kibanteki Boeiryoku (Koso)" was changed from the "Basic Defense Force Concept" to the "Standard Defense Force Concept." Following the advice of the Ministry of Defense, this book uses the translations National Defense Plan Guidelines (NDPG) and Standard Defense Force Concept regardless of the year of their official adoption. Also, readers should be advised that this book follows the Japanese custom of listing the surname first, then the first name. It is, therefore, Yoshida Shigeru, for instance, instead of Shigeru Yoshida, the usage often found in western literature.

Author's Note to the English Edition

Today, Japan's security policy is undergoing the greatest transformation in its postwar history. This will be a change from the uniquely Japanese postwar pacifism that has made the Japanese evade anything military as much as possible to a new posture toward positive engagement in international security affairs that considers the use of military power ("defense capabilities" in Japanese jargon) a given. This transformation started gradually in the 1990s after the end of the cold war. It accelerated after the turn of the century when the Japan Self-Defense Forces (JSDF) participated in international anti-terrorist operations after the September 11, 2001, attacks in the United States and rapidly escalated further when the second Abe Shinzo cabinet was formed in 2012. It is predicted that, under the Abe cabinet's slogan "Proactive Contributor to Peace," the JSDF will play an increasingly important role in days to come.

This does not mean, however, that postwar pacifism has completely vanished from Japan. The criticisms heard from a wide range of people in Japan against the Abe cabinet's attempt at revising security policy—particularly the cabinet's positive attitude toward the exercise of the right of collective self-defense—attest to this. To begin with, the notion of postwar pacifism had come to be shared widely in Japan based on people's broad acceptance of the current Constitution, which renounces war and the possession of armed force. The constitutional renunciation derived from a sense of guilt in Japan about allowing the military to exercise arbitrary power before World War II and about the tremendous damage that Japan had inflicted on Asian countries, including China, during the war. As a result, an eccentric atmosphere held sway in Japan under which academics were discouraged from even discussing anything military and any journalist who advocated the JSDF or the expansion of defense capabilities was labeled as a hawk. Postwar pacifism is a powerful notion that was firmly embedded in postwar Japan.

It is under this kind of atmosphere that the JSDF was born and nurtured. There were many in Japan who opposed the establishment of the JSDF, which by all accounts looked like a military and was seen to have been formed despite the Constitution's renunciation of war and the possession of arms. Those were the days when members of the JSDF had to refrain from going out in uniform lest they be yelled at by citizens who regarded them as parasites on the taxpayers' money. In a 1958 essay, novelist Oe Kenzaburo, the 1994 Nobel laureate, called students taking the entrance examination of the National Defense Academy the "shame of their generation" and wrote that he wished to discourage all applicants to the academy.

This atmosphere lasted a long time. Postwar Japan experienced a prolonged period in which activists of citizens' movements enthusiastically carried out activities denouncing the JSDF, while a number of journalists wrote critical articles on the JSDF. Meanwhile, many politicians did not pay heed to security issues because those issues did not bring them votes, and the JSDF was put under the stringent oversight of the Defense Agency's bureaucrats. Those bureaucrats of the Defense Agency even interfered with the operations of JSDF troops, turning government-military relations in Japan into government-bureaucrats-military relations. Control of the uniformed team by civil officials emerged instead of civilian control.

From the more general perspective of the public, the JSDF has earned increasingly higher esteem as it continues to demonstrate its devotion not only to rescue and relief operations in a homeland infested with frequent earthquakes, typhoons, and other natural disasters but also to such scientific endeavors as the Antarctic observation. Thus, the percentage of people who support the presence of the JSDF has exceeded 60 percent since the 1960s. It should be noted, however, that this should be viewed as the support rate for the JSDF's disaster relief and other peacetime activities.

As a matter of fact, public opinion in Japan was without failure split whenever the JSDF was deployed to engage in military-related activities. The divide in public opinion was seen when Maritime Self-Defense Force minesweepers were dispatched to the Persian Gulf in 1991, when JSDF troops participated in the U.N. peacekeeping operations in Cambodia on the basis of the Act on Cooperation for United Nations Peacekeeping Operations and Other Operations enacted in 1992, and each time since 2001 that the JSDF has participated in anti-terrorist operations.

As Japan's security policy undergoes transformation, the role of the JSDF has become all the more important. The mode of government-military relations, which have been characterized by the control of the uniformed team by civil officials, is also changing due to the escalation of the mission and authority of the uniformed team (i.e., the JSDF). These evolutions and the changes in Japan's postwar security policies are difficult to understand even for the Japanese people. And, unfortunately, only a few documents are available on this issue in languages other than Japanese.

Today, when Japan's role and responsibility have become even more important because of the drastic changes in the international security environment, I believe it is extremely important for foreign readers to understand what kind of security policy Japan has pursued so far and what the JSDF is capable of. In this sense, I very much hope that the English translation and publication herewith of my book *Sengo seiji to Jieitai* (The Self-Defense Forces and Postwar Politics in Japan) as a volume in the Japan Library series of the Japan Publishing Industry Foundation for Culture will contribute to promote overseas understanding on the history of Japan's security policies.

Readers should be reminded that the Japanese original of the present volume was published in 2006. In the more than ten years since its publication, there have been remarkable changes in Japan's security policies. This is why I decided to add a completely new postscript to the English version in order to provide overseas readers with an overview of Japan's security policy after 2006. The appendix has also been updated to include more documents.

I am truly grateful that my work on the Japan Self-Defense Forces in the context of Japan's postwar politics is included in the Japan Library collection. I wish to take this opportunity to express my heartfelt gratitude to all of those who made the English translation and publication possible. It is my truest wish that this book can make a humble contribution to the promotion of overseas readers' understanding of Japan's security policy and the Self-Defense Forces.

Sado Akihiro
October 2016

Prologue

Military of a Nation that Renounces War

Characteristics of Japan's Postwar Politics

The year 2005 was the sixtieth anniversary of the end of World War II. Considered in Japan to mark the completion of the first cycle of one's life and the beginning of a new cycle, a person's sixtieth birthday is an opportune occasion to review the path one has traveled. It would seem, therefore, to be high time for Japan, too, to look back on the path it has taken since its defeat in the war.

Many of the systems that Japan constructed in the postwar days are said to be in need of reform. Nowadays, a review of the systems that have operated in Japan in the realms of politics, the economy, and society as a whole is under way.

In the course of this review, the issue of continuity/discontinuity between prewar and postwar days surfaces. This concerns the question of where—in which areas—prewar mechanisms have been greatly altered or, conversely, left essentially unchanged. Certainly, postwar Japan has been managed under the current Constitution, which is a completely different state system from that of prewar Japan under the Meiji Constitution. Yet seeing as though not all the leaders or legal systems in Japan were replaced after the war, it is only natural for some continuity from prewar days to be found in postwar institutions. This includes perceptions about how institutions should be managed. If continuity is indeed an issue, it should be particularly important to explore the range and degree of continuity and its implications.

Without a doubt the most outstanding change from prewar days pertains to policies concerning national security. Encountering an external threat in the form of the arrival of Commodore Matthew C. Perry's fleet in 1853, Japan underwent the Meiji Restoration and converted itself into a modern nation. It had since pursued a state that put heavy emphasis on national security, strengthening its military buildup under the slogan of "rich country, strong army." Ironically, though, it was arbitrary conduct by the military, the central institution of national security, which rushed prewar Japan into a quixotic war and resulted in the defeat that meant the devastation of the entire state system. During the occupation period after the war, Japan was guided by the U.S. decision to democratize and demilitarize Japan to adopt a democratic and nonmilitary path and enact a pacifist constitution that renounces possession of military forces. In other words, Japan underwent a 180-degree turn from a heavily militaristic state to a thoroughly pacifist nation.

Changes in the international environment, including intensification of the cold war, however, did not allow Japan to remain a nation without arms. Triggered by the eruption of the Korean War in 1950, a National Police Reserve was established in July and soon expanded to the National Safety Forces. The Japan Self-Defense Forces (JSDF), which was mandated to defend Japan against direct invasions, was formed in 1954. Since then, the JSDF has expanded its defense capabilities and grown into a world-class armed force. In 2004, it celebrated its fiftieth anniversary.

It should be noted that the JSDF's path of development has not always been smooth. The JSDF has had to experience the pain of growth under the huge constraint of a pacifist constitution. Occasionally, even the legality of the JSDF's very existence was questioned. When Japan regained its independence from the occupation forces in 1951, the Japanese government decided to make the security arrangements with the United States the lynchpin of its own security. This was tantamount to basically relying on the United States for Japan's defense. Against this backdrop, the newly established JSDF had to explore what role it should play within the framework of the security arrangements with the United States. And it must be pointed out here that Japan's postwar politics has hardly exercised any initiative in this soul-searching exploration.

Naturally, national security is one of the most important issues for a nation state, and in today's world the military still plays a central role in any nation's security. Armed forces are the state's organ for attending to military affairs, and the strongest force for organized violence. As such, one of the most important political issues for a government is to decide where to place the military in the state apparatus. In postwar Japan, under the pacifist constitution and in the face of the nation-wide aversion to wars and anything military, the government has concentrated its attention on domestic affairs, leaving the critical issue of the nation's security up to the security arrangements with the United States. To put it differently, it has been the main characteristic of postwar Japanese politics to avoid dealing with military-related affairs as much as possible. And politicians have tried to prevent national defense from becoming a political issue. Thus, a mood that it is utterly unthinkable to use the JSDF for purposes other than disaster relief and civic cooperation is firmly embedded in Japan.

The Hard-to-See JSDF
The situation, however, has changed drastically since the end of the cold war, as evidenced by the results of the January 2003 public survey conducted by the Cabinet Office. Against the backdrop of such newly emerged issues as the nuclear threat from North Korea, an unstable Middle East, and cross-border terrorist attacks, as symbolized by the September 11, 2001, World Trade Center incident, Japanese are feeling a heightened sense of crisis (see fig. 1). People's interest in the JSDF is also on the rise, as shown by figure 2. People's attitude toward the JSDF has grown more favorable, partly thanks to a series of successful international cooperation efforts by the JSDF after the end of the cold war (fig. 3). Moreover, the proportion of survey respondents in favor of an expansion of the JSDF's military capabilities roughly doubled in recent years from that of the immediate post–cold war days (fig. 4). This is an interesting contrast to the rather low and even

Figure 1. Risk of Japan Being Involved in a War

(All charts are based on the Cabinet Office's Public Opinion Survey, January 2003.)

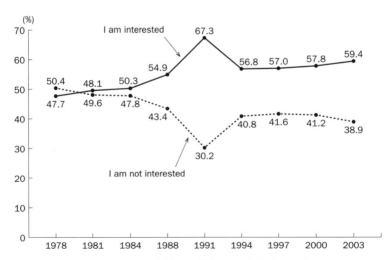

Figure 2. Interest in the JSDF and National Defense Issues

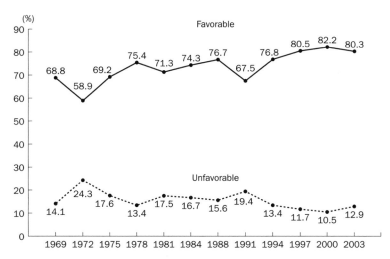

Figure 3. Overall Impression of the JSDF

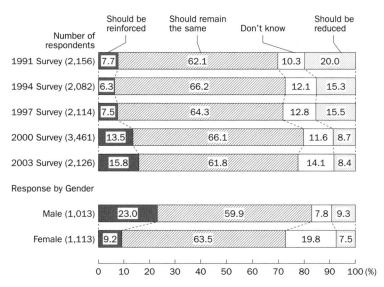

Figure 4. Defense Capabilities of the JSDF

annually declining willingness among respondents to defend the country (fig. 5). The proportion of respondents who intend to cooperate with the JSDF one way or another in the event of a foreign invasion, however, has been increasing (fig. 6). These apparently contradictory responses can be interpreted as the Japanese people's aversion to taking up arms to defend the country, long instilled by the thorough pacifism of postwar days, coexisting together with their expectations of the JSDF, to which they are willing to render cooperation. It seems beyond doubt, therefore, that the JSDF has succeeded in gaining the Japanese people's trust.

Survey results also show that the reality of the JSDF still remains obscure to outsiders and there is a persistent perception that the JSDF is closed to the outside (fig. 7). Perhaps reflecting the heightened sense of crisis among the Japanese, people have become more interested in knowing the concrete substance of Japan's defense policy (fig. 8), which exposes the fact that the substance of Japan's defense policy actually remains relatively unknown. The Japanese people's basic perceptions of the JSDF can be summarized as follows: the JSDF is an organization that the Japanese people count on and trust but which is largely closed to the outside world and, therefore, remains unfathomable. There is no knowing specifically how it is going to defend Japan, either. And this perception is a result of Japan's postwar politics, which has treated anything to do with defense or military affairs as some kind of taboo and tried to keep the JSDF's presence invisible to people as much as possible, except for disaster relief and civic cooperation activities such as at the time of the Olympic Games. The Japanese government, which has kept national defense issues at arm's length and not actively wrestled with them, is to blame for the fact that people in Japan are unfamiliar with the substance of the country's defense policies.

Structure of This Book
How, then, was the JSDF established, and how did it evolve to its present state? What kinds of defense policies have been devised in postwar Japan? The basic mission of this book is to clarify how the JSDF grew

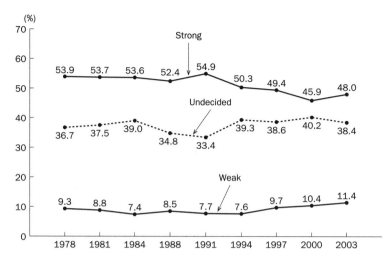

Figure 5. Enthusiasm for Defending the Country

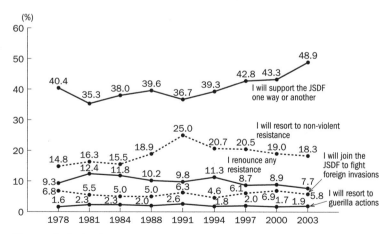

Figure 6. Attitude toward Foreign Invasions

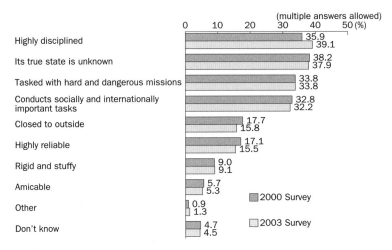

Figure 7. Impression of the JSDF (multiple answers allowed)

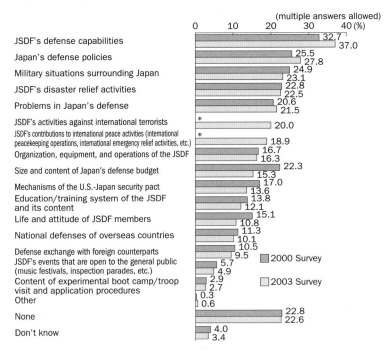

Figure 8. What I'd Like to Learn More about the JSDF and Japan's Defense (multiple answers allowed)

to its present state against the backdrop of postwar politics that considered military-related affairs a taboo. To accomplish this mission, let us begin with an exploration of the JSDF's position in Japan's postwar politics.

Having learned a lesson from the arbitrary conduct of the military in prewar days, the Japanese government has placed the JSDF under strict civilian control. This civilian control in the Japanese context is characterized as "negative civilian control" or "negative control" in which any military element is treated negatively. Simply put, it is a mechanism to minimize the use of the JSDF and make it as difficult as possible for a military organization to act. The mechanism consists of the following two constraints: (a) the institutional and organizational constraint symbolized by the term *bunkan tosei* (control by civil officials) and (b) the fiscal constraint on long-term planning in the form of the series of Defense Build-up Plans. Under these two constraints, the military organization is subjected to strict control. Moreover, the issue of defense itself has been given only low priority in the agenda of policy makers. The present author intends to explore how postwar politics in Japan has treated the JSDF in the context of these two constraints.

This book is divided into four parts. Part one, "Beginning of the Rearmament of Japan," briefly reviews the history from Japan's defeat in the war through the founding of the JSDF. "The Birth and Growth of the JSDF," part two, outlines the history of the JSDF from its founding through the late 1970s when the distinctively Japanese defense policy system called the National Defense Program Guidelines was first adopted. This section mainly discusses how, over the course of the transformation from the National Police Reserve to the National Safety Forces and, eventually, the Japan Self-Defense Forces, control by civil officials was established between the JSDF and the Defense Agency (present-day Ministry of Defense), what the significance of the Defense Build-up Plan system is, and why the National Defense Program Guidelines system came to be adopted.

Part three, "During the Second Cold War," covers the period up to the end of the cold war. Following the Guidelines for Japan-U.S. Defense Cooperation, which was adopted around the same time as the National Defense Program Guidelines, Japan "fought" the cold war as a prominent ally of the United States within the framework of bilateral security cooperation. Thus emerged a situation in Japan where two different defense doctrines were instituted simultaneously.

As a matter of fact, perceptions about the role of the JSDF under the U.S.-Japan security cooperation regime roughly fall into two camps. One line of thinking supports expanding Japan's self-reliance concerning the country's defense, while the other line of thinking supports increasing reliance on the U.S.-Japan security cooperation. The former line of thinking, known as the autonomous defense argument, advocates expanding the role of the JSDF. According to the latter line of thinking, the role of the JSDF should be reduced. As the JSDF's role expands so would the role and responsibility of military professionals (the so-called uniformed team). If, however, the path for greater reliance on the U.S.-Japan security cooperation is chosen, the very raison d'etre of the JSDF will be called into question. Thus, what role should be given to the JSDF in the overall framework of the security arrangements with the United States has been a salient issue since the establishment of the JSDF.

The National Defense Program Guidelines was originally formulated on the premise that Japan would become more self-reliant in the country's defense. In contrast, the Guidelines for Japan-U.S. Defense Cooperation placed U.S.-Japan security cooperation at the heart of Japan's defense. Section three reviews how, of these two different directions, Japan has chosen the direction that would deepen its reliance on the U.S.-Japan security alliance.

Part four, "The JSDF and the End of the Cold War," covers the period from the end of the cold war in 1989 to the present. Although it was expected that the role of the U.S.-Japan security regime itself would be reviewed once the cold war ended, post–cold war confusion in the international order, particularly the instability of East Asia, led to further strengthening of the bilateral security cooperation and, at the same time, expansion of the role of the JSDF. Over the course of time, the National Defense Program Guidelines was revised twice. In what way, then, and how much has the position of the military in Japan's politics changed, as the role of the JSDF expanded? This section tries to find an answer to this question by analyzing the contents of the two revisions of the National Defense Program Guidelines.

Part I

Beginning of the Rearmament of Japan

Chapter 1

Does Establishment of the National Police Reserve Constitute the Rearmament of Japan?

Dissolution of the Imperial Army/Navy and Former Military Personnel

Japan accepted the Potsdam Declaration and surrendered to the Allied powers in August 1945. Accordingly, the Imperial Japanese Army and Navy, which had once prided themselves on their mightiness, were disarmed. The United States, the central figure in the occupation of Japan, had been determined to promote the democratization and demilitarization of Japan as the foundation of its occupation policies. As a result, the Imperial Japanese Army and Navy were dissolved except for small numbers of personnel and equipment engaged mainly in demobilization and minesweeping operations. When the new Constitution was enacted in November 1946, under which Japan forever renounced war, the country started down its postwar path under the conditions of strict disarmament and thorough pacifism. From that time until the Police Reserve Act was promulgated and put into effect on August 10, 1950, no domestic military organization to defend Japan existed.

While disarmament of the military of a war-defeated country is a matter of course, it had not been decided from the beginning that Japan would renounce military armaments for the long-term future. The basic right of a sovereign country to rebuild its military in due time even if it is temporarily disarmed after defeat in a war is internationally recognized. Naturally, from the very day of surrender, former generals and officers of the now dissolved Imperial Army and Navy, too, had been contemplating how and what type of military Japan should rebuild. These former army and navy personnel held differing opinions on the involvement of former military personnel in rearmament as well as what military organizations to rebuild. Because these differences later came to play a significant role, let us start this chapter with an exploration of the conduct of former military personnel in the immediate postwar days.

First, how did former Imperial Japanese Army people behave? In prewar days, the Imperial Japanese Army was the leading player in what was called the domination of politics by the military. After the defeat, however, most of the army's leading figures disappeared from the center stage of politics—either because of suicide, death in battle, or arrest as war criminals. The effect on the former army both in terms of its organization as well as the solidarity among its members was devastating. While many ideas were discussed concerning the proposition to preserve a body of the armed forces as the nucleus of a future army—including preserving the Imperial Guard, forming new troops to guard the Imperial Palace, and including former military police members in an expanded police force—all were turned down by the Supreme Commander for the Allied Powers (popularly known as the GHQ). Thus, the former Imperial Japanese Army failed to pool the human resources or retain the traditions necessary to rebuild an army in the future.

As for former army officers, only a handful of former generals and field-grade officers remained active as GHQ liaisons, compilers of history related to General Douglas MacArthur, or advisors to Prime Minister Yoshida Shigeru. Moreover, these former army generals/officers were divided into several separate groups among which there hardly was any communication or liaison, making their activities unorganized and isolated from each other. Among these groups, the one centered around former Colonel Hattori Takushiro and backed up by Major General Charles Willoughby, chief of intelligence on General MacArthur's staff (the so-called G2), showed interest in actively engaging in the rearmament of Japan. For instance, as discussed in detail later, when the National Police Reserve was founded in 1950, Hattori's group acted vigorously to enable its members to assume leading positions in this new organization.

Let us turn our attention now to the former Imperial Japanese Navy. It goes without saying that a navy is tantamount to naught without warships. And a warship is an aggregate of highly sophisticated science and technology, requiring superior skills and extreme discipline to operate it, not to mention a fleet of ships. Therefore, in order to rebuild the navy in the future, it was more imperative for the former Imperial Navy to pass on its skills and traditions than was the case for the army. From this viewpoint, it was fortunate that some former Imperial Navy personnel as well as vessels were recruited not only to transport the demobilized troops back from the Chinese continent and the Southeast Asia/Pacific regions but also to engage in minesweeping activities in seas around mainland Japan, which had been infested with innumerable sea mines. The minesweeping activities were eventually taken on by the Maritime Safety Agency, which was founded in 1948. Even though minesweeping was a small-scale operation, it provided an opportunity for participating former Imperial Navy personnel to pass on their expertise, skills, and knowledge to next generations. Some former navy personnel joined the newly established Maritime Self-Defense Force (MSDF), formed in 1954, after participating in the minesweeping operations, and some of them rose all the way to chief of staff, the highest position at the MSDF.

Belonging to a somewhat smaller establishment than the Imperial Japanese Army, veterans of the former Imperial Navy were able to maintain solid cohesion even after the end of the war. It was Vice Admiral Hoshina Zenshiro, former director of the Navy Ministry of Japan's Bureau of Naval Affairs at the end of the war, who actively took initiative in the rebuilding of the navy. Hoshina gathered former captains and commanders who had served in the Navy Ministry as division chiefs around Admiral Nomura Kichisaburo, former foreign minister and Japanese ambassador to the United States who had numerous friends and acquaintances in the U.S. Navy. In such a way (we'll look at the details later), the former Imperial Navy was able to act more cohesively than the former Imperial Army in the period immediately following the war.

Postwar Reconstruction and the Yoshida Doctrine

It was the GHQ's demilitarization policy that had the greatest impact on the rearmament debate in the early stages. As discussed earlier, disarmament following defeat in a war does not automatically lead to the renouncing of war or demilitarization. In fact, even Japan was temporarily

Yoshida Shigeru (Source: Yoshikawa Kobunkan)

disarmed, and people in Japan believed that the country would naturally rearm itself as the peace treaty was signed to end the occupation. Yet a new constitution was promulgated that renounced war eternally. This was the result of the thorough democratization and demilitarization—to the extent of idealism—imposed by the GHQ in the early stage of the occupation. Undoubtedly, the Japanese people, particularly the mass media and intellectuals, were favorably disposed toward this pacifism manifested by the new Constitution as the basic path that postwar Japan should pursue. While today the interpretation that, even under a constitution that renounces war and armed forces, Japan has an inherent right to self-defense as a sovereign nation is prevailing, when the new Constitution was promulgated, even the right to self-defense was subject to debate. It is beyond doubt that enactment of such a constitution became a great barrier to Japan's rearmament.

Aside from the rearmament issue, the issue that was of utmost importance for postwar Japan was restoration of the national land and economy, which had been devastated by the war, and accomplishment of independence from the occupation. It was Yoshida Shigeru that took leadership in coping with the political turmoil immediately following the defeat and pursuing goals of postwar reconstruction and early independence. From the time that Yoshida formed his second cabinet in October 1948, backed up by MacArthur, until his fifth cabinet stepped down en masse in 1954, Yoshida remained at the center of Japanese politics as prime minister. And it was "top priority to economic recovery and rejection of rearmament" that remained Yoshida's basic stance in pursuit of postwar restoration and independence. As the National Police Reserve was established and then became the National Security Forces and, eventually, the JSDF, however, Yoshida's stance converted to "top priority to economic recovery with light armament." This stance became known as the Yoshida Doctrine. Simply put, it was a policy to give top priority to economic reconstruction, forgoing the highly costly reinforcement of defense capabilities by heavily relying on security arrangements with the United States for the country's security. Yoshida was convinced that international trade should be the main engine of development for postwar Japan.

A former diplomat, Yoshida was elected president of the Jiyuto, —pinch-hitting for Hatoyama Ichiro who had been purged by the GHQ—to become prime minister. Because he had had no power base in political parties, he promoted ex-bureaucrat legislators and nurtured them as his entourage. This was what later came to be known as the Yoshida School. "Graduates" from this powerful presence in postwar politics included Ikeda Hayato and Sato Eisaku. Both Ikeda and Sato, who later became prime ministers themselves in the 1960s, were regarded as being among the mainstream of the conservatives, which emphasized relations with the United States. When the Jiyuto and Nihon Minshuto parties merged into the Liberal Democratic Party (LDP), Ikeda and Sato succeeded in securing the support of the majority of the new party. Both of them also became loyal successors of the "top priority to economic recovery with light armament" policy that had been advocated by Yoshida. In other words, Yoshida laid the groundwork for the policy to give top priority to economic development and minimize military expenditure, and his successors, including Ikeda and Sato, consolidated the policy as the basic line of postwar conservative politics.

Undoubtedly, the Yoshida Doctrine was the right choice for war-devastated Japan. As we will discuss later, in the course of the deepening of cold war, the United States dropped its earlier goal of democratizing and demilitarizing Japan and, instead, started tena-ciously pressuring Japan toward rearmament and greater defense ca-pabilities. Yoshida, nevertheless, continued to refuse rearmament of Japan, citing its negative impact on economic reconstruction. This, however, does not mean that Yoshida believed that Japan should not rearm even after the signing of the peace treaty and independence. It is certain, in fact, that he was convinced that Japan as an independent sovereign nation had to rearm sometime in the future. Yoshida simply thought that rearmament was premature during his tenure as prime minister. When Japan accomplished recovery and entered the stage of economic growth, Yoshida preached the need for rearmament to his successors. In light of the prevalence for an aversion to war and the military among the Japanese people, Yoshida's successors, however, faithfully adhered to the Yoshida Doctrine and pursued further eco-nomic development.

Cold War and Its Impact
Even granting that the basic policy of "top priority to economic recov-ery with light armament" had been appropriate, there still remains the serious question of whether Japan's security was well assured after the peace treaty was signed and independence regained. And this ques-tion made relations with the United States all the more important.

In the beginning of the occupation, the U.S. government was firmly determined to impose thorough democratization and demili-tarization on Japan. Many of the American officials who joined the GHQ were idealistic individuals who had been under the influence of New Deal programs in the United States. It was under these circum-stances that Japan's new constitution was promulgated.

Meanwhile, on the international scene around that time, the cold war between the United States and the Soviet Union had already be-come prominent in as early as 1947. These changes in international relations affected U.S. policies toward Japan. In other words, U.S. policies shifted from preventing Japan from being a threat in East Asia again through democratization and demilitarization to actively assisting Japan's restoration so as to make the country an anti-communist ally in Asia.

It was under these circumstances that the rearmament of Japan began to be discussed back home in the United States. The GHQ, which was actually in charge of the occupation of Japan, was of the view that rearmament was not necessary. Behind the GHQ's judgment were such considerations as the apprehension on the part of neighboring Asian countries about Japan's rearmament; the contradiction to the initial U.S. policy of demilitarizing Japan; the Japanese people's own aversion to rearmament; and the insignificant military capabilities Japan would have even if it chose to rearm. But most of all, General Douglas MacArthur, supreme commander for the Allied powers, was himself adamantly against Japan's rearmament. As dean of the U.S. Army and a hero of the Pacific War, MacArthur wielded formidable influence on the U.S. government. Thus, even though Washington wanted Japan to be a partner in a joint anti-communist front, it could not ignore MacArthur's opinion.

While the U.S. government wished to expedite the signing of the peace treaty and Japan's independence so as to that much sooner strengthen its relations with an independent Japan, it also began requesting that Japan rearm so that it could defend itself after independence. On the other side of the Pacific, Prime Minister Yoshida continued to reject the U.S. demand for Japan's rearmament with the backing of MacArthur. The GHQ's stance to reject Japan's rearmament continued for some time to come. When the National Police Reserve was founded at the time of the Korean War, this stance of the GHQ led to its indecisiveness about the nature of the newly established institution—that is, whether it was to be a clearly military organization or merely a reinforced police force. As a result, an institution with an obscure nature was born.

Even as the Japanese government and the GHQ opposed the rearmament of Japan, they agreed on the need to strengthen the police force as a public safety measure. Public order in Japan had deteriorated owing to the defeat in the war and the GHQ's democratization policies, and frequent labor disputes escalated public unrest. Illegal activities by the Japanese Communist Party and other entities also became rampant against the backdrop of a deepening cold war and the civil war in China that ended with the victory of the Communist Party of China. In the case of Japan, it can be said that intensification of the cold war manifested itself as further deterioration of domestic public order. This phenomenon of the cold war manifesting as a domestic public order problem continued for quite some time longer, and it became a unique feature of Japan's security issue. In any event, in those days, the police force in Japan had undergone significant reforms, including dissolution of the Home Ministry (a cabinet-level ministry that had managed the internal affairs of the Empire of Japan, including the police) by the GHQ and division of the police force into national police and municipal police. These and other reforms, contrary to initial intentions, resulted in a weakening of police capabilities. Thus, strengthening the police force was a major concern in those days. And it was the eruption of the Korean War that made addressing this issue all the more urgent and salient.

Establishment of the National Police Reserve
The Korean War erupted on June 25, 1950, with tremendous impact on Japan's rearmament controversy. When the U.S. and South Korean forces were cornered to Busan by North Korean offensives, U.S. forces stationed in Japan were mobilized to assist them. Because the U.S. forces stationed in Japan had been, a backing to support Japan's defense and the maintenance of public order, their absence would leave Japan powerless in the face of a crisis. It was considered that such a military vacuum in Japan, if left unattended, could put the country in danger of a direct, external invasion and/or an indirect invasion (taking advantage of social unrest and confusion to engineer a revolution).

Thus, on July 8, 1950, General MacArthur sent a letter to Prime Minister Yoshida instructing him to establish a 75,000-strong National Police Reserve and to reinforce the Maritime Safety Agency by 8,000 new recruits in order to supplement police and maritime safety capabilities. In response, the Yoshida government on August 10 promulgated a cabinet ordinance on the National Police Reserve as a so-called Potsdam Order requiring no Diet approval. The cabinet ordinance was enacted immediately. Thus was launched the National Police Reserve.

This incident is commonly regarded as the beginning of the rearmament of Japan. We shall examine important issues related to the National Police Reserve, including this common view, in the following paragraphs.

National Police Reserve (Source: Yoshikawa Kobunkan)

First and foremost is the fact that the National Police Reserve was founded under the GHQ's initiative. From the Japanese government's side, the order from General MacArthur to establish this organization appeared totally out of the blue. Being at a loss about what kind of organization it was requested to establish, the government simply followed the GHQ's instructions. Once the National Police Reserve was established, the GHQ organized a board of advisors to instruct the Japanese side on the specifics of its order.

Second, it was ex-bureaucrats of the former Home Ministry's Police Bureau who actually took charge of organizing the National Police Reserve. These ex-bureaucrats assumed that the new organization should emulate a police organization. The National Police Reserve ordinance specified the task of the new organization as "acting on the prime minister's order when a special need arises for maintenance of public order" and limited its activities to "the range of ordinary police missions." Thus, the nature of the National Police Reserve, which was more akin to a police force than a military force, was deeply influenced by these stipulations in the ordinance and by the ex-bureaucrats of the former Home Ministry's Police Bureau. Also influential in determining the nature of the National Police Reserve were constraints on the GHQ to establish an organization that did not go against the Constitution—even though the GHQ had envisioned that the National Police Reserve should be the foundation of a future Japanese army. Thus, even though the National Police Reserve was a military organization in terms of its composition and equipment, which was modeled after the U.S. Army, legally it was defined as a police force. All of this gave the National Police Reserve a highly obscure presence.

The National Police Reserve consisted of 75,000 troops and 100 administrative staff members. Ex-bureaucrats of the former Home Ministry's Police Bureau occupied key positions and seized leadership of the newly founded organization. The position of superintendent-general, or commander-in-chief of the National Police Reserve, was assumed by Hayashi Keizo, a former bureaucrat of the Home Ministry who later became the first chairman of the Joint Staff Council of the JSDF. Hayashi's appointment heralded the long stretch of strong influence that ex–Home Ministry bureaucrats came to wield in the Defense Agency until the 1970s. At first, appointments of these ex-bureaucrats were intended to exclude veterans of the former Imperial Army/Navy as much as possible from the National Police Reserve. Over time, former imperial military members were recruited out of necessity to manage the troops. The ex–Home Ministry bureaucrats paid close attention to thoroughly blocking any influence by former Imperial Army/Navy veterans from affecting the National Police Reserve.

In this sense, the attempt by Hattori Takushiro and others who had been in leadership positions in the former Imperial Army to participate in the National Police Reserve had a lasting impact. The instigator of this attempt was Major General Charles Willoughby, who had taken the side of the military National Police Reserve advocates in the intra-GHQ arguments. Willoughby engineered to recruit former members of the Imperial Japanese Army as senior officials of the National Police Reserve so as to let them command and train National Police Reserve recruits. While this attempt was crippled by a complaint from Prime Minister Yoshida to General MacArthur, it stirred strong anxiety among police bureaucrats in leading positions within the National Police Reserve; they feared that former military personnel could come in and turn the National Police Reserve into an organization resembling the former Imperial Army at any time. It was this anxiety that made ex–Home Ministry bureaucrats firmly determined to suppress the power of the uniformed team (uniformed officers and soldiers) as much as possible lest the National Police Reserve should become a military organization like the former Imperial Army. Because Hattori's group continued to exhibit dubious behavior—including approaching Hatoyama Ichiro, who was anti Yoshida—resurrection of the influence of former Imperial Army elements remained a very worrisome possibility for the police bureaucrats who formed the core of civil officers within the National Police Reserve, then the National Safety Forces, and next the JSDF.

And it was the notion of civilian control that became the theoretical pillar that allowed police bureaucrats to suppress the rise of the uniformed team. Civilian control was a new concept that had not existed during the time of the Imperial Army. At first, the Japanese side had a hard time understanding the explanation of this idea provided by the U.S. side. Nevertheless, civil officers, in time, learned to use it as the basic premise when they established the National Safety Forces and the JSDF.

One point of reference that those civil officers relied on when they applied the concept of civilian control was American political scientist/sociologist Harold Lasswell. Author of the treatise "The Garrison State," Lasswell argued that men in uniform had a stronger predilection for fighting a war than civilians did. Lasswell warned about the danger of a free country becoming militarized (or, in his terminology, a garrison state). Because it was reputed that Japan in 1937 had been closest to what Lasswell called a garrison state, his theory was readily acceptable to the bureaucrats of the internal bureau who had experienced the arbitrary conduct of the military and the resultant war. Today, Lasswell is criticized for excessively overrating the role of the military. But it is significant that his theory functioned to support the theoretical pillar of civilian control that the internal bureau's bureaucrats used to suppress the uniformed team.

Chapter 2

From National Safety Forces to Japan Self-Defense Forces

Treaty of Peace with Japan and the U.S.-Japan Security Treaty

The goal of Japan under occupational rule was to attain both independence and economic recovery. As introduced in the previous chapter, Prime Minister Yoshida Shigeru applied a principle of "top priority to economic recovery and rejection of rearmament" to his negotiations for a peace treaty with the United States. This principle, however, would leave unaddressed the crucial issue of how to assure Japan's security when it regained independence without military power. Yoshida was not a naive idealist who believed that unarmed neutrality would ensure a country's security. What Yoshida decided to rely on as a means for security was the U.S. defense of Japan by means of bilateral security cooperation.

Yoshida was not the only one to face the issue of how to guarantee Japan's security under a constitution that renounces possession of a military. During the occupation period—a time in which constitutional reform was utterly impossible—many discussions were held about security in Japan after the country had signed a peace treaty and regained independence. Prominent among them was the argument of Ashida Hitoshi, foreign minister of the Katayama Tetsu cabinet who later became prime minister himself. Ashida argued that in the event of an emergency, the U.S. military should be deployed to Japan to defend it. This scenario, in a way, could be regarded as a prototype of the security arrangements with the United States. Whereas Ashida argued for the stationing of U.S. troops in Japan during an emergency, the U.S.-Japan Security Treaty that Yoshida actually concluded with the United States called for the permanent stationing of U.S. troops in Japan. Thus, it was decided that Japan should pursue the path of economic reconstruction and basically rely on the United States for defense of the country.

In the end, Japan achieved its return to the international community by simultaneously concluding the Treaty of Peace with Japan (Treaty of San Francisco) and the U.S.-Japan Security Treaty. What is noteworthy here is the basic nature of the U.S.-Japan security pact, which was essentially a swap of military bases for soldiers. In other words, Japan renounced possession of the military capabilities to defend itself and requested the United States to defend it. In return for the U.S. commitment to Japan's defense, Japan became obliged to offer military bases to the U.S. forces within Japan. This meant that the U.S. military, an occupation force that was supposed to depart after the peace treaty was signed and independence regained, would continue to be stationed in Japan as stipulated by the U.S.-Japan Security Treaty.

In the eyes of the Japanese people, who had been looking forward to living free from the occupation forces, this continued stationing in Japan of U.S. forces appeared to be a perpetuation of the occupation. At that time, the Korean War had not yet ended, and the Japanese people were exposed to an increasing number of crimes committed by American soldiers returning from the battlefield. Also, some citizens living near the military bases suffered from the expansion of training fields for the U.S. troops. These incidents provoked people's nationalistic sentiment, resulting in a chain of anti–U.S. base activities in various locations. Examples are local protests against American bases in Uchinada (Ishikawa prefecture), which grew fiercer after 1953; the Sunagawa Struggle (Tachikawa, Tokyo) that started in 1955; and the strong outcry over the January 1957 killing of a Japanese housewife by an American serviceman (Girard Incident in Gunma prefecture). Along with the anti–nuclear test movements triggered by the contamination of the Japanese fishing boat *Daigo Fukuryu Maru* by the nucle-

Table 1. Trends in U.S. Bases in Japan

Year	Total number of troops	Army	Navy	Air Force	Number of military bases	Space in square meters	Number of arrests made	Remarks
1952	260,000	—	—	—	2,824	1,352,636	1,431	Enactment of Peace Treaty with Japan
1953	250,000	—	—	—	1,282	1,341,301	4,152	Protests in Uchinada getting fiercer
1954	210,000	—	—	—	728	1,299,927	6,215	
1955	150,000	—	—	—	658	1,296,364	6,952	
1956	117,000	—	—	—	565	1,121,225	7,326	Sunagawa Incident Prime Minister Kishi–President Eisenhower talk
1957	77,000	17,000	20,000	40,000	457	1,005,390	5,173	Girard Incident
1958	65,000	10,000	18,000	37,000	368	660,528	3,329	
1959	58,000	6,000	17,000	35,000	272	494,693	2,578	
1960	46,000	5,000	14,000	27,000	241	335,204	2,005	U.S.-Japan Security Treaty revised
1961	45,000	6,000	14,000	25,000	187	311,751	1,766	
1962	45,000	6,000	13,000	26,000	164	305,152	1,993	
1963	46,000	6,000	14,000	26,000	163	307,898	1,782	
1964	46,000	6,000	14,000	26,000	159	305,864	1,658	Olympic Games in Tokyo
1965	40,000	6,000	13,000	21,000	148	306,824	1,376	Vietnam War becomes full-scale war
1966	34,700	4,600	12,000	18,100	142	304,632	1,350	
1967	39,300	8,300	11,400	19,600	140	305,443	1,119	

Notes: 1. The base month differs year by year; figures in the table should be interpreted as round figures for each year.
2. Number of troops is taken from *Anpo kanren shiryoshu* [Reference materials related to the U.S.-Japan Security Treaty], number of U.S. bases and their square meters are from *Boei nenkan 88-nendoban* [Yearbook on national defense, 1988], and number of arrests are taken from *Anpo joyaku taisei-shi 3-kan* [History of U.S.-Japan security pact regime, vol. 3].

29

ar fallout from the U.S. test of a thermonuclear device on Bikini Atoll (1954), anti–U.S. military base and anti-U.S. movements were on the rise in Japan in the 1950s.

The peace treaty and independence allowed Japanese politicians who had been purged by the GHQ or arrested as war criminals to return to politics. Encouraged by this, anti-Yoshida conservative elements began to criticize what appeared to be Yoshida's lopsided devotion to the United States and argue for more independent foreign policy, a self-reliant defense, constitutional revision, and the rearmament of Japan. Leading figures in this faction included Hatoyama Ichiro, Ishibashi Tanzan, Kishi Nobusuke, Ashida Hitoshi, and Shigemitsu Mamoru. The first three later formed their own cabinets after Yoshida. It should be noted, however, that Hatoyama and Ishibashi had a different policy priority from Shigemitsu and Ashida (who together founded the Kaishinto political party). While Hatoyama and his associates put emphasis on constitutional revision, they had not formed a clear-cut stance toward the rearmament of Japan. In contrast, Ashida was of the view that Japan should own an explicitly military organization, and he came to play a major role in the future establishment of the Japan Self-Defense Forces (JSDF). In any event, the anti-Yoshida faction was united in its wish to eliminate U.S. forces and bases from Japan by having Japan possess its own military.

From National Police Reserve to National Security Forces
It should be noted here that the call for rearmament was not only heard within Japan. As introduced earlier, the United States repeatedly stressed the need for Japan's rearmament during its peace treaty negotiations with Japan. Given the condition of U.S.-Japan relations in those days, it can be said that the pressure for rearmament and greater defense capabilities from the United States was stronger than that from within Japan. Backed up by such U.S. pressure, Prime Minister Yoshida announced in the Diet in January 1952 that the National Police Reserve would be dissolved in October 1952 and replaced by a "defensive force." This defensive force later took the form of the National Security Forces. But the problem was that the basic stance of the

United States toward Japan's defensive capabilities and that of the Japanese government were far apart from one another.

One of the major factors behind this discrepancy was the increasing intensification of the Korean War and the threat of the Soviet military in the Far East. In the midst of these circumstances, General MacArthur, a powerful sympathizer and supporter of Yoshida's rejection of the U.S. demand for rearmament, was dismissed. Given this new situation, not only the U.S. government but also the U.S. forces stationed in Japan began to contemplate making the National Police Reserve more heavily armed and expanding its complements. Their proposition was to remake the 75,000-strong National Police Reserve (as of 1952) into a well-balanced force of 300,000 to 325,000 troops composed of 10 divisions. This was in total conflict with Yoshida's vision of, for the time being, pursuing economic recovery with as light armament as possible so that a military that suited Japan could be built up over the long run. In the midst of this conflict of views between the Japanese and American governments, the National Safety Agency Act was promulgated on July 31, 1952, to be enacted on August 1.

U.S. pressure on Japan to expand its defense capabilities continued even after the establishment of the National Safety Forces. Negotiations on this issue between the two governments ran into rough waters and became entangled with the U.S. proposition on the provision of military assistance to Japan: The United States wanted Japan to procure the necessary equipment under the Mutual Security Act (MSA). When Yoshida's special envoy, Ikeda Hayato, had a talk with Walter Robertson, assistant secretary of state for far eastern affairs, in October 1953, he presented a private proposal for a five-year plan for Japan's defense. The plan included expansion of the ground force to 180,000 strong in three years starting in 1954. Nevertheless, the two failed to strike a clear agreement. At the end of the talk, a joint statement was released announcing adoption of the Japanese proposal for a gradual increase of defense capabilities. This outcome left the U.S. side unsatisfied with the Japanese attitude toward the expansion of its defense capabilities, and it gave the Japanese the impression that Japan had committed to forming a ground force of 180,000 troops.

The fact of the matter is that Ikeda's private proposal for a five-year plan had been worked out by Ikeda and Ministry of Finance bureaucrats who were close to Ikeda. The National Safety Agency played no part in it. Moreover, the agency was not directly informed of the concrete contents of the Ikeda-Robertson talk, either. This episode goes to show that in the Yoshida government the expansion of defense capabilities was discussed not from the angle of necessity for Japan's defense but from the angle of extra budgetary expenditures, which is what the Ministry of Finance was concerned about.

The National Safety Agency, founded in August 1952, was, legally speaking, an organization for public safety and security. Directly dealing with foreign invasions was not among its prospective missions. In this sense, the National Safety Agency was no different from the National Police Reserve. The National Safety Agency's armed troops consisted of the National Safety Forces, a ground force whose missions were inherited from the National Police Reserve, and the Safety Security Force, successor of the Coastal Safety Force, of the Maritime Safety Agency. These organs later evolved into the Ground Self-Defense Force and the Maritime Self-Defense Force, respectively. Because these two forces followed different paths of evolution, however, their organizational structure was also different. In a nutshell, since the days of the National Police Reserve, the ground force had been developed as much as possible with the exclusion of influence from the former Imperial Japanese Army, while the former Imperial Japanese Navy played a significant role in developing the maritime defense force. How, then, was the maritime defense force founded?

The Maritime Safety Agency and the Y Committee

The seas around Japan after the war became a theater of vicious crimes including fish poaching, smuggling, and illegal immigration. Even piracy had become rampant, which was unthinkable when the Imperial Japanese Navy had been around. On top of these problems, the Korean peninsula experienced a cholera outbreak, which had to be stopped at border lest it should spread in Japan. Thus, the Maritime Safety Agency, which was mandated to improve maritime security around Japan, was established. Once established, the agency allowed former Imperial Navy personnel to participate heavily. Incorporating the aforementioned minesweeping team into the agency was one example. The appointments of Yamamoto Yoshio, former rear-admiral and the last director of the Navy Ministry's Bureau of Naval Affairs, and former Captain Oku Sanji as assistants to the agency's director-general as well as of former Captain Watanabe Yasuji to director of the Department of Vessel Management were other examples. Furthermore, General MacArthur issued a memorandum to the effect that less than 10,000 former Imperial Navy personnel could be employed by the agency. In the end, a total of 3,000 former Imperial Navy officers and seamen (1,000 officers and 2,000 commissioned officers and seamen) were hired. Because maritime security operations required high-level technical knowledge and skills, the GHQ had to permit the employment of former Imperial Navy personnel.

Thus, former Imperial Navy generals and senior officers flocked to carry out efforts toward rebuilding the navy. At their center were Yamamoto Yoshio; Nagasawa Hiroshi, director of the Second Demobilization Bureau and former director of Division One of the Naval Affairs Bureau; Yoshida Eizo, director of the Archives Division and former director of Division Two of the Naval Affairs Bureau; as well as aforementioned Admiral Nomura Kichisaburo, former foreign minister and Japanese ambassador to the United States, and Vice Admiral Hoshina Zenshiro, former director of the Navy Ministry's Bureau of Naval Affairs at the end of the war. One of the representative activities of those former navy men was establishment of the Study Group on Rebuilding the New Japanese Navy (Shin-Kaigun Saiken Kenkyukai), which they secretly founded on January 24, 1951. These former Imperial Navy men also actively engaged in making sure that former navy officers and seamen were employed by the newly established Maritime Safety Agency. They continued to exercise formidable influence over the agency's staff, many of which later became the core of the Maritime Self-Defense Force. And all of this was in stark contrast to the Imperial Army veterans, who had been divided and scattered into numerous groups among which no effective communication occurred. Even Colonel Hattori Takushiro's group, which aimed to be at the heart of the rearmament of Japan, hardly communicated with former army generals, confining its activities among former mid-level staff officers.

One remarkable characteristic of the former Imperial Navy group's rearmament plan was its emphasis on the importance of relations with the United States. This group was foresighted enough to make Nomura Kichisaburo, who had been well connected with the U.S. military, the center of its efforts. As a result, such U.S. Navy leaders as Vice Admiral Charles Turner Joy, Commander Naval Forces, Far East; Chief of Staff Ralph A. Ofstie; and Deputy Chief of Staff Arleigh A. Burke, who later assumed the highest post in the U.S. Navy, chief of naval operations, became powerful supporters of the efforts by Nomura, Hoshina, and their associates. As eloquently revealed in Nomura's remark to U.S. Secretary of State John Foster Dulles, who visited Japan for the peace treaty negotiations, that "the most important foundation is the U.S.-Japan military alliance," the Nomura group's emphasis on relations with the United States put the military alliance first. Moreover, when Hoshina briefed the Study Group on Rebuilding the New Japanese Navy plan to Arleigh Burke, one of the most outstanding Japan sympathizers in the U.S. Navy, he declared that the new Japanese navy would be "an object of cooperation with the United States Navy." Thus, Hoshina revealed that the group was planning to build a navy that, within the framework of the U.S.-Japan military alliance, could collaborate with the U.S. Navy. It is an important point to be kept in mind that these ideas were at the foundation of the establishment of today's Maritime Self-Defense Force.

The setting up of the so-called Y Committee within the Maritime Safety Agency clearly demonstrated the U.S. Navy's favorable attitude toward the rebuilding of the Japanese navy. Although the U.S. government communicated to the Japanese government in October 1951 that it would lend a total of 68 vessels to Japan, the organization on the Japanese side that would receive the vessels remained undetermined. Possible recipient organizations included the existing Maritime Safety

Agency, the Japanese navy to be rebuilt anew, or a newly established coast guard. A U.S.-Japan joint study committee was set up to decide which Japanese organization would be responsible for managing and operating the lent vessels. This joint committee was called the Y Committee. Before the end of World War II, the Japanese military used to abbreviate army as A, navy as B, and civilian as C; reading the alphabet in reverse made Y the navy.

At this Y Committee, which was composed of representatives of the Maritime Safety Agency and eight former Imperial Navy men including Yamamoto, Yoshida, and Nagasawa, members held fierce discussions on the position of the organization that was to be assigned to manage and operate vessels lent from the United States. Committee members from the Maritime Safety Agency opposed setting up a new organization that was envisioned to become independent from the agency in the future, because doing so could contribute to a resurrection of the old navy. They argued that lent vessels should be managed and operated by the agency. Ex–Imperial Navy members, however, had been determined to establish a "small navy" from the beginning.

It was the U.S. Naval Forces, Far East, that put an end to this unending argument. The U.S. Naval Forces, Far East supported the argument of the ex–Imperial Navy group and approved establishment of an organization that was expected to be separated from and independent from the agency in the future. Thus, on April 26, 1952, the Coastal Safety Force of the Maritime Safety Agency was established. Three months later, on August 1, the Coastal Safety Force was separated from the agency to become the Safety Security Force. The way for the rebuilding of the Japanese navy was, thus, paved by the collaboration between former Imperial Navy elements and the U.S. Navy.

Three-Party Agreement on the Founding of the Japan Self-Defense Forces

The Yoshida government managed to reject the U.S. demand for a significant expansion of Japan's defense capabilities by proposing, instead, a gradual increase in capabilities. However, in terms of domestic politics, the Yoshida government experienced hardship in the face of mounting criticism from the anti-Yoshida faction of what it saw as Yoshida's lopsided devotion to relations with the United States. In the general election in April following the dissolution of the House of Representatives in March 1953 (the so-called *bakayaro* dissolution), Yoshida's Jiyuto party saw its seats fall from 222 before the election to 199 after the election. It managed to remain the dominant party in the Diet, but it failed to win the majority. Even though Yoshida formed a minority cabinet, it was far from a stable government, forcing him to explore collaboration with Kaishinto, the number-two party.

At this point, the rearmament issue became a stumbling block to collaboration between the two parties. The Kaishinto's Ashida Hitoshi had aggressively argued for the self-initiated rearmament of Japan, and the party had already started exploring means to realize Japan's rearmament around Ashida's argument. As a matter of fact, when the Kaishinto was founded in February 1952, it had already adopted a party decision of "creation of a democratic defense force commensurate with Japan's national strength." In its fourth party convention in February 1953, the Kaishinto also adopted a "basic stance toward national defense," which included a policy to "set up an intra-party special committee to study a scheme for self-defense." Accordingly, the party set up a special committee on defense in July and appointed Ashida as its chairman. Since then, the Kaishinto had continued to actively address issues of rearmament and amendment of the National Safety Agency Act with its special committee on national defense as the central player.

The heads of the two parties, Yoshida and Shigemitsu, conducted talks on September 27, 1953, in order to nurture cooperative relations between the Jiyuto and the Kaishinto. Although the discrepancy of views between the two parties was large, in the end, they somehow succeeded in reaching an agreement on "drafting a long-term plan of expansion of defense capabilities commensurate with Japan's national strength to instantaneously respond to a gradual decrease in the occupation forces" and "reforming the Act on National Safety Agency and remaking the National Security Forces into Self-Defense Forces, for the time being, so that Japan can respond to direct invasions." Thus,

Japan had at this point started moving toward the establishment of the JSDF.

After the above Yoshida-Shigemitsu talk, three conservative parties (Jiyuto, Kaishinto, and Nippon Jiyuto) went into negotiations on revising the National Safety Agency Act and establishing the JSDF. The Kaishinto assumed leadership. Of the members of the Kaishinto, Ashida played a particularly important role in these negotiations. The Kaishinto had been of the view that rearmament was possible without revision of the Constitution, and with this conviction as the base, Ashida devoted his utmost efforts to establishing an organization with a clearly military nature that could respond to direct foreign invasions. The Jiyuto side resisted Ashida's argument in order to obscure the military nature of the new organization as much as possible. Lest it should be doubted as having changed its line toward rearmament, the Jiyuto instead wanted to establish a security force–like organization as an extension of the existing National Security Forces. The Jiyuto's argument was supported by civil officials who wished to protect the primacy of civil officials (or control by civil officials) that had been established within the National Security Forces in the face of a rise in the uniformed team's power.

Issues discussed during the three-party negotiation included (a) the position and composition of the National Defense Council; (b) missions of the JSDF; (c) promotion of the National Safety Agency to a ministry; (d) whether there should be both an act on the establishment of the Defense Agency and one on establishment of the JSDF; (e) the creation of a Joint Staff Council; and (f) restriction on qualifications for promotion to top positions in the internal bureau of the Defense Agency. Agreement was reached on all but the first issue on the basis of the Kaishinto's argument. It was agreed to discuss the organization and composition of the National Defense Council again, after the Defense Agency was actually established.

More concretely, it was agreed that responding to direct invasions was to be clearly included among the missions of the JSDF. This gave the JSDF two major missions—responding to direct invasions and maintaining internal security—that essentially made it the same as the military of other countries. While the issue of whether the National Safety Agency should be made a ministry was shelved for the time being, the Kaishinto's argument that separate acts on the establishment of the Defense Agency and the JSDF should be instituted was adopted. The National Safety Agency bureaucrats' argument that it was too premature to create a Joint Staff Council was rejected, and its establishment was agreed upon. Over the protestations of bureaucrats, it was agreed to suspend restrictions on the uniformed members to be promoted to top positions in the internal bureau of the Defense Agency.

In this way, agreement was reached among the three conservative parties to establish the JSDF with a clearly military nature and a stated main mission of repelling direct invasions.

What, then, happened to the primacy of civil officials over the uniformed team in the JSDF, which had been maintained in the National Police Reserve and the National Security Forces? Did suspension of the restriction on qualifications for promotion to top positions in the internal bureau of the Defense Agency affect this primacy of civil officials over the uniformed team? To come right to the conclusion, it did not. To begin with, immediately below the director-general of the National Safety Agency/Defense Agency were an internal bureau composed of the director-general's secretariat as well as various bureaus staffed by civil officials, on the one hand, and a staff office comprised of the uniformed team, on the other. These existed to assist the director-general. Article 10 of the National Safety Agency Act defined relations between these two assisting organs and stipulated the mandates of the director-general's secretariat and various bureaus staffed by civil officials as follows:

To assist the director-general in giving instructions to first and second chiefs of staff on drafting various policies of the National Safety Forces and the Safety Security Force as well as basic implementation plans. The director-general is mandated to determine basic policies on management and operations of the National Safety Forces and the Safety Security Force and to give instructions on these policies to first and second chiefs of staff, who will then produce their own policies and basic implementation plans based on these instructions. <u>The director-general's secretariat and various bureaus are responsible for producing these draft instructions of the director-general.</u> (underline added)

To put it another way, regarding the mandate of the director-general's secretariat and various bureaus, the system of primacy of civil officials was maintained by Article 10 of the National Safety Agency Act, which de facto superordinated the internal bureau over the uniformed team, and by Article 16, which excluded the uniformed team from the internal bureau by imposing restrictions on qualifications for promotion to top positions in the internal bureau.

Even when the restriction on qualifications for promotion to top positions in the internal bureau was lifted when the JSDF and the Defense Agency were established, civil officials of the internal bureau were still the ones to determine promotion to leadership positions. Thus, promotion from the uniformed team to key leadership positions in the internal bureau had actually never taken place. Moreover, the spirit of Article 10 of the National Safety Agency Act was succeeded by Article 20 of the Act for Establishment of the Defense Agency, which said that "The director-general's secretariat and all the bureau chiefs are mandated to assist the director-general to attend to the following tasks in their respective jurisdictions." Thus, in the end, the system of primacy of civil officials over the uniformed team was preserved even when the Defense Agency and the JSDF were founded.

Part II

The Birth and Growth of the JSDF

Chapter 3

The Defense Agency
and the JSDF

Establishment of the "Control by Civil Officials" System

The Defense Agency and the Ground/Maritime/Air Self-Defense Forces were launched in July 1954. With its origins in the National Police Reserve—a mere supplementary force to the police—a military organization mandated to respond to direct invasions from outside was now finally established in postwar Japan. In order to prevent a recurrence of the domination of politics by the military seen in prewar days, mobilization of the Japan Self-Defense Forces (JSDF) was put under strict legal control. For instance, even in the case of mobilization in response to a direct invasion, the prime minister must obtain approval from the National Diet either before or after the mobilization. In the case of public security operations carried out in response to an indirect invasion, the prime minister is required to obtain post facto approval from the Diet. Moreover, to prevent the uniformed team from behaving arbitrarily with the organizational principle, the civilian control principle that had been introduced at the time of the establishment of the National Police Reserve was also adopted by the newly founded Defense Agency. The problem is, however, that what was established as civilian control in Japan's context at that time was more "control by powerful civil officials (officials of the inner bureau)" than the "control by civilians" that is prevalent in western countries. Allow me to dwell on this point a little more.

Figure 9 is an organizational chart of the Defense Agency and the

JSDF when they were founded. As discussed in the previous chapter, the restriction on qualifications for promotion to top positions in the internal bureau was lifted when the Self-Defense Force Law and the Act for Establishment of the Defense Agency were enacted. Nevertheless, members of the uniformed team—that is, members of the JSDF—had never been promoted to leadership posts in the agency's internal bureau. And the Act for Establishment of the Defense Agency explicitly stated that the "director general of the secretariat of the minister of state for defense and all the bureau chiefs are mandated to assist the director-general by attending to the following tasks in their respective jurisdictions," thus granting a wide range of authority to the internal bureau. In fact, de facto the internal bureau came to interfere with troop operations (so-called matters of military command), an area in which the uniformed team was supposed to enjoy great power. It is beyond doubt that a defense organization where civil officials possessed and exercised such strong power was quite peculiar compared with defense organizations of other countries in the world.

Ex-bureaucrats of the former Home Ministry's Police Bureau had been at the center of this internal bureau since the establishment of the National Police Reserve. Having suffered from the arbitrary conduct of the Imperial Japanese Army and Navy in prewar days, they were all permeated with something akin to a sense of mission to prevent the new organization from becoming anything like the former Japanese military at any cost. As we saw in chapter 1, the Hattori group, which was, by all accounts, a ghost of the prewar military, would not stop interfering with the founding of the new organization. Therefore, it was feared that, even though a decade had already passed since Japan's defeat, resurrection of the former military or prewar militarism was not altogether unthinkable.

The central figure among the bureaucrats of the internal bureau was Kaihara Osamu, who had participated in the planning of the National Police Reserve Act; joined the National Safety Agency first as director of the security division; and then moved on to become the Defense Agency's director of defense, Policy Division 1; director-general, Bureau of Defense Policy; and director-general, Secretariat of

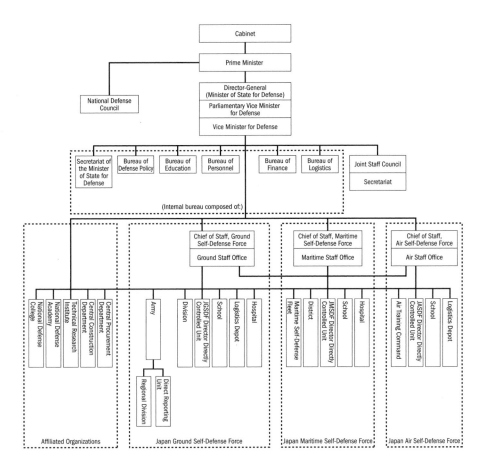

Figure 9. Organizational Chart of the Newly Established Defense Agency

Source: *Jieitai 10-nen-shi* [Ten-year history of the Japan Self-Defense Forces], p.78.*

---

* Boeicho Jieitai 10-nen-shi Henshu Iinkai, ed. *Jieitai 10-nen-shi* [Ten-year history of the Japan Self-Defense Forces]. Tokyo: Okurasho Zoheikyoku, 1961.

the Minister of State for Defense. Thus, having assumed key policy positions in the Defense Agency one after another, he earned the nickname of "Emperor Kaihara." Keenly aware through his own experience just how irrational and problematic the Imperial Army and Navy had been, Kaihara held an extremely low opinion of military organizations and staff officers. And it was bureaucrats of the internal bureau of the Defense Agency centered around Kaihara who pushed ahead with control by civil officials with the main aim of suppressing the power of the uniformed team as much as possible.

It should be noted that in those days there was already criticism that control by the internal bureau permeated all corners of the organization. In response to such criticism, the government considered introducing a councilor system modeled after the assistant secretary system of the U.S. Department of Defense in place of the traditional bureau-division system. In other words, it was a proposition to place political appointees as assistants to the director-general of the Defense Agency. Space does not allow me to go into details, so let it suffice to say that resistance from the internal bureau's top senior officials allowed only a half-baked adaptation of the proposed system: only the director-general of the Secretariat of the Minister of State for Defense and chiefs of bureaus became councilors. In other words, the director-general of the Defense Agency (minister of state for defense) became to be assisted by the director-general of the Secretariat of the Minister of State for Defense and chiefs of various bureaus of the internal bureau, who were also councilors. Accordingly, there was no change in the primacy of the civil officials of the internal bureau within the Defense Agency.

Who Makes the Long-Term Plan?

When discussing an issue of defense policy, one important factor is the long-term defense plan. Defensive equipage such as naval vessels and airplanes, if not small guns and automobiles, are aggregates of sophisticated science and technology requiring long periods of time as well as deep coffers to develop. To ensure the most effective allocation of the limited funds available for upgrading equipage and improving troop capabilities, long-term planning is indispensable. And to develop a long-term plan, there first needs to be a basic defense plan, which provides the premise for the long-term plan. The defense plan sets forth the basic ideas concerning what threats Japan may need to defend itself from, how Japan can be defended from those enemies, what roles the ground, maritime, and air self-defense forces should play in the defense of Japan, and what kind of equipage is required for these self-defense forces to defend Japan.

The need for a long-term plan had already been advocated from around the time of establishment of the National Safety Forces. The argument was triggered by the need to respond to the U.S. demand that Japan's defense capabilities be expanded and also by expectations from the defense industries that began to sprout in Japan during the Korean War. In September 1952, soon after the establishment of the National Safety Agency, the Systems Investigative Committee (Seido Chosa Iinkai) was founded. Composed of the deputy director-general of the National Safety Agency as chairman, the first chief of staff (ground force) and the second chief of staff (maritime) as members, and the internal bureau's bureau chiefs, directors, and pertinent directors of the ground and maritime staff offices as participants, this committee discussed a variety of issues related to the defense of Japan. It was this committee that deliberated and drafted all the proposals—from the first one in March 1953 in anticipation of U.S. Secretary of State John Foster Dulles' visit to Japan in May through the tenth one in April 1955—that became the foundation of Japan's initial long-term defense plan.

Even though the committee continued its deliberations until the early days of the newly established Defense Agency, in the end it fell short of producing and deciding on a finalized long-term plan. This was because the committee lacked the coordination capabilities required to produce a long-term plan. To begin with, to come up with a defense plan that would be the foundation of a long-term plan, one had to decide which force—i.e., ground, maritime, or air—should be the core of the defensive arrangement. And, even before that, in the case of Japan's defense in those days, there was the question of the extent to which Japan should rely on the security arrangements with the United States. Being fully reliant on bilateral security cooperation with the United States would make the U.S. military the major player in the defense of Japan. In that case, the role of the JSDF would be a highly limited one requiring only small-scale military capabilities. In contrast, if reliance on the United States were limited, then the role of the JSDF would naturally be larger, requiring greater military capabilities and grander strategies. In the discussions at that time, the argument that the role of the air and maritime forces in defending Japan would be greater than that of the ground force was quite a weighty one.

It would have been impossible for such an organization as the Systems Investigative Committee to coordinate these and other issues among the pertinent bureaus and departments and produce a long-term plan that took into account fiscal constraints. In the end, the Defense Policy Division of the Defense Agency's Defense Policy Bureau, which had a strong mandate regarding the defense administration as a whole, was appointed to coordinate the long-term defense planning.

It should be noted that there was one more organization that could have possibly taken on the task of producing such a long-term plan: the Joint Staff Council. With its chairman being the highest post of the Ground/Maritime/Air Self-Defense Forces, the Joint Staff Council was supposed to be tasked with coordinating the Ground/Maritime/Air Staff Offices. In actuality, however, the authority of the Joint Staff Council had been limited from the beginning. It, thus, was not capable of coordinating views among the three Self-Defense Forces and producing a long-term defense plan.

To improve the situation, Kaihara, director of the Defense Agency's Defense Policy Division 1 in charge of drafting a long-term defense plan at that time, issued a written instruction in the name of the director-general of the Defense Agency to the Joint Staff Council to devise a long-term defense plan. Hayashi Keizo, chairman of the Joint Staff Council, replied verbally that the council was not capable of doing so. Reminiscing later, Kaihara said that he regretted not having requested a reply in writing, because the document would have proved that the Defense Agency's internal bureau was engaged in the long-term defense planning because it was the only organization capable of doing so. In any event, at the time of the founding of the Defense Agency and the JSDF, it had already been recognized that the internal bureau of the Defense Agency (Defense Policy Bureau) would be in charge of long-term defense planning, by far the most important task of all.

Compilation of Basic Policy on National Defense
Thus, as we have seen, the Defense Policy Division, Defense Policy Bureau of the Defense Agency was put in charge of producing Japan's long-term defense plan. The Basic Policy on National Defense (May 20, 1957) and the First Defense Build-up Plan (three-year government plan, June 14, 1957) were compiled under the Kishi Nobusuke cabinet. It should be recalled that, during the preceding Hatoyama cabinet, Foreign Minister Shigemitsu Mamoru's negotiations with the United States on the revision of the U.S.-Japan security pact had failed because Shigemitsu did not hide his intention to win the total withdrawal of U.S. forces from Japan. Having learned a lesson from this failure, Prime Minister Kishi was determined to stress his support of security cooperation with the United States. On the basis of this, it is believed that Kishi intended to propose concrete plans for improving Japan's self-defense capabilities, which would hopefully facilitate the withdrawal of U.S. ground forces from Japan, significantly remedy the U.S. bases issue in Japan, and establish a foothold for revision of the security pact. With these wishes in mind, Kishi urged the Defense Agency to formulate the Basic Policy on National Defense and the First Defense Build-up Plan in time for his trip to the United States. What, then, were the contents of these two documents? Let us first look into the Basic Policy on National Defense.

The Basic Policy on National Defense defines the objective of national defense as (a) preventing direct and indirect aggression, (b) repelling any such aggression, and (c) safeguarding the independence and peace of Japan by means of the following four concise basic policies:

(1) Supporting the activities of the United Nations, promoting international collaboration, and, thereby, making a commitment to the realization of world peace.
(2) Stabilizing the livelihood of the people, fostering patriotism, and thereby, establishing the necessary basis for national security.
(3) Building up rational defense capabilities by steps within the limit necessary for self-defense in accordance with the nation's strength and situation.
(4) Dealing with external aggression <u>based on the security arrangements with the United States</u> until the United Nations will be able to fulfill its function in stopping such aggression effectively in the future (underline added).

What is important here is that this policy of "dealing with external aggression <u>based on the security arrangements with the United States</u>" (underline added) became the foundation of subsequent defense policy in Japan. Thus, the Japanese government's policy to place the security arrangements with the United States at the heart of its national defense was explicitly declared, paving the way for revision of the U.S.-Japan Security Treaty that Kishi had aimed at.

Moreover, the policy also had the effect of sealing off the earlier argument for a more autonomous defense arrangement. The uniformed team of the Defense Agency, in particular, had argued that, because it would be militarily unreasonable for Japan to rely solely on the security pact with the United States for its defense, Japan should try to improve its defensive capabilities in those areas where Japan could contribute to its defense most effectively. If Japan's defense policy should incorporate more elements of autonomous engagement, then naturally the views of the uniformed team, who were military professionals, had to be given weight in long-term defense planning. As such, it was quite conceivable that any long-term planning initiative would fall into the hands of the uniformed team. Against this fear, making the security arrangement with the United States the basis of Japan's defense would seal off arguments stressing autonomous defense efforts, minimizing the risk of assertions by the uniformed team carrying too much weight.

Kaihara, the central person behind the Basic Policy on National Defense, was of the view that, "Basically, no country in the world will attack a Japan in which U.S. forces are stationed," and, if indeed some country dared to attack Japan, "Then we have no other option than to rely on the Americans to take care of it. We are not capable of it nor will we be in the foreseeable future" (*Kaihara Osamu oraruhisutori* [Kaihara Osamu's oral history]*). On the premise that the JSDF's capabilities were regarded as being extremely low, Kaihara took a view that could even be called "sole dependence on security arrangements with the United States." From this perspective, Kaihara tried to suppress the possibility of the uniformed team's influence looming larger by strongly stressing that the U.S.-Japan security pact was the foundation of Japan's defense.

It should be noted that the Basic Policy on National Defense made one more important contribution. As plainly stated in point number three above, the Basic Policy clearly gave consideration to political situations and, particularly, fiscal constraints. While it was only natural for financial considerations to be included in national defense planning, it was nevertheless noteworthy that the Basic Policy deliberately mentioned in writing the need to consider fiscal constraints, thus signifying that fiscal circumstances would always play a large part in defense policy planning. And this consideration of fiscal constraints was also repeated, almost verbosely, in the First Defense Build-up Plan that was formulated soon after the Basic Policy. For instance:

1. As the first step in building defense capabilities of minimum necessity in accordance with national strength and circumstances, following the Basic Policy on National Defense, a de-

---

* *Kaihara Osamu oraruhisutori* [Kaihara Osamu's oral history]. Tokyo: National Graduate Institute for Policy Studies, 2001, p.20.

fense build-up plan for the years 1958 through 1960 (1962 for some portion) has been produced.

. . .

5. When pursing these goals, we should constantly keep in mind that the economic stability of Japan should not be disturbed. Particularly, when deciding on year-by-year expansion of defense capabilities, we should be flexible, paying due consideration to fiscal conditions and the balance with other measures for the stabilization of people's livelihoods.

The First Defense Build-up Plan was a long-term plan that set a goal to expand the Ground Self-Defense Force (GSDF) to 180,000 troops and build up core defense capabilities around the GSDF. This first plan was, for one thing, an attempt at showing compliance with the commitment to the United States made at the Ikeda-Robertson talks in 1953. Also behind this plan was the political consideration, so to speak, of making withdrawal of U.S. ground forces from Japan easier by upgrading the defense capabilities of the GSDF.

Both the declaration of the central position occupied by security arrangements with the United States in Japan's defense plans and the attention paid to the financial aspect of defense buildup as put forth in the Basic Policy on National Defense and the First Defense Build-up Plan proved to be very effective in sealing off any argument for defense buildup based on Japan's own defense initiative. And this, in turn, successfully suppressed an increase of influence by the uniformed team, making the primacy of civil officials in Japan's defense policies all the more clear-cut. But, as we will see when we revisit this theme later, this did not automatically mean that the system of control by civil officials was immediately embedded in Japan.

Campaign against the U.S.-Japan Security Treaty and the JSDF
This section looks into relations between the revision of the U.S.-Japan Security Treaty and Japan's defense policies, particularly concerning

the JSDF. Prime Minister Kishi aimed to correct inequalities in the existing U.S.-Japan Security Treaty as much as possible. From that angle, it can be said that the revision of 1960 was a successful one. But this does not mean that the U.S. base problem, which was deemed to be a symbol of Japan's subjugation to the United States, was solved once and for all. Kishi's hardline political style manifested in the revision of the treaty as well as the prior revision of the Police Duties Execution Act, and Kishi's personal history—which included his membership in the Tojo Hideki cabinet and detention as a suspected war criminal—triggered strong repulsion toward the U.S.-Japan Security Treaty with the rise of nationalism. This campaign against the U.S.-Japan security pact had long-lasting influences on subsequent defense policies and the position of the JSDF. The next few paragraphs review these briefly.

The first issue that has to be discussed about relations between politics and the JSDF is that of the use of the JSDF. After the bilateral security pact was revised, Prime Minister Kishi was expecting U.S. President Dwight D. Eisenhower to visit Japan. With the rise of the campaign against the U.S.-Japan security pact, Kishi grew apprehensive about security at the time of the presidential visit. When police authorities said they were not confident that the police force could guarantee the safety of the guest, Kishi lodged a request with the Defense Agency's director-general for the JSDF's participation in a public safety operation. It is said that not only Kishi but also such central figures in the Kishi government as Finance Minister Sato Eisaku, Minister for International Trade and Industry Ikeda Hayato, and Kawashima Shojiro, secretary-general of the Liberal Democratic Party, were openly supportive of mobilizing the JSDF for this purpose. As introduced earlier, being direct disciples of Yoshida Shigeru, both Ikeda and Sato were in the mainstream of conservative politics in Japan. They both became prime ministers after Kishi, and they were quite instrumental in helping the Yoshida Doctrine radicate in the Japanese politics. Nevertheless, at the time of the rise of the campaign against the U.S.-Japan security pact, they both were supportive of mobilizing the JSDF.

As we have seen, at the time of the three-party consultation on the establishment of the Self-Defense Forces, Yoshida's Jiyuto had been of the view that it was desirable to obscure the military nature of the new organization as much as possible and, instead, establish a security force–like orga-

Campaign against the U.S.-Japan Security Treaty
(Source: The Mainichi Newspapers)

nization mainly to respond to indirect invasions as an extension of the National Security Forces. And it should be pointed out that there was a perception among public order authorities that the rise of the campaign against the U.S.-Japan Security Treaty was akin to an indirect invasion backed by the international communist movement. It was believed that even the former Jiyuto politicians and direct disciples of Yoshida, such as Sato and Ikeda, did not oppose mobilization of the JSDF in such cases of indirect invasion.

But it was the Defense Agency that resisted the requests for the JSDF's mobilization to the last. Akagi Munenori, director-general of the Defense Agency (state minister for defense) at that time reminisced that, at the Defense Agency, both civil officials of the inner bureau and the uniformed team acted in unison against mobilization. According to Kato Yozo, director of the Defense Policy Bureau at that time, Akagi, too, had at first been of the view that mobilization would be inevitable. If that was indeed the case, then politicians were more positive about mobilization of the JSDF, while both the inner bureau and the uniformed team of the Defense Agency opposed mobilization. In other words, as far as mobilization of the JSDF was concerned, officials of the Defense Agency were much more cautious than the politicians.

In the end, the JSDF were not mobilized, President Eisenhower cancelled his visit, and the Kishi cabinet resigned en masse upon en-actment of the new U.S.-Japan Security Treaty. From this point on, this episode was referred to as a success story of the Defense Agency repel-ling the demand for mobilization of the JSDF. With this, the idea be-came embedded in the minds of the Japanese people that it was a good thing that the JSDF were not mobilized. This experience of fail-ing to mobilize the JSDF even in such a major public safety crisis made Japanese politicians all the more cautious about the use of the JSDF. Having blocked politicians' easy reliance on the JSDF, bureaucrats of the Defense Agency, for their part, became all the more self-confident about their role at the center of Japan's defense policies.

Defense Initiative Divided
The turmoil around revision of the U.S.-Japan Security Treaty also ended up affecting the defense policies of the GSDF. Actually, even prior to this turmoil, signs had been spotted since the Kishi-Eisenhow-er talks in 1957, which decided the withdrawal of U.S. ground forces from Japan, that the target of anti-military base movements in Japan was shifting from the U.S. military to the GSDF. According to Sugita Ichiji, the then chief of staff of the GSDF, the highest post in the force, anti-government and anti-military base activities, including anti–U.S.-Japan security pact movements, as well as such labor dis-putes as the Miike coal mine dispute, were all perceived in those days as having the backing of the international communist movement (i.e., the Soviet Union and China). At that time, some in Japan perceived that the country was "on the eve of revolution." In the face of citizens' movements against their own bases and training grounds, the GSDF itself became rapidly concerned about domestic security issues.

Importantly, when the U.S.-Japan Security Treaty was revised, the clause that said, "including assistance given at the express request of the Jap-anese Government to put down large-scale internal riots and distur-bances in Japan, caused through instigation or intervention by an outside power or powers" was struck from cases in which U.S. troops stationed in Japan would be mobilized. This clause had been criticized because it sounded very much like colonial rule. Elimination of this clause, however, also meant that, from that point on, Japan alone would be responsible for suppressing any large-scale riots and disturbances. As such, it would have to be the police force and the JSDF that actually had to cope with these troubles. Because the police force would not be able to handle a situation bad enough to be described as a civil war, the revision of the U.S.-Japan Security Treaty magnified the JSDF's responsibility for domestic security. In fact, at the time Japan's internal security was perceived to be worsening, so the GSDF made maintaining domestic security and responding to indirect invasions its mission target. This stress on internal security and indirect invasions continued to be the GSDF's basic stance throughout the 1960s until defense capabilities against invasions from the north, particularly in Hokkaido, were reinforced in the 1970s, so that Japan could "cope with small-scale, regionally limited battles." As we will discuss later in detail, there occurred an issue called the "reorganization of 13 divisions," through which the division of labor with the police and the JSDF's own policy toward internal security were determined. At the root of this issue was also this stress on responding to internal security problems.

After the mobilization of the JSDF was rejected at the time of the campaign against the U.S.-Japan Security Treaty, the use of the JSDF for maintenance of public order was never considered, and the police became the central force for internal security. By developing the riot police unit, which enjoyed state-of-the-art equipment and concentrated police authority to an extent unheard of overseas, Japan's police coped with a variety of problems, including the student riots of the 1960s.

While the maintenance of security within Japan became the main task of the GSDF, the Maritime Self-Defense Force (MSDF) had been operating according to a completely different policy—that is, maritime escort missions and a special focus on anti-submarine warfare. As indicated by the fact that the MSDF had been strongly supported by the U.S. Navy at the time of its founding, it enjoyed presupposed collaboration with the U.S. Navy in its operations. In short, the MSDF positioned itself as a supplementary force to the U.S. Navy. This self-perception of the MSDF was well symbolized by an operation scheme calling for a blockade of the Korea, Tsugaru, and Soya Straits in order to block Soviet submarines' advances to the Pacific Ocean. Based on the lesson from World War II when supply shipments were cut off by submarine-centered operations and on the need to collaborate with the U.S. Navy, the MSDF trained troops on the assumption that antisubmarine operations were their basic mission. Coastal defense in the case of direct invasions from external enemies never was its central concern.

The differences in the policies of the GSDF and the MSDF also led to major differences in their relations with the U.S. military. If, as in the case of the GSDF, the major mission were to deal with indirect invasions within Japan and internal security, the possibility of joint operations with the U.S. military would be extremely small. Because the MSDF, in contrast, had assumed collaborations with the U.S. Navy as its basic stance from the beginning, it conducted joint drills with the U.S. Navy quite intensively from the early days of its founding. This contributed to the close relations between the MSDF and the U.S. Navy.

This line of thinking of the MSDF was unacceptable to the inner bureau of the Defense Agency, the central organ of defense plan making, particularly Kaihara and his associates. Declaring that the maritime escort that the MSDF proposed would be utterly impossible, Kaihara was convinced that the MSDF's mission was confined to coastal and inshore defenses. As long as Kaihara remained in the center of the inner bureau, therefore, improvement of the equipage that the MSDF wished for would be kept in check.

Chapter 4

The Build Up of Defense Capabilities and a Series of Defense Build-up Plans

Setback for the Akagi Plan

The previous chapter chronicled the process toward the formulation of the Basic Policy on National Defense and the First Defense Build-up Plan. It should be noted that Prime Minister Kishi Nobusuke did not involve himself in the substance of these documents. Also discussed earlier were Kishi's main aims when he instructed that these documents be compiled promptly. First, Kishi aimed to stress the importance that Japan attached to security cooperation with the United States. Second, he aimed to propose concrete plans to improve Japan's self-defense capabilities to satisfy U.S. expectations, establish a foothold for revising the security pact, and significantly improve the issues pertaining to U.S. bases in Japan by facilitating the withdrawal of U.S. ground forces from Japan. These goals were why Kishi rushed these documents into completion in time for his trip to the United States.

Kishi's promise to the U.S. government to expand Japan's defense efforts, however, ended up causing two new problems. One was the issue of organizational reform, as represented by the proposed promotion of the Defense Agency to a ministry. The other was the issue of new defense buildup plans following on the First Defense Build-up Plan. Both of these new issues harbored the potential to gravely affect the primacy of civil officials in Japan's defense policy. And it was when Kaihara Osamu, chief drafter of the two documents, was seconded to the Ministry of Foreign Affairs from the Defense Agency, stationed at the Japanese embassy in Washington, D.C., that these two issues loomed large.

First, let us look into the issue of organizational reform. It encompassed two areas: the proposed promotion of the Defense Agency to a ministry and a strengthening of the Joint Staff Office as a part of internal reform of the Defense Agency/Japan Self-Defense Forces. To come right to the conclusion, neither of these scenarios was realized. Although promotion of the Defense Agency to a ministry had been advocated chiefly by the National Defense Division of the governing Liberal Democratic Party (LDP), the party postponed submitting its bill to that effect due to the reform of the Police Duties Execution Act and the riots against the U.S.-Japan Security Treaty. When the Kishi cabinet was succeeded by the Ikeda Hayato cabinet, which wished to concentrate on economic growth and stay away from defense issues as much as possible, it was decided to shelve the idea of promoting the Defense Agency to a ministry.

As for the strengthening of the Joint Staff Office, although a draft proposal satisfactory to the uniformed team had been devised, the decision was made to minimize legislation by handling most of the points included in the proposal with the prime minister's directives. This decision was taken out of consideration for the political turmoil of the time. To avoid more confusion after the security pact riots, submission of the bill was delayed. By the time the bill was submitted, officials involved in the preparation of the bill had been transferred to other departments or bureaus. Thus, the plan backfired. Handling some of the proposals with the prime minister's directives became virtually impossible. Nor was it possible to pass the bill, because the necessary supplementary directives were not established. At this point, the plan to strengthen the Joint Staff Office fell apart.

The second issue was about long-term defense planning. The First Defense Build-up Plan was a three-year plan covering fiscal years 1958 through 1960. Therefore, a new long-term plan beginning in fiscal year 1961 was necessary. This meant that the plan had to be decided before March 31, 1961. The so-called Akagi Plan, a long-term plan published in July 1959 under the name of Akagi Munenori, director-general of the Defense Agency, was devised to meet this need. The Akagi Plan gave priority to improvement of air and maritime defense capabilities over that of ground capabilities, which was a major departure from the First Defense Build-up Plan that had stressed the role of the Ground Self-Defense Force (GSDF).

The Akagi Plan aimed at appropriating ¥290 billion, or 2 to 2.5 percent of the projected national income in fiscal 1965, the year the plan would end, to defense buildup. Financial authorities including the Ministry of Finance, however, criticized this amount as being fiscally unrealistic.

Akagi Munenori (Source: The Mainichi Newspapers)

Formulating such a budget would be impossible, they claimed. Cautious voices were heard even from within the LDP against approving the second defense buildup plan before signing a revised U.S.-Japan Security Treaty. Waiting until the treaty was signed made it impossible for the plan to be officially adopted before the end of 1959.

Although the Defense Agency responded to the criticism from the Finance Ministry by reducing the plan's budget so as to expedite approval in 1960, in the end, the Akagi Plan was never officially adopted. The greatest cause of this setback was actually opposition from within the Defense Agency. More concretely, when Kaihara returned to the Defense Agency's Defense Policy Bureau from his post in Washington, D.C., he started a campaign against the Akagi Plan. Kaihara found the plan to be financially infeasible and problematic because its buildup plan prioritized unnecessary equipage such as a helicopter carrier. Kaihara's campaign succeeded in forcing reconsideration of the Akagi Plan.

It was true that, as Kaihara pointed out, certain problem areas in the Akagi Plan, including defects in its estimates of necessary expenses, did need review. Whether these problems were really serious enough to require the full reconsideration of the plan overall, however, was questionable. The true reason behind Kaihara's adamant opposition to the Akagi Plan was believed to be the abundant inclusion in the plan of the uniformed team's views and opinions. At the outset, the Akagi Plan said:

> Because Japan's defense capabilities are for self-defense, they should be considered within the range of a defensive strategy. Therefore, Japan will rely on the U.S. military for offensive strategy. Taking into consideration the possibility that assistance from the U.S. military could fluctuate depending on the situation, however, we should equip ourselves with the capability to conduct military operations single-handedly, at least for the initial period, against substantially formidable military invasion in order to maintain the self-initiative of our operations. And we should build up our capability to cope mainly on our own with military invasions other than large-scale invasions, as well as indirect invasions. (underline added)

The above line of thinking accepted, to a considerable extent, the argument for Japan's own self-initiative, which had once been sealed off. It was obvious that acceptance of this line of thinking would allow expansion of the uniformed team's power and influence. It is believed that Kaihara strongly opposed the Akagi Plan because he was very much aware of this danger.

In the end, the Akagi Plan was shelved for thorough reconsideration. And Kaihara, who was now director of the Defense Policy Bureau was designated to draft the Second Defense Build-up Plan. Thus, the path for the uniformed team's power to be expanded was blocked once again both in the realm of organizational reform and long-term defense planning.

Deliberations on the Second Defense Build-up Plan
How, then, was the Second Defense Build-up Plan decided and what were its contents? Concerning the decision-making process regarding the content of the second plan, particularly close attention was paid to

fiscal constraints and relations with the United States. Let us look into this process in detail through the examples of the proposals to reorganize the GSDF into 13 divisions, to reinforce it to a force of 180,000 troops, and to build a helicopter carrier for the Maritime Self-Defense Force (MSDF). These proposals became salient issues during the deliberations.

The proposal to reorganize the GSDF was an organizational change that involved switching from the conventional 100,000 troops divided into six district divisions (12,700 strong each) and four combined brigades (approximately 6,100 strong each), for a total of ten units or about 100,000 troops, to 13 divisions each consisting of some 9,000 soldiers as its standard complement. Having realized that troop organization modeled after that of the U.S. Army could not effectively cope with Japan's distinctive topology and other tactical alterations, the proposal aimed to (1) downsize and improve mobility; (2) improve troops' independence and operational flexibility; (3) develop troop leaders (sergeant-class) with the ability to command; and (4) qualitatively improve configurations and equipage by taking advantage of recent advances in tactics and military technologies. In short, the main aim of the proposal was to downsize the GSDF divisions. It was hoped that these downsizing efforts would facilitate (1) an increase in the number of division headquarters; (2) intensified linkages with local administrative authorities because troops would be nimbler; (3) promptness of troops' actions; (4) efficiency in disaster relief operations; and (5) improved public order in metropolitan areas such as the Tokyo-Yokohama area and the Osaka-Kobe area.

Whether these expectations were actually realized, however, is another story. As discussed earlier, the maintenance of public security had been made the basic mission of the GSDF under its Chief of Staff Sugita Ichiji. The proposed reorganization of the GSDF divisions upheld this basic stance of the GSDF and, therefore, its prompt realization was hoped for. Incidentally, the expense accompanying this reorganization was estimated to be kept at the relatively low level of about ¥300 million required for facility improvement and other reforms.

Along with the proposed reorganization of the GSDF into 13 divisions, the expansion of the GSDF's complement to 180,000 strong was another important issue. This proposed expansion had been considered to be Japan's longstanding commitment to the United States since the Ikeda-Robertson talk in 1953. As such, meeting this commitment was thought of as an important piece of homework for Japan.

Moving on to the issue related to the MSDF—what was construction of a helicopter carrier all about? As we have seen, the MSDF had made the protection of maritime traffic its objective and considered anti-submarine operations to be its chief mission. As it became increasingly difficult to accomplish this mission only with fixed-wing aircrafts and naval vessels because of remarkable innovations in submarine technologies, including the introduction of missile submarines, the Second Defense Build-up Plan proposed introducing a helicopter carrier that would allow the MSDF to carry out anti-submarine operations more effectively. The problem is that the plan called for construction of a 10,000-ton vessel with formidable speed and 27 heavy helicopters (including spare helicopters), which would altogether cost as much as ¥19,575 million. Judging that it would be impossible for Japan to singlehandedly bear the cost, the MSDF requested financial support from the U.S. Navy. As a result, it was decided that the Japanese government would appropriate ¥12,252 million or 62.8 percent of the total, while the U.S. side would contribute the remaining 37.2 percent. The U.S. Navy's commitment was taken as evidence of its high expectations for the MSDF to build a helicopter carrier.

How, then, were the above problems settled? Seeing as reorganization of the GSDF into 13 divisions would not be too costly and the sooner GSDF facilities could be upgraded the better, it was decided that the reorganization would be carried out separately from the Second Defense Build-up Plan. The remaining two proposals—expansion of the GSDF to 180,000 troops and construction of a helicopter carrier—did not enjoy a similar happy ending.

Expanding the GSDF to 180,000 troops was a promise that Japan had made at the time of the Ikeda-Robertson talk, and building a helicopter carrier—an endeavor supported by the U.S. Navy—was considered to be a symbol of U.S-Japan collaboration. But in the end, while achieving a force of 180,000 troops remained a goal, the GSDF was reinforced to 175,000 troops, and construction of a helicopter carrier was shelved because of high costs and less urgency.

What is noteworthy here was that Prime Minister Ikeda had at first rejected the argument that expansion of the GSDF to 180,000 troops had been a promise to the United States, saying, "It is not necessary." While in the end it was decided that the figure of 180,000 would remain as a goal in consideration of good relations with the United States, Ikeda's determination to prioritize fiscal soundness remained firm. This affected other members of his cabinet as well. In short, Ikeda, who was a direct disciple of Yoshida Shigeru, faithfully pursued the line of emphasis on economic growth with light armament started by Yoshida. And the Defense Agency and the Ministry of Finance supported Ikeda's stance.

At this juncture, the stance taken by the Defense Agency merits attention. When members of the Legislators' Roundtable of the National Defense Council were briefed on the Defense Agency's attitude toward the government budget, Sakomizu Hisatsune, director-general of the Economic Planning Agency and a member of the roundtable, criticized the Defense Agency's attitude, "It is for the Ministry of Finance to say that the defense budget should be 2 percent or 5 percent of GNP. It is not right for the Defense Agency to restrain itself, quoting these figures." Behind this remark was the Defense Agency's custom to draft defense buildup plans based on the logic of fiscal soundness, when in actuality it should have negotiated with the Finance Ministry to win the budget for its defense buildup plans based on defense necessities. As a matter of fact, since the time of the First Defense Build-up Plan, the Ministry of Finance had dispatched officials to the Defense Policy Division of the Defense Agency so that they could take part in drafting long-term defense plans. By having seconded Finance Ministry officials closely examine the requests submitted by the three self-defense forces using the Finance Ministry's budgetary assessment method, Kaihara intended to suppress demands from the uniformed team. From the Second Defense Build-up Plan on, a pattern became established to discuss defense buildup plans in terms of how many items could be added within the boundary of a certain percentage of GNP. To be sure, demands from the uniformed team tended to be excessive, and, therefore, it was indeed necessary to suppress these demands from the viewpoint of fiscal feasibility. In fact, Kaihara succeeded in cornering the Akagi Plan to the point of thorough reconsideration, relying on the Finance Ministry's methodology. In other words, this was an example of the Finance Ministry's methodology functioning as an effective tool to suppress the uniformed team's demands.

As a corollary, however, the Defense Agency now had to use the logic of the Ministry of Finance to discuss its defense plans. This not only led to an expansion of the Finance Ministry's influence in defense planning but also temporarily deprived the Defense Agency of its determination to build up defense plans from the basics.

Content of the Second Defense Build-up Plan and Its Political Implications

In terms of content, the Second Defense Build-up Plan had the following major characteristics.

First, it set forth the Basic Policy on National Defense as its premise and clarified its stance to place the security arrangements with the United States at the heart of Japan's defense. It rejected the argument adopted in the Akagi Plan that the security arrangements with the United States were inadequate and, instead, declared that Japan would basically rely on the United States for its defense. In other words, the Second Defense Build-up Plan confirmed that the chief actor in the defense of Japan would be the United States.

The second characteristic was its attitude toward defense buildup per se. Although, as we saw earlier, the inner bureau of the Defense Agency had succeeded in suppressing the uniformed team's self-assertion, it was only natural that it could not deny the very raison d'être of the JSDF. An answer, therefore, had to be found to make suppression of the uniformed team compatible with the raison d'être of the JSDF. A clause in the Second Defense Build-up Plan tried to solve this dilemma. It read that Japan "committed to build up defense forces able to cope effectively with an aggression at or lower than the level of a local war, using conventional weapons under the security arrangements with the United States." In a nutshell, in the Second Defense Build-up Plan, the role of the JSDF became confined to responses to extremely limited situations. With this basic stance, the Second Defense Build-up Plan mainly focused on upgrading the defense capabilities constructed under the First Defense Build-up Plan and renewing outdated equipage.

The third characteristic was what it prioritized. In the end, construction of a helicopter carrier, which not only the MSDF and the U.S. Navy but also the LDP's National Defense Division had strongly requested, was rejected, while the reorganization of the GSDF into 13 divisions was realized, separate from the Second Defense Build-up Plan. This goes to show that, in actuality, the defense buildup this time gave more weight toward the GSDF than the MSDF and the Air Self-Defense Force. And this means that the Defense Agency de facto rejected the line of emphasis on maritime and air defense set forth by the Akagi Plan.

Given these characteristics of the Second Defense Build-up Plan, then, how did it affect relations between the Defense Agency's inner bureau and the uniformed team? In other words, what happened to the system of primacy of civil officials over the uniformed team, which was a Japanese version of civilian control? As discussed earlier, the uniformed team's proactive participation in the formulation of defense policy was blocked when the Akagi Plan was cornered into being reconsidered. By rejecting the requests from the LDP's National Defense Division during deliberations on the Second Defense Build-up Plan, it can be said that the Defense Agency's inner bureau strengthened its position regarding the planning of defense policies. On top of that, the policy to continue to put security arrangements with the United States at the center of Japan's defense was once again reconfirmed by the Second Defense Build-up Plan with the purpose of eliminating the chance for the uniformed team of the Defense Agency to proactively participate in defense policy making.

But the problem is that, because Japan at this point decided to rely almost completely on the United States for its defense, any room for Japan to independently formulate its defense plans became extremely limited. Japan's dependence on the United States for its defense called into question the raison d'être of the JSDF, and, as explained, a clause "committing [Japan] to build up defense forces able to cope effectively with an aggression at or lower than the level of a local war, using conventional weapons under the security arrangements with the United States," was included in the Second Defense Build-up Plan in response to this dilemma. But incorporation of this clause also confined the Defense Agency's work to the boundaries of the clause. In other words, seeing as Japan depended on the United States for its defense, the Defense Agency was not tasked with formulating Japan's own defense plan or promoting joint defense with the United States. Rather, the central task of the agency would be to manage the JSDF, an organization mandated to repel "an aggression at or lower than the level of a local war, using conventional weapons." Thus, the process that the inner bureau of the Defense Agency had applied to strengthen the system of "primacy of civil officials" ironically resulted in promoting the conversion of the Defense Agency from a policy formulating authority to a mere body that managed and operated the JSDF.

In the face of this situation, the inner bureau of the Defense Agency decided to devote its energy to strengthening the Japanese people's sense of the JSDF's presence in their daily lives. For instance, the Second Defense Build-up Plan included a clause stating, "in order to become a defense power that stays close to people's daily lives, the JSDF intends to devote itself to various measures of civil cooperation including disaster rescue operations and public works as well as noise prevention activities." Such a clause was not in the First Defense Build-up Plan.

Disaster rescue operations were one of the JSDF missions that was stipulated in the Self-Defense Forces Act, and the JSDF had been engaged in this service even before the above clause was explicitly added. The fact that this clause was nevertheless deliberately added to the Second Defense Build-up Plan signified that this activity was now recognized to be one of the central missions of the JSDF. It is indeed quite conceivable that people's increased exposure to the JSDF's involvement in such non-defense-related activities as disaster relief, backup for the 1965 Tokyo Olympic Games, and support for Antarctic exploration—all matters of great concern among the Japanese people— were effective in popularizing the JSDF among the citizens.

The Directive on the Defense Agency's Public Relations Activities had already been issued in July 1960, around which time the Defense Agency's public relations activities became active. On June 28, 1961, around the time the Second Defense Build-up Plan was adopted, a booklet portraying the ideal JSDF member in democratic Japan was published. The booklet was titled *Jieikan no kokorogamae* (Desired mindset for JSDF members). It read, "The JSDF should always be one with the Japanese people . . . JSDF members must always be of one mind with the Japanese people and take pride in serving the public beyond their own self-interest." The Defense Agency's strong desire to stress that the JSDF was always on the people's side and to embed this image in people's minds is certainly evident in the above phrase. Also, sometime later (in 1967) a PR movie on the JSDF, *Kagaku no kyoi* (Wonders of science), was released. As shown by these examples, public relations became an important task for the Defense Agency around this time, along with management of the JSDF. It was through these activities that the JSDF became a familiar presence in people's minds in the 1960s.

The LDP's Defense Policy Tribe and the Argument for an Independent National Defense

On November 16, 1960, as the Second Defense Build-up Plan was being deliberated in Japan, an important decision related to Japan's defense was made in the United States. This is known as the dollar defense policy. Based on this policy, U.S. Secretary of State Christian Herter handed a memorandum to James Riddleberger, director of the International Cooperation Administration (ICA), announcing the change of overseas procurement plans related to nineteen countries, including Japan, Germany, France, and Britain. Japan was the recipient of the largest amount of overseas procurements with ICA funds, reaching the level of $115.8 million in one year between July 1959 and June 1960. And this procurement was to be reduced drastically. This was a big shock to Japan because it had enjoyed assistance from the United States at the time of the First Defense Build-up Plan and expected the same for the Second Defense Build-up Plan. Japan knew that the United States would reduce assistance for the Second Defense Build-up Plan, but it did not occur to the Japanese government that the reduction would be so huge.

Japan's defense industry, which had started growing since the Korean War, and LDP members concerned about defense experienced a heightened sense of crisis at these developments. Moreover, voices were heard in the United States, which was in the midst of a heated cold war with the Soviet Union, nagging Japan for not making more self-help efforts in terms of defense buildup even though it had already graduated from postwar recovery and had entered a period of high economic growth. For instance, in his speech at the Senate on April 22, 1963, Senator Frank Church demanded the termination of military aid to Japan, saying, "If we cannot even display our ability to terminate assistance to the nominal defense forces that Japan maintains in fear of displeasing the Japanese government, Lord, have mercy on the United States of America." His proposition was adopted at the Senate Foreign Relations Committee by unanimous decision. The sense of crisis felt by Japan's defense industry and the defense policy tribe in the Diet further intensified at the Ikeda Hayato cabinet's passive attitude toward national defense issues as displayed during deliberations on the Second Defense Build-up Plan. These contingents began to criticize the government fiercely.

At the center of the concerned LDP members were Hoshina Zenshiro, former vice-admiral of the Imperial Japanese Navy who had been deeply involved in the establishment of the MSDF, and Funada Naka, who had once served as director-general of the Defense Agency. There were a few others, including other former Defense Agency director-generals, who flocked together to form the so-called *kokubozoku* (defense policy tribe). In terms of their depth of engagement in defense issues and how active they were in defense-related activities, it seems beyond doubt that Hoshina and Funada were by far the central figures. The two shared a basic stance toward defense policy that emphasized the importance of maritime defense and the security arrangements with the United States. This was basically the same position that the MSDF took. Yet it was quite different from those advocating the settlement of the U.S. base problem in the 1950s through the buildup of independent defense capabilities and from Nakasone Yasuhiro and other successors of this argument. Therefore, even though Hoshina, Funada, and their associates were positive about strengthening defense capabilities, they nevertheless strongly opposed the withdrawal of U.S. bases from Japan or revision of the U.S.-Japan Security Treaty.

Another characteristic of the likes of Hoshina and Funada was their strong ties with the defense industry in Japan. During his days at the Imperial Japanese Navy, Hoshina was chief of the Navy Ministry's Naval Affairs Bureau, which had been in charge of naval build-up planning. Through this assignment he had become acquainted with Ishikawa Ichiro, who later became president of the Federation of Economic Organizations (Keidanren). It is said that Ishikawa rendered assistance to Hoshina when the latter ran for the National Diet. Hoshina had participated in Keidanren's Defense Production Committee, a committee for promotion of the defense industry in Japan, since its inception. After he was elected to the House of Representatives, he remained an active member of the LDP's National Defense Division, serving as a pipe between the LDP and the defense industry as well as pertinent government bureaus and agencies, starting with the Defense Agency. Funada, for his part, had been a longstanding friend since student days with Uemura Kogoro, who had served on Keidanren's Defense Production Committee as a facilitator on the business side. From this connection, Funada became interested in defense productions.

Diet members with a special interest in national defense—characterized by their emphasis on the importance of maritime defense and the security arrangements with the United States as well as their strong ties with the defense industry in Japan—strongly criticized the Ikeda cabinet, which remained passive toward national defense. At the same time, these critics also actively sought to promote the nationalization of defense equipage in order to mitigate damages to Japan's defense industry should the United States withdraw military assistance. And it was this nationalization of defense equipage that came to be insisted on as a concrete step to promote an independent national defense from the time of the Second Defense Build-up Plan through the Third Defense Build-up Plan.

It should be recalled here that the argument for an independent national defense in the 1950s, in contrast, aimed at settlement of the U.S. military base problem by expanding Japan's own defense capabilities. Taking this course, it was thought, could infringe on the very foundation of the security arrangements with the United States and, therefore, affect the arrangements as a whole. From the viewpoint of the defense policy tribe—including Hoshina and Funada, who believed in the said arrangements—this had to be avoided at any cost. Nevertheless, the base issue persisted and the government continued to be criticized repeatedly by opposition parties for its subordination to the United States. Accusations of dependence on the United States had to be suppressed lest anti-government movements, such as the earlier anti–U.S.-Japan Security Treaty campaign, should recur, stimulating people's nationalistic sentiments. To accomplish this, the government had to stress that Japan was self-reliant in its defense and actively advocate an independent national defense. The nationalization of defense equipage was one argument for self-reliant defense that would not involve the base issue.

Thus, at the National Diet during the period of the Second and Third Defense Build-up Plans, the argument for self-reliant defense was explained to mean the nationalization of defense equipage, and deliberations were conducted along that line. But this explanation also caused some problems. The most serious was that of the connection between politics and the procurement of defense equipage. Many kinds of defense equipage, including highly sophisticated electronic equipment and state-of-the-art jet fighters, were quite expensive. In

Japan, which procured most of such equipage from the United States, it is said that fierce commercial battles involving trading companies were fought around the introduction of the next-generation jet fighter (FX). Although details of these battles that involved huge amounts of money are unknown, it is said that politicians, particularly those of the defense policy tribe, were quite active behind the scenes.

During this period, when the JSDF was moving from its embryonic stage into a growth stage, politicians actively engaged in the national defense issue tended to be more concerned about defense equipage than the content of defense policies. It would be appropriate to say that they left the contents of defense policies and their implementation to the Defense Agency and mainly concentrated their attention on the defense equipage issue. In fact, when questioned about the LDP's National Defense Division having reached a settlement with Mitsubishi and Toshiba on production of the Nike and Hawk anti-aircraft missiles, the director of the Defense Agency's Bureau of Finance replied, "I am aware of those settlements."

Reflecting on this trend, Kaihara testified as follows:

It is wrong for the LDP's National Defense Division to make decisions on such matters, isn't it? As I wrote in my book, it is like the LDP's Land, Infrastructure and Transport Division deciding which train the Japan National Railway should buy. I say it is absurd, but undoubtedly it happened. And this must be one of the causes for the confusion around the issue of the production of defense equipage.

Politicians wanted to become involved in the production of defense equipage, which called for a humongous amount of funding. And in truth, the inner bureau of the Defense Agency did try to act as a shield to protect the newly established Defense Agency from being confused by these political interferences. This attempt by the inner bureau succeeded some of the times, while other times, the agency's bureaucrats themselves became entangled in the interferences. As the defense issue itself became a kind of taboo after the anti–U.S.-Japan Security

Treaty campaign, opposition Diet members started attacking the very presence of the JSDF, while those interested in defense issues—a rare presence among members of the governing party—were more concerned about the defense industry than defense policies. It was in the mid-1960s that this pattern became established in Japan.

Adoption of the Third Defense Build-up Plan and Its Implications
The Third Defense Build-up Plan was formulated as a five-year plan covering the period of 1967 through 1971. Even though it was formulated by the same Sato Eisaku cabinet that had criticized the Ikeda cabinet's passive attitude toward the defense issue, the content of the Third Defense Build-up Plan was essentially an extension of the content of the Second Defense Build-up Plan. Prime Minister Sato himself did not wish for a large-scale increase in the defense budget; he preferred to follow the basic line of the Second Defense Build-up Plan. In fact, deliberations on the Third Defense Build-up Plan were characterized by time and energy (much more so than in the case of the Second Defense Build-up Plan) devoted to discussing the size of the budget, rather than talk about the basic issues of the national defense policy.

The background to this situation is noteworthy. First, the Ikeda cabinet, which was formed in the midst of the confusion surrounding the anti–U.S.-Japan Security Treaty campaign, was characterized by a low profile and an emphasis on economic growth. During the Ikeda cabinet's tenure, discussion on defense issues became almost taboo. For instance, public opinion polls in 1958, soon after the peace treaty/independence, showed that 15 percent of respondents were absolute pacifists who felt that "War is bad no matter what," while 75 percent of respondents felt that "War may be necessary to defeat evil and to maintain peace," showing a conditional tolerance to war. In contrast, the same poll in 1967, when the Third Defense Build-up Plan was formulated, showed that 77 percent of respondents were absolute pacifists as opposed to the 22 percent of respondents who said, "War may be unavoidable to defend the country." This was a complete reversal of the 1958 results. The 1967 poll revealed a trend among the Japanese people to view war and the presence of the military as a war machine itself as evil (*Zusetsu sengo yoron-shi* [Illustrated history of postwar public opinions]*).

The Mitsuya Kenkyu (Mitsuya Study, or "Three Arrows" contingency planning) incident in 1965 symbolized this trend. Mitsuya Kenkyu was an intra-JSDF contingency simulation on the eruption of a second Korean War. The purpose of the simulation was to predict such a war's prospective impact on Japan and Japan's possible responses, which included suspending the Constitution. The inner bureau of the Defense Agency participated in the simulation. Having learned of the exercise, a Diet member from the Japan Socialist Party took it up at a Diet session. Even Prime Minister Sato at first criticized the exercise as a violation of civilian control, which further aggravated the political confusion. For quite some time after this exposé, the Diet and mass media were filled with criticisms of Mitsuya Kenkyu, and the Defense Agency had to busy itself with coping with them.

Objectively speaking, it was only natural for the JSDF, which was mainly mandated to repel direct invasions, to simulate emergencies. In fact, it would have been a negligence of duty if the JSDF had not conducted studies on how to respond in the case of an emergency. And it was this "natural thing for the JSDF to do" that came under criticism during the Mitsuya Kenkyu incident. The logic of the criticizers was that a study simulating an emergency was in fact a plan to cause an emergency. While the number of people subscribing to this logic has decreased drastically, there still exist a few today who resort to this logic. But in the 1960s, this kind of logic went unchallenged. It seems beyond a doubt that, under the circumstances of the time, it must have been difficult to have serious debates on national defense.

There was a second reason that the deliberations on the Third Defense Build-up Plan failed to address basic defense policy issues. As will be explained in more detail later, the argument for review of the security arrangements with the United States gained momentum around that time against the backdrop of an intensification of the

---

* NHK Hoso Yoron Chosa-sho, ed. *Zusetsu sengo yoron-shi, dai 2-han* [Illustrated history of postwar public opinions, second edition], Tokyo: NHK Books, 1982, p.164

Vietnam War and the rise of opposition to automatic renewal of the U.S.-Japan Security Treaty in 1970. And among Japanese government leaders, including Prime Minister Sato, awareness was on the rise that, even though the Third Defense Build-up Plan would essentially follow the pattern of the Second Defense Build-up Plan, serious exploration had to be made into desirable forms of independent defense policy as well as security arrangements with the United States. The Ministry of Finance, which had begun to have a greater influence on defense policy, insisted on a full-fledged examination of national defense policy. This created an ironical picture because the Defense Agency wanted to avoid serious soul-searching about defense policy. Prompt cabinet approval of the Third Defense Build-up Plan was the Defense Agency's top priority.

It was not unreasonable for the Defense Agency to make formulation of the Third Defense Build-up Plan a top priority because the plan could affect annual operations. Even though the Defense Agency had become something akin to a managerial agency for the JSDF, it still must not have been amusing for its bureaucrats to witness the Ministry of Finance further increasing its influence on defense policies by leading discussions on basic defense policy issues during deliberations of the Third Defense Build-up Plan. Moreover, having become confident about their role at the center of defense policy formulation through the experiences of playing an important role in rejecting mobilization of the JSDF during the anti–U.S.-Japan Security Treaty riots and forcing a thorough reconsideration of the Akagi Plan, bureaucrats of the Defense Agency's inner bureau failed to maintain a close liaison with the office of the prime minister. In the end, though, the Defense Agency's argument that the government should avoid wasting time unproductively discussing basic issues of defense policy was adopted, perhaps assisted by the practical necessity to obtain prompt cabinet approval of the Third Defense Build-up Plan.

Let us turn our attention to the content of the Third Defense Build-up Plan thus adopted. While the plan showed characteristics making it an extension of the Second Defense Build-up Plan, it nevertheless contained several features not seen in the Second Plan. One was an emphasis on maritime defense capabilities. Another was the promotion of the nationalization of defense equipage.

As far as the former was concerned, the policy to attach weight to maritime defense capabilities was explicitly incorporated in the Third Defense Build-up Plan. As a matter of fact, in the outline of the Third Defense Build-up Plan approved by the National Defense Council and the Cabinet on November 24, 1966, the "General Policy" section stated that "Improvement of defense capabilities this time gives weight to maritime defense capabilities in adjacent seas and air defense capabilities over important regions as well as the mobility of various functions." In terms of proportion of the defense budget, the Second Defense Build-up Plan allocated 43.4 percent for ground forces, 23.1 percent for maritime forces, and 30.8 percent for air forces. Under the Third Defense Build-up Plan, the proportions were 41.2 percent for ground forces, 24.5 percent for maritime forces, and 24.5 percent for air forces. Only the proportion for maritime defense increased. A look at the growth rate of expenditures reveals that expenditure for ground and air defenses increased by 1.7 times and 1.4 times, respectively, and that for maritime defense expanded by as much as 1.9 times. The figures clearly reveal the explicit emphasis on capabilities of the Maritime Self-Defense Force.

As for the emphasis on promoting the nationalization of defense equipage, both the LDP's defense policy tribe members and Prime Minister Sato himself showed strong interest in this proposition. In the outline of the Third Defense Build-up Plan, the following statement was incorporated in the "General Policy" section: "It is so resolved that technological research and development should be promoted so that it can contribute to the modernization of defense equipage and to improving domestic technological standards, while, at the same time, it will facilitate the appropriate nationalization of defense equipage and thereby contribute to nurturing the foundation of Japan's defense." From this point on, the nationalization of defense equipage advanced rapidly.

Thus, although the Third Defense Build-up Plan had been envisioned as an extension of the Second Plan, it ended up incorporating content different from the Second Plan. Behind this change in the game plan were shifts within the Defense Agency itself. Most of all, the generational change in the agency witnessed the first generation of top leaders from the day of the agency's establishment being replaced by the rising new generation that had been active as young officials during the agency's embryonic days. Most symbolic of this generational change was the departure of Kaihara Osamu, who had been so powerful as to be nicknamed "Emperor Kaihara," for a new post as a member of the National Defense Council. Given that Kaihara was one of the most outstanding officials of the inner bureau of the Defense Agency who had supported the organization throughout its founding days, nobody had doubted that Kaihara would become administrative vice minister someday. Partly due to inter-factional conflicts within the LDP, however, Kaihara had to retire from the agency with director-general of the secretariat as his last post.

While Kaihara's downfall itself was a product of interference by politics into the administrative branch of government, it was nevertheless true that a new generation had already grown inside the agency. Unlike Kaihara's generation, which had devoted its energy to suppression of the uniformed team and taken the primacy of civil officials for granted, this new generation of Defense Agency bureaucrats had a fairer view of the uniformed team as military professionals. The new generation bureaucrats were unhappy that the Defense agency had been degraded to a managerial body for the JSDF; they were anxious to convert the agency back into a policy formulating authority. The new generation bureaucrats were aware of the problems that the long-term defense plans so far had harbored and of the need to reexamine the position and role of the JSDF. This was the generation that came to play the central role in the 1970s.

Chapter 5

The Nakasone Plan and
the Argument for Autonomous
National Defense

Rise of the Argument for Autonomous National Defense

The period from the mid-1960s, when the Third Defense Build-up Plan was formulated and deliberated, through the late 1960s saw a resurgence of the argument for a more autonomous national defense in Japan. During this period, such phrases as "autonomous national defense" and "autonomous diplomacy" became major themes in magazines and other media. Behind the resurgence of this chorus demanding "autonomy" was, among other reasons, the intensification of the Vietnam War, the rise of a new type of military base problem called "pollution caused by U.S. bases," and the renewal of the U.S.-Japan Security Treaty in 1970.

Of these developments, full-scale military interference in Vietnam by the United States from 1965, triggered by the Gulf of Tonkin incident in August 1964, stimulated the rise in Japan of anti–Vietnam War demonstrations and arguments that Japan was also liable to be involved in the war in Vietnam. Other issues such as problems related to the U.S. military bases became entangled in the anti–Vietnam War movement. According to opinion polls in those days, the ratio of respondents who were concerned about the Vietnam War consistently exceeded 70 percent throughout the 1960s. Those who thought that Japan might be involved in the war comprised 17 percent in 1963 and 18 percent in 1964 but showed a steep rise to 43 percent in 1965, as the Vietnam War intensified. In 1967, the same ratio reached 50 per-

cent. It should be added, however, that the ratio of those who supported the U.S.-Japan Security Treaty consistently exceeded 30 percent
throughout the period. While the rise of the anti–Vietnam War movement in Japan did not automatically lead to a public majority in opposition to the U.S.-Japan security pact, it is beyond doubt that people at
that time questioned the Japanese government's attitude toward the
Vietnam War.

The rise of the anti–Vietnam War movement was also related to
the U.S. military base issue. During the 1960s, many of the issues people had with the bases took the form of "pollution caused by U.S. bases"—in other words, situations in which citizens living and working in
the vicinities of the U.S. bases were victims of base activities, such as
the noise pollution from aircraft. Because U.S. bases in Japan were
mostly located in densely populated areas, such as Kanagawa prefecture, the base problem easily caught people's attention. On top of that,
U.S. military–related incidents erupted one after another during this
period. For example, from the mid-1960s port calls by U.S. nuclear
submarines and nuclear carriers became frequent, accidents involving
radiation leakage occurred, and military aircrafts crashed. These incidents undoubtedly gave momentum to the anti–U.S.-Japan Security
Treaty movement and other campaigns.

Renewal of the U.S.-Japan Security Treaty, which was scheduled to
expire in 1970, was a third factor behind the resurgence of an argument for more autonomous national defense in Japan. It was debated
whether the treaty should be extended to a new expiration date (say,
ten more years, for instance), automatically renewed as stipulated in
the treaty, or revised or even abolished as opposition parties demanded. Essentially, the argument was about what to do with the security
arrangements with the United States.

All of the above developments intermingled to stimulate the Japanese people's nationalistic sentiment once again, reinvigorating arguments for more autonomous national defense and diplomacy. It was
under these circumstances and at the particular timing of deliberations and decision making on the Third Defense Build-up Plan that all
the political parties—not only the ruling Liberal Democratic Party

(LDP) but also the Japan Socialist Party, the Komeito Party, the Democratic Socialist Party, and the Communist Party of Japan—announced respective policies clarifying their own security policy and stance toward the security arrangements with the United States.

What made the problem even more complicated for the Sato Eisaku government of the time was the issue of the return of Okinawa to Japan and U.S. President Richard Nixon's Guam Doctrine. Prime Minister Sato had pursued the reversion of Okinawa as his government's top priority, but the consent of the U.S. government was indispensable to realizing reversion. In order to make the reversion possible when the bases in Okinawa were being used by the U.S. military for the Vietnam War, it was necessary to construct a relationship of mutual trust with the United States that was appropriate for an ally (although "ally" was not used in those days). This meant accepting as many U.S. requests as possible. When Richard Nixon became president of the United States in 1969, he put forth in Guam what came to be known as the Nixon Doctrine (or the Guam Doctrine). The doctrine was a declaration that the United States would terminate unnecessary interferences in Asia and that those countries that could afford to do so should be in charge of their own security in general. This included Japan, which, having just reached a basic agreement on the reversion of Okinawa with the United States, now had to negotiate a schedule for the return. The Guam Doctrine forced Japan to assume the primary responsibility of defending itself from then on.

Thus, during the Sato government, the argument for autonomous national defense became conspicuous, with proponents calling for "the Japanese people's mettle to defend their own country." And at the time, the "U.S.-Japan Security Treaty as supplement" theory—which held that the "chief responsibility for Japan's defense should be at Japan's self-initiative, with Japan's efforts to be supplemented by the U.S.-Japan Security Treaty"—gave substance to the autonomous national defense argument.

Nakasone Yasuhiro and the Autonomous National Defense Argument

While this theory of the U.S.-Japan Security Treaty functioning as a supplement to Japan's own self-defense initiatives became advocated repeatedly from around 1969, the concrete substance of autonomous defense supplemented by the U.S.-Japan pact remained obscure. The theory was not advocated on the basis of a concrete examination on what the Japan Self-Defense Forces (JSDF) could and could not do or what cooperation the U.S. military could or could not render as a supplement to Japan's own efforts. It was mainly the Sato government and the governing LDP that insisted on the idea merely as a way to ride the rising tide of the autonomous national defense argument at the time.

In the midst of these arguments, Nakasone Yasuhiro was appointed director-general of the Defense Agency (in other words, state minister for defense) in January 1970. Nakasone had been known for his aggressive argument for autonomous national defense from the days when he was a member of the Kaishinto party, to which Ashida Hitoshi, a strong advocate of the rearmament of Japan, belonged. It was said that director-general of the Defense Agency was the position Nakasone wanted for himself, and so people were watching closely to see what kind of defense policy this new minister for defense would pursue in the midst of heightened arguments for autonomous national defense. Nakasone aggressively argued for autonomous national defense from the beginning, and later he set forth a long-term defense plan called the Nakasone Plan. Nakasone proposed that this plan incorporating his own defense policy ideas should come into effect after the Third Defense Build-up Plan expired.

Let's take a look at the content of the Nakasone Plan. Its "five principles of autonomous defense" (Jishu Boei 5-Gensoku) represented long-held ideas of Nakasone's. The five principles were: (1) Japan should abide by its Constitution and respect the principle of "exclusive self-defense"; (2) a balance should be maintained between foreign and security policies; (3) civilian control should be firmly observed; (4) the "three non-nuclear principles" should be preserved; and (5) the JSDF should perform the main functions of Japan's defense, with the

U.S.-Japan alliance playing a complementary role.* Overall, Nakasone's plan was a manifest for Japan to pursue the path of a "conventional nation" comparable to the western powers, something akin to the more recent notion of a "normal nation" advocated by Ozawa Ichiro. This path of a conventional nation was based on a balance-of-power view incorporating such notions as defense capabilities exclusively for self-defense and status as a non-nuclear middle power. What, then, were the main features of Nakasone's "autonomous defense"?

A major characteristic of Nakasone's argument for autonomous defense was the weight he gave to the issue of nationalism in Japan. Nakasone's stance was far apart from the "nationalization of defense equipage equals autonomous defense" formula adopted in the 1960s by the LDP's defense policy tribe members. Most symbolic was his approach to the military base issue. He had long insisted on the complete withdrawal of U.S. bases from Japan, except for a few exceptions, since the 1950s. After he became state minister for defense, Nakasone continued to propose withdrawal of the U.S. bases by means of transferring them to the newly reinforced JSDF. Nakasone was of the view that the base issue was easily connected to nationalism. But nationalism had been in the hands of the progressive political forces in Japan and needed to be reclaimed by the conservative forces, he felt. According to Nakasone, settling the base issue was the way to put nationalism back in the hands of the conservatives.

Another idea of his that Nakasone wanted realized early was regular meetings between the U.S. and Japanese defense ministers. While there already was a Japan–United States Security Consultative Committee (SCC), a bilateral consultative body on security issues stipulated by Article 4 of the U.S.-Japan Security Treaty, its representation was asymmetrical. The minister of foreign affairs and the director-general of the Defense Agency participated from the Japanese side, while the U.S. side was represented by the American ambassador to Japan and the commander-in-chief of the U.S. Pacific Command. Nakasone's

---

* Soeya Yoshihide, David A. Welch, and Tadokoro Masayuki, eds. *Japan as a 'Normal Country'?: A Nation in Search of Its Place in the World*. Toronto: University of Toronto Press, 2011.

proposal was to establish a new consultative body with more equal representation from two sides. While the composition of the SCC symbolized the relative positions of Japan and the United States concerning security relations in those days, Nakasone must have been aware when he attempted to remedy the unequal representation that criticism of Japan's dependence on the United States could provoke nationalistic sentiment among the Japanese people.

Nakasone's arguments for change, some of which were related to long-term defense plans that we will discuss later, provoked criticisms from various corners including inside the LDP. For instance, Nakasone's proposal that the U.S. bases be transferred to the JSDF after its capabilities were expanded was essentially tantamount to arguing for the stationing of U.S. troops in Japan only during emergency situations. Many LDP members saw Nakasone's proposition as something that touched on the very foundation of the security arrangements with the United States and thus demanded a transformation in the nature of the arrangements. Nakasone was criticized not only by those who placed the U.S.-Japan security pact at the center of Japan's defense, including the LDP's defense policy tribe, but also by the successors of the Yoshida Doctrine. Prime Minister Sato, who wished to minimize intra-party confusion in anticipation of renewal of the security pact and the LDP presidential election, abstained from enthusiastically supporting Nakasone's arguments.

Nakasone also attempted to revise the Basic Policy for National Defense in order to explicitly advocate autonomous defense. In the end, however, he failed.

Significance of the Nakasone Plan

Let's take a closer look at the long-term defense plan that was drafted to succeed the Third Defense Build-up Plan while Nakasone was chief of the Defense Agency. Claiming that he had formulated a long-term defense plan from a new perspective instead of as a mere extension of traditional long-term plans, Nakasone named his plan the New Defense Build-up Plan instead of the Fourth Defense Build-up Plan. Nakasone's vision was for the plan to be accomplished in ten years.

A note of caution is in order here. No matter how well versed Nakasone might have been about defense issues—in fact, he had actively remarked on such issues—it would have been impossible for him to give detailed instructions on all the specifics of a long-term defense plan. As a matter of fact, formulation of the plan to succeed the Third Defense Build-up Plan had already been started when Nakasone's predecessor, Arita Kiichi, was director-general of the Defense Agency. The successor plan's basic line had been decided at that time. Before Nakasone was appointed as the Defense Agency's chief, he instructed the agency's inner bureau to study what it would take to realize a national defense chiefly reliant on the JSDF. The result of the study astonished Nakasone because the scale necessary to accomplish what Nakasone envisioned was estimated to be humongous. It was these same officials of the Defense Agency's inner bureau that played the central role in formulating the New Defense Build-up Plan.

Where, then, do we see Nakasone's influences in the long-term defense plan? One obvious influence of Nakasone was the high visibility of the plan—much more so than previous plans. Another influence was Nakasone Plan's most important feature: the notion of a "standing armed force" (which in itself was an invention of the Defense Agency's inner bureau). Because this notion is closely related to the Concept of Basic Defense Capability of later days, we will come back to it later in this book. Other than that, it appears that regarding the plan's contents, a distinctive "Nakasone color" could be spotted in (1) the emphasis on maritime and air defenses; (2) the emphasis on nationalization of defense equipage by promoting scientific research and development; (3) the emphasis on the importance of logistical support systems; and (4) the limitation of defense capabilities.

The emphasis on maritime and air defense buildup represented what Nakasone had long advocated as "the military power to sustain Japan's diplomatic power." The nationalization of defense equipage, according to Nakasone, would be necessary to enable autonomous defense, which should be supported by enhanced scientific research and development capabilities.

The third item—emphasis on the importance of logistical support—was particularly noteworthy. This item was believed to have been influenced by the contents of a report by the Group to Diagnose Japan's Defense and Defense Agency/JSDF (Nippon no Boei to Boeicho/ Jieitai o Shindan Suru Kai), a group of private intellectuals that Nakasone put together when he was appointed the Defense Agency's chief. Not only did the report emphasize the importance of the procurement of ammunitions, which had long been found problematic, it also addressed the need to improve the social standing of the JSDF and the working environments of its members. This last point related to the serious difficulties the JSDF had been facing in recruiting members.

The limitation of Japan's defense capabilities, the final item reflecting Nakasone's influence, was very much related to the outcome of the Nakasone Plan itself.

As the Defense Agency's draft of the plan to succeed the Third Defense Build-up Plan—the fourth in the series of defense plans— began to take shape, its budgetary scale became a subject of controversy, along with Nakasone's aggressive assertion of autonomous defense. The budgets for the Second and Third Defense Build-up Plans had doubled from the budgets of their preceding plans, and the budget for the fourth plan was expected to be humongous if past trends continued. Thus, voices began to be raised, particularly from among opposition parties, questioning whether some kind of check should be imposed on the expansion of defense capabilities. In the end, the draft budget for this plan to succeed the Third Defense Build-up Plan loomed at ¥5,195 billion, excluding a regular pay-scale increase, which was 2.2 times more than the budget for the Third Defense Build-up Plan. As mentioned, Nakasone envisioned his long-term defense plan to be accomplished in ten years, and this draft of the plan to succeed the Third Defense Build-up Plan represented the first five of the ten years. During the first five years, Nakasone intended to accomplish up to 80 percent of the ultimate goal, including procurement of equipages. The second five years would be spent further enhancing the accomplishments of the first five years. It was therefore obvious that Nakasone did not expect any large-scale budget increase after the draft budget was passed. In other words, the scale of the draft budget was considered to be the maximum limit of the defense expenditure at that time.

Nonetheless, this draft defense build-up plan, with its emphasis on autonomous defense and its gigantic budget scale, coupled with Nakasone's proposal on the military base issue that provoked protests even from LDP members, came to be criticized, both domestically and internationally, as a sign of the resurgence of militarism in Japan. This showed that the notion of a limitation of defense capabilities incorporated in the newly formulated plan was way inadequate, making it necessary to more explicitly clarify the ultimate goal of a defense buildup or the limitation of defense capabilities.

The Nakasone Plan and the Fourth Defense Build-up Plan

Judging from its content, Nakasone's New Defense Build-up Plan can be recognized as an attempt at making defense plans, as Nakasone put it, "adaptive to Japan's own strategies and tactics" rather than mere defense equipage procurement plans like the Second and Third Defense Build-up Plans. In the midst of the criticisms of Nakasone's argument for autonomous defense from within the LDP as well as domestic and international accusations of an alleged resurgence of militarism in Japan, Nakasone's New Defense Build-up Plan also faced harsh criticisms. Most representative were the Ministry of Finance's criticism of the plan's budgetary scale and the National Defense Council's criticism of the plan's contents. The National Defense Council, whose secretary-general at that time was Kaihara Osamu, was critical of the basic thrusts of the New Defense Build-up Plan, including the importance it attached to maritime defense. In the face of such strong opposition from the Finance Ministry and the National Defense Council, revision of the proposed plan became inevitable.

The first and second Nixon Shocks, which took place immediately after Nakasone was replaced by Masuda Kaneshichi as director-general of the Defense Agency, made the flow toward revising and scaling down the proposed defense buildup plan irreversible. The first Nixon Shock attacked Japan when U.S. President Nixon visited China in July 1971; the timing of Nixon's visit delayed deliberations on the

New Defense Build-up Plan, which had already been behind schedule at the Finance Ministry and the National Defense Council, into the next fiscal year. More impactful on Japan, however, was the second Nixon Shock. This occurred in August 1971, when the United States unilaterally cancelled the direct international convertibility of the U.S. dollar to gold. Because of this, it was predicted that Japan would be forced to spend more for its defense and that it would also face problems procuring arms and weapons from the United States. It was also feared that confusion in international financial exchange would affect Japan's finances. In the end, Nishimura Naomi, at this time the new director-general of the Defense Agency, decided to significantly revise the proposed plan, and the Defense Agency immediately started the process of reexamination. (It should be noted that, after Nakasone left the Defense Agency, the proposed draft plan came to be called the Fourth Defense Build-up Plan, following the pattern of the first through third plans.)

Nishimura had originally been an official of the former Home Ministry and a close personal friend to Kaihara. Reexamination of this draft defense buildup plan under Nishimura, therefore, meant that Kaihara's views would substantially influence the plan's revision. Without going into detail, in the process toward formulation of the revised Fourth Defense Build-up Plan, it was Kaihara who took the leadership in drastically revising and downsizing the draft plan. On January 28, 1972, an "Outline of the Fourth Defense Build-up Plan: Kaihara's Personal Proposal" was circulated at the four-minister meeting (among Finance Minister Mizuta Mikio, Defense Agency Director-General Esaki Masumi, Economic Planning Agency Director-General Kimura Toshio, and Chief Cabinet Secretary Takeshita Noboru) among concerned ministries/agencies. It was on the basis of this document that the outline of the fourth plan was formulated. After Kaihara's personal proposal was circulated, it was deliberated almost every day at the councilors' meetings of the National Defense Council and at Diet members' roundtables. Finally, the Outline of the Fourth Defense Build-up Plan was approved by the National Defense Council on February 7, 1972. The Cabinet approved it the next day.

The Outline of the Fourth Defense Build-up Plan opened with these words:

1. Basics of National Defense
The basic policy of Japan's national defense is, in full compliance with the Basic Policy on National Policy, to establish friendly relations with neighboring countries, pursue diplomatic measures to mitigate international tensions, carry out various domestic policy measures to promote economic and social developments, build up defense capabilities to repel foreign invasions on the basis of the U.S.-Japan Security Treaty regime, and, thereby, defend democratic Japan's independence and peace.

Because Kaihara took leadership in revising the Fourth Defense Build-up Plan, it in the end complied fully with the Basic Policy on National Defense that Nakasone had wished to reform so badly. Pursuit of a more autonomous defense, so conspicuous in the Nakasone Plan, mostly disappeared. Instead, the Fourth Defense Build-up Plan was transformed into a plan centered around security arrangements with the United States. In other words, it became de facto an extension of the Third Defense Build-up Plan.

Once the Outline of the Fourth Defense Build-up Plan was determined, discussions on details commenced. Discussions centered less on the essence of the plan and more on such issues as types of equipage to be procured and in what quantities. At this point, the Nakasone Plan was de facto thwarted and the debate on whether Japan should pursue more autonomous defense or rely on security arrangements with the United States was once again sealed. It was President Nixon's Guam Doctrine of July 25, 1969, that gave momentum to arguments for autonomous defense in Japan; those arguments, having generated unprecedented levels of attention, culminated in the Nakasone Plan. Ironically, it was a second Nixon declaration, in the form of the Nixon Shock, that forced the Nakasone Plan to be completely revamped.

What Nakasone pursued was twofold: departure from dependence on the United States for the country's defense and expansion of the range of autonomous defense as well as greater equality in Japan's relations with the United States. Both pursuits appear to have been thwarted, along with the Nakasone Plan, at least on the surface. What really happened to these two goals?

Chapter 6

Formulation of the National Defense Program Guidelines

Two Critical Issues Concerning Japan's Defense Policy

The argument for more autonomous national defense, which had been on the rise in Japan since the late 1960s, also necessitated review of Japan's defense capabilities—in other words, the role of the Japan Self-Defense Forces (JSDF). Simply put, even if Japan chose the option of security arrangements with the United States as a complement to its own autonomous defense efforts, it would be necessary to review how much the JSDF could do and how its capabilities could be configured to defend Japan under the U.S.-Japan Security Treaty. It was against this backdrop that Nakasone Yasuhiro proposed his New Defense Build-up Plan. As we saw in the previous chapter, however, not only did Nakasone's plan end up being drastically revised, it also provoked criticism of a resurgence of militarism in Japan, imposing on Japan a new important task of clarifying the limitations of its defense capabilities.

Yet the situation that provoked the rise of the argument for autonomous defense itself remained essentially unchanged. As a matter of fact, after the two Nixon Shocks in 1971, a sense of mistrust toward the United States grew stronger among the Japanese people. This further propelled momentum for the argument for Japan's increased autonomy in national defense. Therefore, the 1970s was a decade when Japan was urged to respond simultaneously to the two critical issues of clarifying the role of Japan's own defense capabilities, on the one hand, and deciding on the limitations of its own defense capabilities, on the other. It was Kubo Takuya, director of the Defense Policy Bureau of the Defense Agency under Director-General Nakasone and later administrative vice minister for defense, who tried to theorize Japan's defense policy in order to respond to these two critical issues. Also, originally from the former Home Ministry's Police Bureau, Kubo belonged to a slightly younger generation than that of Kaihara Osamu. Kubo had been engaged in Japan's defense issues since his days at the National Safety

Kubo Takuya (Source: The Mainichi Newspapers)

Agency and had assumed various posts back and forth between the Defense Agency and the National Police Agency. Kubo had been personally very much interested in defense issues, and he had been engaged in all the long-term defense plannings since the First Defense Build-up Plan in one way or another. He was, thus, an official who had been expected to be a new-generation leader of the Defense Agency. Kaihara and his fellow "first generation" officials had devoted their energy to firmly establishing the primacy of civil officials over the uniformed team within the Defense Agency, eliminating interferences from former military personnel and politicians and suppressing the rise of the uniformed team as much as possible. In contrast, Kubo was discontent with the degrading of the Defense Agency to a mere managing/coordinating agency and expressed his wish to restore the agency's position as a policy authority. Whether the Defense Agency could really transform itself into a policy authority was put to the test by the above important issues of the 1970s. After returning from the National Police Agency to the Defense Agency as its director of the Defense Policy Bureau, Kubo had to tackle these two issues, while laboriously attending to deliberations on Nakasone's New Defense Build-up Plan.

Kubo was instrumental in elaborating the notion of "defense capabilities in peacetime." While it is believed that this notion later evolved into the Concept of Basic Defense Capability, a careful study of the idea would reveal that its basis was an idea first put forth by the Nakasone Plan. In essence, it was the idea of a standing force—but we will come back to this idea later when the Concept of Basic Defense Capability is discussed in detail.

In any event, as soon as Kubo could put together his ideas, he circulated among Defense Agency officials what he called a "KB personal treatise." He welcomed feedback from readers and often shared his views with non–Defense Agency readers of popular magazines. He also published a number of books and treatises, making him a vocal Defense Agency official along with Kaihara, who had become a commentator after his retirement and published a number of books.

Formulation of a Defense Build-up Plan to Succeed the Fourth Plan
The Fourth Defense Build-up Plan was formulated as an extension of the Third Defense Build-up Plan; it was a significantly revised and downsized version of Nakasone's New Defense Build-up Plan. The Outline of the Fourth Defense Build-up Plan was approved by the Sato Eisaku cabinet on February 7, 1972, giving the plan its basic stances. The plan's key elements were approved on October 9 in the same year. The October approval took place under the Tanaka Kakuei government that had taken over from the long administration of the Sato cabinet in July.

It was soon after the Fourth Defense Build-up Plan was approved that discussions on defense capabilities in peacetime got into full swing. At the time—in the aftermath of the first Oil Crisis of 1973— Japan was believed to have entered a period of lower growth after years of rapid growth, which seriously affected Japan's defense budget. The Fourth Defense Build-up Plan was an unfortunate long-term plan in the sense that not only was it subject to large-scale revisions and downscaling due to the highly disarrayed deliberation process, but it also contained many plans that were never realized at the implementation stage. This was particularly true for aspects of the plan pertaining to the Maritime Self-Defense Force.

Under these economic conditions and an international situation that can be summarily described as détente, how to formulate a long-term defense plan to succeed the Fourth Defense Build-up Plan while avoiding a process of disarrayed deliberations became a crucial issue for the Defense Agency. In other words, the time had come to reexamine what shape a long-term defense plan itself should take in Japan.

Kubo Takuya had already addressed the issues of the significance of Japan's defense capabilities and limitations of peacetime defense capabilities in his attempt to theorize defense policy. It was Natsume Haruo, Nishihiro Seiki, and Hoshuyama Noboru, Defense Agency officials through and through who belonged to a yet younger generation than that of Kubo, who tackled the concrete task of formulating a long-term defense plan to succeed the Fourth Defense Build-up Plan. Their efforts culminated in the National Defense Program Guidelines (Boei Keikaku no Taiko, NDPG henceforth).

While the Defense Agency was tackling the task of formulating a new plan to succeed the Fourth Defense Build-up Plan under the circumstances of low economic growth and general détente, Sakata Michita was appointed to director-general of the Defense Agency in the Miki Takeo cabinet. Known as a party politician of the education policy tribe, Sakata had had almost no dealings with national defense. It might be said that because of this, Sakata could be free from the restraint of the past entanglement surrounding defense policy. Sakata decided that the clarification of Japan's peacetime defense capabilities and the strengthening of security arrangements with the United States were the two most important issues for him to pursue. Finding the formulation of defense policies in closed chambers to be undesirable, Sakata proactively promoted the transparency of defense policy making. He revived publication of the whitepaper on defense, which had been suspended after the first issue during the Nakasone days, and launched a Committee to Think about Japan's Defense (Boei o Kangaeru Kai) among private intellectuals and experts.

While the purpose of the Committee to Think about Japan's Defense was to discuss a basic stance toward formulation of a defense plan to succeed the Fourth Defense Build-up Plan, the group actually discussed a wide range of topics related to the role of Japan's defense capabilities. The substance of discussions in this group was the essence of what later became the Concept of Basic Defense Capability (Kiban-teki Boeiryoku Koso). It should be pointed out here that a key member of the group, Professor Kosaka Masataka of Kyoto University, shared a very similar idea of defense with Kubo and the group found it easy to adopt the Concept of Basic Defense Capability as a model of peacetime defense capabilities for Japan. Thus, the content of the "Summary of Discussion" published by the Committee to Think about Japan's Defense essentially overlapped the Concept of Basic Defense Capability.

After Kubo was promoted to administrative vice-minister of defense, he continued to push formulation of the next defense build-up plan, which culminated in compilation of the NDPG. What, then, was the substance of this NDPG? And what was the idea behind the Concept of Basic Defense Capability that provided the foundation for the NDPG? The following section explores these questions.

Formulation of the National Defense Program Guidelines
The first National Defense Program Guidelines (the First NDPG) officially approved in October 1976 was the first full-fledged formulation of Japan's own defense plans in twenty years since the establishment of the Defense Agency/JSDF. It was an attempt at reviewing the long-term defense planning up to the Fourth Defense Build-up Plan and clarifying the significance of defense capabilities for Japan. Although it has been customary when discussing the NDPG to refer only to the Concept of Basic Defense Capability that provided its basic stance on defense buildup, the NDPG should be evaluated in a more comprehensive manner that includes the adoption of previously untried methods such as the midterm accomplishments evaluation method (*chugyo*) and the proposal on strengthening the Joint Staff Office.

The long-term defense plans up to the Fourth Defense Build-up Plan had subscribed to the concept of a "required defense force"—that is, that Japan's defense capabilities should match the power of an aggressor. This in itself was nothing unusual; it is the very basic idea of defense buildup. In the case of Japan, however, its presumed aggressor was the Soviet Union, and the Soviet Union's military capabilities, even when limited to those in the Far East region, were enormous. Thus, when Japan calculated the defense capabilities necessary to match Soviet power, it became clear that building up adequate capabilities would not be possible. Moreover, as long as the three branches of the JSDF were not allowed to participate in the formulation of basic defense policy and as long as each branch planned its own buildup based on independent, branch-specific defense policies, any long-term defense plan would become a budget scramble. Also, because each branch of the JSDF tried to procure equipages in line with its own defense plan and within the constraints of a limited budget, a long-term defense buildup plan tended to look like a shopping list for state-of-the-art equipages.

The fact of the matter is that in those days defense buildup became quite a distorted picture of state-of-the-art equipages being introduced despite a dearth of supplies, including indispensable ammunitions (see fig. 10). Each branch of the JSDF accumulated resentment at the inability to procure necessary equipages to its satisfaction owing to strict outside assessments, including by the Ministry of Finance. It was in response to these situations that the Concept of Basic Defense Capability was adopted.

Assuming that there was a low probability for Japan to be attacked by a large-scale direct invasion—with the exception of the eruption of war between the United States and the Soviet Union, which would de facto be another world war—the Concept of Basic Defense Capability assumed that a threat to be anticipated and prepared for was that of "a local war by a limited, small-scale military unit." The ability to respond to a local war by a limited, small-scale military unit sufficed as Japan's peacetime defense capabilities according to the Concept of Basic Defense Capability, which advocated defense buildup within the range necessary for rejecting direct invasions. The term used for this was "rejection power."

Kosaka Masataka, who as mentioned was a key member of the Committee to Think about Japan's Defense, also referred to rejection power. In fact, it was the defense capabilities that constituted rejection

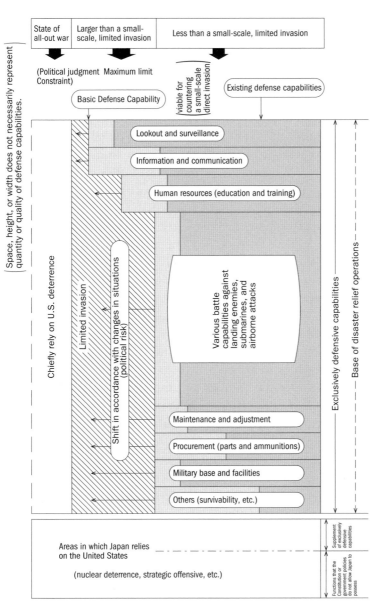

| State of all-out war | Larger than a small-scale, limited invasion | Less than a small-scale, limited invasion |

(Political judgment Constraint) Maximum limit

Basic Defense Capability

viable for countering a small-scale direct invasion

Existing defense capabilities

(Space, height, or width does not necessarily represent quantity or quality of defense capabilities.)

Lookout and surveillance

Information and communication

Human resources (education and training)

Chiefly rely on U.S. deterrence

Limited invasion

Shift in accordance with changes in situations (political risk)

Various battle capabilities against landing enemies, submarines, and airborne attacks

Maintenance and adjustment

Procurement (parts and ammunitions)

Military base and facilities

Others (survivability, etc.)

Exclusively defensive capabilities

Base of disaster relief operations

Areas in which Japan relies on the United States

(nuclear deterrence, strategic offensive, etc.)

Supplement of exclusively defensive capabilities

Functions that the Constitution or government policies do not allow Japan to possess

Figure 10. Concept of Basic Defense Capability

power that had been discussed as a standing force in Nakasone's New Defense Build-up Plan. As shown in figure 10, it was decided that it would be adequate in peacetime to build up just enough defense capabilities to reject direct invasions (which was the substance of the Concept of Basic Defense Capability) and that doing so would allow Japan to attain a more comprehensive defense buildup, including bolstering hitherto inadequate logistic support.

To accomplish this type of comprehensive defense buildup, it became necessary to coordinate among the three branches of the JSDF in a comprehensive manner. The Joint Staff Office should have been in charge of such coordination, but seeing as its authority at that time was not strong enough, strengthening of the Joint Staff Office was advocated. As we will see in the process of the formulation of the Guidelines for Japan-U.S. Defense Cooperation later, this office began to gradually accumulate power from this period on.

In more concrete terms, then, what was the scale of this basic defense capability? The table of defense buildup goals in the NDPG is one depiction. The rolling plan system known as the midterm accomplishments evaluation method, or *chugyo*, was introduced to accomplish these defense buildup goals. In contrast to conventional defense buildup plans, which were five-year fixed government plans approved by the National Defense Council and the Cabinet, the *chugyo* was an internal document of the Defense Agency that was subject to revision every three years according to what had actually been accomplished under the plans. Because conventional defense buildup plans were government plans, they were often subject to assessments and revision requests by the Ministry of Finance twice: once during the formulation stage and once at the final implementation stage. In other words, under the conventional system, defense policy had been constrained twice by the fiscal authority. Behind adoption of the *chugyo* was the Defense Agency's wish to limit inspection by the financial authority to one time, which would ensure independence of defense policy.

Formulation of the NDPG appeared to provide the Defense Agency with a way out from under the constraints of financial authority imposed on its long-term planning, opening a new possibility to formulate a plan that gave more weight to the needs of defense policy. As soon as the NDPG and the Concept of Basic Defense Capability were formulated, however, they became targets of fierce criticism.

NDPG Criticized

It appeared that the greatest cause of the fierce criticism heaped on the Concept of Basic Defense Capability was the emphasis that Kubo placed on the "threat removal theory" as the concept's premise when he explained the concept as its spokesperson. To be sure, the international situation that the NDPG assumed was characterized by détente under which there hardly was any possibility that Japan would face a large-scale direct invasion. And this was what Kubo emphasized as the removal of threat. In actuality, however, when calculating the necessary basic defense capability for Japan, a threat from a local war by a limited, small-scale military unit was used as the yardstick. That was, by no means, a situation that could be called a state of "removal of threat" from the first place. When coupled with the arms buildup of the Soviet Union, which became conspicuous around this time, plus arguments for the end of détente, the NDPG came to be criticized as already being out of date regarding international situations when it was formulated.

Of all the criticisms of the NDPG from every direction, the fiercest one was heard from the uniformed team of the Defense Agency. It was Director-General Sakata's policy to give the uniformed team opportunities to speak freely, and it helped the uniformed team to be more vocal. Although few incumbent officials made remarks, veterans became quite vocal about the threat removal theory, which they found to be already outdated. While the Concept of Basic Defense Capability proposed the prompt expansion of defense capabilities to the necessary level in case of emergency, the uniformed team veterans strongly criticized that as unrealistic and infeasible.

These and other criticisms did not lead to immediate reexamination of the NDPG. After all, the NDPG tested a new possibility in defense buildup on the basis of a review of traditional long-term defense planning, and it was an attempt at answering the two major issues in

Table 2. Key Positions of the Defense Agency's Inner Bureau

	Administrative Vice Minister of Defense	Director-General, Secretariat of the Minister of State for Defense	Director, Bureau of Defense Policy
1954	Masuhara Keikichi** (Home Ministry)	July 1 Toga Muneo** (Home Ministry)	September 11 Hayashi Kazuo
1955			
1956			
1957	June 15 Imai Hisashi** (Home Ministry)		August 2 Kato Yozo* (Home Ministry)
1958			
1959			
1960	December 27 Toga Muneo** (Home Ministry)	December 27 Kato Yozo* (Home Ministry)	December 27 Kaihara Osamu* (Home Ministry)
1961			
1962			
1963	August 2 Kato Yozo* (Home Ministry)	August 2 Miwa Yoshio* (Home Ministry)	
1964	November 17 Miwa Yoshio* (Home Ministry)	November 17 Obata Hisao* (Ministry of Communications)	
1965		June 16 Kaihara Osamu* (Home Ministry)	June 16 Shimada Yutaka* (Home Ministry)
1966			
1967	December 5 Obata Hisao* (Ministry of Communications)	July 28 Shimada Yutaka* (Home Ministry)	July 28 Shishido Motoo* (Home Ministry)
1968			
1969			
1970	November 20 Utsumi Hitoshi** (Home Ministry)	November 20 Shishido Motoo* (Home Ministry)	November 2 Kubo Takuya*** (Home Ministry)
1971			
1972	May 23 Shimada Yutaka* (Home Ministry)	June 2 Tashiro Kazumasa** (Ministry of Finance)	
1973		November 2 Maruyama Ko*** (Home Ministry)	
1974	June 7 Tashiro Kazumasa** (Ministry of Finance)	June 7 Saito Ichiro** (National Police Agency)	June 7 Maruyama Ko*** (Home Ministry)
1975	July 15 Kubo Takuya*** (Home Ministry)	July 15 Tamaki Seiji* (National Personnel Authority)	
1976	July 16 Maruyama Ko*** (Home Ministry)	July 16 Watari Akira** (Ministry of Finance)	July 16 Ito Keiichi* (National Personnel Authority)
1977		July 15 Takeoka Katsumi** (National Police Agency)	
1978	November 1 Watari Akira** (Ministry of Finance)	November 1 Shiota Akira** (Ministry of Home Affairs)	November 1 Hara Toru** (Ministry of Finance)
1979			
1980	June 6 Hara Toru** (Ministry of Finance)	June 6 Natsume Haruo* (Procurement Agency)	June 6 Shiota Akira** (Ministry of Home Affairs)
1981			
1982	July 9 Yoshino Minoru*** (Ministry of Finance)	July 9 Sasa Atsuyuki** (National Police Agency)	July 9 Natsume Haruo* (Procurement Agency)
1983	June 29 Natsume Haruo* (Procurement Agency)		June 29 Yazaki Shinji*** (Ministry of Finance)
1984		July 1 Nishihiro Seiki (Defense Agency)	
1985	June 25 Yazaki Shinji*** (Ministry of Finance)	June 25 Anakura Muneo** (Ministry of Finance)	June 25 Nishihiro Seiki (Defense Agency)
1986		June 10 Tomoto Kazutaka (Defense Agency)	
1987	June 23 Anakura Muneo** (Ministry of Finance)	June 23 Yoda Tomoharu** (National Police Agency)	
1988	June 14 Nishihiro Seiki (Defense Agency)		June 14 Hiyoshi Akira*** (Ministry of Finance)

Notes: 1. Dates preceding names are dates when the person came into office; the person's office of origin is in parentheses. Asterisks after a name indicate the depth of the person's affiliation with the Defense Agency defined by Hirose as follows:

* Officials who had been transferred from other government bureaus/agencies and subsequently continued to work at the Defense Agency

** Officials from other government bureaus/agencies who were promoted to executive positions (director of bureau and higher) of the Defense Agency without experiencing major posts in the agency

Director, Bureau of Finance	Director, Bureau of Education	Director, Bureau of Personnel	Director, Bureau of Logistics
August 2 Kitajima Takeo** (Ministry of Finance)			
			April 17 Oyama Yuji** (Ministry of International Trade and Industry)
June 13 Yamashita Taketoshi** (Ministry of Finance)		August 2 Yamamoto Yukio	
	April 1 Obata Hisao* (Ministry of Communications)		October 9 Tsukamoto Toshio** (Ministry of International Trade and Industry)
June 24 Kimura Hidehiro** (Ministry of Finance)		July 13 Ono Hiroshi	
			July 7 Kubo Tadao** (Ministry of International Trade and Industry)
May 16 Ueda Katsuro** (Ministry of Finance)			June 1 Ito Saburo** (Ministry of International Trade and Industry)
	August 2 Hotta Masataka* (Home Ministry)		
May 8 Kimura Fudeo** (Ministry of Finance)	November 17 Shimada Yutaka* (Home Ministry)		October 6 Kunii Makoto*** (Ministry of International Trade and Industry)
	June 16 Shishido Motoo* (Home Ministry)		
August 4 Sasaki Tatsuo** (Ministry of Finance)	June 1 Nakai Ryoichi** (Home Ministry)	June 1 Shishido Motoo* (Home Ministry)	August 10 Morita Mikio, October 23 Kabaya Tomohide
		July 28 Aso Shigeru* (Home Ministry)	
	Bureau of Education and Bureau of Personnel merged to Bureau of Personnel and Education on June 15		
September 2 Tashiro Kazumasa** (Ministry of Finance)	November 21 Utsumi Hitoshi** (Home Ministry)		
	November 2 Eto Atsuo** (Home Ministry)		September 1 Kurobe Yuzuru** (Ministry of International Trade and Industry)
June 20 Odamura Shiro*** (Ministry of Finance)	June 2 Takase Tadao* (National Police Agency)		November 24 Yamaguchi Eiichi** (Ministry of International Trade and Industry)
July 2 Watari Akira** (Ministry of Finance)	August 19 Imaizumi Masataka*** (National Police Agency)		
			August 1 Eguchi Hiromichi** (Ministry of International Trade and Industry)
July 16 Hara Toru** (Ministry of Finance)	January 13 Takeoka Katsumi** (National Police Agency)		
			July 15 Mabuchi Naozo** (Ministry of International Trade and Industry)
November 1 Watanabe Isuke* (Ministry of Home Affairs)	July 15 Watanabe Isuke* (Ministry of Home Affairs)		November 16 Kurabe Yukio** (Ministry of International Trade and Industry)
June 6 Yoshino Minoru*** (Ministry of Finance)	November 1 Natsume Haruo* (Procurement Agency)		June 6 Wada Hiroshi ** (Ministry of International Trade and Industry)
July 23 Yazaki Shinji*** (Ministry of Finance)	June 6 Sasa Atsuyuki** (National Policy Agency)		
			June 11 Kinoshita Hiroo** (Ministry of International Trade and Industry)
June 29 Anakura Muneo** (Ministry of Finance)	July 9 Ueno Takashi (Defense Agency)		
	Director, Bureau of Education and Training July 1 Odaka Tokio	Director, Bureau of Personnel July 1 Tomofuji Kazutaka	June 19 Yamada Katsuhisa** (Ministry of International Trade and Industry)
June 25 Ikeda Hisakatsu (Defense Agency)	June 1 Yoda Tomoji** (National Police Agency)	June 1 Matsumoto Munekazu* (Procurement Agency)	June 10 Kamata Kichiro** (Ministry of International Trade and Industry)
June 23 Hiyoshi Akira*** (Ministry of Finance)	June 23 Hasegawa Hiroshi (Defense Agency)		June 23 Yamamoto Masashi** (Ministry of International Trade and Industry)
		June 14 Kodama Yoshio (Defense Agency)	

*** Officials who had important working experiences in the Defense Agency before being promoted to its executive positions
Names without parenthesized information or asterisks are those whose office of origin or mode of affiliation was unknown as of the time of writing.
2. Such acting titles as *dairi* and *jimutoriatsukai* are omitted.
3. Produced by the author chiefly on the basis of Hirose Katsuya, *Kanryo to gunjin* [Bureaucrats and military], Tokyo: Iwanami Shoten, 1989, *Boei nenkan* [Defense yearbook].

Japan's defense policy in the 1970s—the significance of defense capabilities for Japan and defense capabilities in peacetime. Besides, the situation was such that an increase in the defense budget could not be expected owing to the post–oil crisis downturn of the world economy and the need for fiscal reconstruction in Japan.

Around the same time as the NDPG was announced, the Japanese government decided to limit the defense budget to within 1 percent of annual GNP. From the viewpoint of holding down the defense budget, the importance of the NDPG, which set an upper limit on peacetime defense capabilities, was all the more appreciated.

Also around that time, the Defense Agency was experiencing an internal change in personnel in the sense that more and more officials originally from other government bureaus and agencies, including the Ministry of Finance, were promoted to its key positions in place of officials from the former Home Ministry's Police Bureau (see table 2). Although Administrative Vice Minister of Defense Kubo was directly succeeded by Maruyama Ko, another ex-police bureaucrat, three subsequent administrative vice minister posts were assumed by officials originally from the Ministry of Finance. Some of those administrative vice ministers from outside of the agency had not experienced the post of director of the Bureau of Defense Policy, a post at the very core of defense policy formulation. Thus, as officials who had started their careers at the Defense Agency grew to assume mid-level management positions, an increasing number of top positions within the agency became to be occupied by outsiders with scarce knowledge or firsthand experience of the reality of defense policy. Under these circumstances, therefore, fundamental discussions on Japan's defense policy were never deepened.

Part III

During the Second Cold War

Chapter 7

Formulation of the Guidelines for Japan-U.S. Defense Cooperation

From Détente to the Second Cold War

The years from the early 1970s through the mid-1970s were marked by cabinet approval of the Fourth Defense Build-up Plan and deliberations on the plan to follow it. Those deliberations yielded what later was adopted as the National Defense Program Guidelines (Boei Keikaku no Taiko or Taiko; NDPG). Globally, this period was characterized by détente, during which the earlier state of fierce confrontation between the United States and the Soviet Union evolved into steps toward international peace and stability symbolized by the U.S.-China rapprochement and the signing of the Strategic Arms Limitation Talks Agreement (SALT I) by the United States and the Soviet Union on May 26, 1972. In Asia, China appeared to be at last regaining stability from the confusion caused by the Cultural Revolution and, most of all, China-U.S. rapprochement made China more tolerant toward the U.S.-Japan Security Treaty, which was a positive development for Japan's security environment. Moreover, the Vietnam War, which had intensified since the mid-1960s, at last ended, while north-south dialogue was being proposed on the Korean peninsula, signifying a trend toward greater stabilization in the region surrounding Japan. It was these international situations that provided the basic premises for the formulation of the NDPG.

By the time the NDPG was officially adopted in the mid-1970s, however, détente had already begun to show signs of fraying. The greatest cause of this was the instability in the international situation because of turmoil in the Middle East and the Soviet military expansion that reached even Asia. While the Middle East problem was not something that started in the 1970s, the fourth Arab-Israeli War (Yom Kippur War) in 1973 and the oil crisis it triggered propelled the world economy into a chaotic situation. Oil-producing countries in the Middle East, which came together in the Organization of the Petroleum Exporting Countries (OPEC), finally made their entry into international politics in the 1970s as critical actors possessing a strategic resource called oil. It became obvious, then, that the situation and developments in the Middle East would greatly affect the world economy. Social changes in this region, including the Iranian Revolution, became a serious instability factor.

The second cause of instability—the expansion of Soviet military capabilities—manifested itself as an attempt by the Soviet Union to increase its presence in Asia and the Indian Ocean as the United States tried to reduce its influences in Asia with the end of the Vietnam War. The Soviet Union secured a military base in Vietnam, started very active diplomacy within Asia, and intensified its naval activities in the Indian Ocean. As evidenced by the activities in the Indian Ocean, it was obvious that the Soviet Union's main concern was the situation in the Middle East; in fact, the Soviet Union strengthened its relations with Iran and Iraq during this period.

The Soviet Union's expansion of arms buildup at this time was particularly conspicuous regarding its navy. In contrast to the U.S. Navy, which had to be downsized due to financial aggravation caused by the Vietnam War, expansion of the Soviet Navy was remarkable (see fig. 11). The expansion transformed the Soviet Navy from a traditional coastal force to a blue sea navy, as was proven by the worldwide naval exercise OKEAN, conducted in 1970 and, in a larger scale, in 1975. These exercises put U.S. security authorities and experts on alert regarding the Soviet Union's steady expansion of arms buildup at a time when the Vietnam War–weary United States had let its guard down after signing SALT I.

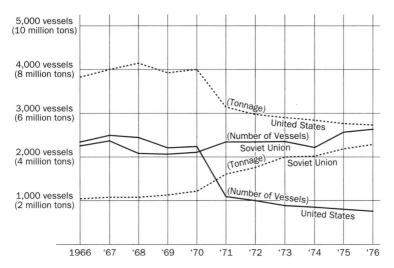

Figure 11. Shift in Naval Forces in the United States and the Soviet Union

Source: Boei Nenkan Kankokai, ed. *Boei nenkan 1980-nendo ban* [Defense yearbook, 1980], Tokyo: Boei Media Center, p.161.

Soviet Military Expansion and the JSDF

Soviet military expansion in the Far East took the form of strengthening its Pacific Fleet and deploying troops to the Kuril Islands. Earlier when the Soviet Union had reinforced its navy, it had usually been to strengthen fleets in the Atlantic region such as the Baltic Sea and the Black Sea. In the 1970s, however, the Soviet Navy deployed *Minsk*, its second Kiev-class aircraft carrier, to the Pacific Fleet and significantly increased the number of nuclear submarines in the fleet. Submarines in the Soviet Pacific Fleet had always been a threat to the U.S. Navy, and the deployment of these new vessels further increased that threat. The threat was felt even more keenly at that time because the military capabilities of the U.S. Navy were reduced owing to significant downsizing.

The Soviet Union's military reinforcements in the Far East were not confined to its navy; in 1978, it started deploying ground forces on the Kuril Islands. Moreover, the Tupolev Tu-22M (Backfire), a supersonic long-range strategic and maritime strike bomber, was also deployed in the Far East, making the Soviet military in the Far East a serious and formidable threat to the United States in the latter half of the 1970s. And, as we will discuss later, this became one of the causes for the U.S. demand that Japan expand its defense capabilities.

Where did the Japan Self-Defense Forces (JSDF) stand on these developments? Having successfully withstood the ordeal surrounding renewal of the U.S.-Japan Security Treaty in 1970, the Ground Self-Defense Force (GSDF) was shifting the emphasis of its strategy from responses to indirect invasions and maintenance of public order in the 1960s to the handling of limited direct invasions. Limiting the likely target of direct invasions from outside to Hokkaido, the GSDF reinforced its troops deployed on the island. This action was basically in alignment with the notion of response to limited small-scale armed offenses set forth in the NDPG.

At the same time, the Maritime Self-Defense Force (MSDF) was further deepening its cooperation with the U.S. Navy. After the reinforcements under the Third Defense Build-up Plan, the MSDF had in the 1970s at last grown to a military organization that was recognized by the U.S. Navy. Through frequent joint exercises with its American counterpart, the MSDF succeeded in earning respect for its high morale and proficiency. As symbolized by its operation to contain Soviet submarines by blockading three straits (Korea, Tsugaru, and Soya) to supplement the U.S. Navy's anti-submarine capabilities in the Pacific, the MSDF had been nurtured with cooperation with the U.S. Navy as a basic assumption. From the viewpoint of a U.S. Navy facing steadily dwindling military capabilities, the MSDF's anti-submarine capabilities were precious additional forces. With the revision of the U.S. Navy's training manual in the mid-1970s, relations between the two navies became even more tightly knit. The MSDF, on its part, continued to further improve its anti-submarine capabilities as a "detachment force" of the U.S. Navy.

Such a policy of the MSDF was fundamentally different from the GSDF's stance to stand ready to meet direct invasions to the homeland. As a matter of fact, the MSDF's capabilities to deliver an attack on troop transports heading for homeland Japan were extremely limited. From beginning to end, the chief mission of the MSDF had been anti-submarine operations, and this was symbolically manifested in the sinking of the *Dai-10 Yuyomaru*, an LPG gas tanker, in November 1974. When the *Dai-10 Yuyomaru* collided with a Liberian cargo ship, killing 33 crew members, and sat burning in Tokyo Bay, the MSDF was deployed as a last resort to sink the burning vessel. From the launching of the attack on November 27 until the sinking of the vessel in the evening of November 28, the operation took close to 30 hours. The MSDF was criticized for having taken too long to sink the vessel even if the target was a tanker weighing over 40,000 tons with numerous partitions in the hull that made the vessel hard to sink. Geared to attack submarines with torpedoes tailored for anti-submarine operations, and with scarcely any large-caliber anti-ship guns, however, this result was inevitable for the MSDF.

The fundamental difference in the basic policies of the GSDF and the MSDF was attributable to the different weight the two organizations gave to homeland defense. Given its nature, it was only natural for the GSDF to focus most of its attention on homeland defense. And given its history since its origin, the MSDF had always followed a basic policy of conducting joint operations with the U.S. Navy. Its attention was mainly focused on protecting the sea lines of communication (chiefly anti-submarine operations) and blockading the Korea, Tsugaru, and Soya straits around Japan. From the viewpoint of the MSDF with its close partnership with the U.S. Navy, emergencies on the Korean peninsula and in the Middle East appeared much more imminent than direct invasions of the homeland. The MSDF stance, actually, was at variance with the content of the NDPG, which had been formulated in anticipation of direct foreign invasions to the homeland. This discrepancy later came to have an important meaning when the Guidelines for Japan-U.S. Defense Cooperation were formulated. The next section looks at how the Guidelines were formulated.

Materialization of U.S.-Japan Military Cooperation

It was Maruyama Ko, director of the Bureau of Defense Policy under

Administrative Vice Minister of Defense Kubo Takuya before he himself succeeded Kubo, who earnestly promoted defense cooperation between Japan and the United States. Maruyama's efforts culminated in the Guidelines for Japan-U.S. Defense Cooperation. Maruyama, too, was originally from the former Home Ministry's Police Bureau and, although he had once served as director of the General Affairs Division of the Minister's Secretariat of the Defense Agency, he had not been at the center of Japan's national defense administration until he became director-general of the Minister's Secretariat of the Defense Agency. In contrast to Kaihara Osamu, who had remained engaged in national defense policy since his National Safety Agency days, or Kubo, who had participated in all of the defense build-up plans even though he was transferred back and forth between the Defense Agency and the National Police Agency, Maruyama was an outsider in the inner bureau of the Defense Agency. Staying away almost entirely from formulation of the NDPG, which was an aggregate of all the problems that past defense build-up plans had had, Maruyama devoted himself to the strengthening of U.S.-Japan defense cooperation. Maruyama himself reminisced that he had been concerned about the absence of consultations on concrete matters in Japan's defense plans between Japan and the United States and so decided to concentrate on this issue when he was appointed director of the Bureau of Defense Policy.

What Maruyama decided at this point was to set up a mechanism to consult about concrete applications of the security treaty between Japan and the United States and to launch a regular consultation between cabinet members in charge of defense issues of the two countries. Concerning the first initiative, the Security Consultative Committee (SCC), the Security Subcommittee (SSC), and the Security Consultative Group (SCG) between the two countries already existed. But the SCC had an inherent structural problem in the sense that, while Japan was represented by the foreign minister and the director-general of the Defense Agency, the U.S. side was represented by the ambassador to Japan and the commander-in-chief of the U.S. Pacific Command. Moreover, the SCC was an organ for dealing with basic issues of the bilateral security pact. The SSC, in contrast, was a vice-ministerial–level meeting convened occasionally to compare notes. The SCG was started as a forum to discuss more specific issues of security cooperation by Foreign Minister Ohira Masayoshi and U.S. Ambassador to Japan Robert Ingersoll in January 1973; however, under the initiative of the Ministry of Foreign Affairs, it was functioning as a mechanism to exchange views between the two sides. Therefore, Maruyama thought that there should be a new mechanism for consultations on specific matters regarding the contents of Japan's defense plans.

This notion of a mechanism for consultations on specific matters in the contents of Japan's defense plans had its genesis in a proposition to change the composition of the SCC's members. This proposition was made when Nakasone Yasuhiro was director-general of the Defense Agency. Nakasone aimed to obtain symmetry of representation at the SCC between the two sides by upgrading the U.S. members to cabinet minister level. In the end, the asymmetry within the SCC remained unattended to. While mutual visits by Minister of State for Defense Nakasone and Secretary of Defense Melvin Laird were realized, further reforms, such as a change in the composition of SCC members, were found to be hard to realize. As a stopgap measure, it was decided that a regular minister-level meeting between Japan and the United States would be launched; this meeting was hoped to make the two countries equal partners.

Maruyama became director of the Bureau of Defense Policy after Miki Takeo formed his cabinet. When Maruyama emphasized the need to establish a mechanism to consult on concrete applications of the bilateral security pact and proposed a minister-level regular meeting between the two countries to Sakata Michita, director-general of the Defense Agency, Sakata concurred. This conversation later culminated in U.S. Secretary of Defense James Schlesinger's visit to Japan, Schlesinger's talk with Sakata, and establishment of the Subcommittee for Defense Cooperation (SDC).

What puzzled Maruyama was why the bilateral consultations on specific matters regarding U.S.-Japan joint activities had lagged behind from the first place. The delay derived from the notion in Japan's defense policy that the presence of the U.S. military bases in Japan itself was deterrence; this thinking allowed the Japanese side to pay little attention to the possibility of joint activities with the U.S. military. Kaihara, who had been a central figure in Japan's defense policy in the 1950s through the 1960s, for one, was of the view that, like himself, the U.S. military did not hold the JSDF's capabilities in high esteem and, therefore, joint activities between the two would never take place. As we will see later, Kubo essentially believed in autonomous defense of the homeland; he hardly recognized the need for joint U.S.-Japan activities. More than that, Kubo was quite skeptical about the promotion of U.S.-Japan cooperation that Maruyama was advocating. Thus, there emerged a situation within the Defense Agency in which formulation of the NDPG along the autonomous defense argument centered around Kubo, on the one hand, and efforts to promote U.S.-Japan defense cooperation centered around Maruyama, on the other hand. These two lines were pursued simultaneously with hardly any coordination between them.

Behind this simultaneous pursuit of two parallel lines inside the Defense Agency was the presence of Director-General Sakata. Having had little dealing with national defense as he was originally a member of the education policy tribe, Sakata was free from entanglements of past history when he decided to go ahead with what he thought to be best. The two key issues facing Sakata when he became director-general of the Defense Agency were (1) how to set limitations on peacetime defense capabilities and (2) how to define the meaning of defense capabilities for Japan. In order to respond to these issues, Sakata decided to adopt the Concept of Basic Defense Capability and formulate the NDPG. At the same time, Sakata was convinced that it would be possible to build up a robust defense system by further strengthening security cooperation with the United States, thus preventing Japan's defense capabilities from becoming unnecessarily large. Sakata agreed with and endorsed Maruyama when he said that if the reality of security arrangements with the United States was hollow then cooperative relations between the two countries had to be made closer.

Significance of the Formulation of the Guidelines for Japan-U.S. Defense Cooperation

Securing the support of Director-General Sakata, Maruyama devoted himself to the concrete realization of defense cooperation with the United States and succeeded in launching a minister-level regular meeting between the two countries and establishing the Subcommittee for Defense Cooperation (SDC). Maruyama topped off his contributions with the compilation of the Guidelines for Japan-U.S. Defense Cooperation in November 1978.

A close look at the contents of the Guidelines reveals two major problems. One was about their range of application, and the other concerned their relationship with the NDPG, which had been approved by the Cabinet earlier.

Let us take up the first problem. Article 5 of the U.S.-Japan Security Treaty addressed defense of the homeland Japan, while Article 6 referred to peace and security in the Far East. From a purely military perspective, the uniformed teams of both countries believed the possibility for turmoil on the Korean peninsula, with spillover effects, was much higher than the much-talked-about direct invasions of Hokkaido. Japan and Korea were viewed to share a common destiny and, from that viewpoint, the stipulation on Japan's homeland defense in Article 5 and that on use of military bases in Article 6 were considered to be two sides of the same coin and inseparable. Therefore, the uniformed team expected that the Guidelines, too, would advocate the promotion of U.S.-Japan defense cooperation including what was stipulated by Article 6. In the end, however, because of domestic politics, the Guidelines featured only U.S.-Japan cooperation as set forth by Article 5. Bilateral cooperation vis-à-vis the so-called emergency-at-the-periphery scenario as stipulated by Article 6 had to await formulation of the New Guidelines some 20 years later.

Nevertheless, the issue of U.S.-Japan cooperation in maritime defense had an important meaning. As introduced earlier, there had been a disparity of views among the three branches of the JSDF concerning bilateral cooperation in the defense of Japan, with each one giving particular weight to different things. The GSDF, for instance, was destined to be stuck with homeland defense, and it had to figure out how to cooperate with the U.S. military in this field. It was the same for the Air Self-Defense Force (ASDF) in the sense that its target of defense was the homeland from beginning to end. And, as we have repeatedly observed, this was not the case for the MSDF. In retrospect, it was highly significant for the MSDF, which had always thought primarily of joint actions with the U.S. Navy, that the Guidelines officially stipulated U.S.-Japan cooperation in maritime defense as follows:

(b) Maritime Operations:
The Maritime Self-Defense Force (MSDF) and U.S. Navy will jointly conduct maritime operations for the defense of surrounding waters and the protection of sea lines of communication.
The MSDF will primarily conduct operations for the protection of major ports and straits in Japan, anti-submarine operations, and operations for the protection of ships and other operations in the surrounding waters.
U.S. Naval Forces will support MSDF operations and conduct operations, including those that which may involve the use of task forces providing additional mobility and strike power, with the objective of repelling enemy forces. (underline added)

Whereas U.S.-Japan cooperation was limited to defense of Japan's homeland in the cases of the GSDF and the ASDF, the Guidelines characteristically included protection of sea lines of communication beyond the defense of surrounding waters of Japan as a field of joint operations with the U.S. Navy. This was beyond the range of cooperation stipulated by the NDPG, which said:

(2) Maritime Self-Defense Force
(i) The MSDF must possess one fleet escort force as a mobile operating ship unit in order to quickly respond to aggressive action and such situations at sea. The fleet escort force must be able to maintain at least one escort flotilla on alert at all times.
(ii) The MSDF must possess, as ship units assigned to coastal sur-

veillance and defense, surface anti-submarine capability of at least one ship division in operational readiness at all times in each assigned sea district.
(iii) The MSDF must maintain submarine units, anti-submarine helicopter units and minesweeping units, providing the capability for surveillance and defense missions as well as minesweeping at important harbors and major straits when such necessity arises.
(iv) The MSDF must maintain fixed-wing anti-submarine aircraft units in order to provide the capability of carrying out such missions as surveillance and patrol of the nearby seas and surface ship protection.

Thus, the NDPG did not include the kind of cooperation underlined in the above quote from the Guidelines. What should be noted here is how the underlined portion relates to the National Defense Program Guidelines, which was the second problem. As we have said, in the NDPG the role of the JSDF was confined to that of homeland defense and nothing beyond. Kubo, who was believed to have played an important role in formulating the Concept of Basic Defense Capability, saw the security arrangements with the United States as deterrence. On the basis of this, he defined the Concept of Basic Defense Capability for Japan as follows:

Because it is hard to imagine a large-scale invasion of Japan given today's international situation, and while it is hard to deny the possibility of a small-scale, surprise attack invasion, Japan should be equipped with emergency readiness to respond to the latter type of threat with its own defense capabilities.

Therefore, from Kubo's viewpoint, even though the Concept of Basic Defense Capability was underpinned by the security arrangements with the United States, it was conceived as a means to improve the autonomy of Japan's national defense.

To put it differently, too much reliance on security cooperation with the United States was feared to adversely affect the autonomy of

Japan's national defense. Kubo was of the view that the basic expectation of the United States was for Japan to be prepared to defend the homeland and its surrounding areas. Expectations that Japan would protect vast sea lines of communication and the Indian Ocean would probably not be incorporated in U.S. policy toward Japan, he felt, even though some might voice their hopes on this issue. At the same time, Kubo was aware of the gap between the U.S. expectations and the priority that Japan placed on homeland defense. He was worried, therefore, that it might become necessary to make the United States understand the true state of Japan's defense and its readiness for autonomous defense. Contrary to Kubo's wishful thinking, however, a situation emerged sooner than expected in which Japan's stance toward defense centered around homeland defense clashed with a U.S. request for Japan's defense buildup centered around maritime and air defenses.

Chapter 8

What Comprehensive Security Is

U.S. Demands for Japan's Defense Buildup

How, then, was it possible to produce Guidelines for Japan-U.S. Defense Cooperation (Guidelines) with portions inconsistent with the National Defense Program Guidelines (NDPG)? The Guidelines, as revealed earlier, were endorsed in the initial stage by Director-General of the Defense Agency Sakata Michita, but it was after the Fukuda Takeo cabinet replaced the Miki Takeo cabinet in 1978 that the Guidelines were officially adopted.

It seems reasonable to say that the conditions of U.S.-Japan relations in those days impacted the content of the Guidelines. Prime Minister Miki announced his resignation on December 17, 1976, after the National Defense Council had approved the NDPG on October 29. The Fukuda cabinet formed on December 24. (Around this time, too, Mihara Asao was appointed director-general of the Defense Agency.) These changes in Japan coincided with the change of the U.S. administration from the Gerald Ford presidency to that of Jimmy Carter. What Fukuda faced when he took over was much more strained economic friction with the United States and tougher demands from Washington for Japan's defense buildup.

Because space does not allow me to go into the details of the bilateral economic friction, I intend to focus on the latter issue here. The Annual Defense Department Report for fiscal year 1978 published on January 17, 1977, emphasized throughout the military threats posed by the Soviet Union. The report stated, for instance, that no matter what Soviet intentions might be, it was beyond doubt that the Soviet Union had continued earnest and steadfast efforts to build up its military might and that, should the United States fail to counter these efforts, the Soviet Union would become the dominant military power. As we saw in the previous chapter, the Soviet Union's expansion of its military capabilities was remarkable in those days. The reinforcement of the Soviet Navy—and particularly its deployment to the Indian Ocean, which had great bearing on the Middle East, as well as the expansion of Soviet military capabilities in the Far East, as symbolized by the deployment of such equipages as the Tupolev Tu-22M (Backfire)— had come to pose a serious threat to the United States.

At that time, the United States was downsizing its naval capabilities on a large scale owing to massive cuts in the military budget. It was also looking at revising its post–Vietnam War strategy toward the goal of a new, highly mobile army and primacy of the navy. At this critical juncture, the formulation of new U.S. strategies was greatly impacted by the expansion of Soviet military capabilities.

The same Annual Defense Department Report also referred to the importance of strengthening cooperative relations with Japan. Therefore, faced with the Carter administration's determination to withdraw U.S. troops stationed in South Korea and the new U.S. security strategy based on the threat posed by the Soviet Union, Japan found itself in a situation that demanded it play a larger role in its own defense. On top of that, trade friction with the United States had intensified, forcing the Fukuda cabinet to adjust Japan's relations with the United States in both bilateral trade and defense cooperation.

The Fukuda cabinet decided to deal with the trade friction by accelerating Japan's economic growth. In answer to the demand that Japan play a more active role in its defense, the Cabinet decided to actively pursue U.S.-Japan defense cooperation. This strategy happened to be strongly advocated by the Defense Agency under Vice Minister Maruyama Ko at that time. As indicated by U.S. Secretary of Defense Harold Brown's visit to Japan in June 1977 and the reciprocal visit by Director-General of the Defense Agency Mihara Asao in September of the same year, the exchange of views on defense issues between Japan and the United States had become much more active than before since the formation of the Fukuda cabinet. In December 1977, the F15 Eagle was designated as the next generation mainstay fighter and the P3C Orion was decided on as the anti-submarine patrol aircraft. One hundred units of the former and forty-five units of the latter were ordered. And on November 27, 1978, the Japan-U.S. Security Consultative Committee decided to approve the Guidelines, which were the symbol of U.S.-Japan defense cooperation.

Japanese Politics Averse to Defense Issues
With the formulation of the Guidelines, Japan now had two mutually inconsistent defense policy lines—the NDPG and the Guidelines. Nor was there any coordination undertaken to align the NDPG with the Guidelines, the later comer. Except for the Maritime Self-Defense Force (MSDF), other branches of the Japan Self-Defense Forces (JSDF), particularly the Ground Self-Defense Force (GSDF), had hardly consulted with the U.S. military on joint actions, and it was only after the formulation of the Guidelines that bilateral consultation began to be studied and explored. The situation at the time did not allow for a reexamination of the NDPG as the basic stance of Japan's defense. Nor was any willingness for policy coordination detected within the Defense Agency, where some executive positions were occupied by bureaucrats originally from the Ministry of Finance. More concretely, the Defense Agency in those days was sandwiched between the Ministry of Finance's determination to curb expansion of the defense budget as a way to reconstruct government finances, on the one hand, and the U.S. pressure for Japan to bolster its defense capabilities, on the other. The agency was struggling to secure the defense budget for fiscal year 1980 at the level of 0.9 percent of GNP; it had its hands full with the need to respond to domestic and international situations, scarcely leaving space for promotion of the U.S.-Japan cooperation stipulated in the Guidelines. From the viewpoint of core officials of the Defense Agency, there was no need to change the line set forth by the NDPG seeing as Prime Minister Ohira Masayoshi, who had succeeded

Fukuda Takeo, was supportive of the NDPG. Besides, perhaps the Defense Agency at that time had little room to promote further U.S.-Japan cooperation as stipulated by the Guidelines.

It is noteworthy here that it was bureaucrats of the Defense Agency's inner bureau

Kurisu Hiroomi, chairman, Joint Staff Council, in the press conference to announce his resignation (Source: The Mainichi Newspapers)

that played the central role in the formulation of both the NDPG and the Guidelines. Although Director-General Sakata actively engaged himself in defense policy to an almost unusual extent, he had to follow the initiative of the inner bureau officials when it came to policy content. Thus, while it should have been legislators who took the initiative in defense policy, the central issue for a country's security, there was no change in the structure for defense policy formulation centered around the Defense Agency's inner bureau. As long as the governing party and the opposition parties were in conflict over the basics of security policy, it would not be possible to deepen realistic debates on defense policy in the political realm. The aforementioned tendency to regard anything to do with war or military as a taboo still persisted among legislators and, thus, the majority of politicians stayed away from engaging in discussions on defense issues.

It was Chairman, Joint Staff Council Kurisu Hiroomi's advocacy of extrajudicial actions by the JSDF in case of emergency and his subsequent dismissal that symbolized the air of the time. Revealing in 1978 that, when a direct invasion to Japan occurred, the current legal system of Japan was too insufficient to allow the JSDF to respond to the crisis, Kurisu admitted that, under current conditions, in order to cope with the emergency, the JSDF would have to act extrajudicially. Kanemaru Shin, director-general of the Defense Agency at that time, removed Kurisu from duty for making that remark publicly. In fact, Kurisu had repeatedly made several controversial remarks before this publicly, leading to his eventual dismissal.

What Kurisu argued, however, was in itself justifiable. From the viewpoint of Kurisu, who was originally from the GSDF, the JSDF could not fulfill its responsibility when it could not properly respond to threats unless it resorted to extrajudicial actions, even though the JSDF had developed the strategy to respond to a presumed invasion of Hokkaido.

In order to overcome this deadlock, legislation dealing with military emergencies should have been passed as promptly as possible. Even though this legislation had been studied inside the Defense Agency in the 1960s, it became a subject that legislators shied away from after the Mitsuya Kenkyu (Mitsuya Study, or "Three Arrows" contingency planning) became politicized in 1965. The formulation of legislation in preparation for military emergencies had at last been started during the Fukuda cabinet, but even that was left to bureaucrats, and politicians did not take any initiative in it. How averse politicians were to realistic discussions on defense policy should be obvious from the fact that it took more than twenty years after the Kurisu incident—until 2003—for a legislation dealing with military emergencies to pass. Not all politicians, however, refused to actively tackle Japan's security issue before the end of the cold war. One prominent political leader who was very much concerned about implementing a security policy that was appropriate for Japan was Ohira Masayoshi.

Ohira Masayoshi and the Notion of Comprehensive Security
The Fukuda cabinet resigned en masse on December 6, 1977, after the official adoption of the Guidelines, to be succeeded by the Ohira Masayoshi cabinet on the following day. Having succeeded to the presidency of the Liberal Democratic Party's Kochikai faction from Ikeda Hayato, who had faithfully inherited Yoshida Shigeru's "priority to economic growth with light armament" line, Ohira belonged to the so-called conservative mainstream. Ohira was rather negative toward the strengthening of defensive capabilities. He distinguished himself

from other traditional successors of the Yoshida Doctrine in his determination to not stop at merely rejecting the U.S. demand for more defense capabilities but to formulate his own security strategy for Japan instead. Ohira's security strategy took the form of the notion of "comprehensive security."

When he ran for the election for the Liberal Democratic Party presidency announced on November 1, 1977, Ohira revealed his own political agenda called "The Power of Pluralism for Politics," in which he proposed one basic strategy and two plans for future nation building. The one basic strategy was comprehensive security. Ohira analyzed that, as the promotion of U.S.-Japan cooperation had become more of a focus since the days of the Fukuda cabinet, more attention began to be paid to the military aspect of Japan's security. Against this backdrop, Ohira proposed that, while Japan should not ignore the military aspect of the security arrangements, it should restrict its military capability to a "moderate but high quality" level. Along with this, Ohira proposed that Japan should further enhance its security arrangements with the United States and upgrade Japan's domestic politics in order to improve Japan's security comprehensively. This idea sounded like an echo of the view of Kubo Takuya, who was instrumental in the formulation of the NDPG, and of the similar-minded Kyoto University professor Kosaka Masataka. Kosaka was one of the academics that Ohira had frequently consulted with. It is safe to say that the views of Kosaka and Kubo were reflected in Ohira's proposal.

It is well known that Ohira, in preparation for his long reign, launched nine policy study committees to deliberate long-term policies in various fields. One of those nine was the Comprehensive National Security Study Group, started in April 1979 to discuss issues related to security. The group was chaired by Inoki Masamichi, professor emeritus of Kyoto University and former president of the National Defense Academy who had become president of the newly founded Research Institute of Peace and Security (RIPS), a nongovernmental organization established by business circles and Defense Agency affiliates. Iida Tsuneo, professor of Nagoya University, and Kosaka were its executive members. Other members included such academics as

Kimura Hiroshi, professor of Hokkaido University; Sase Masanori, professor of the National Defense Academy; Sato Seizaburo, professor of the University of Tokyo; and Nakajima Mineo, professor of the Tokyo University of Foreign Studies. Intellectuals such as writers Sono Ayako and Eto Jun and architect Kurokawa Kisho were also members. Members from officialdom were Sasa Atsuyuki from the Defense Agency, Watanabe Koji from the Ministry of Foreign Affairs, and Kinoshita Hiroo from the Ministry of International Trade and Industry. Altogether, the Comprehensive National Security Study Group had 25 members, including secretaries and advisors.

Particularly noteworthy here is that Kosaka, as an executive member of the group, was at the heart of the effort to compile the group's final report. Inoki, chairman of the Comprehensive National Security Study Group, had long been close to Kosaka since his Kyoto University days. After retiring from officialdom in November 1978, Kubo became executive director of RIPS in December. Kubo, the former vice-minister for defense who became the secretary-general of the National Defense Council, was the de facto leader of RIPS where Inoki was president. Therefore, it seems beyond doubt that the discussions at the Comprehensive National Security Study Group strongly reflected the opinions of Kubo and Kosaka. To be more specific, it had been decided that the argument for comprehensive security as it pertained to national defense would be discussed on the basis of the NDPG and the Concept of Basic Defense Capability on which the NDPG was constructed. The final report of the group was completed in July 1979. The report, however, was never utilized by Prime Minister Ohira, who passed away in June 1980 in the midst of the general election.

Tension in International Situations and the Second Cold War
During the period when Prime Minister Ohira entrusted substantiation of the comprehensive security policy to the Comprehensive National Security Study Group, pressure from the United States on Japan's defense buildup became increasingly stronger. For instance, at the eleventh meeting of the Japan-U.S. Security Consultative Committee on July 31, 1979, the U.S. side requested the expansion of Japan's

maritime defense capabilities so that it could protect the sea lanes surrounding Japan by itself. Also, the United States Senate Committee on Foreign Relations published a report on September 17, 1979, advocating the further strengthening of U.S.-Japan cooperation. A request for Japan's defense buildup also came from Secretary of Defense Brown when he visited Japan on October 20 that same year. These demands from the United States made the Japanese government agonize over how to respond to them while pursuing the reconstruction of government finances.

Also during that period, the international situation underwent a drastic change. A revolution erupted in Iran, where the U.S. Embassy was seized by revolutionaries. Meanwhile, Japanese companies continued to purchase Iranian oil, worsening American public opinion toward Japan. This added another headache for the Japanese government to cope with.

It was under these circumstances that the Soviet troops invaded Afghanistan. That incident thoroughly hardened the Carter administration's attitude toward the Soviet Union, and the world entered the so-called second cold war. In January 1980, President Carter announced the Carter Doctrine in his State of the Union speech. He declared, "Let our position be absolutely clear: An attempt by any outside force to gain control of the Persian Gulf region will be regarded as an assault on the vital interests of the United States of America, and such an assault will be repelled by any means necessary, including military force."

During this course of affairs, the so-called swing strategy was revealed. In order to deploy the U.S. Navy to the Indian Ocean facing the Middle East, it would be necessary to keep the Pacific Seventh Fleet, in particular, in a constant state of strategic flexibility so that it could "swing" (to flash points) on a global scale. In order to secure the capabilities to be deployed in the Indian Ocean from among the already downsized U.S. Navy, the United States would need much more cooperation from its allies than before.

Critics of the NDPG had hitherto argued that the international situation called détente, which was the basic premise of the NDPG, had already ceased to exist when the Soviet Union expanded its military capabilities. Critics of the NDPG took the Soviet invasion of Afghanistan as proof that they had been correct.

Aside from the redeployment of Soviet ground forces in the Kuril Islands since 1978, which we noted in an earlier chapter, construction of a new military base was confirmed on these islands in September 1979. Together with deployment of the Tupolev Tu-22M (Backfire) bomber in the Far East, these developments heightened tension vis-à-vis the military situation in East Asia.

From Ohira's viewpoint, the international situation changed greatly before the final report on comprehensive security, on which he had placed high hopes, could be compiled, thus forcing Japan to squarely face the strong demands for defense buildup from the United States. The specific initial requests from the United States were (1) an increase in the defense budget with specific goal figures and (2) the prompt accomplishment of the aims set by the Defense Agency's mid-term accomplishments evaluation method (*chugyo*). As the Ronald Reagan administration succeeded the Carter administration in the United States, U.S.-Japan joint operations against the Soviet Union became an important issue. But, during the Ohira cabinet days, it was these two requests from the United States that Japan was forced to deal with.

What exactly were the issues surrounding the prompt accomplishment of the *chugyo* goals? As chapter 6 discussed, it had been decided to amend the fixed five-year plan system that had been adopted up to the Fourth Defense Build-up Plan by accomplishing annually what was set forth in the table of defense buildup goals attached to the NDPG. Because such long-term enterprises as defense buildup call for some multi-year, interim targets, however, the *chugyo* system was introduced. The *chugyo* system was a mid-term plan that set forth goals to be accomplished in a certain period of time as milestones toward the ultimate goals stipulated by the NDPG. Being an internal document of the Defense Agency, the *chugyo* did not require approval by the National Defense Council or the Cabinet. The *chugyo* plan pursued at the time under discussion was the *53 Chugyo* (after the 53rd

Year of Showa), covering the period from fiscal year 1980 through fiscal year 1984. The *53 Chugyo* was believed to aim at the improvement of JSDF equipage on the assumption that the defense budget would be raised to the level of 1 percent of GNP in five years. If this *chugyo* were accomplished, it was said, all the NDPG goals would be mostly realized.

The United States was demanding that the completion of the *53 Chugyo* be expedited by one year. This demand became one of the important pending issues for the Japanese government. In fact, U.S.-Japan relations in the latter years of the Ohira cabinet were almost entirely focused on this particular issue. Within the Japanese government, confrontation emerged between the Ministry of Foreign Affairs, which was supportive of accelerating the *53 Chugyo* out of consideration for the United States, on the one hand, and the Defense Agency, on the other, which had at last taken leadership in defense policy formulation by separating long-term defense plans from government approval. Even Ohira's visit to the United States in April 1980 only highlighted the discrepancy of attitudes toward the acceleration of the *53 Chugyo* between the two countries. In the end, Ohira failed to find proactive measures to bridge the gap with the United States. This failure was followed by the passing of a no-confidence motion and the subsequent general election during which Ohira suddenly passed away.

Comprehensive Security and the NDPG

As pointed out earlier, the Final Report on Comprehensive Security was not compiled before the passing of Prime Minister Ohira. Considering that Japan had so far been preoccupied with only the pros and cons of security arrangements with the United States and the constitutional issue, the final report submitted on July 22 to Acting Prime Minister Ito Masayoshi may be evaluated as a good summation of all the problems that Japan was facing in the field of security and issues for the future. What really mattered was how policy proposals contained in the report were reflected in actual political situations. The following two points stood out in this regard.

The first was about limiting the role of the military. From the beginning, the comprehensive security policy had been perceived as a means to avoid too much emphasis on the military aspect of U.S.-Japan cooperation by applying a more multidimensional approach to security policy, including the political and economic aspects of it. In other words, the military aspect of security was only one element of the whole from the beginning, and it was hoped that the concept of comprehensive security would dilute attention on the military aspect (which had begun to surface substantially since the formulation of the Guidelines).

Thus, what was developed in the discussion of the military aspect in the final report was basically an argument for autonomous defense of homeland Japan rather than as an exploration of broader U.S.-Japan cooperation. This does not mean, though, that the final report ignored the emerging situation in those days that could be described as the second cold war. The report pointed out that, "the military balance between the United States and the Soviet Union has changed . . . since the mid-1960s as the Soviet Union has continued to build up its military force," giving an accurate analysis on the impact of the Soviet Union's expansion of its military power on international politics. The report continued on to say, "As a result, U.S. military power is no longer able to provide its allies and friends with nearly full security. . . . The changes outlined above have had the effect in Japan's case of augmenting the task of military security." In other words, the report said, "The United States is no longer able to provide a high degree of security, and in maintaining regional balance of power, the military capabilities of the countries in the region have grown in importance."

The problem with this final report, however, is that the discussion stopped there. The above quotes were followed by the statement that, "Thus it has come about that Japan must seriously consider self-reliant efforts for the first time since World War II. More than just retaining overall friendly relations with the United States, it has become necessary for Japan to prepare for well-functioning military relations with America as well." The report failed to elaborate on specifically what was meant by "well-functioning military relations" to supplement "overall friendly relations." After this statement, the report referred to "the end of American supremacy" in military affairs, which points to wider diplomatic implications and switches the focus of argument to the issue of Japan's diplomatic role.

This report was distinct from others in concluding that, militarily, Japan had to increase its autonomous defense capabilities. And it was "rejection power," a concept that had been stylized by Kosaka and Kubo, which was introduced in the discussion of self-defense capabilities. Criticizing the failure to accomplish even what had been set forth by the NDPG, the report flatly claimed that, "Remedying the above-mentioned deficiencies [in strengthening self-defense capabilities] is a task deserving high priority. Such a remedy would be nothing more than the implementation of the National Defense Program Guidelines."

By that time, however—and we will discuss this in more detail later—what the United States was requesting of Japan had gone beyond the mere expansion of its defense capabilities and escalated to asking for joint actions against Soviet military threats. The Final Report on Comprehensive Security failed to propose how to respond to this new situation. Taking into consideration the political situation in Japan in those days where even an argument for increased defense capabilities became controversial, the notion of joint anti-Soviet military actions with the United States might not even have been perceived yet in the minds of the report's authors. In this regard, it can be said that the actual political situation had outpaced the supposition of the report (or discussions on security in Japan in those days).

The second point of importance regarding the report was the death of Prime Minister Ohira. To begin with, the nine policy study committees, including that on comprehensive security, had been launched with Ohira's strong hopes of accomplishing change. In that sense, they would not have existed without Ohira. Even though the Final Report on Comprehensive Security was submitted to Acting Prime Minister Ito after the untimely death of Ohira, the Suzuki Zenko cabinet that succeeded the Ohira cabinet ended up failing to effectively utilize the report. The report was a soul-searching effort to think about Japan's security in the face of strong U.S. pressure for the expansion of defense capabilities and the issue of U.S.-Japan joint actions, which would continue to unfold in the days ahead. Nevertheless, no attempt was ever made to apply the proposals included in the report to real politics. With the demise of its strongest patron, Prime Minister Ohira, this report containing important policy proposals on comprehensive security lost the chance to be of use in actual policies in real politics.

Chapter 9

Toward a Stronger U.S.-Japan Alliance

The Reagan Administration and Sea Lane Defense

Under the circumstances termed the second cold war, U.S. pressure on Japan to expand its defense capabilities grew increasingly fiercer. This pressure coupled with the heightened economic friction between the two countries meant that overall U.S.-Japan relations became quite strained in the 1980s.

With the switch in the United States from the Carter administration to the Ronald Reagan administration, U.S. pressure for an expansion of Japan's defense buildup also underwent a change. The Reagan administration started to treat Japan on a par with European countries but at the same time requested that Japan share the burden of defense with the United States. As we saw in the previous chapter, U.S. pressure for Japan's defense buildup during the Carter administration had taken the form of requesting that the concrete target figures in the defense budget be realized. This approach ended up failing to produce clear-cut results. Consequently, rather than continuing to openly denounce the Japanese government, the Reagan administration opted for a policy that called for consulting on bilateral defense cooperation on the basis of mutual roles and tasks instead of stressing specific defense budget targets in terms of a percentage of Japan's GNP. In the Annual Defense Department Report for fiscal year 1981, Secretary Harold Brown of the Carter administration had already appealed for joint operations among Japan, the United States, and Europe to contain the Soviet Union, along with the establishment of rapid deployment forces in preparation for conflicts in the Persian Gulf and other regions. It was the Reagan administration's intention to lure Japan into voluntary cooperation with the United States by promoting the above trilateral cooperation, particularly in the defense of sea lanes and, in this way, treating Japan on a par with Europe.

When it comes to these issues of sea lanes and division of labor in regional defense, the Guidelines for Japan-U.S. Defense Cooperation (Guidelines) had profound significance. While the Guidelines went beyond the National Defense Plan Guidelines (NDPG) to address the issue of the protection of maritime traffic, that was not all. The English version of the Guidelines said the following about the protection of maritime traffic:

(b) Maritime Operations
The Maritime Self-Defense Force (MSDF) and U.S. Navy will jointly conduct maritime operations for the defense of surrounding waters and <u>the protection of sea lines of communication</u>. (underline added)

Sea lines of communication, or SLOC for short, is a military term often referred to in the books of American naval historian Alfred Thayer Mahan. The term is used to describe the primary maritime routes between ports, logistics, and naval forces. To protect SLOC in the U.S.-Japan context entails protection of and cooperation with the U.S. Navy's military supplies replenishment missions. Oga Ryohei, who was chief of staff of the MSDF when the Guidelines were formulated, explained that "sea lane" as referred in the Guidelines was synonymous with SLOC. Oga stated, "The United States, Japan's ally across the vast Pacific Ocean, needs forward deployment of its troops [to defend Japan]. The survival of Japan and the <u>security of military strategic sea lanes</u> are of crucial significance to the U.S. defense of Japan" (underline added). Oga also pointed out elsewhere that the range of the "1,000 nautical miles defense," which later became a source of controversy, was merely a two-day action for MSDF vessels. According to Oga, "maintenance of maritime supremacy" and "security of sea lanes" were two concepts that replaced the Imperial Japanese Navy's concept of "command of the seas," and, in fact, they became the goals of modern navies. Although sea lane is often taken to mean a shipping lane for maritime transport, equating sea lane defense with the protection of shipping lanes, leaders of the MSDF, at least, did not perceive the term that way. This perception gap became a source of controversy later (see figures 12a and 12b).

Suzuki Zenko Cabinet and the Worsening of U.S.-Japan Relations
Reflecting the complicated power relations within the ruling Liberal Democratic Party (LDP) at that time, Ohira was succeed by Suzuki Zenko, who also belonged to the same Kochikai faction. Setting forth the reconstruction of government finances and administrative reform as its two basic tasks, the Suzuki cabinet was not very enthusiastic about defense buildup. It inherited the Ohira cabinet's basic stance toward the defense issue—that is, the advocacy of comprehensive security. This policy was manifested, for instance, in the setting up of a Ministerial Conference on Comprehensive Security in December 1980. Having inherited the Ohira cabinet's policy also meant that Prime Minister Suzuki himself did not have a clear-cut defense policy of his own. Having long devoted himself to LDP party affairs, Suzuki had dealt with foreign affairs almost entirely in the realm of agricultural relations (fishery in particular). As such, he had had little experience with the national defense issue. Compared to Ohira's attempt to develop his own security policy in the form of a comprehensive security concept, Suzuki's attitude toward security had to be characterized as that of a stopgap measure for responding to problems as they emerged.

It was at the Suzuki-Reagan talk in May 1981 that the discrepancy of views between the Suzuki cabinet and the Reagan administration surfaced. The Reagan administration wanted Japan to share the burden of defense, particularly around the sea lanes. Prime Minister Suzuki told President Reagan that Japan shared the U.S. perception of the current international situation. Japan understood, according to Suzuki, the need for expanding its defense buildup; nevertheless, it

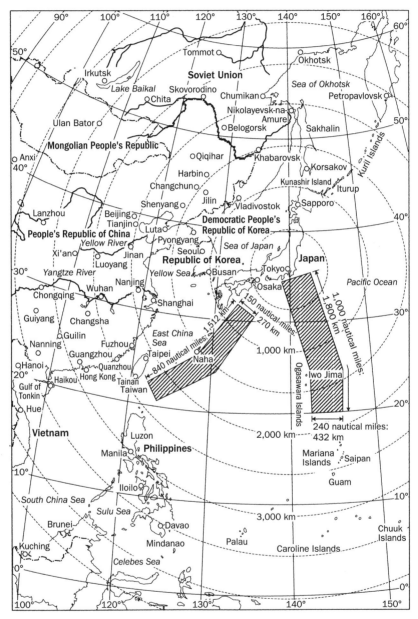

Figure 12a. Conceptual Depiction of Shipping Lanes

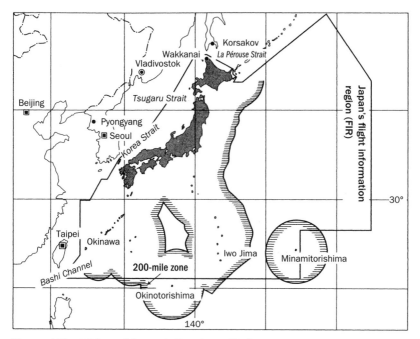

Figure 12b. A Map of Japan's Sea Lane Defense

Note: Figure 12a is a conceptual depiction of shipping lanes as envisioned by the Defense Agency at an early stage. While this was the image that was often envisioned while talking about sea lanes, the actual sea lanes pictured in the minds of officials of the two counties since the late 1970s are more accurately depicted in figure 12b.

Sources: (Figure 12a) Kaihara Osamu, *Watashi no kokubo hakusho* (My own defense white paper), Tokyo: Jiji Tsushinsha, 1975, p.132.
(Figure 12b) Oga Ryohei, *Shi rein no himitsu: Beiso senryaku no hazama de* (Secret of sea lanes: Sandwiched between U.S. and Soviet strategies), Tokyo: Chobunsha, 1983, p.183.

would not be possible for the defense budget alone to stand out from other budgets owing to the financial and political constraints in Japan. In response, the U.S. side requested Japan to share the burden of defending the seas surrounding Japan with the U.S. Navy, stating that if Japan could do so, that would reduce the burden on the U.S. Navy enough to allow it to deploy its capabilities to the Indian Ocean region. On this point, U.S. Secretary of Defense Casper Weinberger stated as follows:

> The United States believes it important to construct powerful and effective partnership with Japan for the defense of sea lanes in the region north of the Philippines and west of Guam. Because Soviet naval power and air power in this region have been expanded massively, it is of utmost urgency for the United States and Japan to collaborate to counter and balance out these Soviet moves in the next five years or so. And when Japan and the United States sufficiently enhance these capabilities, it will become possible for a portion of U.S. naval vessels to be deployed to the Indian Ocean.

Prime Minister Suzuki refrained from concurring with this request from the U.S. side. Instead, he replied that, while Japan would escalate its defense efforts, it asked for U.S. understanding of Japan's domestic situation. In other words, Suzuki would not commit himself clearly to the American request. Suzuki's attitude planted the seeds for a controversy later.

The joint statement released after the Suzuki-Reagan talks termed U.S.-Japan relations an "alliance" for the first time. Section 8 of the joint statement states:

> In insuring peace and stability in the region and the defense of Japan, they acknowledged the desirability of an appropriate division of roles between Japan and the United States. The Prime Minister stated that Japan, on its own initiative and in accordance with its Constitution and basic defense policy, will seek to make

even greater efforts for improving its defense capabilities in Japanese territories and in its surrounding sea and air space, and for further alleviating the financial burden of U.S. forces in Japan. (underline added)

The wording here resulted in further confusion in the Japanese government's explanation. The underlined portion appears to say that Japan and the United States agreed on the division of labor between themselves. In the press conference after his talk with President Reagan, Prime Minister Suzuki said, "It is only a matter of course for Japan to defend at least the seas surrounding the archipelago, which are our own turf. As for a few hundred miles in the surrounding ocean area and the 1,000 miles of the sea lanes, we are pursuing a policy of strengthening our defense capabilities within the range of self-defense in full compliance with our Constitution." This statement was interpreted by the U.S. side as Japan's admission that sea lane defense was included in the division of labor between the two countries. In the U.S. perception, sea lane defense was actually the aforementioned SLOC, while in Prime Minister Suzuki's understanding, sea lanes merely meant the transportation routes, or shipping lanes, for goods heading toward Japan. In the same press conference, Prime Minister Suzuki promised that Japan would make utmost efforts to defend the shipping lanes for Japan, but he showed extreme reluctance toward U.S.-Japan cooperation beyond that. Yet the U.S. side took Suzuki's announcement as his endorsement of a bilateral agreement on the division of labor in the defense of SLOC.

Returning home from Washington, Suzuki denied that agreement on a U.S.-Japan military division of labor had been reached. He denounced the Ministry of Foreign Affairs by saying that the joint statement had already been written before his talk with President Reagan, and, therefore, it did not reflect his views. This disunity within the Japanese government in the end resulted in the resignation of Foreign Minister Ito Masayoshi. As the result of this confusion in Japanese politics, U.S.-Japan relations in this period worsened significantly, along with the intensification of bilateral economic friction. The Suzu-

ki cabinet ended up earning the mistrust of the U.S. government.

Progress in Practical Defense Collaboration

Even as U.S. discontent with and mistrust in the Suzuki cabinet increasingly
deepened, practical defense collaboration between the two countries advanced to a significant degree between
the U.S. military and the uniformed
teams of the MSDF and the Air Self-
Defense Forces (ASDF), particularly in
maritime operations. The MSDF had
taken part in the Rim of the Pacific Exercise in the spring of 1980 (Rimpack
'80), after which U.S.-Japan coopera-

The MSDF's escort ships sailing
toward Hawaii for the Rim of the
Pacific Exercise (Source: The Mainichi Newspapers)

tion in maritime defense further progressed. A U.S. Department of
Defense official disclosed that a U.S.-Japan joint operation in preparation for a Soviet invasion was being formulated by the uniformed
teams of the two countries. A joint drill was started between the ASDF
and the U.S. Air Force stationed in Hawaii at Misawa Air Base in Aomori prefecture. The new escort ship that the MSDF was planning to
build at that time was a helicopter carrying missile ship; the plan to
build this vessel was in response to the U.S. request for anti-submarine
and anti-air capabilities, revealing the good communications between
the two militaries. Moreover, it was announced that the ASDF's inter-
ceptor-fighters to engage in policing Japan's territorial airspace would
be armed with live anti-air missiles. And Yata Tsugio, chief of staff of
the MSDF, disclosed that the MSDF's vessels and patrol aircrafts would
start carrying live torpedoes. All of this projected the impression that
JSDF troops were ready for war in concert with the U.S. military.

Also, information exchange on military technologies and the stan-
dardization of weapons began to be promoted in earnest from this
time. Furthermore, the promotion of fleet rehabilitation and modern-

ization (FRAM) so as to mount missiles onboard vessels in active duty in order to enhance the anti-air and anti-submarine capabilities of MSDF fleets was adopted as an official line at the Defense Agency.

Incidentally, it was reported by the media that, at the Cabinet meeting on February 6, 1981, participants proposed one after another that the government should listen more closely to what the uniformed team had to say, that there should be better communication between the two, and that Prime Minister Suzuki also showed willingness to have dialogues with the uniformed team. This reporting clearly showed that the position of the uniformed team had significantly improved. In other words, while Japanese government leaders hesitated to make a step toward the promotion of defense cooperation with the United States, collaboration between practitioners on both sides, the uniformed team in particular, was steadfastly advancing from where it was possible.

Furthermore, as obvious from the controversy around the joint statement issued after the Suzuki-Reagan talks, Japan's Ministry of Foreign Affairs was of a policy that U.S.-Japan cooperation should be promoted. The question was, therefore, how positive Japanese government leaders could be toward this cause. At the Japan-U.S. Security Consultative Committee (SCC) meeting convened in June 1981 in Hawaii, the U.S. side requested Japan's effort to enhance its defense capabilities in the areas of (1) effective as well as survivable (ability to sustain functions to accomplish missions) conventional combat capabilities to defend the territory of Japan, and (2) maritime and air capabilities sufficient to effectively defend seas surrounding Japan and sea lanes in Northwest Pacific within 1,000 miles against Soviet threats, including Backfire and nuclear submarines. During this consultation, other, broader requests were also made of Japan, such as military technology exchange, support of the U.S. military stationed in South Korea, and financial assistance to American troops stationed in Japan (so-called host nation support). The Suzuki cabinet's basically reluctant attitude toward defense cooperation with the United States, nevertheless, remained unchanged. While practical U.S.-Japan collaboration had already been advanced where possible, any further cooperation had to await political decisions. The situation had already come to the point where increasingly fierce economic friction would make the further worsening of U.S.-Japan relations unavoidable unless a political decision on the deepening of bilateral cooperation was made. Then came the Nakasone Yasuhiro cabinet. As soon as Nakasone became prime minister, he started working actively toward improvement of the U.S.-Japan relations.

The Nakasone Cabinet and the Defense Burden Sharing Issue

After the Suzuki cabinet resigned en masse, Nakasone became the prime minister on November 27, 1982. Prior to his trip to the United States in January 1983, Nakasone made a decision on January 14 to provide weapons technology to the United States in response to the U.S. proposal for a bilateral military technology exchange that had been made at the June 1981 SCC meeting. Truth be told, there had been hardly any consultations within the government on how to respond to U.S. requests. Nakasone nonetheless presented Japan's positive response to one of the important pending issues in preparation for his trip to the United States.

In Washington, Nakasone met President Reagan and the two heads of governments confirmed the alliance relations between the two countries. Of all the moves Nakasone made while in Washington, however, the one with the greatest impact on the United States was his interview with the *Washington Post*. In this interview, Nakasone declared that Japan would be an "unsinkable aircraft carrier" against the Soviet Backfires (although later it came out that Nakasone did not use this particular expression) and even talked about protection of the ocean area west of Guam, something which Weinberger had proposed during his talks with Suzuki. While these remarks stirred up a big controversy inside Japan, they were highly welcomed in the United States as an explicit expression of Japan's resolution to launch joint actions with the United States. Nakasone reminisced, "It would have taken no less than two years for ordinary measures to dispel the air of serious distrust and suspicion of Japan that permeated Washington. But my words instantaneously cleared the air." It seems beyond doubt that Nakasone's words did contribute greatly to the improvement of bilateral relations.

It should be recalled that Nakasone, out of his sympathy with nationalism in Japan, had originally been an advocate of autonomous defense. With the advance of bilateral cooperation after Nakasone formed his cabinet, people repeatedly questioned if he had converted to being an advocate of the U.S.-Japan alliance.

As explained in the earlier discussion of Nakasone's ideas when he was director-general of the Defense Agency, his argument for autonomous national defense had several important characteristics. One was his solicitude to nationalism in Japan. Another was his aspiration for an autonomous state modeled after Europe, which he cherished as an ideal state. For instance, out of his solicitude to nationalism, he advocated the transfer of U.S. military bases in Japan to the JSDF in order to settle the military base dispute, which was a symbol of the rise of nationalism in Japan. Owing to the downsizing and consolidation of military bases based on the Kanto Plain Consolidation Plan (KPCP), which had been agreed on between the two countries in 1973, however, the so-called military base dispute had already been mostly settled in mainland Japan. This meant to Nakasone that he had been substantially liberated from the yoke of nationalism. In other words, the necessity for Nakasone to continue to uphold the slogan of autonomy had been significantly reduced.

What the United States required of Japan in those days was its participation in anti-Soviet joint operations on a par with the European countries. To be treated on a par with European countries had also been Nakasone's own long-standing contention and wish since his days as Defense Agency chief. Nakasone was thus determined to promote joint operations in which Japan and the United States participated on an equal footing.

Questioned later on his intention behind his remark, which had been misquoted as advocating "Japan as an unsinkable aircraft carrier," Nakasone harked back as follows:

While the concept of the defense of Japan includes the defense of straits and sea lanes, I believe the most fundamental thing is to block an invasion by Soviet Backfires by covering the entire airspace over Japan with defense networks. Backfire is a powerful bomber, and once we face an emergency in which it demonstrates its abilities over the Japanese archipelago or the Pacific Ocean, we should be prepared for unavoidable and substantial damage to U.S.-Japan defense cooperation. Therefore, in case of emergency, we must convert the archipelago to something like a big ship surrounded by high walls to block invasion by hostile foreign aircraft. That was the message I wanted to convey in the interview.

In a nutshell, Nakasone was saying that he would make the Japanese archipelago a shield to block Soviet air offensives centered on the Backfire bombers. It was an offer of voluntary military cooperation and joint operations with the United States on a par with European countries in response to the Reagan administration's request. It was an offer from a totally different position than that of the heavy dependence on security arrangements with the United States seen in the 1960s. The offer came from a position that coincided with Nakasone's own belief in establishing parity with the United States in bilateral cooperation.

The progress made toward this direction under Prime Minister Nakasone included the following: it was agreed at the Subcommittee for Defense Cooperation in March 1983 that a joint study would be launched on the defense of sea lanes; joint command post drills with the U.S. military were carried out by the ASDF in 1984 and the MSDF in 1985; deployment of U.S. Air Force F16 fighters to Misawa Air Base in Aomori prefecture progressed; and in 1987 the two nations agreed on joint development of the next generation fighter supporter (FSX) based on the Nakasone cabinet's decision to provide the United States with weapons technology. As these examples indicate, the conflict between the argument for autonomous homeland defense crystalized in the NDPG, on the one hand, and the argument for primacy of defense cooperation with the United States as stressed by the Guidelines, on the other, began to point explicitly in the direction of the U.S.-Japan alliance after the formation of the Nakasone cabinet.

Substantive Transformation of the NDPG

As the U.S.-Japan cooperation stipulated by the Guidelines was placed at the heart of Japan's defense by the Nakasone cabinet, the contents of the NDPG were substantially transformed. Among measures that Japan had taken to upgrade bilateral defense cooperation, the U.S. side particularly appreciated the formulation of the Mid-Term Defense Build-up Plan in 1985 and the increase of Japan's defense budget for 1986 to exceed the ceiling of 1 percent of GNP. The former was a plan on defense buildup for the 1986–1990 period that originally had been designated to be the *59 Chugyo* (the Defense Agency's internal document on a midterm accomplishments evaluation method; 59 represented the 59th Year of Showa) to follow the *53 Chugyo* and *56 Chugyo* plans. After being approved by the National Defense Council and the Cabinet, the *59 Chugyo* was upgraded to a governmental midterm defense build-up plan.

Since the NDPG was first adopted, the Defense Agency had been utilizing its internal *chugyo* document as a tool for taking control of national defense policy planning. With the upgrading of what had been meant to be the *59 Chugyo* to an official government plan, however, the older system of defense build-up plans that had applied up to the Fourth Defense Build-up Plan was de facto resurrected. The upgrade was in response to the U.S. government's request to expedite the accomplishment of *chugyo* goals; the idea to expedite the accomplishment of *chugyo* goals and upgrade the *chugyo* itself to a government plan surfaced during the Carter administration. By upgrading *chugyo* to a government plan, however, defense buildup plans once again became liable to interferences from other governmental ministries and agencies, most notably the Ministry of Finance. It appears that why the *chugyo* system had been adopted in the first place was either forgotten or neglected.

The transformation of the contents of the NDPG was not confined to the system of defense planning, either. In its mission statement, the Mid-Term Defense Build-up Plan said that "under the basic framework of the National Defense Program Guidelines, this plan aims to accomplish the level of defense capabilities set forth by said Guidelines," thus explicitly stating that the NDPG was the foundation of the Mid-Term Plan. But this statement was followed by the following elaborations:

> In light of international military situations as well as trends in the technological levels of various countries, in order to build up effective defense capabilities to cope with these developments, special attention should be paid not only to the improvement of the individual capabilities of the GSDF, the MSDF, and the ASDF, but also particularly to the facilitation of organic cooperation among the three forces and the maximization of the effect of integrated operations.

Accordingly, in the case of the MSDF, which was the central force of U.S.-Japan defense cooperation, for instance, "in order to improve defense capabilities in sea areas surrounding Japan and secure safe maritime traffic," the following measures were proposed:

> (1) In order to improve and modernize the defense capabilities of MSDF vessels, escort ships, submarines, minesweepers, missile ships, and supply ships should be built. Equipping escort ships with missiles should be promoted in order to enhance not only their anti-submarine capabilities but also their anti-ship and anti-air capabilities. In so doing, on the basis of the results of studies on the maritime anti-air defense system that will be conducted separately, ways to improve the capabilities of the anti-air missile system onboard escort ships should be explored and the necessary measures should be taken; and
> (2) In order to improve and modernize the defense capabilities of aircrafts, fixed-wing submarine patrol aircrafts (P-3C), anti-submarine helicopters (including new-type ship-based anti-submarine helicopters), and minesweeping helicopters (MH-53E) should be utilized.

As we discovered earlier in this book, in the NDPG, which was based on the premise of defense with a basic defense capability that could cope with limited and small-scale invasions, the basic idea was defense of the homeland Japan, not U.S.-Japan defense cooperation. Thus, the NDPG was centered around the defense of the coasts and sea areas surrounding Japan, and it included only maritime escort that could be attended to by fixed-wing aircrafts and other aircrafts. In contrast, in the Mid-Term Defense Build-up Plan, defense of maritime traffic became a major goal. The Mid-Term Plan emphasized the improvement of anti-air capabilities, which later resulted in the introduction of Aegis destroyers to the MSDF. Moreover, on September 18, 1985, when the Mid-Term Plan was approved by the National Defense Council and the Cabinet, the quantities to be purchased were raised from 155 to 187 in the case of the F15 fighter and from 75 to 100 in the case of the P-3C. With these developments, preparations for the confinement of Soviet submarines and aircrafts were established.

The above changes show that, although the Mid-Term Defense Build-up Plan claimed to have been based on the NDPG, it actually declared that Japan would aim at defense buildup to enable containment of the Soviet military under the overall policy of strengthening U.S.-Japan cooperation. By stepping into the realm of defense cooperation with the United States around sea lane defense, it was obvious that the Mid-Term Plan would cause discrepancy with the homeland defense-oriented NDPG. It should be recalled that, together with the defense budget ceiling at less than 1 percent of GNP established at around the same time, the NDPG had been regarded as a tool to restrict the expansion of defense expenditure. For this reason, opposition parties at the National Diet criticized the government's attempt at expanding defense capabilities as being at variance with the NDPG. Since the world in those days was still in the midst of the cold war, revision of the NDPG would, without doubt, have stirred fierce controversy in the Diet. Therefore, substantive transformation of the NDPG was pursued, instead, by way of the Mid-Term Defense Build-up Plan. Thus, Japan "fought" the cold war with the U.S. military by upgrading its anti-naval and anti-air capabilities.

The JSDF and the End of the Cold War

As we have seen, U.S.-Japan cooperation in the area of defense deepened at a stroke in the 1980s. It was the result of an agreement on and pursuit of the policy of promoting bilateral cooperation by bureaucrats of the Defense Agency, the JSDF, and the Ministry of Foreign Affairs and Prime Minister Nakasone at the top of the government. Thanks to this, Japan and the United States won out the cold war. What kind of influence, then, did this "victory" have on the JSDF and its relations with politics in Japan?

One thing to be pointed out first is the great role the MSDF played in U.S.-Japan defense cooperation. It can be said that the MSDF, which had been created and developed on the premise of joint actions with the U.S. Navy, well lived up to the U.S. Navy's expectations by exerting its capabilities in full. The cooperation between the U.S. and Japanese naval forces was so close that some diplomacy experts claim the essence of U.S.-Japan security cooperation to be "navy to navy" relations. This degree of closeness, however, also meant that MSDF activities regarding bilateral defense cooperation stood out starkly from the other branches of the JSDF. Truth be told, even within the Defense Agency, the defense of sea lanes was predominantly perceived as defense of shipping lanes. Core bureaucrats of the agency's inner bureau perceived the NDPG as the basic document of Japan's defense, and substantive U.S.-Japan defense cooperation beyond the NDPG was unconceivable to them. They also assessed that it would be impossible for Japan's defense capabilities to be engaged in sea lane defense beyond what was included in the NDPG. Thus, it appears that the MSDF had gone ahead with substantive cooperation with the U.S. Navy to a degree beyond the inner bureau's assumption. It can be said that the MSDF was indeed engaged in defense cooperation with the U.S. Navy one step ahead of other branches of the JSDF.

The MSDF's engagement in defense cooperation with the United States caused the following problem. It was only natural for the MSDF to become the central player in U.S.-Japan defense cooperation because sea lane defense, which was at the center of the MSDF's defense plan, was de facto the substance of bilateral defense cooperation.

While collaboration with the U.S. military was absolutely essential for the ASDF, there was hardly any role that the GSDF could play given that its basic mission was to defend the homeland. As has already been pointed out, the basic concepts of defense were different between the GSDF and the MSDF. Given this background, the deepening of U.S.-Japan defense cooperation in the 1980s meant that, in the circumstance of the second cold war where the chief adversary was the Soviet Union, the MSDF's basic strategy was adopted as the basic strategy of the JSDF as a whole. If that were indeed the case, Japan's basic defense strategy would have to be reconsidered again when the second cold war ended with the disappearance of the Soviet Union. When that happened, discussions on what Japan's basic defense strategy should be would need to consider these questions: Would basic defense strategy again be centered around homeland defense along the lines of the NDPG, to which the inner bureau of the Defense Agency adhered, and what would be the role of the MSDF, which had played the role of defending the sea lanes? Compared to these "should haves," what kind of discussions really took place when the second cold war was over? In the post–second cold war international relations, what position was the JSDF given in Japan's security policy?

Part IV

The JSDF and the End of the Cold War

Chapter 10

Lessons from the Gulf War

The JSDF and International Contributions

As preceding chapters have said, near the end of the cold war, Japan actively promoted defense cooperation with the United States, centered around the Maritime Self-Defense Force (MSDF). With the end of the cold war—in which Japan was able to stand on the side of the "winners"—the arrival of peace was expected. Even though it took time for a clear-cut picture of the post–cold war international order to emerge, the new situation forced the three branches of the Japan Self-Defense Forces (JSDF) to review their defense policies, which were basically centered around anti-Soviet operations. Moreover, the end of the cold war also spurred reconsideration of the significance of the security arrangements with the United States and the role of the JSDF. Even before the end of the cold war, the possibility that the JSDF could be given a new and important role—that is, international contributions—had emerged.

Since the 1960s, Japan's stature in the international community had increased as Japan grew into a world economic power. Starting with its participation in the first Group of Eight Summit Meeting (G8, although it was G6 at that time) in 1975, Japan began to be requested to make international contributions commensurate with its economic strength, as a country with profound influences on world politics and the world economy, and as a beneficiary of the stability in international society. Japan's international contribution was most visible in the form of overseas development assistance centered on official development aid (ODA), which was rapidly expanded in the 1970s. In addition to extending cooperation for economic development, Japan began to consider contributing to the peace and security of international society, including participating in United Nations' peacekeeping activities.

As a matter of fact, some at the Ministry of Foreign Affairs had started contemplating how best Japan could contribute to U.N. activities from the early days of Japan's membership in the body. It was in the 1970s that the idea of contribution began to be actively explored. Nevertheless, such explorations stayed strictly within the foreign ministry; there was no consultation with the Defense Agency, nor did this avenue of thinking escalate to an all-government level of soul searching. Also, there was no consensus about dispatching the JSDF to participate in U.N. peacekeeping activities. On the contrary, in light of the political situation in Japan at the time, the government had to remain cautious about the overseas dispatch of the JSDF. Nonetheless, the fact remains that the idea of making an international contribution aside from overseas economic aid was being explored in Japan while the United States and Japan were deepening their cooperation during the cold war.

It was at this particular point of time that an occasion arose in which Japan had to consider dispatching JSDF personnel overseas on a mission that was totally unrelated to the framework of U.S.-Japan security cooperation—that is, minesweeping operations in the Persian Gulf necessitated by the Iran-Iraq War. Started in 1980, the Iran-Iraq War was still being fought after seven years, during which the Persian Gulf, an area heavily trafficked by oil tankers, was mined. The situation posed a grave threat to safe sea traffic there. Thus, in 1987, the Reagan administration, which had been enjoying a cordial "alliance" with the Nakasone cabinet, requested the latter to render assistance for the minesweeping operations in the Gulf. If Japan accepted this request, then naturally the MSDF's minesweeping unit would be entrusted with the task. The request forced the Japanese government to seriously consider dispatching JSDF troops overseas for non-training purposes for the first time.

Prime Minister Nakasone himself and the Ministry of Foreign Affairs were eager to comply with the U.S. request. It is well known, however, that due to Chief Cabinet Secretary Gotoda Masaharu's adamant opposition, the government decided to forgo the dispatch of the JSDF at that time. Gotoda pointed out that sending JSDF personnel to an area where a truce had not yet been achieved could risk their being involved in the war. Incidentally, Gotoda had been deeply involved in the founding of the National Police Reserve, and he was always extremely cautious when it came to the overseas dispatch of the JSDF, including for peacekeeping operations (PKO). Gotoda entered the Home Ministry in the same year as Kaihara Osamu, a powerful figure in the Defense Agency until the 1960s. Gotoda and his generation were commonly infused with the intention to restrict the activities of the uniformed team. Their attitude perhaps could be summarized as a thorough distrust of any military organization.

Not long after the dispatch of the MSDF to the Persian Gulf under the Nakasone cabinet was aborted, another chance to make use of the JSDF for international cooperation presented itself, this time in the name of cooperation with the United Nations. The chance came in the form of the three new pillars of diplomacy announced by the Takeshita Noboru cabinet formed in November 1987. The Takeshita cabinet promoted the slogan of "A Japan Contributing to a Better World" and announced it would actively pursue this goal through three pillars of contribution: (1) strengthening cooperation for peace, (2) enhancing ODA, and (3) promoting international cultural exchanges. The Cabinet envisioned accomplishing the first pillar mainly through Japan's participation in U.N. peacekeeping operations. This pillar was the result of advice that Prime Minister Takeshita received from the Ministry of Foreign Affairs to the effect that, in light of the transformation of the cold war after Gorbachev's ascent to power and the positive developments toward peace in Cambodia, Japan should actively engage in building peace in its surrounding regions. Still, this debate on Japan's international contribution again remained confined only to within the foreign ministry and failed to provoke an all-govern-

ment discussion. The Defense Agency, for its part, had not even started detailed studies on JSDF participation in U.N. activities, betraying
the stark difference in the degree of enthusiasm for this cause between the two organizations.

Significance of the Gulf War

Just as it appeared that opportunities for JSDF activities had expanded, the cold war ended. The end of the cold war pressed Japan to re-
consider security arrangements with the United States and the role of
the JSDF. But there wasn't enough time for the Japanese government
to carefully study its course of action before other international incidents occurred that further complicated discussions in Japan.

The Iraqi invasion of Kuwait in August 1990 and the subsequent
eruption of the Gulf War in January 1991 were two such incidents.
These incidents tested Japan's ability to make concrete contributions
to a crisis and a war that erupted in the Middle East, a crucially important region not only for Japan but also for the entire world. Even
though Japan even raised taxes so that it could give financial assistance
to the U.S.-led Coalition of the Gulf War, it failed to win high esteem
from the international community for that kind of support. Japan
ended up experiencing a deep sense of failure over this.

Although Japan had been ahead of other countries in imposing
economic sanctions on Iraq in the early stage of the crisis, it nevertheless failed to earn international respect. This disappointing outcome
was attributable to political confusion in domestic politics accompanying the delay in forming a consensus on dispatching the JSDF as Japan's contribution to the multinational coalition forces. Consequently,
Japan ended up providing only financial assistance to the coalition.

It might be said that Japan was paying the price for having in-
dulged in a futile argument on whether the JSDF was constitutional
or unconstitutional and avoided more concrete and realistic discussions on the placement of the JSDF in the state apparatus and how to
utilize it.

The Gulf War showed that, when dispatching the JSDF overseas
was considered for reasons other than the defense of Japan, all kinds

of problems concerning the absolute necessity of such dispatch and the constitutional constraints would come to the fore. As if to prove that collaboration between the U.S. Navy and the MSDF was the core of bilateral security cooperation, the Commander, U.S. Naval Forces Japan had sounded out the Maritime Staff Office on the dispatch of MSDF minesweepers and an MSDF escort of the U.S. Navy's aircraft carrier USS *Midway* when it sailed out of Yokosuka in as early as August–September, soon after the Iraqi invasion of Kuwait. It is reported that the Maritime Staff Office turned down this request without consulting with higher authorities. Perhaps, in the eyes of the U.S. Navy, the MSDF, with which it had "fought" the cold war together, appeared to be a partner with which to fight the Gulf War. However, under the circumstances at the time, it was not possible for JSDF troops to be deployed in the Middle East, because such action would go far beyond the defense of seas surrounding Japan.

As more and more countries began to participate in the coalition force deployed in the Gulf region, however, Japan, which continued to contribute only financial assistance without making any human contribution whatsoever, began to feel more pressure from the international community as a whole, but most strongly from the United States. The Japanese government and the ruling Liberal Democratic Party (LDP) were, thus, pressed by the necessity to make some kind of human contribution centered on the dispatch of JSDF troops. As mentioned, participation in UN peacekeeping operations, including dispatching the JSDF, had been studied at the Ministry of Foreign Affairs prior to this mounting pressure, but the topic remained a mere internal exploration without any serious consultation with the Defense Agency, the Cabinet Legislation Bureau, or any other pertinent authorities. To further complicate the situation, what was being considered this time was not the JSDF's participation in PKO activities after a truce was established. A battle could erupt anytime, and even if it were assumed that JSDF troops would never participate in a battle, whether dispatching the JSDF under such circumstances was constitutional or not was open to debate. And this led to a discussion on the status of the JSDF personnel who would be dispatched.

Space does not allow me to go into details, but in a nutshell, the debate was a conflict between two camps: the Ministry of Foreign Affairs and the Defense Agency. The Ministry of Foreign Affairs insisted on designating JSDF personnel to be dispatched to the coalition force as "temporarily transferred" or "on leave" out of consideration for constitutional constraints and other political aspects, including the dovish sentiment of Prime Minister Kaifu Toshiki. The Defense Agency insisted that dispatched personnel be treated as having a concurrent appointment, thus retaining their status as JSDF personnel. The Defense Agency argued that status as JSDF personnel was required to operate JSDF vessels and aircrafts, command troop activities, and handle firearms. The Defense Agency was both fearful that it would be deprived of its new task of contributing to peace in the post–cold war world by other government organizations and hopeful about finally being in center stage. The Defense Agency was also apprehensive about the complications—such as insurance—arising from the risks that could touch JSDF personnel dispatched on a dangerous overseas mission.

When Prime Minister Kaifu announced that dispatch of the JSDF would take the form of subcontracting, the decision was criticized by the LDP. The ruling party's opposition ended up overturning the decision for "concurrent appointment" status of JSDF personnel that the Defense Agency had wanted, revealing the disarray within the government. The United Nations Peace Cooperation Bill was hastily drafted, and the National Diet deliberations on this bill fell into total confusion, exposing the inconsistency in government explanations. In the end, the bill was scrapped and the JSDF was not dispatched to the Middle East during the Gulf War.

The Gulf War did more than just cause great confusion in politics in Japan. Its true historical significance was in its profound influence on subsequent politics in Japan, particularly on the country's security policy. In the political realm, Japan failed to win the respect of the international community despite the massive amount of financial assistance it had provided. Even worse, Japan's assistance was denounced as being "too little, too late." After this experience, a sense of having been traumatized (known as Gulf War trauma in Japan) lingered with the Japanese government. It became obsessed with an urge to respond to U.S. requests as soon as possible, foreshadowing future conducts such as Japan's action after the terrorist attacks in the United States on September 11, 2001 (9/11).

Of yet greater significance, though, was the change in people's awareness in Japan. Through this bitter experience, people in Japan became suspicious of discussions within Japan on military affairs. The formation of a multilateral coalition force can be judged to be the best choice available for exercising the collective security function of the United Nations when formation of a U.N. force is extremely difficult. And yet, Japan only reacted—and negatively, at that—to the single issue of exercising military power; criticisms of the United States as the center of the multilateral coalition were conspicuous. This "anything military is bad and evil no matter what" attitude of the Japanese people, a dominant argument in postwar politics in Japan, was shattered by international common sense when Japan's contribution was criticized as too little, too late. This defeat made the Japanese people realize that, when Japan rendered international cooperation, financial assistance was not enough; Japan should also make human contributions, including dispatching the JSDF when necessary. This realization had the effect of breaking the traditional taboo. It should be hastily added that this realization did not emerge among the Japanese people immediately after the Gulf War. It actually required some time for information on the debate over Japan's actions in the international community to reach and spread among the Japanese people. And the successful actual dispatch of the JSDF overseas that was carried out later drove the realization home.

Overseas Dispatch of the JSDF

During the Gulf War, it was believed that Iraq laid some 1,200 mines along the Kuwaiti coast, posing a serious threat to safe navigation in the Persian Gulf. Although multilateral minesweeping operations were conducted with the participation of the United States, the United Kingdom, Italy, Germany, the Netherlands, Saudi Arabia, Turkey, France, Belgium, and some other countries, the task was overwhelming, particularly given the tropical environment. There naturally emerged criticism of Japan's absence from the minesweeping operations. After all, being dependent on oil from the Middle East for as much as 70 percent of its domestic demand, didn't Japan have the greatest stake in safe navigation in the Persian Gulf? Having failed to make any human contribution during the Gulf War, the Japanese government judged that, with the end of the war, conditions were right for the dispatch of MSDF minesweepers. After the necessary preparations were carried out under strict confidentiality so as not to provoke criticism from within Japan, six MSDF minesweepers were dispatched to the Persian Gulf in April 1991. At this point, no legislative preparations had been made whatsoever to legitimize the dispatch. Article 99 of the Self-Defense Forces Act, which prescribes minesweeping operations as a role of the MSDF, was used as the grounds to legitimize the dispatch.

The six minesweepers that sailed from the MSDF Kure Naval Base—amid 60 fishing boats boarded by protestors against the dispatch—arrived in the Persian Gulf after a 31-day, 7,000 nautical-mile voyage. Once it started operations, the MSDF minesweeping fleet earned the high esteem of other participating troops as well as of countries along the Persian Gulf where the mines were. Having completed its mission on September 11, the flotilla returned to Kure Naval Base on October 30. The welcome ceremony was attended by Prime Minister Kaifu and Ikeda Yukihiko, director-general of the Defense Agency. Thus, the first overseas dispatch of the MSDF was a huge success.

Even more impressive for the Japanese people than this minesweeping operation in the Persian Gulf were the JSDF's activities in Cambodia. Having learned a lesson from the bitter experiences of the Gulf War, the Japanese government decided to actively engage in peacekeeping in Cambodia by cooperating with the country's effort to hold an election to establish a new government and by assisting various local reconstruction endeavors. Also learning a lesson from the miscarriage of the United Nations Peace Cooperation Bill at the time of the Gulf War, the ruling LDP secured an agreement with the Komeito Party and the Democratic Socialist Party (DSP) to coordinate the necessary political conditions to allow enactment of the Act on Cooperation with the United Nations Peacekeeping Operations and Other Operations in June 1992.

Actually, PKO activities in Cambodia by the United Nations had already started in March 1992. The JSDF's participation was conducted in a hectic manner, starting with the enactment of the Act on Cooperation with United Nations Peacekeeping Operations and Other Operations in June, followed by dispatch of an investigative team on July 1, approval of JSDF dispatch by the cabinet on September 8 before the selected personnel departed for Cambodia on September 17 to take part in PKO activities. Readers should be reminded, however, that, this time, due political consideration had been paid to maintaining the LDP-Komeito-DSP agreement, including a freeze on PKF (peacekeeping force) operations and the five-point principle on PKO participation, before the dispatch, putting Japan's participation in PKO activities under tight restrictions. We shall come back to this point in detail later.

In any event, Japan's participation in PKO activities in Cambodia attracted a great deal of interest, almost to the point of abnormal, as symbolized by the 300 press corps personnel dispatched from Japanese media organizations to cover the activities of the 600 PKO members. While two Japanese lives were lost among the civilian police and U.N. volunteers, there were no casualties involving JSDF personnel. With the successful implementation of the election, U.N. PKO activities in Cambodia were successfully completed. The JSDF's mission in Cambodia became a feather in the cap of Japan's postwar diplomacy to be referred to repeatedly in days to come. Moreover, the JSDF's contributions were highly appreciated internationally. This was widely reported in Japan, giving momentum to Japan's future PKO activities.

The JSDF and PKO

After these successful dispatches of the JSDF to the Persian Gulf and Cambodia, the activities of the JSDF came to be held in high regard and cases of the JSDF being dispatched overseas increased accordingly (see tables 3 and 4). Along with disaster relief activities, which became increasingly important for the JSDF after the Great Hanshin Earthquake in 1995, international cooperation has now become one of the most important post–cold war activities of the JSDF.

Nevertheless, it is also true that there is a limit to PKO activities by the JSDF. Setting aside the minesweeping operations in the Persian Gulf, to which MSDF minesweepers were dispatched on the basis of the Self-Defense Forces Act, even the participation in PKO activities in Cambodia, for which a special law was enacted, were conducted under the restrictions already mentioned—a freeze of PKF operations and the five-point principle on PKO participation—in order to secure agreement among the LDP, the DSP, and the Komeito to enact the law. The five-point principle on PKO participation states that PKO participation should be contingent on: (1) existence of a ceasefire agreement between parties to a conflict; (2) agreement by the parties concerned, including the country where a PKO is carried out, on Japan's participation; (3) activities being conducted in a strictly impartial manner; (4) the suspension of participation at any time, or the termination of participation if after a short period of suspension any of the above conditions one through three ceases to be satisfied; and (5) the use of weapons only to the minimum necessary to protect the life or person of oneself or other unit members.

As a matter of fact, when two Japanese lives were lost in Cambodia, withdrawal of the JSDF was seriously discussed. Today, the freeze of PKF operations has been lifted and the restrictions on the use of weapons have been significantly relaxed through a series of amendments. Nevertheless, compared with other countries that participate in PKO activities, JSDF personnel are still under numerous restrictions regarding the use of weapons—so much so that not a small number of dispatched JSDF personnel question if they can really defend themselves and their comrades. Moreover, because, legally speaking, the JSDF is not a military, when its personnel carry weapons overseas, the weapons have to undergo procedures required for the export of goods. There also have been cases in which restrictions on the JSDF posed an obstacle to effective coordination with troops dispatched by other participating countries. Furthermore, the irony of a military organization that, by definition, must be able to defend itself from outside aggressions being in need of protection by other military organizations raised the most fundamental question of why Japan dispatched such a "military" organization in the first place.

As we will explain in detail later, the new National Defense Program Guidelines adopted in December 2004 (2004 NDPG) to cope with new threats in the twenty-first century gives an important position to the JSDF's international cooperation activities. Therefore, instances of the JSDF being dispatched overseas are likely to continue to increase. Nevertheless, there remains a risk that the JSDF's presence overseas may fail to receive as much high esteem from the international community as expected due to the numerous constraints on its activities and its lack of self-defense capabilities. The obstacles mentioned above to dispatching the JSDF still have to be overcome. Meanwhile, today dispatch of the JSDF overseas is no longer contained to PKO activities; nowadays the JSDF is mobilized to assist overseas anti-terrorist activities. Thus, it should be said that a limit has already been reached for Japan to continue to dispatch the JSDF in the same fashion as in the past.

Table 3. International Peace Cooperation Activities by the JSDF (as of May 31, 2006)

		Period of dispatch	Number of personnel	Total number of personnel	Description of principal tasks
United Nations Transitional Authority in Cambodia (UNTAC)	Cease-fire monitors	September 1992–September 1993	8	16	· Monitor custody of weapons collected and observance of cease-fire · Monitor observance of cease-fire at the border
	Engineering unit	September 1992–September 1993	600	1,200	· Repair roads, bridges and other infrastructure · Supply fuel and water to UNTAC components and other groups · Supply food and accommodation, provide facilities needed for work and medical care to UNTAC component personnel
United Nations Operation in Mozambique (ONUMOZ)	Headquarters staff	May 1993–January 1995	5	10	· Draft mid-and long-term plans, plan and coordinate transport operations at ONUMOZ Headquarters
	Transport coordination unit	May 1993–January 1995	48	144	· Support customs clearance work and provide other transport-related technical coordination in the allocation of transport
Relief Operations for Rwandan Refugees	Rwandan refugee relief unit	September–December 1994	260		· Medical care, prevention of epidemics, water supplies
	Air transport unit	September–December 1994	118		· Airlift members of Rwandan refugee relief units and additional supplies between Nairobi (Kenya) and Goma (former Republic of Zaire and present Democratic Republic of Congo) · Make use of spare capacity to airlift personnel and supplies of humanitarian international organizations engaged in refugee relief operations
United Nations Disengagement Observer Force (UNDOF)	Headquarters staff	February 1996–	2	22	· Create PR and budgets for UNDOF operations, plan and coordinate transport, maintenance and other operations at UNDOF Headquarters
	Transport unit	February 1996–	43	903	· Transport food and other supplies · Store goods at supply warehouses, repair roads and other infrastructure, maintain heavy machinery, conduct firefighting and snow clearance
Humanitarian Assistance to East Timor	Air transport unit	November 1999–February 2000	113		· Air transport of aid materials for UNHCR · Use of spare capacity for the air transportation of UNHCR-related personnel
Relief Operations for Afghanistan Refugees	Air transport unit	October 2001	138		· Air transport of aid materials for UNHCR
United Nations Transitional Administration in East Timor (UNTAET) United Nations Mission in East Timor (UNMISET) from May 20, 2002	Headquarters staff	February 2002–June 2005	7 (10 for the first Headquarters staff)	17	· Plan and coordinate engineering and logistics operations at military headquarters
	Engineering unit	March 2002–June 2005	405 (680 each for the first and second units, 522 for the third unit)	2,287	· Maintain and repair roads and bridges that are necessary for PKO unit activities · Maintain reservoirs used by units of other nations and local inhabitants that are in Dili and other locations · Civic assistance
Relief Operations for Iraqi Refugees	Air transport unit	March–April, 2003	50		· Air transport of aid materials for UNHCR
Relief Operations for Iraqi Victims	Air transport unit	July–August, 2003	98		· Air transport of materials for the relief of Iraqi victims

Notes: 1. Other operations have included support activities in the areas of transport and supply carried out by units of the MSDF (in Cambodia and East Timor) and the ASDF (in Cambodia, Mozambique, the Golan Heights, East Timor, and Afghanistan).
2. An advance unit of 23 people was additionally sent as part the Rwandan refugee relief effort.
3. Source: Ministry of Defense and SDF

Table 4. International Disaster Relief Activities by the JSDF

		Period of dispatch	Number of personnel	Total number of personnel	Description of principal tasks
International disaster relief activities in Honduras (hurricane)	Medical unit	November 13–December 9, 1998	80		· Medical treatment and disease control in the Republic of Honduras
	Air transport unit		105		· Transportation of equipment for medical units, etc. between Japan and Honduras · Air transport of equipment and other materials between the United States and Honduras
Transportation of materials for international disaster relief activities in Turkey (earthquake)	Maritime transport unit	September 23–November 22, 1999	426		· Marine transportation of materials necessary for international disaster relief activities in the Republic of Turkey (e.g. temporary dwellings)
International disaster relief activities in India (earthquake)	Material support unit	February 5–11, 2001	16		· Delivery of aid materials and technical instruction on aid materials
	Air transport unit		78		· Transport of aid materials and support units, etc.
International disaster relief activities in Iran (earthquake)	Air transport unit	December 30, 2003-January 6, 2004	31		· Air transport of aid materials
International disaster relief activities in Thailand (earthquake, tsunami)	Dispatched maritime unit	December 28, 2004–January 1, 2005	590		· Search and rescue activities for the disaster struck victims around Thailand and its sea
International disaster relief activities in Indonesia (earthquake, tsunami)	Joint liaison office	January 6–March 23, 2005	22		· Joint arrangements for the international disaster relief activities · Communication and coordination with authorities and foreign forces involved in the international disaster relief activities
International disaster relief activities in Indonesia (earthquake, tsunami)	Medical/Air support unit	January 6–March 23, 2005	228		· Air transport of aid materials · Medical treatment and disease control
	Maritime transport unit		593		· Maritime transport of GSDF International Disaster Relief Teams · Support for the activities of GSDF International Disaster Relief Teams · Transport of aid materials
	Air transport unit		82		· Air Transport of aid materials
International disaster relief activities off Kamchatka Peninsula, Russia	Maritime transport unit	August 5–10, 2005	346		· Rescue of a Russian submarine
International disaster relief activities in Pakistan (earthquake)	Air support unit	October 12–December 2, 2005	147		· Air transport in connection with relief activities
	Air transport unit		114		· Air transport of GSDF International Disaster Relief Teams

Notes: 1. For International disaster relief activities in Iran, a fixing team was sent to Singapore separately because of the mechanical problem of transport aircraft on the way to Iran.
2. Eleven officers dispatched by GSDF, MSDF and ASDF are included in the number of personnel of the liaison office in Indonesia for the international disaster relief activities.
3. Source: Ministry of Defense and SDF

Chapter 11

Multilateral Security Cooperation vs. the U.S.-Japan Alliance

The Defense Agency–Foreign Ministry Confrontation

After the end of the cold war, as we've seen, reconsideration of the role of the Japan Self-Defense Forces (JSDF) did not proceed as it should have. This was partly because the Japanese government's hands were kept full with the Gulf War. Another reason was that the cold war had ended mainly in Europe, with little affect in Asia where remnants of the cold war still lingered in the form of China-Taiwan relations and the two Koreas. It was, nevertheless, beyond doubt that, thanks to the collapse of the Soviet Union, by far the most formidable threat during the cold war, the overall threat in Asia, too, was greatly reduced. Amid the chorus of voices demanding a share of the "peace dividend" after the end of the cold war, expectations arose concerning arms reduction, particularly in western countries. This wave of expectations also reached Japan.

At the same time, the JSDF was asked to perform new tasks, most notably in regard to activities connected with peacekeeping operations (PKO). Although these new tasks were not a part of the JSDF's main mission of defending the country from outside adversaries, as the JSDF became increasingly engaged in these new tasks, handling them became more of an important role for the organization. And the more these activities were widely covered by the mass media, the more it appeared in people's minds as if those activities were the JSDF's main tasks.

Thus, the role of the JSDF in post–cold war days came to be argued over from two angles: arms reduction and international cooperation. In order to promote arms reduction, however, it was necessary to formulate a security policy that was suitable to the post–cold war international environment. And in order to discuss what degree of arms reduction would be appropriate, it was first necessary to clarify the role of the JSDF in the new international environment. Until the JSDF's role was clarified, discussion on the appropriate degree of arms reduction would be meaningless. So it was that the positioning of U.S.-Japan security cooperation became a major issue in contemplating the post–cold war security policy of Japan.

In fact, a conflict of views emerged on this particular issue between the Defense Agency and the Ministry of Foreign Affairs. Put another way, the difference of opinion took the form of a conflict between the argument for multilateral security cooperation, including reevaluation of the United Nations, represented by the Defense Agency, and the argument for putting U.S.-Japan security arrangements at the center of Japan's security policy, as advocated by the Ministry of Foreign Affairs.

Attributing the malfunctioning of the United Nations mostly to constraints on the function of its Security Council because of the confrontation between the United States and the Soviet Union, the argument for a review of U.N. functions and roles after the end of the cold war gained momentum. Against this backdrop, the Defense Agency argued that Japan should promote multilateral security cooperation globally through more active participation in U.N. peacekeeping activities, while at the same time retaining the U.S.-Japan security pact as the foundation of Japan's security policy. Actually, voices advocating this kind of multilateral security cooperation had already been heard from among senior officials of the Defense Agency since the 1980s.

In contrast, it was the view of the Ministry of Foreign Affairs that Japan should adhere to regional security and the defense of Japan centered around the U.S.-Japan security pact. When, and if, the ministry's argument went, the line of multilateral security cooperation was pursued, closer cooperation with the United Nations would inevitably dilute intimacy with the United States, no matter how much the central position of the security arrangements with the United States was stressed. The Ministry of Foreign Affairs was adamantly against anything that could lower the relative weight of U.S.-Japan security cooperation.

This confrontation can be attributed to the differing viewpoints between the two offices on the security arrangements with the United States. Unlike bureaucrats of the Defense Agency up until the 1960s, when Japan had been totally dependent on the U.S.-Japan security pact for its defense, officials of the Defense Agency, who had been with the agency from the beginning of their careers and were promoted to senior positions therein in the 1980s, had experienced firsthand the debates on autonomous diplomacy and national defense in the late 1960s through 1970s. It was these bureaucrats who did the soul-searching on what defense capabilities were suitable to Japan—all in the crossfire of criticisms of excessive reliance on the United States, on the one hand, and the resurrection of militarism, on the other.

As the result of these soul-searching efforts, the first National Defense Program Guidelines (Boei Keikaku no Taiko, or NDPG) based on the Concept of Basic Defense Capability was formulated in 1976. This NDPG was formulated to clarify the role of Japan's defense capabilities at a time when the function of the security arrangements with the United States as a deterrent was a given. Naturally, the NDPG strongly advocated Japan's own autonomous defense efforts, particularly regarding defense of the homeland Japan. A typical example of this in the NDPG is found in the following statement:

Should direct aggression occur, Japan will repel such aggression at the earliest possible stage by taking immediate responsive action and trying to conduct an integrated, systematic operation of its defense capability. Japan will repel limited and small-scale aggression, in principle, without external assistance. In cases where the unassisted repelling of aggression is not feasible, due to scale, type or other factors of such aggression, Japan will continue an unyielding resistance by mobilizing all available forces until such time as cooperation from the United States is introduced, thus rebuffing such aggression.

As exemplified by the anti–U.S. military base movement in the 1950s and the anti–U.S.-Japan Security Treaty campaign in the 1960s, nationalism in Japan is likely to take the form of an anti-U.S. movement. That being the case, bureaucrats of the Defense Agency had to pursue defense buildup while at the same time placing the security arrangements with the United States at the heart of security policy. They seemed to have grown to share a sense of crisis that complete reliance on the United States would be detrimental to Japan's own defense buildup. This thinking was beyond the understanding of foreign ministry officials, who single-mindedly believed in the absolute value of the U.S.-Japan security cooperation. However, after the political realignment in 1993—as the result of the collapse of the "1955 system" (a two-party system of government in Japan led by the Liberal Democratic Party [LDP] with the Japan Socialist Party in opposition)—post–cold war security policy began to be reexamined in earnest against the backdrop of the above discrepancy within the government.

The Advisory Group on Defense Issues

The reexamination of Japan's defense capabilities from the dual angles of arms reduction and international cooperation escalating to the level of the formulation of a new NDPG was mainly due to two developments: One was a trend in Japan where defense issues became less and less of a taboo since the Gulf War, and the other was more realistic policy dialogue facilitated by the former opposition forces' participation in the government as a result of collapse of the 1955 system. Of particular significance was the formation of a cabinet by Murayama Tomiichi, chairman of the Japan Socialist Party (present day Social Democratic Party), which had long advocated unarmed neutrality as the party line. Prime Minister Murayama officially recognized the U.S.-Japan Security Treaty and converted the party's policy to accept the JSDF as constitutional. With this historic conversion, conditions were complete for Japan's defense policy, which had been mainly deliberated by the Defense Agency's inner bureau, to be discussed more widely in the political arena.

The Advisory Group on Defense Issues (also known as the Higuchi Group) launched by the Hosokawa Morihiro cabinet played an extremely important role in the discussions of Japan's security policy in the immediate post–cold war days. It was these discussions that led to the formulation of the new National Defense Program Guidelines of 1995. The Hosokawa cabinet was a non-LDP coalition cabinet formed following the collapse of the 1955 system; Prime Minister Hosokawa, it is believed, had wished to reexamine Japan's security policy bearing in mind the trend toward arms control. And it was the Advisory Group on Defense Issues under the chairmanship of Higuchi Hirotaro, chairman of Asahi Breweries, Inc., that conducted the reexamination of Japan's security policy. The group consisted of the following members:

Chairman:
Higuchi Hirotaro, Chairman the Board, Asahi Breweries, Ltd.
Acting Chairman:
Moroi Ken, Chairman, Chichibu Cement Co, Ltd.
Members:
Inoguchi Kuniko, Professor, Sophia University
Okawara Yoshio, Executive Adviser, Keidanren (former Japanese Ambassador to the United States)
Gyoten Toyoo, Chairman of the Board of Directors, The Bank of Tokyo, Ltd. (former Vice Minister of Finance for International Affairs)
Sakuma Makoto, Consultant to the President, Nippon Telegraph and Telephone Corporation (former Chairman, Joint Staff Council)
Nishihiro Seiki, Adviser, The Tokyo Marine and Fire Insurance Co, Ltd. (former Administrative Vice Minister of Defense)
Fukukawa Shinji, Vice Chairman of the Board, Kobe Steel, Ltd. (former Administrative Vice Minister of International Trade and Industry)

Watanabe Akio, Professor, Aoyama Gakuin University

Prime Minister Hosokawa decided to launch this group while he heard briefings on the status of Japan's defense policy from defense professionals and experts. The Defense Agency was instrumental in the actual organization of the group under the initiative of Nishihiro Seiki, who was also appointed as a member of the group. The first Defense Agency career bureaucrat who made it to the post of administrative vice-minister of defense, Nishihiro was one of the most outstanding Defense Agency bureaucrats, along with Kaihara Osamu and Kubo Takuya. Having been deeply involved in the formulation of the Concept of Basic Defense Capability and the first National Defense Program Guidelines, it is believed that Nishihiro continued to retain a powerful influence on Japan's defense policy even after his retirement from the agency. Because it was Watanabe Akio, a long-standing and close associate of Nishihiro's, who drafted the final report of the group, it seems safe to say that the discussions at the group reflected the view of the Defense Agency to a significant degree.

Discussions in the Higuchi Group, however, were not necessarily in complete harmony from the beginning. The most conspicuous discrepancy was seen around the notion of multilateral security cooperation, which had already been introduced in the narrative of the conflict between the Defense Agency and Ministry of Foreign Affairs. The group included former ambassador to the United States Okawara Yoshio as a member, and the issue of multilateral security cooperation was discussed mainly from the standpoint of the primacy of security arrangements with the United States. In the end, though, it is believed that the final report reflecting the argument of the Defense Agency was drafted by Watanabe. The Report of the Advisory Group on Defense Issues was finalized under the title of "The Modality of Security and Defense Capability of Japan: Outlook for the 21st Century." It should be noted, incidentally, that even though the group was launched by the Hosokawa cabinet, its final report was submitted to the succeeding Murayama cabinet, a reflection of the drastic changes in the political scene in those days.

What specifically did this final report set forth? While the report covered a wide range of issues, in a nutshell, it proposed that (1) Japan should promote global as well as regional multilateral security cooperation; (2) the functions of the U.S.-Japan security cooperation should be enhanced; and (3) Japan should pursue proactive and constructive security policy, maintaining highly reliable and efficient defense capabilities of its own.

The fact of the matter is that the content of this final report gave a shock to the United States because it gave Americans the impression that Japan might begin to keep its distance from the security arrangements with the United States. This led to anxiety among U.S. security professionals that Japan might not trust the U.S. commitment to maintain its presence in Asia; this anxiety spurred further security dialogues with Japan.

The Nye Initiative

The United States in those days was under Bill Clinton's Democrat administration. Having defeated the incumbent President George Bush by emphasizing the importance of economic policies, it is said that President Clinton at first was not too much interested in security cooperation with Japan. And yet, it so happened that the passing of the worst season of U.S.-Japan economic friction, due to a worsening of Japan's economic conditions and the tentative settlement of pending issues including the U.S.-Japan Framework for a New Economic Partnership, coincided with the season of political realignment in Japan. Problems such as the turmoil in the East Asian security situation also happened in this period. Against this backdrop, voices requesting the reevaluation of the U.S.-Japan security arrangements gained momentum in the United States. It was at this very timing that the Higuchi Group's final report was published.

The U.S. government reacted by having Japan hands at the State Department and other Japan specialists make a quick assessment of Japan's true intention. At the same time, fearing that not only Japan but also other Asian countries, including Korea, may have been worried about a reduction of the U.S. presence in Asia, Washington hurriedly put together U.S. strategies toward Asia. Joseph Nye, Jr., the former Harvard professor who had been appointed as assistant secretary of defense for international security affairs, became the central figure in this endeavor. With the consent of Secretary of Defense William Perry, Nye authored a U.S. strategy that explicitly emphasized the U.S. presence in Asia. This new East Asian strategy of the United States called the Nye initiative was compiled into the East Asia Strategic Report in February 1995, half a year after the final report of the Higuchi Group was released.

The main feature of the Nye Report was high praise of Japan's role in East Asia and clarification of the U.S. intention to maintain its presence in East Asia by announcing its "commitment to maintain a stable forward presence in the region, at the existing level of about 100,000 troops, for the foreseeable future." It was particularly important that, in the process of compilation of the Nye Report, U.S. security experts with extensive knowledge of and experience with Japan repeatedly exchanged views with Japanese bureaucrats, particularly those of the Defense Agency on the divisional deputy-director level, including those "Japan desk" officials stationed in the United States.

U.S. concern about the Higuchi Group's report was frequently conveyed to the Japanese side through these occasions. In response to the U.S. side, which in the Nye Report gave a high score to Japan's role and clarified its intention to maintain its presence in East Asia, the Japanese side reassured its American counterparts that the Higuchi Report had not slighted the U.S.-Japan alliance at all and that the multilateral security cooperation that the report had advocated was centered around the U.S.-Japan security arrangements being at its core. Nevertheless, the Japanese side became increasingly convinced that the Higuchi Report should be revised to stress the primacy of the security arrangements with the United States more clearly in order to erase American concerns. Because, coincidentally, a need to reconfirm the functions of the U.S.-Japan security cooperation arose at that time, triggered by such developments as the nuclear crisis on the Korean peninsula, the Japanese side decided to conduct a thorough review of its defense policy in post–cold war days. This decision culminated in the formulation of the new National Defense Program Guidelines and the Japan-U.S. Joint Declaration on Security Alliance for the 21st Century.

Revision of the NDPG

The Defense Agency launched an intra-agency committee to review the defense posture of Japan in February 1994 and began revising the NDPG for the first time in some twenty years. Although it was the aforementioned Higuchi Report that had provided the premise for this review endeavor, discussions at the commission continued even after publication of said report. The commission was composed of top leaders of the Defense Agency, including its director-general (minister of state for defense), parliamentary vice-minister of defense, administrative vice-minister, director-general of the Secretariat of the Minister of State for Defense, director-general of the Bureau of Defense Policy, chairman of the Joint Staff Council, and the chiefs of staff of all three forces of the JSDF. It was unprecedented for members of the uniformed team to participate in the formulation of national defense policy, which had previously been conducted almost exclusively by the inner bureau of the Defense Agency, particularly its Bureau of Defense Policy.

In November 1995, the commission laid forth a new set of guidelines for Japan's defense capability. The resultant National Defense Program Guidelines in and after FY 1996 (henceforth Second NDPG) had four distinctive features. First, in conjunction with the issue of arms control, which had been argued about since the end of the cold war, the Second NDPG set a certain direction for the downsizing mainly of the Ground Self-Defense Force (GSDF) through enhanced efficiency. The general direction of the downsizing of the JSDF as a whole had already been decided before the Second NDPG. Seeing as enhancement of the GSDF's efficiency had long been discussed and the GSDF in fact had never realized its full complement, it had been agreed that downsizing should start with the GSDF. Because it was improper for only the GSDF to be the victim of downsizing, however, the Maritime Self-Defense Force and the Air Self-Defense Force were also reduced in size. Still, the GSDF, which had the largest number of personnel, received the largest cut, reducing its size from 180,000 strong to 160,000 strong (see table 5).

The second feature of the Second NDPG was clarification of the increased role of the JSDF. Both the JSDF's international cooperation activities, which became conspicuous after the end of the cold war, and its large-scale disaster relief operations, including those after the Great Hanshin Earthquake, were featured as important tasks of the JSDF. Thus, while on the one hand downsizing through enhancing efficiency was promoted, on the other hand, the range of JSDF tasks continued to be expanded to include international cooperation, disaster relief, and, as we will see later, responses to situations in areas surrounding Japan.

The third characteristic was the Second NDPG's emphasis on the importance of the U.S.-Japan security arrangements. As we've seen, there had been a conflict before the formulation of the Second NDPG between advocates of multilateral security cooperation and advocates of the alliance with the United States, who adamantly refused anything that could dilute the importance of the alliance. While the former school was represented by the Defense Agency, the Ministry of Foreign Affairs was the chief advocate of the latter. The Higuchi Report clearly took the side of the former argument, which inadvertently elicited an unexpected result: a sense of distrust of Japan's attitude (that is, a sense that Japan was putting itself a little distant from the U.S.-Japan security arrangements) in the United States. The Second NDPG thoroughly stressed the importance of U.S.-Japan security cooperation as if to banish all suspicion among the Americans. This was obvious, for instance, from the thirteen references in the Second NDPG to the U.S.-Japan security arrangement, in contrast to only the one reference to it in the First NDPG of 1976. In fact, throughout the text, the credibility of the U.S.-Japan security arrangements was stressed incessantly in the Second NDPG.

Moreover, fourthly, responses to situations in areas surrounding Japan was also included in the Second NDPG. This was because the need for U.S.-Japan security cooperation beyond homeland defense

Table 5. Trends in Defense Buildup Goals Shown by NDPG Appendices

	Equipage	1976 NDPG	1995 NDPG	2004 NDPG	2004/1976 (%)	2004/1995 (%)
GSDF	# of personnel	180,000	160,000	155,000	approx 86%	approx 97%
	# of tanks	approx 1,200	approx 900	approx 600	approx 50%	approx 67%
	# of artilleries	approx 1,000	approx 900	approx 600	approx 60%	approx 67%
MSDF	# of escort ships	approx 60	approx 50	approx 47	approx 75%	approx 90%
	# of submarines	16	16	16	100	100
	# of operational aircrafts	approx 220	approx 170	approx 150	approx 70%	approx 88%
ASDF	# of operational aircrafts	approx 430	approx 400	approx 350	approx 80%	approx 87%
	(of which # of fighters)	approx 350	approx 300	approx 260	approx 75%	approx 87%

Source: Constructed by author based on Ministry of Defense's *Defense of Japan 2005*

was heightened owing to instability in the East Asian region, as typically represented by nuclear issues on the Korean peninsula. With the inclusion of this awareness of the new need, the Second NDPG prompted U.S.-Japan discussions on the actual realization of bilateral cooperation. This led to the release of the Japan-U.S. Joint Declaration on Security Alliance for the 21st Century in April 1996 and revision of the Guidelines for Japan-U.S. Defense Cooperation (Guidelines) in 1997. Simply put, the difference between the old and new Guidelines was that movement toward actual realization of their content was started almost immediately in the case of the new Guidelines. U.S.-Japan cooperation was, thus, reinforced again, and the actual realization of bilateral cooperation was pursued in the midst of redefinition or reconfirmation of the security arrangements with the United States.

Chapter 12

In the Midst of Redefinition of the U.S.-Japan Security Arrangements

National Defense Program Guidelines in and after FY1996 and the Concept of Basic Defense Capability

It should be recalled that the National Defense Program Guidelines in and after FY1996 (Second NDPG) explicitly stressed the importance of the security arrangements with the United States and set forth the expansion of Japan Self-Defense Forces (JSDF) activities. It was hoped that the Second NDPG would continue to provide a basic guideline for Japan's defense policy for the next fifteen years or so. In actuality, however, it had to undergo reexamination in less than ten years, which meant the formulation of yet another, third NDPG.

This circumstance was at least partly attributable to the need to cope with the newly emerged threats symbolized by the September 11, 2001, terrorist attacks in the United States. But that wasn't all. As a matter of fact, because there had been a lot of uncertainties about the post–cold war international order at the time of the formulation of the Second NDPG, some areas of Japan's defense capabilities had not been thoroughly examined. Let us look into these areas in relation to the Concept of Basic Defense Capability that had provided the premise for the formulation of the older, first NDPG.

When the Second NDPG was formulated, it was declared that the Concept of Basic Defense Capability would continue to be adopted as the basic guideline for defense buildup. It is indeed true that, with the end of the cold war, there no longer was the need to promote defense cooperation between U.S. and Japanese naval forces to protect sea lanes (meaning burden sharing for the regions to be defended was no longer necessary). The demise of the Soviet Union made it unnecessary for Japan to prevent a Soviet invasion into the Pacific Ocean by making the Japanese archipelago a shield against the presumed invader. Since the mid-1980s, the defense buildup required to construct cooperative relations with the U.S. Navy had been pursued beyond capabilities to cope with a limited, small-scale direct invasion, which was the premise behind the Concept of Basic Defense Capability. Now that the conditions surrounding defense capability buildup had changed, it was only natural that homeland defense should once again became a focus of attention and that the Concept of Basic Defense Capability be reevaluated.

In the Second NDPG, however, the basic policy of defending Japan against a limited, small-scale direct invasion was dropped. Moreover, what was stated as (A) below as a manifesto of resolution to defend one's own country in the older NDPG was changed to (B):

(A) Should direct aggression occur, <u>Japan will repel such aggression at the earliest possible stage by taking immediate responsive action and trying to conduct an integrated, systematic operation of its defense capability. Japan will repel limited and small-scale aggression, in principle, without external assistance. In cases where the unassisted repelling of aggression is not feasible, due to scale, type or other factors of such aggression, Japan will continue an unyielding resistance by mobilizing all available forces</u> until such time as cooperation from the United States is introduced, thus rebuffing such aggression. (underline added)

(B) Should direct aggression occur, take immediate responsive action by conducting an integrated and systematic operation of its defense capabilities, in appropriate cooperation with the United States, in order to repel such aggression at the earliest possible stage.

The above comparison clearly shows that the underlined portion in

(A) was almost entirely deleted in (B). The older NDPG was the product of an exploration into Japan's own autonomous defense mainly of the homeland Japan. In contrast, the Second NDPG, which stressed the importance of security arrangements with the United States, became devoid of autonomous posture toward national defense. It must have been judged that the hypothesis of a limited and small-scale invasion was itself unrealistic and, once an invasion to Japan occurred, it would inevitably call for joint operations with the U.S. military to cope with it, making the underlined portion redundant.

Yet immediately after the formulation of the Second NDPG, voices questioning the wisdom of suppressing autonomy in defense of one's own country had already been raised openly. In fact, not all of the threats, including international terrorism and other newer threats, are to be met in collaboration with the U.S. military from beginning to end. There must be problems that Japan has to cope with on its own. If that is indeed the case, the question remains if a security policy that depends solely on the security arrangements with the United States can construct an effective defense against such threats.

Another problem with the Second NDPG was the ambiguity about the basis for the Concept of Basic Defense Capability when the supposition of a limited, small-scale invasion was eliminated. In fact, it was not transparent at all against what threat defense capabilities were to be constructed when downsizing in the name of efficiency was conducted along with, quite ironically, the expansion of roles that the JSDF was expected to play. The Joint Staff Council should have been aggrandized so that it could deliberate which basic threats to Japan ought to be prepared for and thus clarify the roles of the three forces of the JSDF. But little progress was made in strengthening the Joint Staff Council despite the constant calls for such heard nearly every year. In the end, the Defense Agency had to resort to purchasing equipages to cope with its newly imposed roles while putting up with overall downsizing. Although politicians became increasingly interested in defense issues from that time onward, their interest was not yet adequate enough to look into the specific contents of equipages and their efficiency. All told, it should be concluded that the Second NDPG was of a transitional nature reflecting a shift from the confusion in the immediate post–cold war days to the recent manifestation of new threats. It could also be said that the actual changes in the international situation turned out to be much more drastic than drafters of the Second NDPG had anticipated.

Thus, the JSDF's attitude toward national defense, its most central mission, remained ambiguous, even though the Second NDPG had claimed to adhere to the Concept of Basic Defense Capability. Meanwhile, examinations were continued to formulate the new Guidelines for Japan-U.S. Defense Cooperation, including an in-depth look into the concrete contents of the bilateral cooperation.

Situations in Areas Surrounding Japan and the New Guidelines

The 1955 system of Japanese politics collapsed in 1993 and the Hosokawa Morihiro cabinet was formed. From this point on, Japanese politics entered a season of drastic political realignment. As far as the national defense issue was concerned, the Higuchi Group launched in February 1994 conducted a full-fledged examination of post–cold war defense policy. And it so happened that this season in Japan coincided with the nuclear crisis caused by North Korea, which brought home to Japanese the importance of the security arrangements with the United States and, at the same time, provided renewed impetus for Japan to materialize U.S.-Japan defense cooperation.

In March 1996, the year the Second NDPG was officially adopted, China dared a military exercise in the waters surrounding Taiwan, presumably to obstruct the first presidential election in the Republic of China. Missiles were fired and naval and air force drills using live ammunition were conducted from March 5 through 25. Fearing further intensification of the tension in the Taiwan Strait, the United States deployed an aircraft carrier to the region. The situation regained normalcy after the election in Taiwan.

Without a doubt, these international developments concerning North Korea and China refocused attention and effort on materializing U.S.-Japan cooperation in responses to situations in areas surrounding Japan, as was incorporated in the Second NDPG. And this led to the formulation of the new Guidelines for Japan-U.S. Defense Cooperation in September 1997.

Compared to the older Guidelines, the new Guidelines had the two new features of (1) responses to situations in areas surrounding Japan, known as the Article 6 situations, being included from the beginning of its formulation and (2) legislative preparations to validate such responses. In contrast, the older Guidelines mainly focused on homeland defense (Article 5 situations) in consideration of the domestic situation in Japan in those days, and preparation of legislation to underpin responses to Article 6 situations was hardly implemented. Behind the inclusion of these new features was active involvement of politics in the defense issue, which will be discussed later. But, first, let us consider the anatomy of the content of the new Guidelines.

In the new Guidelines, U.S.-Japan cooperation was called for in the three areas of (1) cooperation under normal circumstances; (2) actions in response to an armed attack against Japan; and (3) cooperation in situations in areas surrounding Japan. Of these three, the most important area of the bilateral cooperation was cooperation in situations in areas surrounding Japan. Regarding this, the functions and fields of cooperation of the two countries included (1) cooperation in activities initiated by either government; (2) Japan's support for U.S. forces activities; and (3) U.S.-Japan operational cooperation. Of these three functions, (1) set forth bilateral cooperation in the protection of citizens, which any sovereign state should provide, and international activities. International activities belonged to the type of bilateral cooperation that had to be conducted promptly when such situations in areas surrounding Japan as the protection of Japanese citizens staying in the affected areas emerged. The fact of the matter was that specifics had hardly been contemplated in Japan even on such basic moves.

After the announcement of the new Guidelines, tenacious arguments commenced between China and Japan on the definition of "situations in areas surrounding Japan." The argument—that is, whether "situations" was a geographical concept or not—became politicized between the two countries. Certainly, from the viewpoint of the security issue as a whole, what constituted situations in areas surrounding Japan was an important issue. What was most important from the viewpoint of the JSDF, however, was cooperation with the United States in the area of the second point—Japan's support for U.S. forces activities—when the JSDF had to respond to situations in areas surrounding Japan on a full scale. This "Japan's support for U.S. forces activities" was to be mostly conducted in the area known as rear area support. It should be obvious from The Guidelines for Japan-U.S. Defense Cooperation (September 23, 1997) in the appendix how versatile that area actually is. Even those activities that were assumed to be conducted within the framework of the Japanese Constitution were significantly wide-ranging. While the JSDF in those days appeared to be capable of accomplishing these tasks, it should be noted that the JSDF was requested to cope with these situations even as it was under pressure for rationalization and downsizing. Whether the JSDF could actually handle the mission bestowed on it depended on what actually happened, of course. Nonetheless, taking up its mission would have, beyond a doubt, meant the further expansion of its role.

The formulation of the new Guidelines also necessitated pertinent legislation. While the new missions were within the bounds of the current Constitution, were they to be actually implemented, supportive legislation would have been found to be inadequate in many areas. But bureaucrats alone could not attend to the task of new legislation, as was clearly shown by the delay in legislative preparations for the older Guidelines after the retirement of Administrative Vice Minister of Defense Maruyama Ko, whose enthusiasm for promoting the necessary legal infrastructure had not been carried on by his successors. In contrast, legal preparations for new missions stipulated by the new Guidelines were actively pursued, starting with the Act on Measures to Ensure the Peace and Security of Japan in Perilous Situations in Areas Surrounding Japan enacted in 1999. This change was attributable to people's recognition of the importance of the security issue and to politicians' active involvement in the issue after experiencing the end of the cold war and the political realignment in Japan.

Toward Active Civilian Control

Political realignment in Japan after the collapse of the 1955 system was first triggered by political reform attempts. After the Lockheed incident in 1976, scandals involving politics and money erupted one after another. For instance, the Takeshita Noboru cabinet, which had been expected to be a long and stable government, fell because of the Recruit scandal in 1988. Having suffered from its loss of the majority in the House of Councilors election as well as from a fall in support ratings, the ruling Liberal Democratic Party (LDP) experienced a swell of voices from within demanding political reform to settle money and politics problems. The timing of these rising expectations for political reform in Japan coincided with the end of the cold war and the Gulf War. Political reform, therefore, was not only a matter of political scandals involving money but also a matter of instituting a policy decision-making system suitable to the new age.

In the end, political reform this time converged into reform of the medium-size constituency system (the electoral system that allows three to five candidates to run from one district) that had been the hotbed of the LDP's faction politics. Under this system, election results were bound to be influenced by candidates' personal popularity, including their private services to the constituency, resulting in a dearth of policy debates among political parties during a campaign. To remedy this situation, a single-seat constituency system was adopted after the collapse of the 1955 system to promote more policy-oriented politics in Japan. It still is open to debate how effective this new system has been in ending constituency service–oriented politics and fostering more policy-oriented politics. Nevertheless, it is beyond doubt that the single-seat constituency system did undermine faction politics, which had long characterized LDP politics, and activated policy debates among political parties. Whereas the debate on national defense during the cold war almost sounded like a theological argument, discussion of the security issue after the Gulf War became an important political issue calling for concrete responses from Japan in the form of dispatching the JSDF overseas and responding to the nuclear crisis on the Korean peninsula.

It was of great significance that the
Japan Socialist Party (JSP) came to participate in the government at this point
through the changes explained earlier.
For one thing, this had the effect of almost instantly diminishing taboos in
the discussions of security affairs. This
was a drastic change, considering that
once there had been an atmosphere to
prohibit even the discussion of concrete
defense policies.

It should be noted, however, that
the Second NDPG was formulated
during a season of political upheaval in
Japan, as symbolized by four ministers
of state for defense coming and going
in two years. Bureaucrats were still the

Okinawans' Indignation Meeting
against the Okinawa Rape Incident
of September 4, 1995 (Source: The
Mainichi Newspapers)

prime movers during this period. Yet as the content of the Second
NDPG shows, Japan was entering a period of transition in which the
old pattern of the bureaucracy taking the initiative in defense policy
gave way to the new paradigm of active involvement by politicians. By
the time the LDP-JSP coalition government was formed, the upheaval
in politics had begun to subside, allowing politicians to be involved in
national defense policies more earnestly. A chain of international
problems, such as the nuclear crisis on the Korean peninsula and the
tension in the Taiwan Strait, further encouraged the politicians' involvement.

Although it is beyond the scope of this book on the JSDF, this
period also witnessed the intensification of citizens' movements that
had been demanding the withdrawal of U.S. military bases from Okinawa since the Okinawa rape incident on September 4, 1995. Under
the security arrangements with the United States, which were essentially a system of barter between (American) soldiers and (Japanese)
military bases, citizens' movements demanding the return of military
bases in Okinawa, where 75 percent of U.S. bases in Japan were con-

centrated, were an issue that related directly to Japan's security. And this was indeed a problem that politicians had to cope with, because bureaucrats alone could not handle it. As Japan was increasingly urged to carry out the concrete materialization of U.S.-Japan defense cooperation, politicians no longer could evade decisions, whether they liked it or not.

The active involvement of politicians in defense affairs, however, did not automatically mean that they immediately became able to play a prominent role in security affairs, including specific defense policies, thus replacing bureaucrats. In any event, and even though their stage might have been prepared by bureaucrats, the fact remains that Japanese politicians, who had shown a tendency to distance themselves from any decision related to national defense, started to actively engage in and make decisions on these policies. Formulation of the new Guidelines, which had assumed the Article 6 situations, and the Act on Measures to Ensure the Peace and Security of Japan in Perilous Situations in Areas Surrounding Japan would not have been possible without the support of politicians.

Moreover, there erupted a chain of events toward the end of the 1990s that magnified the Japanese people's sense of crisis about the country's defense. Two of these events were the North Korean launch of a missile that flew over Japan in August 1998 and the spotting of two suspicious boats with false markings off the Noto peninsula in 1999. This second event made the Japanese government issue an order for maritime security operations for the first time in its postwar history. It was under these circumstances that politicians began to make decisions on national defense themselves—something they had long shied away from. This also represented a major shift from what was termed "passive civilian control"—that is, how to get by without using the JSDF—to "active civilian control," or regulating when and how to use the JSDF. One big piece of homework still remained, though, to make the JSDF "usable": legislation concerning emergency situations.

Chapter 13

New Threats and the New NDPG

Toward a "Usable" JSDF

Since the Mitsuya Kenkyu (Mitsuya Study, or "Three Arrows" contingency planning) incident in 1965, studying the implementation of legislation concerning emergency situations had been, so to speak, a political taboo. Such legislation was considered during the Fukuda Takeo cabinet, under which the formulation of the first Guidelines for Japan-U.S. Defense Cooperation had been promoted. At the time, the investigation into such legislation attracted people's attention partly due to the advocacy of extrajudicial actions by the Japan Self-Defense Forces (JSDF) in case of emergency by Kurisu Hiroomi, chairman of the Joint Staff Council. A series of interim reports on the legislation concerning emergency situations had been made, including an interim report on laws and ordinances under the jurisdiction of the Defense Agency (Category 1) in 1984, an interim report on laws and ordinances under the jurisdiction of other ministries/agencies (Category 2) in 1984, and an interim report on laws and ordinances under obscure jurisdictions (Category 3) in 1988. Nevertheless, these endeavors remained a mere study, perhaps due to the evasiveness of other ministries concerning involvement in national defense affairs and a lack of enthusiasm among politicians for drafting a bill. In the end, legislators, who had not yet graduated from the mindset of "negative civilian control," were not able to overcome the accusation that this legislation concerning emergency situations was for the purpose of actually using the JSDF for military purposes.

It was after the mid-1990s that the above situation changed drastically. Owing to the JSDF's successful involvement in activities connected to United Nations' peacekeeping operations (PKO) and the resulting favorable international repercussions, the argument in Japan against the use of the JSDF no matter what lost its persuasive power. As political realignment facilitated policy debates among political parties, national security became a concrete issue and attracted the attention of the Japanese people. As the materialization of U.S.-Japan security cooperation advanced against the backdrop of crises in East Asia and as the new Guidelines for Japan-U.S. Defense Cooperation began to be formulated, the ruling Liberal Democratic Party's Research Commission on Security published a memorandum titled "Gaidorain no minaoshi to aratana hoseido ni mukete" (Toward review of the guidelines and necessary new legislation). The memorandum proposed further efforts toward the study and enactment of legislation concerning emergency situations. It showed that the time had come, at last, for legislators in Japan to get serious about promulgating laws in preparation for emergency situations.

After the Act on Measures to Ensure the Peace and Security of Japan in Perilous Situations in Areas Surrounding Japan and other legislation concerning emergency situations were drafted and promulgated in 1999 and 2000, it became an issue that legislation concerning emergency situations within Japan, which should have been handled before legislation on emergencies in surrounding areas, had lagged behind. Certainly, properly speaking, legislation on homeland defense should be enacted before legislation on international contingencies. But in Japan's case, the order was reversed, with legislation on the JSDF's overseas activities—be it U.N. PKO activities or emergencies in areas surrounding Japan—being prepared first. This was the result of Japan's treating symptoms by responding to problems that arose one after another while procrastinating on what should be first priority—legislation concerning emergency situations threatening the homeland—out of fear of stirring up domestic controversy. This episode eloquently represents a typical pattern of Japanese political behavior—that is, procrastinating on the priority issue and treating symptoms by responding to immediate problems as they emerge.

In March 2000, the LDP, the Jiyuto (Ozawa Jiyuto or Liberal Party), and the New Komeito Party reached an agreement on expediting legislation concerning emergency situations within Japan. Prime Minister Mori Yoshiro referenced this legislation in his policy speech in April 2000 and announced the start of discussions on said legislation in his administrative policy speech in January 2001. Subsequently, after a season of domestic and international turbulence, including formation of the Koizumi Jun'ichiro cabinet and the September 11, 2001 (9/11 henceforth) terrorist attacks in the United States, three defense bills designed to deal with a military attack from abroad were enacted in June 2003. These bills were supported by an overwhelming majority in both houses (about 90 percent at the House of Representatives and about 84 percent at the House of Councilors). This symbolized the great change from the days of the cold war when the confrontation between the government party and the opposition parties had not allowed any serious deliberation on these issues. In any event, it took close to a half century after the founding of the JSDF for legislation on homeland defense, by far the most basic task for the JSDF, to be enacted.

9/11 and the JSDF

It is safe to say that the series of four coordinated terrorist attacks on the United States on the morning of September 11, 2001, greatly changed subsequent notions of security and responses to threats to security. Accusing the Taliban regime in Afghanistan for sheltering the Islamic terrorist group known as al-Qaeda, which was believed to be responsible for the attacks, the United States launched attacks to topple the Afghan government. After that, the U.S. military invaded Iraq under President Saddam Hussein under the pretext that Iraq had failed to abandon its weapons of mass destruction program in violation of U.N. Resolution 687. Not only was a "preventive war" as an exercise of the right to self-defense talked about openly, such a war was actually carried out by the United States, which boasted the most powerful military might in the modern world.

While the pros and cons of U.S. actions after 9/11, particularly the invasion of Iraq, will probably continue to be debated in years to come, they also brought up an important issue directly related to the JSDF. Whereas before 9/11 the JSDF's international cooperation activities had been confined to within the framework of U.N. PKO, after 9/11, they were carried out in the name of anti-terrorist operations without a U.N. resolution. A special anti-terrorism law was enacted as a temporary statute, legitimizing the JSDF's participation in anti-terrorist war assistance activities, albeit under the condition that the JSDF would not participate in actual battles during its rear area support mission. This was indeed a groundbreaking change in the history of the JSDF.

Participation in activities in Iraq was particularly controversial. The purpose of the JSDF's overseas activities is to render humanitarian and reconstruction assistance in rear areas. But even after President George Bush's declaration that the war had ended, battles, including terrorist attacks, still continued in Iraq. The situation caused a confrontation in Japan between the government parties and the opposition parties over the basic policy of not sending the JSDF to war zones. The Law Concerning the Special Measures on Humanitarian and Reconstruction Assistance in Iraq, under which the JSDF was dispatched to Iraq, stipulates as follows:

> The activities based on this Law are implemented in the Japanese territory and the following areas where no combat ("Combat" means, throughout this Law, an act, undertaken as part of an international armed conflict, of killing or injuring a person, or destroying an object) is taking place and it is deemed that there will be no combat through the period of the implementation of these activities.*

Thus, the Japanese government's legal definition of areas where the

---

* Hayashi Mika, "The Japanese Law Concerning the Special Measures on Humanitarian and Reconstruction Assistance in Iraq: Translator's Introduction," *Pacific Rim Law & Policy Journal*, vol. XIII, no. 3 (June 2004).

JSDF was to be dispatched was those areas where acts of combat prohibited by the Japanese Constitution were not taking place. Acts of combat were defined as the organizational and premeditated use of force by a state and/or its equivalent.

According to this definition, the activities of terrorists, who are not a state or its equivalent, are not acts of combat; therefore, areas where terrorists terrorize are not, legally speaking, combat areas. It follows, then, that non-combat areas are not automatically safe zones. The assertion that an area under terrorist attack is a combat zone is rejected as a view of those ignorant of the legal definition. That may be so legally, but the question is whether or not the decision on the JSDF's dispatch based on this legal definition is really justifiable.

It is said that while the threat of interstate warfare has diminished drastically, one of the greatest threats in today's world comes from terrorists with international networks. The weapons used by terrorist groups have also become much more destructive, and some of them are even comparable to the weapons used by formal military organizations. When and if a terrorist organization decides to attack the JSDF with a will, the JSDF should be prepared to sustain considerable damage. Such damage would be a price to pay for dispatching the JSDF to dangerous zones under harsh conditions, in contrast to earlier international cooperation activities that had been conducted in areas where a truce had been achieved, albeit tentatively, such as the Persian Gulf and Cambodia. This goes to show that there has emerged a gap between legal explanations and the reality.

It is the mission of a military organization to be deployed when the national interest is at stake—even to a dangerous zone. It was precisely because it was a dangerous zone that the JSDF, an armed force, was dispatched instead of nongovernmental organizations. But the Japanese government's legal explanations sound more like a justification for stressing that the JSDF's overseas activities are carried out within the framework of the Constitution. Seen from a different angle, it can be said that the method of deciding the mode of dispatch for the JSDF in accordance with the Constitution has already reached a limit.

New Threats and the Council on Security and Defense Capabilities
The global security environment in the twenty-first century has become highly complex and diversified. Rampant international terrorist activities, most notoriously symbolized by 9/11, and ethnic conflicts are examples. Even in East Asia directly adjacent to Japan, there has been no dearth of sources of instability, including North Korea's nuclear development program, China-Taiwan relations, and various territorial issues involving the development of natural resources. While the threat from classical, state vs. state warfare has diminished significantly, the threat from terrorist organizations equipped with international networks and powerful weapons has grown immensely. Although there is little possibility for a world war to erupt today such as those we saw in the twentieth century, the probability of military conflict between states over, say, natural resources or territories, is not altogether nil. Thus, while traditional threats from interstate wars have not been entirely eliminated, East Asia has increasingly been exposed to new and tangible threats, including terrorism.

Facing these new threats, the National Defense Program Guidelines in and after FY1996 (Second NDPG revised in November 1995 after the end of the cold war) could no longer cope with the many emerging situations. In order to study defense capabilities for Japan to cope with the age of new threats, the Council on Security and Defense Capabilities (Araki Council) was launched in April 2004. It was composed of the following members:

Chairman:
Araki Hiroshi, Advisor, Tokyo Electric Power Company
Deputy Chairman:
Cho Fujio, President, Toyota Motor Corporation
Members:
Furukawa Teijiro, Former Deputy Chief Cabinet Secretary
Hiwatari Yumi, Professor, Faculty of Foreign Studies, Sophia University
Iokibe Makoto, Professor, Faculty of Law, Kobe University
Nishimoto Tetsuya, President, Japan Mine Action Service; former

Self-Defense Forces Joint Staff Council Chairman
Sato Ken, Deputy Chairman, Institute for International Policy Studies; former Administrative Vice Minister of Defense
Tanaka Akihiko, Professor, Institute of Oriental Culture, University of Tokyo
Yamazaki Masakazu, President, University of East Asia
Yanai Shunji, Professor, Chuo University; former Japanese Ambassador to the United States

Mandated to study basic security strategies for Japan toward the formulation of a yet newer NDPG, the council met thirteen times between April and October 2004. Its final report was submitted to Prime Minister Koizumi Jun'ichiro. The report called for an "Integrated Security Strategy, the security strategy that Japan should adopt in this complex twenty-first-century security environment." The Integrated Security Strategy had two major goals. The first was "to prevent a direct threat from reaching Japan and, in the event that it does reach Japan, to minimize the damage"—in other words, defend Japan. The second goal was "to reduce the chances of threats arising in various parts of the world . . ." (improvement of the international security environment). And the report proposed "three approaches to achieve these goals: (a) Japan's own efforts, (b) cooperation with an alliance partner, and (c) cooperation with the international community."

While the Second NDPG of 1995 stressed the centrality of the security arrangements with the United States to the extent of excessive reliance on them, it was short of an autonomous posture toward national defense. In contrast, the first approach listed in the Council's final report, "Japan's own efforts," was a reflection of the increase of things that Japan should do on its own in the face of new threats. It is also noteworthy that the notion of multilateral security cooperation, which had been proposed by the Higuchi Group prior to the formulation of the Second NDPG, was again explicitly proposed in the Araki Council's report in the form of the third approach—that is, cooperation with the international community.

In terms of the defense capabilities that Japan should possess, although the council's report proclaimed that it would uphold valid elements of the Concept of Basic Defense Capability, the council found the concept to be inadequate in the current security environment and set forth the notion of a "multi-functional flexible defense force." To quote the relevant portion of the report:

> Basically, the capabilities required of the SDF are those that contribute to the various approaches outlined in the section dealing with the Integrated Security Strategy. From the perspective of Japan's defense, the SDF must have a rapid-response capability and the ability to collect and analyze information when faced with a variety of threats arising from conflicts between states, such as those involving ballistic missiles, and also certain "basic" capabilities to respond to a possible revival of traditional threats. It must also have the ability to respond to acts of terrorism by non-state actors and also maintain and strengthen the capacity to deal with major natural disasters. There is the need for an appropriate division of roles to ensure the effective functioning of the Japan-U.S. alliance. In addition, we will have to take actions for confidence building with our neighbors and promote regional cooperation. In terms of improving the international security environment, the SDF should also be capable of participating in international peace cooperation activities. For this purpose, the SDF should participate in cooperative activities with the United States and security dialogue with other countries. The future Defense Force will, thus, need to be capable of fulfilling a number of functions, as discussed here.

Thus, the JSDF was expected to possess the versatile capabilities outlined above. Given such constraints as the low birthrate of recent years and the financial crunch facing the Japanese government, however, the report pointed out the importance of constructing a system that allowed the JSDF to fulfill various functions effectively by making good use of and trying various combinations of existing organizations as well as reviewing cooperation with allies. It was judged that, in light of the JSDF's past track record, it would be possible to fulfill a number of the functions without greatly expanding the scale of the JSDF.

What, then, was the content of this new NDPG formulated on the basis of the recommendations of the Araki Council?

Adoption of the Third NDPG

The National Defense Program Guidelines, FY2005– (Third NDPG henceforth), which was approved by the Security Council and the Cabinet on December 10, 2004, was formulated on the basis of the Araki Council's basic lines of argument (see appendix for its text). At the outset, this Third NDPG said:

> The first objective of Japan's security policy is to prevent any threat from reaching Japan and, in the event that it does, repel it and minimize any damage. The second objective is to improve the international security environment so as to reduce the chances that any threat will reach Japan in the first place.

Furthermore, the Third NDPG also stated that "[Japan's] security depends first and foremost on its own efforts." Clearly, the Third NDPG also stressed the importance of autonomous efforts and adopted the Araki Council's recommendations as its basic stance toward Japan's defense capabilities.

More specifically, on the basis of the Araki Council's notion of a multi-functional flexible defense force, the Third NDPG referred to such new threats and diverse situations as ballistic missile attacks, guerrillas and special operations forces attacks, the invasion of Japan's offshore islands, patrol and surveillance in the seas and airspace surrounding Japan, and response to a violation of Japan's airspace and an intrusion by armed special-purpose ships and other similar vessels. The Third NDPG proposed the buildup of capabilities to respond to these scenarios.

As for preparations to deal with a full-scale invasion, the Third NDPG proposed modification of the current defense force building concept that emphasized cold war–type anti-tank warfare, anti-submarine warfare, and anti-air warfare. At the same time, it stressed that Japan should continue to maintain the most basic capabilities of its defense forces. The Third NDPG also emphasized the necessity to make proactive efforts to improve the international security environment. In addition, the Third NDPG proposed the enhancement of joint operation capabilities, the strengthening of intelligence capabilities, and the incorporation of advances in science and technology into the defense forces. Overall, the Third NDPG should be evaluated as having taken significant steps forward from previous NDPGs and as being well suited to the current security environment of the world.

But it was also true that the Third NDPG harbored a major problem: it was never clear what specific kinds of defense capabilities Japan should possess. The main text of the Third NDPG gave a considerably clear-cut account of the new threats facing Japan and advocated the buildup of capabilities to cope with these new threats. But it was the annex tables attached to the text that laid out the concrete substances of the defense capabilities that Japan aimed to possess. Seeing these tables, it was not altogether clear what specific kind of defense buildup could be pursued with capabilities that were reduced even from those at the time of the Second NDPG of 1995 (see tables 6 and 7). No matter how promising the text might sound, it could be regarded as a mere slogan if the text wasn't backed up by explicit and concrete defense capability compositions.

As we've seen, the missions and roles of the JSDF have continued to be expanded. The JSDF is now also expected to conduct such high-cost research as missile defense. In contrast to Europe where the end of the cold war accelerated arms reduction, tensions in East Asia linger on, including regarding the North Korean nuclear development program and China-Taiwan relations, while the armaments of neighboring countries also continue to expand. It was against this backdrop that the Third NDPG was formulated. While the Ground Self-Defense Force (GSDF) was allowed to retain 155,000 troops, which approximated its actual full complement, one may wonder if that complement would be adequate to cope with international terrorist attacks, special operations force attacks, an invasion of Japan's offshore islands, and the increasing need for international cooperation. Also, although the text of the Third NDPG states that security for sea traffic is essential, the maritime defense capabilities indispensable for sea lane defense were actually downsized. Undoubtedly, the government's financial problems were behind the fact that downsizing occurred in spite of the expansion in the JSDF's tasks.

When one looks at the budget structure of the JSDF, for instance, for fiscal year 2005, of the total budget of ¥4,830.1 billion, the fixed costs of personnel and provisions expenses occupied 44.6 percent of the total, while obligatory outlay expenses (expenditures that are postponed so as to extend the payment period of portions of the obligatory outlay expenses from their respective fiscal years to later fiscal years) were 35.9 percent of the total, and general material expenses including procurement of new equipages (activity cost) were only 19.4 percent (¥937.7 billion) of the total. It was within such a budget that the JSDF was expected to explore defense capabilities that could cope with new challenges and do so on the assumption that it could simultaneously accomplish a reduction of equipages from the cold war days, rationalization, and a review of troop organization.

It goes without saying that the importance of financial aspects was well recognized when the new defense capabilities were studied. The final report of the Araki Council clearly stated, "It should be possible to perform many functions without enlarging the size of the force." It must have been under strong pressure from the Ministry of Finance that in actuality the JSDF was downsized rather than maintained at status quo. It is reported, for instance, that the finance ministry had originally insisted on reducing the 160,000-strong GSDF to 120,000 personnel, the 50 escort ships of the Maritime Self-Defense Force to 38, and the 300 jetfighters of the Air Self-Defense Force to 216. It is believed that the ministry wished to minimize the scale of the Mid-Term Defense Program (the defense buildup plan renewed every five years together with the NDPG) for fiscal years 2005–2009.

Examining the Third NDPG, it can be said that the end result, or final report, looked like proposals from the Defense Agency and the Ministry of Finance had been added and then halved. Taking into con-

Table 6. Compositions and Scale of Equipages of Ground/Maritime/Air Self-Defense Forces in the National Defense Program Guidelines in and after FY1996

	Personnel		160,000
	Regular		145,000
Ground Self-Defense Force	Reserve (Ready reserve personnel)		15,000
Ground Self-Defense Force	Major units	Regionally deployed units	8 divisions 6 brigades
Ground Self-Defense Force	Major units	Mobile operation units	1 armored division 1 airborne brigade 1 helicopter brigade
Ground Self-Defense Force	Major units	Surface-to-air guided missile units	8 anti-aircraft artillery groups
Ground Self-Defense Force	Major equipment	Tanks	approx. 900
Ground Self-Defense Force	Major equipment	Main artillery	approx. 900
Maritime Self-Defense Force	Major units	Destroyer units (for mobile operations)	4 flotillas
Maritime Self-Defense Force	Major units	Destroyer units (regional district units)	7 divisions
Maritime Self-Defense Force	Major units	Submarine units	6 divisions
Maritime Self-Defense Force	Major units	Minesweeper unit	1 flotilla
Maritime Self-Defense Force	Major units	Patrol aircraft units	13 squadrons
Maritime Self-Defense Force	Major equipment	Destroyers	approx. 50
Maritime Self-Defense Force	Major equipment	Submarines	16
Maritime Self-Defense Force	Major equipment	Combat aircraft	approx. 170
Air Self-Defense Force	Major units	Air warning and control units	8 warning groups 20 warning squadrons 1 airborne early-warning group
Air Self-Defense Force	Major units	Fighter aircraft units	9 squadrons
Air Self-Defense Force	Major units	Fighter supporter units	3 squadrons
Air Self-Defense Force	Major units	Air reconnaissance units	1 squadron
Air Self-Defense Force	Major units	Air transport units	3 squadrons
Air Self-Defense Force	Major units	Surface-to-air guided missile units	6 groups
Air Self-Defense Force	Major equipment	Combat aircraft	approx. 400
Air Self-Defense Force	Major equipment	Of which fighters	approx. 300

Source: Ministry of Defense, *Defense of Japan 2005*. Tokyo: Ministry of Defense, 2006, p. 105.

Table 7. Compositions and Scale of Equipages of Ground/Maritime/Air Self-Defense Forces in the National Defense Program Guidelines, FY2005–

Ground Self-Defense Force	Personnel		155,000
	Regular		148,000
	Reserve (Ready reserve personnel)		7,000
	Major units	Regionally deployed units	8 divisions
			6 brigades
		Mobile operation units	1 armored division
			Central readiness group
		Surface-to-air guided missile units	8 anti-aircraft artillery groups
	Major equipment	Tanks	approx. 600
		Main artillery	approx. 600
Maritime Self-Defense Force	Major units	Destroyer units (for mobile operations)	4 flotillas (8 divisions)
		Destroyer units (regional district units)	5 divisions
		Submarine units	4 divisions
		Minesweeper unit	1 flotilla
		Patrol aircraft units	9 squadrons
	Major equipment	Destroyers	47
		Submarines	16
		Combat aircraft	approx. 150
Air Self-Defense Force	Major units	Air warning and control units	8 warning groups
			20 warning squadrons
			1 airborne early-warning group (2 squadrons)
		Fighter aircraft units	12 squadrons
		Air reconnaissance units	1 squadron
		Air transport units	3 squadrons
		Aerial refueling/transport unit	1 squadron
		Surface-to-air guided missile units	6 groups
	Major equipment	Combat aircraft	approx. 350
		Of which fighters	approx. 260
Assets and major units for ballistic missile defense		Aegis-equipped destroyers	4
		Air warning and control units	7 warning groups
			4 warning squadrons
		Surface-to-air guided missile units	3 groups

Source: Ministry of Defense, *Defense of Japan 2005*. Tokyo: Ministry of Defense, 2006, p. 105.

sideration that the defense budget had been subject to the government's budget cut plan from the beginning, it can be said that the Defense Agency put up a good resistance. The biggest problem, however, was that formulation of the Third NDPG, which determined the basic policy underpinning the national defense strategy, was constrained not by security considerations but by financial considerations. Even when positive civilian control at last began to be exercised, the problem of Japan's defense being controlled by financial constraints, which had been a problem since the days of a series of Defense Build-up Plans, still remains unsolved.

Chapter 14

The JSDF at a Turning Point

Problems of the JSDF

After the end of the cold war, the role of the Japan Self-Defense Forces (JSDF) expanded greatly. As is obvious from table 8, ever since 1991 the JSDF has been engaged in international cooperation activities almost incessantly and there have been only a few days that JSDF personnel were not working somewhere in the world. In this context, it can be said that the JSDF today is at a major turning point. Simply put, the JSDF is undergoing a conversion from an organization founded on the premise that it <u>would not be used</u> to an organization operating on the assumption that it <u>will actually be used</u>. Put differently, the JSDF's conversion is about a switch from traditional negative civilian control to positive civilian control. Needless to say, in the history of the JSDF this would be a monumental change. What, then, are the issues and problems that lie along the path of the JSDF's pursuit of this transformation?

First, there is a problem inherent in the JSDF itself, and that is the tendency for its three forces to act with little integration. The National Defense Program Guidelines, FY 2005– (Third NDPG) was adopted in 2004 to clarify the mission of national defense, the most central task for the JSDF. The contents of the Third NDPG reflected the recommendations of the Araki Council, which advocated a multi-functional flexible defense force. This Third NDPG was permeated by the new thinking on national defense that included responding to new threats

Table 8. JSDF's Activities in Recent Years

Year	Domestic/international developments			JSDF's activities		
	International developments	Neighboring countries	Law amendments, etc.	Responses to incidents	International peacekeeping cooperation	Disaster relief
1989	Demolition of the Berlin Wall (December)					
1990						
1991	Gulf War (January), Dissolution of the Soviet Union (December)				MSDF vessels minesweeping operations in the Persian Gulf (April–October)	Disaster relief dispatch with the eruption of Fugendake on Mount Unzen (June)
1992			Act on Cooperation for United Nations Peacekeeping Operations and Other Operations (June)		JSDF units dispatched to UNTAC in Cambodia (September–September 1993)	
1993		North Korea conducts ballistic missile test (May)			JSDF units dispatched to the UN operations in Mozambique (May–January 1995)	Disaster relief Dispatch to Hokkaido in response to the earthquake off southwestern Hokkaido (July)
1994			Amendment of Act Concerning Dispatch of Japan Disaster Relief Team (June)/ amendment of Self Defense Forces Law (authority to transport Japanese citizens in foreign countries, November)		JSDF units dispatched to Zaire to assist Rwandan refugees (September–December)	
1995			National Defense Council and Cabinet adopt National Defense Program Outline for the period from FY1996 (November)			Great Hanshin Earthquake (January)/sarin gas attack on the Tokyo subway (March)
1996					UN Disengagement Observer Force dispatched to Golan Heights (January–January–2013)	

Year						
1997			Formulation of new Guidelines for Japan-U.S. Defense Cooperation (September)			Disaster relief team dispatched to oil effluence accident from Nahodka tanker (January)
1998	North Korea launches missile over and beyond Japanese airspace (August)		Amendment of Self-Defense Force Law and Act for Establishment of the Ministry of Defense (enhancement of functions of Joint Staff Office, etc., April)/Revision of the International Peace Cooperation Law (June)		JSDF units dispatched to Honduras (November)	
1999	NATO starts air campaign in Yugoslavia (March)	Spotting of a spy ship off the Noto peninsula (March)	Act Concerning the Measures for Peace and Safety of Japan in Situations in Areas Surrounding Japan and Bill Partially Amending the Self-Defense Forces Law (transportation of Japanese citizens and others in foreign countries) enacted (May)	Maritime security operations (March)	International Emergency Relief Operations in Turkey (September)	Disaster relief team dispatched to the Tokaimura criticality accident (September)
2000			The Special Law for Nuclear Emergency Preparedness comes into force (June)			Disaster relief team dispatched to the eruption of Mount Usu (March)/Disaster relief dispatch to the eruption of Mount Miyake (June)
2001	9/11 terrorist attacks on the U.S.	Suspicious boat incident in waters southwest of Kyushu (December)	The Ship Inspection Operations Law comes into effect (March)/Anti-Terrorism Special Measures Law and Law to Amend the Self-Defense Forces Law (guarding operations, etc.) (November)/A bill introduced to partially amend the Law Concerning Cooperation for UNPKO and Other Operations (December)	Based on the Anti-Terrorism Special Measures Law, various support activities including international airlift of refugees are launched (November–December)	International Emergency Relief Operations in India (January)/International peace cooperation for the relief of Afghan refugees (October)	Assistance to raising sunken fishery training ship Ehime Maru off Hawaii (August)
2002					JSDF personnel dispatched to East Timor (March–September 2012)	
2003	U.S. and U.K. forces begin military operations in Iraq (March)		Three armed attack situation response-related laws enacted (June)			

Source: Constructed by author based on *Whitepaper on Defense 2003*

from various offenders including terrorists. This new thinking was a departure from the Concept of Basic Defense Capability geared toward traditional threats from states and their equivalent. In order to materialize this multi-functional flexible defense force, it would be essential to improve the intelligence capabilities and integrated operations of the three forces of the JSDF. Integrated operations have become all the more important in order to accomplish efficient equipage procurement under stringent financial constraints. The two most important challenges that the JSDF will face in the years to come in pursuing its basic mission of defending Japan are further enhancement of its intelligence capabilities and operation of troops under integrated strategies.

The history of the JSDF, however, shows that its three forces have constructed their own defense plans separately, planned their own equipage systems, and acted independently, paying no attention to what the other two forces are doing. In fact, the promotion of integration is an issue that has been pointed out since the founding days of the JSDF. It is true that, when the very first NDPG was adopted in 1976, the inner bureau of the Defense Agency advocated strengthening the Joint Staff Office. That was accomplished to some extent with momentum gained from, among other efforts, the adoption of the Guidelines for Japan-U.S. Defense Cooperation. It remains to be seen, however, to what degree integrated operations among the three forces can be achieved and, even, whether an integrated strategy can be worked out or not in the first place. The fact that the need to advance integration has been repeated in the Whitepaper on Defense in recent years might betray how difficult it is to accomplish it.

It should be recalled that the Ground, Maritime, and Air Self-Defense Forces are three different organizations with different founding ideas and evolutionary processes. And they have existed like that for over half a century since their founding, separately advancing intra-organizational institutionalization and building up tried and true traditions. Seen from a different angle, it may be undeniable that the bureaucratization and organizational inflexibility of the three forces have also advanced. It calls for strong leadership to realize an integrated strategy and to facilitate integrated operations across the boundaries among the three forces.

Second is the issue of enacting and enforcing the legislation that is necessary for the JSDF's activities. It should be obvious from table 8 that the 1990s, a period when the JSDF's activities were expanded, was a decade that saw the drafting and amendment of legislation to lay the legal foundation for those new activities. What happened in the 1990s was, in a way, a reflection of the nature of the cold war days in Japan, because that was an age of negative civilian control that essentially aimed at the nonuse of the JSDF. During that period, whenever legislation necessary for the JSDF to act—for instance, national emergency legislation—was debated, it stirred up harsh criticism. Critics contended that, "The intention of the advocates of such legislation is to let the JSDF engage in a war." In those days, even the conservative camp did not wish to discuss the actual use of the JSDF, and it did not find it necessary to force legislation through in the face of such resistance. Therefore, the period from the 1990s on has witnessed a flood of backlash from the way things were handled during the cold war days. The enactment of national emergency legislation and civil protection laws at the long last—which had been homework for Japan since the cold war days—thus symbolized the changes of the times.

But the problem is that if the JSDF's activities are to be further expanded, there still remain a number of issues requiring legislation. Also, even when laws are enacted, that is not the end of it. Take the Civil Protection Law, for instance. In order to make it effective, there should be intense consultations among the JSDF, local municipalities, and police authorities so as to, for example, develop concrete plans for conducting evacuations and for coordinating with the JSDF's activities. But because local municipalities have their hands full with local administrative reforms, their responses to the need for consultations are totally uncoordinated. The JSDF, on its part, has hardly had any experience in this kind of consultation with local municipalities and naturally has not accumulated any know-how on how to conduct it. In the days to come, the JSDF will have to build relations with local communities that go well beyond the provision of base maintenance subsidies to localities hosting JSDF bases or grass-roots interchanges with local citizens. This is another new challenge for the JSDF.

As a matter of fact, attempts at local administrative reform have their own problems—for example, there has been a tendency to discuss reform solely from the viewpoint of financial problems. In the present world, where the new types of threats have emerged, relations between the central government and local municipalities in security issues need to change greatly. Article 9 of the Act on Measures to Ensure the Peace and Security of Japan in Perilous Situations in Areas Surrounding Japan enacted in 1999 declares that chiefs of pertinent administrative organizations can, in the context of exercising the authority bestowed on them and in compliance with laws and basic plans, request the necessary cooperation from the heads of local municipalities. Thus, the time has come when national security, which has traditionally been under the central government's exclusive jurisdiction, can no longer be effectively exercised without the cooperation of local governments.

While it is already obvious that the central government alone can no longer cope with all the problems Japan faces today, now even national security has joined the list of matters that the central government cannot handle singlehandedly. The trend in Japan has been toward the direction of stronger authority for local governments under the name of local autonomy, but, seen from a different angle, this also means that the responsibilities of local governments have grown that much greater. And it is also true that local governments' postures toward this issue differ greatly region by region.

The Position of the JSDF in the State Apparatus

By far the most important issue, however, is that of the position of the JSDF within Japan's state apparatus. As the old negative civilian control, which is essentially geared toward the nonuse of the JSDF, is taken over by positive civilian control, which is concerned about how best to use the JSDF, the following two distinct features of Japan's defense must inevitably come under review. The first is *bunkan tosei* (control by civil officials), which has been the traditional means to suppress the influences of the uniformed team. The second is the financial constraints on national defense policy.

As far as control by civil officials is concerned, the following articles of the Act for Establishment of the Ministry of Defense have not been amended to date:

> (Relations among the director-general of the Secretariat of the Minister of State for Defense, the directors-general of bureaus, the chief of staff, the Joint Staff, and the Joint Staff Council)
>
> Article 16: Directors-general of the Secretariat of the Minister of State for Defense and all the bureaus of the Defense Agency should, within respective jurisdictions, assist the minister of state for defense in carrying out the following tasks:
>
> (1) minister of state for defense's instructions addressed to chiefs of staff of the Ground Self-Defense Force (GSDF), Maritime Self-Defense Force (MSDF), or Air Self-Defense Force (ASDF) on the formulation of various policies as well as the basic implementation of plans concerning the GSDF, MSDF, or ASDF;
>
> (2) minister of state for defense's approval of policies and basic implementation plans on matters related to the GSDF, MSDF, or ASDF formulated by chiefs of staff of the respective JSDF forces;
>
> (3) minister of state for defense's instruction or approval on matters which belong to the jurisdiction of the Joint Staff Council; and
>
> (4) minister of state for defense's general supervision of the GSDF, MSDF, or ASDF.

Therefore, the inner bureau of the Defense Agency still has precedence over the uniformed team and exercises authority for general supervision. In actuality, however, since the adoption of the Guidelines for Japan-U.S. Defense Cooperation in 1978, the situation no longer allows the inner bureau to neglect the views of the uniformed team all the time, and the latter's voice has come to carry much more weight than before. As the JSDF's activities are expected to continue to expand, it seems indispensable to construct a system by which the views of JSDF personnel/the uniformed team can be tapped sufficiently. On that particular point, readers should be reminded that review of the Defense Counselor System was recently considered. While it was decided in the end that the current system was to be preserved, it seems beyond doubt that a system of civilian control that is suitable for the new age has to be explored.

Let's turn our attention to the second aspect that calls for review: financial constraints on national defense policy. As we have already seen in the discussion of the Third NDPG, the logic of financial constraints is still powerful. Defense buildup in postwar Japan has never ignored financial logic. It would have been a rehash of the prewar mistake if military logic became absolutely dominant, ignoring all other logic, including that of financial constraints.

The biggest problem is the mindset of officials that financial considerations take precedence over anything else. In as early as 1961, when the National Defense Council was convened to officially adopt the Second Defense Build-up Plan, Sakomizu Hisatsune, director-general of the Economic Planning Agency who was originally from the Ministry of Finance, pointed out that it was problematic to assign a certain budget ceiling to a defense plan at the outset, saying, "It would be improper to determine a defense budget prior to deliberations on the strategic scheme." Having experienced firsthand the arbitrary conducts of the prewar military, Sakomizu's comment carries a lot of weight. Indeed, under normal conditions, it is the most basic of basics for a national defense plan to be formulated first according to the international environment and strategic conditions a country finds itself in. And it would be normal security planning to materialize the defense plan thus formulated in accordance with a country's financial conditions.

On this particular point, it should be recalled that, when the very first NDPG was officially adopted in 1976, a rolling plan system called the midterm accomplishments evaluation method (*chugyo*) was adopted to review the long-term defense plan every three years. Also at that time, it was decided that the planning itself would be done internally within the Defense Agency, rather than having the plan be a subject of governmental decision, and that the plan would be materialized through annual negotiations with the Ministry of Finance. In contrast to conventional defense buildup plans, which were five-year fixed government plans approved by the National Defense Council and the Cabinet, the *chugyo* was an internal document of the Defense Agency that was subject to revision every three years according to what had actually been accomplished. Because conventional defense buildup plans were government plans, they were subject to assessments and revision requests by the Ministry of Finance twice: once during the drafting stage and again at the final implementation stage. In other words, under the conventional system, defense policy had been constrained twice by the fiscal authority. Behind adoption of the *chugyo* was the Defense Agency's wish to limit inspection by the financial authority to one time. This would have allowed at least the initial defense buildup plan to stress the importance of defense plans. Had this *chugyo* remained an internal plan within the Defense Agency, restrictions by the financial authority on the defense buildup plan would have been mitigated. But the *chugyo* was "upgraded" to a government mid-term defense buildup plan by those legislators who had no idea about the Defense Agency's latent intentions.

The fact of the matter was that cuts in the defense budget had been decided from the beginning under the slogan, "structural reform without sanctuary." Prime Minister Koizumi Jun'ichiro touted this stance on the assumption that the financial crunch would worsen. It appears that prime ministers of Japan—who are the top leaders of Japanese politics and who are supposed to be the supreme commander of the JSDF—do not give high priority to the security issue. The Ministry of Finance's sense of mission stemming from the fear of a nightmare financial catastrophe appears to be so firm that the Defense Agency could seemingly overcome it with only considerable difficulty. Given these conditions, it appears that this tradition of financial constraints on national defense policy will remain unchanged for quite some time more to come.

To say a few words in defense of the Ministry of Finance, though, the control by civil officials (or the primacy of civil officials) since the

days of the founding of the JSDF/Defense Agency has not been conducted singlehandedly by the inner bureau of the Defense Agency; in
fact, the Ministry of Finance has also played a role in the endeavor
from the beginning. The Defense Agency has used and relied on the
logic of the finance ministry's assessment to suppress demands from
the uniformed team. Consequently, the finance ministry's influence on
Japan's defense affairs grew large, and from the 1970s on, the ministry
seconded its officials to key positions of the Defense Agency.

The True Meaning of Civilian Control

Truth to be told, it is politicians' aversion to defense affairs that has
played an important role in the control of the uniformed team by civil officials. As the history of the JSDF/Defense Agency since their
founding tells, civil officials of the Japanese government have controlled the country's defense affairs to an almost excessive extent in
the absence of due political initiative. While I have so far taken a critical stance toward excessive control by civil officials and the restrictions
on defense buildup imposed by financial logic, by no means do I insist
that all the demands of the uniformed team be accepted unmodified.
What is called for is to hear the views of civil officials, understand the
requests of the uniformed team and, on the basis of these, watch equipage procurement closely, facilitate integrated operations and more
efficient troop operations, and advise how best to convert the JSDF
into a military organization well-fitted to today's conditions. This is not
the job of the Ministry of Finance but of politicians—who are responsible for the security of the country and its people.

And this is a point that has bearing on recent debates on constitutional amendments in Japan: whether or not the JSDF will become a
full military. As the JSDF's mission continues to be expanded, it is true
that its current status as an organization that is not a military may get
in its way when it pursues its international tasks in, for instance, United Nations' peacekeeping operations. But the expansion of the JSDF's
activities in the 1990s was a political decision. As I have repeatedly
pointed out, the JSDF is now at a turning point of shifting from traditional negative civilian control to positive civilian control. And to exer-

cise positive civilian control, politicians must be made accountable. Ultimately, it boils down to what kind of politicians people elect as their representatives. If the Japanese people choose to grant an explicit position and authority on the JSDF under positive civilian control and expect it to play yet newer roles, they should be clearly aware that the quality of democracy in Japan itself is going to be put to the test.

Postscript

The Transformation of Japan's Security Policy and the JSDF

I. The Changing Security Environment and Japan's Defense Policy

The Changing Security Environment

Japan's security policy has changed greatly in the past ten years. We will consider the substance of this change later. For now, let us briefly touch on the developments in the security environment that are behind the change.

The first development is the declining presence of the United States. While the United States still possesses the world's strongest military, it has shown a tendency to cut down its military might significantly, due to a financial crunch partly caused by U.S. entanglement in Middle Eastern affairs since the 2003 Iraq War. Asian countries, including Japan, have been apprehensive about the isolationist tendency that seems to be on the rise in the United States. The smaller the U.S. presence in Asia becomes, the larger the role that Japan is expected to play.

The second development is China's increased military presence in Asia. Backed up by strong economic growth, China has greatly expanded its military buildup, particularly its naval and air combat capabilities. Not only has China continued to expand its military capabilities annually by some 10 percent over more than ten years, it has also stepped up its actions involving its military power in both the East China and South China Seas. These actions, including China's nine-dash-line claim (or demarcation line pertaining to its claims) in the South China Sea, are aimed at altering the current international order of the seas by force, causing neighboring countries, including Japan, additional concern.

North Korea's actions, such as aggressive missile launching experiments and nuclear development coupled with its brinksmanship-like diplomacy, are the third source of instability in East Asia.

These actions by China and North Korea can be categorized as traditional types of threats from nuclear development and territorial disputes. In contrast, terrorist attacks by radical elements, which are no longer confined to the Middle East, are called new threats. Responses to these have become a major issue in today's world.

Because the backgrounds of these new threats vary case by case— and encompass such issues as the rise of nationalism and the widening disparity owing to advanced globalization—it is difficult to come up with across-the-board measures that are effective in dealing with such threats. Whether in response to traditional threats or new threats, the sharing of information and coordinated actions among the countries concerned, including the United States, are essential. What follows is an analysis of the contents of concrete policies already taken toward this need.

The National Defense Program Guidelines for Fiscal 2011 and Beyond and the China Threat

The terrorist attacks on the United States on September 11, 2001, added threats from international terrorists to the list of major security issues. As introduced in part four of this book, Japan has explored the implementation of security arrangements to cope with newer threats, including international terrorism. One result was the 2004 revision of the National Defense Program Guidelines (Third NDPG). A second result was the approval of the NDPG for fiscal 2011 and beyond (2010 NDPG) by the Security Council and the Cabinet on December 17, 2010. This approval came in the aftermath of the 2009 general election of the House of Representatives, in which the Liberal Democratic Party–New Komeito Party coalition government was taken over by another coalition government among the Democratic Party of Japan, the Social Democratic Party of Japan, and the People's New Party. The

2010 NDPG was unique in introducing the fresh concept of a "dynamic defense force," replacing the traditional Concept of Basic Defense Capability, to cope with rising threats from China and the intensifying financial crunch, and, thereby, renovating Japan's defense capabilities.

It is said that this notion of a dynamic defense force aimed at realizing a defense force in Japan that was truly operational. Construction of the dynamic defense force, according to the 2010 NDPG, called for further structural reforms regarding defense capabilities on the basis of existing capabilities in order to enable more effective and more proactive use of these capabilities. More concretely, it said, "Japan will choose truly necessary functions on which to concentrate resources, and carry out structural reform of the defense forces, thereby producing more outcome with limited resources." This shows that pursuit of the basic line of organizational downsizing for the Japan Self-Defense Forces (JSDF) by streamlining and rationalization, which was started after the end of the cold war, still continued.

While the 2004 NDPG (Third NDPG) had already referred to the threat of China, the 2010 NDPG strongly stressed said threat and set forth countermeasures. Prior to the recent escalation of Chinese activities and while the U.S. military stationed in Japan deployed a considerable number of troops in the Nansei Islands region (a chain of islands extending from southwestern Kyushu to northern Taiwan), the JSDF's defense posture in the region had been limited to the 1st Combined Brigade of the Ground Self-Defense Force (GSDF) and mainly airborne units of the Maritime Self-Defense Force (MSDF) and the Air Self-Defense Force (ASDF), both on Okinawa Island, and a radar site on Miyako Island in the Miyako-Yaeyama area. In other words, this region consisting of numerous islands remained a defense power vacuum. The 2004 NDPG called for strengthening the defense of the Nansei Islands region. The 2010 NDPG, which was formulated after the change of government in 2009, went a step further to state,

> The JSDF will permanently station the minimum necessary units on off-shore islands where the JSDF is not currently stationed. Also, the JSDF will enhance its capability to respond to attacks on

those islands and ensure the security of the surrounding sea and air space by securing bases, mobility, transport capacity and effective countermeasures necessary for conducting operations against such attacks.

More specifically, the GSDF 1st Combined Brigade stationed in Okinawa was reinforced with some 300 additional troops and upgraded to the GSDF 15th Brigade Okinawa. Also, it was decided that a GSDF base, called Camp Yonaguni, was to be opened on Yonaguni Island, the westernmost inhabited island of Japan, equipped with coastal patrol troops and the ASDF's mobile warning and control radar. No JSDF base had been stationed on the island before. At present, construction of the physical base facilities has been completed, and JSDF troops are being deployed there.

Actually, Japan and China are in a serious confrontation over a territorial issue, most typically symbolized by the 2010 Senkaku boat collision incident that occurred on the morning of September 7, 2010, when a Chinese trawler operating in disputed waters near the Senkaku Islands collided with Japan Coast Guard (JCG) patrol boats. In the waters around the Senkaku Islands, which Japan and China both claim, Chinese fishermen have repeated what Japan regards as illegal trawling in its territorial waters. The JCG has observed these activities closely. Prior to this incident, there were cases of Chinese fishermen being arrested in that region for refusing boarding inspections. But this time, the captain of the Chinese trawler deliberately collided with two JCG patrol ships; the captain and his crew were arrested for the malicious obstruction of duty. When the Chinese government high-handedly pressured the Japanese government to release the fishermen—Chinese tactics included the detention of Japanese businessmen stationed in China (who were totally unrelated to the incident) and the embargo of rare earth minerals (which could damage Japanese business)—Tokyo gave in and released the Chinese fishing boat captain.

When the Japanese government purchased the Senkaku Islands from their landowner and nationalized them in 2012, Chinese government vessels began entering Japan's contiguous zone almost daily. Furthermore, they even repeatedly intruded into Japan's territorial sea. The Chinese side has also exhibited such provocative conduct as having a Chinese naval vessel beam fire-control system radar at an MSDF escort ship—which could well be interpreted as commencement of an attack. In recent years, cases of ASDF fighters' scrambling in rapid response to Chinese planes entering areas inside and outside of what Japan considers its airspace over the East China Sea have increased. Each incident only worsens the Japanese people's perception of China. While only a few in Japan had perceived the Soviet Union as a threat during the cold war, today a large number of Japanese perceive China as an actual threat.

Mega Disaster and the JSDF
At 2:46 p.m. on March 11, 2011, a mega, magnitude 9.0 earthquake originating off the coast of Sanriku struck the Pacific coast of northeastern (Tohoku) Japan. It shook up a vast area along the Pacific coast between the Tohoku and Kanto regions and triggered a mega-tsunami as high as 40 meters in places. The tsunami ravaged coastal areas. The damage done by the tsunami, which rode over or even broke through coastal levees, swallowing inland buildings and dwellers, went far beyond anyone's imagination. Moreover, the tsunami completely destroyed all the power facilities at the Fukushima Daiichi Nuclear Power Plant in Fukushima prefecture, nullifying its emergency cooling system. Japan was faced with the unprecedented crisis of an earthquake/mega-tsunami and a nuclear accident combined.

The National Diet went into a spontaneous recess, while the government simultaneously set up an emergency disaster control headquarters and declared an emergency nuclear situation in compliance with the Act on Special Measures Concerning Nuclear Emergency Preparedness. Consequently, the Kan Naoto cabinet at the time was faced not only with the rescue and relief of the earthquake/mega-tsunami victims and the recovery and reconstruction of the affected areas but also the disaster of a nuclear accident. The JSDF ended up playing an outstanding role at this time of crisis.

As many units and personnel as possible of the GSDF were seconded from all over Japan to the GSDF North Eastern Army District Headquarters located in devastated Miyagi prefecture. It was judged to be dangerous to reduce defense capabilities in the Nansei Islands region in light of the intensified confrontation with China over the Senkaku Islands issue; preparedness against unpredictable North Korean behavior should not be scaled down, either, it was felt. Because the GSDF has always been the main target of manpower reduction among the three JSDF forces since the end of the cold war, it was extremely taxing for the GSDF to put together units and personnel to be sent to Tohoku from among its already downsized force.

In any event, it is beyond doubt that the JSDF's rescue and relief activities, to which an unprecedented 100,000 troops were mobilized, had the effect of considerably improving the Japanese people's perception of the JSDF. The selfless devotion demonstrated by JSDF personnel further reinforced people's good impression of the JSDF. Aside from the GSDF, both the MSDF and the ASDF also contributed, particularly in the transport of supplies and people. The integrated operation of the JSDF proposed by the 2004 NDPG was, thus, realized in full scale, not in response to a military emergency, but in response to a mega disaster.

And JSDF personnel handled not just the rescue operations for the earthquake/mega-tsunami victims—responding to the nuclear accident was part of their mandate as well. JSDF personnel had to engage in the cooling operation of the nuclear reactors at Fukushima Daiichi in peril of a meltdown. As it became clear that the measures needed to contain the nuclear accident, such as spraying cooling water by helicopter, would be life threatening, requests for the JSDF's involvement escalated. Some of requests lacked consideration for the lives of JSDF personnel.

II. A Shift in Japan's Security Policy

Establishment of the National Security Council

In the general election in December 2012, the incumbent Democratic Party of Japan was defeated. Once again, a Liberal Democratic Party–New Komeito Party coalition government came into power—that is, the second Abe Shinzo cabinet. It is under this Abe cabinet that Japan's postwar defense policy is about to be transformed drastically.

Three main changes make up this transformation. First is the establishment of the National Security Council (NSC) as the control tower of Japan's security policy. Along with this, a National Security Secretariat has been set up within the Cabinet Secretariat as an office to assist the NSC by engaging in the planning and general coordination of the basic thrusts and essential elements of Japan's diplomatic and defense policies. Second is the National Security Strategy of Japan that was formulated to replace the Basic Policy on National Defense, which was adopted in 1957. Third is the course the Abe cabinet is steering toward approval of the limited exercise of the right of collective self-defense.

The NSC, modeled after the U.S. National Security Council, was founded by reorganizing the National Defense Council, which had accompanied the establishment of the Defense Agency in 1954, and the Security Council of Japan, which had succeeded the function of the National Defense Council. This reorganization was the realization of a proposal made during the first Abe cabinet in 2007 that had ended up being shelved. The Abe cabinet aimed at making the National Security Secretariat, in its role as support for the NSC, a central organ of national security policy, by substantially upgrading the existing Cabinet Security Affairs Office. To accomplish this, the Abe cabinet appointed former Administrative Vice Minister for Foreign Affairs Yachi Shotaro as the National Security Secretariat's first director-general and two assistant chief cabinet secretaries seconded from the Ministry of Foreign Affairs and the Ministry of Defense as its deputy directors-general.

Formulation of the National Security Strategy of Japan

As mentioned, the National Defense Program Guidelines for fiscal 2011 and beyond (2010 NDPG) was approved by the Security Council and the Kan Naoto Democratic Party cabinet on December 17, 2010. Although, normally, the NDPG is revised every five years or so, there was a change of government in 2012, so, consequently, a newer NDPG for fiscal 2014 and beyond (2013 NDPG) was formulated in December 2013. What distinguishes the newest NDPG from previous versions is that the National Security Strategy of Japan, which takes precedence over the NDPG, was formulated at the same time. Thus, it makes sense to look into the content of the National Security Strategy of Japan first.

To begin with, previously there had been no concrete national security strategy in Japan. The United States, in contrast, has used a layered approach to security preparedness composed of a national security strategy, from which military strategies and diplomatic strategies are formulated, in turn from which operational plans are made based on existing military capabilities. And the whole structure is subject to periodical review. This is typical of how national security strategy is formulated in other countries as well, including Australia, the United Kingdom, and the Republic of Korea. Seeing this way of formulating national security strategy stimulated many Japanese experts to stress the need for instituting a similar structure in Japan. Thus, at long last, a national security strategy was formulated for the first time in Japan.

The fact of the matter is that in Japan, the series of National Defense Program Guidelines has been a de facto national security strategy in proxy. The NDPG originated as a document on the basic policy toward defense buildup. Thus, while it is natural for the NDPG to include references to military strategy, including offering perceptions on the international security environment as a premise for desirable defense buildup as well as actual defense buildup, the NDPG is by no means a place to discuss the security strategy of the entire nation. In the absence of the national security strategy that should have existed, however, the NDPG has played the role of a partial surrogate.

What, then, are the actual contents of the National Security Strategy of Japan (hereinafter referred to as the Strategy), which was formulated for the first time in the sixty years since Japan's independence from the occupation? This thirty-two-page document in Japanese, which was compiled essentially on the basis of the contents of past National Defense Program Guidelines since the 1990s, aims at further strengthening Japan's contribution to international security by proposing that Japan should be a "proactive contributor to peace based on the principle of international cooperation."

The Strategy, which is expected to "guide Japan's national security policy over the next decade," gives an overview of Japan's past security strategies and claims that "Japan has adhered to a basic policy of maintaining an exclusively national defense–oriented policy, not becoming a military power that poses a threat to other countries, and observing the Three Non-Nuclear Principles." For these efforts, the Strategy claims that "the course Japan has taken as a peace-loving nation has garnered significant praise and respect from the international community," but stresses that, "Japan must continue these steps to further consolidate such a position." On the basis of these observations, the Strategy analyzes that "surrounded by an increasingly severe security environment and confronted by complex and grave national security challenges, it has become indispensable for Japan to make more proactive efforts in line with the principle of international cooperation." The Strategy advocates Japan's active engagement in international peace by concluding that "achieving its own security as well as peace and stability in the Asia-Pacific region as a proactive contributor to peace based on the principle of international cooperation [is] the fundamental principle of national security that Japan should stand to hold." The term "proactive contributor to peace" is often repeated as a central concept of the Abe cabinet's security policy. While the Abe cabinet has offered no clear definition of this term, it seems safe to interpret it as referring to engagement in issues related to international peace by means of all measures available to Japan.

The Strategy proposes that Japan should achieve the following national security objectives:

— Strengthen the deterrence necessary for maintaining its peace and security and for ensuring its survival, thus deterring threats from directly reaching Japan; at the same time, if by any chance a threat should reach Japan, to defeat such threat and to minimize the damage.

— Improve the security environment of the Asia-Pacific region, and prevent the emergence of and reduce direct threats to Japan, through strengthening the Japan-U.S. Alliance, enhancing the trust and cooperative relationships between Japan and its partners within and outside the Asia-Pacific region, and promoting practical security cooperation.

— Improve the global security environment and build a peaceful, stable, and prosperous international community by strengthening the international order based on universal values and rules, and by playing a leading role in the settlement of disputes, through consistent diplomatic efforts and further personnel contributions.

To summarize these three goals, the first one is about the buildup of Japan's own defense capabilities, while the second is about the U.S.-Japan alliance and partnership with countries surrounding this alliance. The second goal echoes the notion of maritime security cooperation set forth by the Guidelines for Japan-U.S. Defense Cooperation adopted on April 27, 2015, and actually pursued with Australia and member countries of the Association of Southeast Asian Nations (ASEAN). The third goal is an extension of the multilateral security cooperation argument, and, thus, it can be said that it is a modified reiteration of a security issue that has been discussed throughout all the past National Defense Program Guidelines since the 1990s. This is why I said at the outset that the Strategy was compiled essentially on the basis of the contents of past National Defense Program Guidelines since the 1990s.

A Severe View of China
After identifying the above three goals, the Strategy goes on to discuss

the security environment surrounding Japan and issues in international security, including in Asia Pacific. In this context, the Strategy takes a very severe view of China:

> There is an expectation for China to share and comply with international norms, and to play a more active and cooperative role for regional and global issues. Yet China has been rapidly advancing its military capabilities in a wide range of areas through its continued increase in its military budget, without sufficient transparency. In addition, China has taken actions that can be regarded as attempts to change the status quo by coercion based on its own assertions, which are incompatible with the existing order of international law, in the maritime and aerial domains, including the East China Sea and the South China Sea. In particular, China has rapidly expanded and intensified its activities in the seas and airspace around Japan, including intruding into Japan's territorial waters and airspace around the Senkaku Islands. Moreover, China has acted in a way that appears to infringe unduly on the freedom of overflight above the high seas by establishing its own Air Defense Identification Zone over the East China Sea.
>
> Such an external stance and military activities by China, coupled with a lack of transparency in its military affairs and security policy, have become an issue of concern to the international community including Japan. Therefore, the Government of Japan needs to pay careful attention to this situation.

While taking this severe view of China, the Strategy also lays out the following measures to prevent confrontation with China from escalating to a military conflict:

> (2) Stable relations between Japan and China are an essential factor for peace and stability of the Asia-Pacific region. From a broad, as well as a medium- to long-term, perspective, Japan will strive to construct and enhance a Mutually Beneficial Relationship Based on Common Strategic Interests with China in all areas, including

politics, economy, finance, security, culture and personal exchanges. In particular, Japan will continue to encourage China to play a responsible and constructive role for the sake of regional peace, stability and prosperity, to adhere to international norms of behavior, as well as to improve openness and transparency in its advancing military capabilities through its rapidly increasing military budget. As a part of such efforts, through continuing and promoting defense cooperation, Japan will seek to urge improvement in transparency of China's military and security policies, and promote measures such as establishing a framework to avert or prevent unexpected situations. Furthermore, with regard to China's recent attempts to change the status quo by coercion based on its unique assertion in its relations with neighboring countries, including Japan, Japan will urge China to exercise self-restraint and will continue to respond firmly but in a calm manner without escalating the situation.

References to China are made not only in the Strategy but also, quite frequently, in the 2013 NDPG. These are much bolder references than those made about the Soviet Union during cold war days in the Japanese government's annual whitepaper on defense, *Defense of Japan*. Descriptions of the Soviet Union in the *Defense of Japan* were more or less confined to actual facts and were restricted by Japan's official stance that the Soviet Union was not a hypothetical enemy. In the Strategy, in contrast, it is clearly stated that "China has taken actions that can be regarded as attempts to change the status quo by coercion based on its own assertions," that such actions were a violation of international law, and that such actions, in effect, posed a threat to China's neighboring countries, including Japan. The wording in the Strategy reveals that today China is the greatest security issue for Japan and it is the most important theme for Japan's security strategy.

To be sure, it is true that China's conduct has threatened its neighboring countries. Confrontations have erupted frequently with Southeast Asian countries over the territorial rights of the Spratly and Paracel Islands. China reclaimed land and converted the Fiery Cross Reef it

thus in effect controlled into an artificial island on which it constructed a sizable airstrip. While China justifies its conduct by claiming that
both Vietnam and the Philippines also constructed runways on islands
in the same area, the fact of the matter is that these other airstrips are
no match for the one China built. Moreover, China has also constructed military facilities on this artificial island and other islands in the
area. To begin with, it should be recalled that the nine-dash-line that
China insists on by way of claiming those islands is not endorsed by
international law, as indicated by the ruling of an arbitral tribunal in
the Permanent Court of Arbitration in the Hague on July 12, 2016. It
is only natural for these territorial claims by China to cause frictions
and tensions with the surrounding countries.

Furthermore, since the establishment of the so-called Air Defense
Identification Zone over the East China Sea in 2014, China has treated
the area as if it were its own territorial airspace. Troubles have already
occurred between Chinese vessels/aircrafts and the JSDF: the Chinese
side locked fire-control radar on an MSDF vessel/helicopter and a Chinese fighter flew extremely close to a Japanese surveillance plane. The
region encompassing the South China and East China Seas, in which
China is trying to expand its influence, is an important sea area for
surrounding countries because of the sea lanes. These seas are, so to
speak, a global commons, the safety and order of which the countries
concerned should work hand-in-hand to maintain. This is why Japan
wishes to strengthen cooperation with Southeast Asian countries.

Formulation of the National Defense Program Guidelines for FY2014 and Beyond

The National Defense Program Guidelines for FY2014 and beyond
(2013 NDPG), formulated on the basis of the Strategy, were officially
approved on December 17, 2013. While the 2013 NDPG shares a lot in
terms of content with the Strategy, its descriptions of defense policy
are more detailed.

First, for instance, while in the past Japan's defense capabilities
were characterized as being "basic defense capabilities," a "multi-functional flexible defense force," and a "dynamic defense force," the 2013

NDPG proclaims that Japan should aim at building a "dynamic joint defense force." The 2013 NDPG defines the role of Japan's defense forces as "the ultimate guarantee of national security, [which] represent Japan's will and ability to deter threats from directly reaching Japan and defeat them if threats should reach Japan." The 2013 NDPG states that, as the security environment surrounding Japan becomes increasingly tense,

> The defense force also must be an effective one that enables conducting a diverse range of activities that are seamless as well as dynamic and adapting to situations as they demand. To that end, Japan will build a Dynamic Joint Defense Force, which emphasizes both soft and hard aspects of readiness, sustainability, resiliency and connectivity, reinforced by advanced technology and capability for C3I, with a consideration to establish a wide range of infrastructure to support the SDF's operation.

Based on this basic policy, the 2013 NDPG argues that Japan should actively engage in strengthening its alliance with the United States and improving the global security environment. Japan should next practice effective deterrence of and response to various situations, including gray zone situations, such as (1) ensuring the security of the sea and airspace surrounding Japan; (2) responding to an attack on remote islands; (3) responding to ballistic missile attacks; (4) responding in outer space and cyberspace; and (5) responding in times of major disasters.

Second, concerning the basic idea of strengthening architecture of the JSDF, the 2013 NDPG says,

> From the perspective of efficiently developing an effective defense force, the SDF will selectively strengthen the following functions and capabilities in particular, paying attention to enhance joint functions with interoperability with the U.S. forces.
>
> Based on the results of the capability assessments, concerning the defense capability buildup, the SDF will prioritize the de-

velopment of capacities to ensure maritime supremacy and air superiority, which is the prerequisite for effective deterrence and response in various situations, including defense posture buildup in the southwestern region. Furthermore, the JSDF will emphasize the establishment of rapid deployment capabilities with a consideration to establishing a wide-ranging logistical support foundation.

The above basic policy, which clearly defines Japan as a maritime nation, appears to be an appropriate one to cope with the Chinese threat.

It should be noted that, while the JSDF's budget and organizational scale continued to be reduced even as the scope of its missions kept expanding after the end of the cold war, the 2013 NDPG and the Mid-Term Defense Program (fiscal year 2014–fiscal year 2018), which is based on the 2013 NDPG, suggest that the JSDF's organizational scale should be expanded, albeit in small measure. Given the tight fiscal conditions, it might be difficult to significantly increase the defense budget. Nonetheless, it appears that the JSDF has already reached its organizational limit for maintaining the current scale of activities and accomplishing given missions.

The Right of Collective Self-Defense and Revision of the Guidelines for Japan-U.S. Defense Cooperation

Traditionally, the Cabinet Legislation Bureau interpreted that, although Japan is entitled to exercise the right of collective self-defense by international law, the Constitution of Japan does not allow it. But the Abe cabinet overturned this and approved the limited use of the right. This decision is deeply connected to security-related legislation that is pursued by the Abe cabinet and is stirring opposition from Japanese of all walks of life. Those who oppose the cabinet decision argue that this revision of the interpretation goes against the constitution and is, therefore, unconstitutional. And the view that the Abe cabinet's undemocratic conduct—that is, the forcible passage of the bill revising the interpretation of the Constitution—cannot be tolerated in a democratic country is shared widely by common people in Japan. In an unusual development, even people in show business, such as musicians, actors, and TV personalities, who are typically relatively silent on matters of politics, have spoken out against the Abe cabinet's decision.

How, then, should we interpret the Abe cabinet's revision of the interpretation of Japan's right of collective self-defense? The security-related legislation that the Abe cabinet is attempting to promulgate is a central piece of a series of security policy reforms. Content-wise, this reform attempt aims at legislating various measures proposed by the Strategy but is not confined to the legislation now under deliberation. The reform attempt is linked to such other measures as the already-enacted Act on the Protection of Specially Designated Secrets as well as to the reform of the Defense Ministry, to which mass media has paid little attention, obsessed as they are with the topic of collective self-defense.

It has been said that the deliberation methods used by the Abe cabinet—such as deliberating on ten acts simultaneously—makes arguments in the Diet difficult to understand for non-experts. This point is well taken. The rather heavy-handed responses by the defense minister and the prime minister to questions in the Diet have also been problematic. While it is obvious that China is a major target of the current draft security legislation, China is not explicitly mentioned out of diplomatic considerations. This has made the content of the legislation obscure. It is self-evident that the more the JSDF's activities escalate, the higher the risk to its members is. The government's denial of this risk in the Diet made people suspicious because it looked as though the government intended to cover up an inconvenient truth. When draft legislation on a serious and important matter is being deliberated, it is all the more essential to instill a deeper understanding of the legislation among the people. It is highly regrettable that such has not been the case in Japan.

It should be recalled that originally the right of collective self-defense was a concept that the Japanese side utilized at the signing of the first U.S.-Japan Security Treaty in 1951. At that time, Japan brought forth this concept so as to have the protection of the United States. In that sense, Japan has already exercised the right—and in fact, Japan's right of collective self-defense is written in the text of the U.S.-Japan Security Treaty, too.

Today, many tend to believe that Japan cannot exercise the right of collective self-defense at all, but the fact of the matter is that Japan has already exercised it to a limited extent. Prime Minister Kishi Nobusuke replied to Diet questions to that effect when he revised the treaty in 1960. It appears that it was after the above Cabinet Legislation Bureau's interpretation had become firmly fixed in people's minds that the right of collective self-defense became regarded as being un-exercisable. The bureau's interpretation was announced at a time when, under the pacifism of the immediate postwar period, overseas activities by the JSDF were utterly unthinkable. Moreover, this interpretation was issued mostly to appease the National Diet.

The problem is that the interpretation of the right of collective self-defense has been stretched to such an extent that the JSDF's use of weapons overseas is always discussed in conjunction with this right. Thus, when the use of weapons overseas should have been discussed in the context of the United Nations' collective security, instead the right of collective self-defense became spotlighted. It is beyond doubt that, since the days of the formulation of the Constitution, the issue of the right of collective self-defense has been a constraint on the JSDF's active cooperation with the United Nations.

As I have pointed out, the right of collective self-defense has already been exercised to a limited extent. The central theme of the controversy over the right of collective self-defense was about how much this limit on the use of the right should be relaxed. This is what was so controversial. While some argue that all restrictions should be lifted so that the full use of the right becomes possible, due consideration should also be given to the experiences that Japan has accumulated as a pacifist nation. In any event, it seems high time to review once again how the right of collective self-defense and collective security are different and how Japan should deal with each.

The Substance of Defense Ministry Reform

In 2015, the Ministry of Defense underwent a major organizational reform, marking the beginning of a watershed in government-military relations in postwar Japan. Specifically, the watershed I am referring to is the revision of the traditional control of the uniformed team by civil officials. What this means is that the control by civil officials, which had long characterized the government-military relationship in postwar Japan, is now relaxed and relations between civil officials and the uniformed team are more equal.

First and foremost were the changes made inside the inner bureau of the Defense Ministry. Because all the work related to actual troop operations came to be concentrated unitarily in the Joint Staff Office, the ministry's Bureau of Operational Policy was abolished. The bureau's function of designing and planning operation-related legislation is now handled by the Bureau of Defense Policy, within which a Strategic Planning Division was newly established.

The integrity of the inner bureau and the Joint Staff Office was promoted further by transferring civil officials of the inner bureau to the Joint Staff Office to function as director-general for operational policy planning and deputy director-general for operational policy planning to assist the director-general. This integration enabled rationalization of external explanations of troop operations and coordination, which hitherto had been offered out redundantly by the two offices separately.

Aside from these reorganizations within the Defense Ministry and the Joint Staff Office, the Acquisition, Technology and Logistics Agency was newly established, along with the Ground Central Command inside the GSDF to handle the operations of all GSDF troops.

These reforms, which are symbolized by the strengthening of the Joint Staff Office's functions, are responses to the new reality—which is that the JSDF is actually being used and its cooperation with the U.S. military is to be further deepened. When the JSDF collaborates with the U.S. military, the integrated operations of which are far advanced, the JSDF is also required to carry out integrated operations. Also, when the JSDF is engaged in operations at overseas sites, the professional knowledge and experience of its personnel as military experts are indispensable, necessitating revision of the traditional control of the uniformed team by civil officials. When it comes to the actual implementation of integrated operations of the JSDF's three forces, the full accomplishment of such still appears to be far away, as revealed by the first large-scale integrated operations attempted after the Great Tohoku Earthquake and Tsunami. At the time, a thick wall of organizational divisions emerged as a serious obstacle.

In any event, the control of the uniformed team by civil officials, which, many believe, has characterized the government-military relations in postwar Japan, has been drastically revised in response to the new reality in which it should be assumed that the JSDF is actually going to be used as an armed force. The critical question, then, is whether civilian control in Japan can remain intact. It seems safe to say that civilian control is assured by legislative measures. While the control by civil officials has indeed been relaxed, a number of constraints on JSDF activities nonetheless remain, and these constraints are far more restrictive than those placed on militaries in other countries.

The bigger problem, though, is how responsible politicians are going to be. The essence of civilian control is for politicians—that is, legislators elected by the people—to make important decisions on national security and for the military to comply with those decisions. Does this mean that politicians always make the right decisions? Unfortunately, no. Past studies show a number of cases in which large numbers of casualties were caused and unnecessary wars started not by the military, but by politicians' poor judgments.

III. Issues for the Future

High Obstacles to a Normal Military Organization
Today, the roles a military organization is expected to play are changing. The times defy the simplistic characterization of a military organization as a mere war machine.

Of course, for a military organization, fighting an enemy still remains its main mission, and, accordingly, such a body is provided with the equipage, organization, footing, and training necessary to accomplish this main mission. Still, the military has increasingly come to function more as an organization to create a state of peace—not the "positive peace" as advocated by peace research, but peace in the sense of the absence of war. The military does this not only in the form of relief and support for disaster victims but also through such activities as the United Nations' peacekeeping operations, peace building activities, and confidence-building measures.

It is high time that remnants of the distinctively postwar Japanese fixation on "the military = a war machine = evil" is abolished. Much of the criticism of the Abe cabinet has been based on images of more than seventy years ago from World War II. How accurately the Japanese people can perceive the current security situation is a salient issue for Japan.

The government-military relations have two aspects: "peace from the military" and "peace by the military." The former is about how to prevent breaches of the peace by the military such as coups d'état, while the latter is about how to effectively maintain security by the military. Reflecting on the pre–World War II error of letting the military indulge in enormous power and thus allowing it to rush Japan into a war, postwar government-military relations have reflected a keen awareness of the importance of peace from the military. Thus, numerous restrictions are imposed on the JSDF's activities. And while other countries devote attention and energy to how to construct a powerful military, in Japan the focus of attention has long been on how to constrain the JSDF and how best to limit its equipage to only that which can be used for homeland defense. The government parties have shown a tendency to submissively comply with demands along these lines from the opposition parties for the sake of smooth National Diet deliberations.

Changes in the international environment since the end of the cold war, however, tell us the time has come for the JSDF to be expected to actually engage in various activities as an armed force. Today, the range of activities in which the JSDF is involved has greatly expanded. As such, it has become increasingly obvious that the JSDF would not be able to fulfill the roles expected of it as long as the traditional restrictions on it remain in place. Legally speaking, the JSDF is not yet a military. But the time has come to discuss whether the JSDF should become a military—and making it so should entail a constitutional amendment.

In the midst of these changes, a number of problems inherent to the JSDF have come under the spotlight. For instance, according to statistics from 2008, the average age of JSDF personnel was 35.1 years old; this was about five years older than their British counterparts. The higher the average age of JSDF personnel, the higher their wages also become. This pushes up personnel costs, which already occupy some 40 percent of Japan's defense budget. The Ministry of Finance holds the view that the defense budget can be reduced by lowering the average age of JSDF personnel. That view is quite understandable given the current financial crunch. Arguments to the contrary maintain that the aging of JSDF personnel is attributable to the sophistication and specialization of their missions, which necessitate technical expertise. This view is also understandable to a certain extent. Taking into consideration the prospect that tasks for the JSDF which require tremendous amounts of manpower, such as disaster relief, are likely to increase in days to come, the proper age composition of the JSDF is an issue to be studied—although, admittedly, remedying the situation will not be an easy task given the low birthrate in Japan as a whole.

Although the enactment of the Legislation for Peace and Security now allows the JSDF to dispatch personnel to rescue civilians in remote locations, Japan does not possess a military law to govern a JSDF that has not been given the legal status of a military organization. A normal military would be tried under military law should its exercise of military power overseas victimize local civilians. But which law in Japan would apply to JSDF personnel? This and other kinds of legislative preparations are issues to be addressed.

A review of the record of Diet discussions on the provision allowing the JSDF to dispatch personnel to rescue civilians in remote locations reveals an inadequate understanding of the change in the nature of present-day U.N. peacekeeping operations (PKO) from the days when the JSDF first participated in such. Today it is assumed that PKO activities are accompanied by the use of force. In other words, there is a possibility that discussions at the Diet do not fit with reality.

Confusion over Peace

Seven decades after the end of World War II, Japan's security policy is about to be transformed. At this juncture, one often hears of lessons of history. While it seems that perspectives on history differ depending on the relative position of the proponent, one of the most important points to recognize is that it was a mistake for prewar Japan to isolate itself internationally and rely on its military might to forcibly create a self-serving international order. In conjunction with this, it is regrettable that today there have emerged two powerful states in the world attempting to change the existing international order by force. I am referring to Russia and China. To be sure, neither country is likely to start a war easily, and the economic interdependences among these countries and the rest of the world continue to deepen. Still, using military power when and if necessary is the reality in international politics, no matter how much their aversion to war dulls the awareness of such for many in Japan. It is to avoid situations necessitating the use of military power that countries strengthen their respective military capabilities and promote multilateral defense cooperation. And Japan, too, is about to pursue this path.

The important thing is to discuss what Japan should and can do on the basis of the awareness that the current international order is being changed by force. Engaging in this discussion is tantamount to reviewing the way Japan as a sovereign state positions itself in the international community. In so doing, it will become necessary to utilize the image Japan has created throughout these postwar years of itself as a pacifist nation.

Still, the fact remains that Japan's defense-related legal systems, which have been constructed like a complex mosaic under the postwar pacifism, can no longer cope with the fluid international situations. Many countries, particularly those in Southeast Asia, have come to expect a lot from Japan, and Japan should respond to those expectations by carrying out reform of pertinent legal systems. To begin with, such terms as "war zone," "logistical support," and "*ittaika* with the use of force" are used to secure compatibility with Japanese legal systems but are not compatible with international standards. If Japan is determined to actively facilitate overseas activities by the JSDF, the time has come to graduate from parochial legal arguments that are acceptable only within Japan. And these legal reforms will inevitably involve the Constitution, calling for full-scale and earnest discussions on whether or not some elements should be amended, all the while preserving intact the pacifism that permeates the current Constitution. This will be a test of Japan's constitutionalism.

Afterword

The year 2004 was the fiftieth anniversary of the Defense Agency and the Japan Self-Defense Forces (JSDF). The very next year was the sixtieth anniversary of the end of World War II. That same year of 2005, the Liberal Democratic Party, which had been the ruling party for most of its fifty-year history in postwar Japan, unveiled its proposal for amending the Japanese Constitution. The proposal included the party's proposition to formally convert the JSDF into a formal military organization.

The JSDF, which its founder Yoshida Shigeru once called an "inconspicuous presence," has never held a clear-cut position in Japanese society since the days of the National Police Reserve, having been tossed around in a controversy over its constitutionality. Now it appears that the time has finally come for the JSDF to be given an explicit position in the state apparatus. But let me hastily add that there still remains a lot to be discussed, and even the future prospect of a constitutional amendment remains uncertain.

I take great pleasure in the fact that this book is published at this particular timing to review how the JSDF has grown against the backdrop of postwar politics in Japan. It was an utterly unexpected delight when my 2003 book, *Sengo Nippon no boei to seiji* [Defense and politics in postwar Japan], was welcomed both by general readers and critics, who contributed numerous favorable reviews to newspapers, magazines, and professional periodicals. Understandably, though, a few readers complained about the poor accessibility of the book due to its highly academic nature. It is generous of the publisher, Yoshikawa Kobunkan, to have allowed me to revise the content of the earlier book for a wider readership and to broaden its coverage in this book to include the most recent developments. I'm pleased that this book is entering the world as a volume of the Rekishi Bunka Library (Historical

Culture Library) series for general readers.

So much has happened so quickly to the JSDF and the Defense Agency in the two years since the publication of the original book, including the dispatch of JSDF units to Iraq and the formulation of the National Defense Program Guidelines, FY2005– (Third NDPG). Fortunately, the Democratic Party of Japan, the largest opposition party at the time of writing, appears to be prepared to discuss national security affairs squarely—unlike previous opposition parties. It is hoped that politics will no longer put security issues on the back burner and, instead, deepen farsighted debates on the issue for the sake of a better future. As I have pointed out in the text, however, attempting to reform the JSDF could cause further confusion if the attempt is not backed up with a thorough review of the organization's historical evolution. I will be gratified if this book can contribute even a little to the Japanese people's awareness of problems surrounding Japan's security issue.

I wish to take this opportunity to express my gratitude to all of those who assisted me one way or another to complete this book. First and foremost, I am deeply indebted to Professor Ito Takashi of the National Graduate Institute for Policy Studies. In completing this book, I benefitted greatly from his insights and experiences with the oral history of postwar Japan's politics and diplomacy, which occupies a large part of my current research activities, as well as from his documentation of historical data. I have had the pleasure of working with Professor Ito as his research collaborator in collecting oral history from defense policy people and other historical documents since my days at the National Graduate Institute for Policy Studies. It would delight me if readers find some fruits of this collaboration in the present book. Professor Ito's passion for the advancement of historical documentation and historiography does not need my humble introduction. Suffice it to say that I have been extremely fortunate to benefit so much in the pursuit of my own research from assisting Professor Ito's work. I am truly grateful.

I also wish to express my thanks to members of the Study Group on the History of the JSDF and the Defense Agency, particularly Professor Watanabe Akio, one of the leading experts in security studies in Japan, and other participants including Kono Yasuko, Michishita Narishige, Takeda Tomomi, Taira Yoshitoshi, Chonan Masayoshi, Tanaka Yoshitomo, and Nakajima Shingo. The study group has been conducting studies on the condition of historical documents on national defense, including oral history on defense policies. I have benefitted immensely from the intellectual inspiration provided by the group's members.

I also wish to mention Ms. Abe Yukiko of the publisher Yoshikawa Kobunkan. She remained professional but considerate throughout the entire publication process, from the planning of the book all the way to the proofreading. Needless to say, an author cannot publish a book alone. It is a product of collaboration between a writer and an editor, and it is truly thanks to Ms. Abe's dedication to this joint endeavor that the book was successfully published. I also owe much to her special solicitude for allowing me to add a large amount of reference materials in the book's appendix, which is highly unusual for a volume in the Historical Culture Library series.

I wish to take this opportunity to reiterate my deepest gratitude and affection to my parents in Fukuoka, where I was born. No matter how far they get on in years, they still think of their children first.

Last but not least are my wife and children. Since I started working at Chukyo University in Nagoya in April 2004, I have spent most of my time in my workplace, apart from my family. This book could never have been published without the understanding and cooperation of my family, who remained ever tolerant no matter how irregularly I came home and stayed home, during which times I ended up indulging in work even at home. I am eternally indebted to them. It is to my wife and children that I wish to dedicate this book.

Sado Akihiro
December 2005

List of Suggested Readings

There are countless books and documents on Japan's security policies, the history of Japan's defense policies, and the history of the Japan Self-Defense Forces. The primary objective of the following list is to recommend documents that should be useful to readers who wish to study these issues further. Readers should be advised, however, that works on security affairs in general as well as analyses of current international situations and military affairs are not included in the list.

While I am aware that not too many readers of this book are proficient enough in the Japanese language to read academic books written in that language freely, I have, nevertheless, decided to include the following works for the benefit of those who wish to study Japan's security policies in general in the vernacular language.

Official/Semiofficial Documents Published by the Ministry of Defense or Its Affiliated Organizations

Defense of Japan, an annual whitepaper on defense compiled and published by the Ministry of Defense, is available in Japanese and English. See: <http://www.mod.go.jp/e/publ/w_paper/2016.html>.

East Asian Strategic Review, an annual compilation published by the National Institute for Defense Studies, Ministry of Defense, is available both in Japanese and English. See: <http://www.nids.go.jp/english/publication/east-asian/e2015.html>.

General Books

1. Books on Japan's Security Policy in General and/or Security-Related History

Agawa Naoyuki. *Umi no yujo: Beikoku kaigun to Kaijo Jieitai* [Friendship on the seas: The U.S. Navy and the Maritime Self-Defense Force]. Tokyo: Chuo-koron-shinsha, 2001.

Hata Ikuhiko. *Shiroku Nippon saigunbi* [Historical document on Japan's rearmament]. Tokyo: Bungei Shunju, 1976.

Hara Akihisa. *Sengo Nippon to kokusai seiji: Anpo kaitei no seiji rikigaku* [Postwar Japan and international politics: Political dynamics of revision of the U.S.-

Japan security pact]. Tokyo: Chuokoron-sha, 1988.

Hirose Katsuya. *Kanryo to gunjin: Bunmin tosei no genkai* [Bureaucrats and the military: Limitations of civilian control]. Tokyo: Iwanami Shoten, 1989.

Jieitai o Ikasu Kai, ed. *Shin Jieitai ron* [On the Japan Self-Defense Forces, revised]. Tokyo: Kodansha, 2015.

Kusunoki Ayako. *Yoshida Shigeru to anzen hosho seisaku no keisei* [Yoshida Shigeru and the formulation of security policy]. Tokyo: Minerva Shobo, 2009.

Maeda Tetsuo. *Jieitai wa nani o shitekitanoka: Waga kokugun no 40-nen* [What have the Japan Self-Defense Forces been doing?: 40 years of Japan's national military]. Tokyo: Chikuma Shobo, 1990 (Retitled *Jieitai no rekishi* [History of the Japan Self-Defense Forces] in 1994).

Masuda Hiroshi. *Jieitai no tanjo: Nippon no saigunbi to amerika* [Establishment of the Japan Self-Defense Forces: Japan's rearmament and the United States]. Tokyo: Chuokoron-shinsha, 2004.

Nakajima Shingo. *Sengo Nippon no boei seisaku: "Yoshida rosen" o meguru seiji, gaiko, gunji* [Postwar Japan's defense policy: Politics, diplomacy, and military surrounding the Yoshida Doctrine]. Tokyo: Keio University Press, 2006.

NHK Hodohan "Kaijo Jieitai" Shuzaihan, ed. *Kaijo Jieitai wa koshite umareta: "Y bunsho" ga akasu sosetsu no himitsu* [How the Maritime Self-Defense Force was founded: Secrets surrounding the establishment of the Maritime Self-Defense Force as exposed by the "Y Document"]. Tokyo: NHK Publishing, 2003.

Otake Hideo. *Saigunbi to nashonarizumu* [Rearmament and nationalism]. Tokyo: Chuokoron-sha, 1988.

Sado Akihiro. *Sengo Nippon no boei to seiji* [National defense and politics in postwar Japan]. Tokyo: Yoshikawa Kobunkan, 2004.

———. *Jieitai-shi ron: Sei-kan-gun-min no 60-nen* [Historiography of Japan Self-Defense Forces: 60 years of government-bureaucracy-military-civilian relations]. Tokyo: Yoshikawa Kobunkan, 2014.

Sakamoto Kazuya. *Nichibei domei no kizuna: Anpo joyaku to sogosei no mosaku* [Bond of the U.S.-Japan alliance: U.S.-Japan security pact and quest for reciprocity]. Tokyo: Yuhikaku Publishing, 2002.

Sotooka Hidetoshi, Honda Masaru and Miura Toshiaki. *Nichibei domei hanseiki: Anpo to mitsuyaku* [Half a century of the U.S.-Japan alliance: U.S.-Japan security pact and a secret agreement]. Tokyo: The Asahi Shimbun Company, 2001.

Takino Takahiro. *Shutsudo sezu: Jieitai 60-nen no kuno to shudanteki jieiken* [Not to be deployed: 60 years of Japan Self-Defense Forces' agony and the right of collective self-defense]. Tokyo: Poplar Publishing, 2014.

Tanaka Akihiko. *Anzen hosho: Sengo 50-nen no mosaku* [Security: 50 years of postwar exploration]. Tokyo: The Yomiuri Shimbun, 1997.

Uemura Hideki. *Saigunbi to 55-nen taisei* [Rearmament and the 1955 system]. Tokyo: Bokutakusha, 1995.

Yomiuri Shimbun Sengo-shi-han, ed. *Showa sengo-shi: "Saigunbi" no kiseki* [Postwar Showa history: Trajectory of rearmament]. Tokyo: The Yomiuri Shimbun, 1981.

2. Books Written by Authors Affiliated with the Ministry of Defense (formerly the Defense Agency) or the Japan Self-Defense Forces

Hibako Yoshibumi. *Sokudo hittsui* [Prompt deployment to accomplish missions without failure]. Tokyo: Maneimentosha, 2015.

Kaihara Osamu. *Watashi no kokubo hakusho* [My personal defense whitepaper]. Tokyo: Jiji Tsushinsha, 1975.

———. *Nippon boei taisei no uchimaku* [Inside story of Japan's defense posture]. Tokyo: Jiji Press, 1977.

Kato Yozo. *Shiroku Jieitai-shi: Keisatsu Yobitai kara kon'nichi made* [Personal memorandum on the history of the Japan Self-Defense Forces: From the days of the National Police Reserve through today]. Tokyo: Gekkan Seisaku Seiji Gepposha, 1979.

Moriya Takemasa. *Nippon boei hiroku* [Secret record of Japan's defense]. Tokyo: Shinchosha, 2013.

Natsukawa Kazuya and Yamashita Teruo. *Kiro ni tatsu Jieitai: Sengo no hensen kara mirai o uranau* [The Japan Self-Defense Forces at a crossroads: Predicting its future from its postwar evolution]. Tokyo: Bungeisha, 2015.

Oga Ryohei. *Shiren no himitsu: Beiso senryaku no hazamade* [Secret of sea lane: In-between U.S. and Soviet strategies]. Tokyo: Chobunsha, 1983.

Omori Keiji. *Waga kuni no kokubo senryaku* [Japan's national defense strategy]. Tokyo: Naigai Publishing, 2009.

Oriki Ryoichi. *Kuni o mamoru sekinin: Jieitai moto saiko kanbu wa kataru* [Responsibility to defend the country: Monologue of a former top official of the Japan Self-Defense Forces]. Tokyo & Kyoto: PHP Institute, 2015.

Sassa Atsuyuki. *Poritiko-miritari no susume: Nippon no anzen hosho gyosei no genba kara* [Arguing for politico-military: From the actual field of Japan's security administration]. Tokyo: Toshi Shuppan, 1994.

Sato Morio. *Keisatsu Yobitai to saigunbi eno michi: Dai 1-kisei ga mita soshiki no jitsu-zo* [National Police Reserve and road to Japan's Rearmament: The reality of the organization in the eyes of a member of its inaugural class]. Tokyo: Fuyo Shobo Shuppan, 2015.

Sugita Ichiji. *Wasurareteiru anzen hosho* [Security that is forgotten]. Tokyo: Jiji Tsushinsha, 1967.

Tomizawa Akira. *Gyakusetsu no gunji ron* [Paradoxical military theory]. Tokyo: Basilico, 2015.

Tsukamoto Shoichi. *Jieitai no joho sen: Rikubaku dai-2 bucho no kaiso* [Information war of the Japan Self-Defense Forces: Memoir of a director of the 2nd department of the Ground Staff Office]. Tokyo: Soshisha Publishing, 2008.

Yanagisawa Kyoji. *Kensho kantei no Iraku senso: Moto boei kanryo ni yoru hihan to jisei* [Scrutiny of the prime minister's office during the Iraq War: Criticism and self-criticism by a former Defense Agency bureaucrat]. Tokyo: Iwanami Shoten, 2013.

Documents in English

Readers who are interested in overviews of Japan's foreign policy are advised to visit the Japan's Diplomacy Series in the Japan Digital Library of the Japan Institute of International Affairs at:
<http://www2.jiia.or.jp/en/digital_library/japan_s_diplomacy.php>.
Included there is an article by myself, Sado Akihiro, titled "The End of the Cold War and Japan's Participation in Peacekeeping Operations: Overseas Deployment of the Self-Defense Forces."

Auer, J. E. *The Postwar Rearmament of Japanese Maritime Forces, 1945–1971*. London: Praeger, 1973.

Dower, J. *Embracing Defeat: Japan in the Wake of World War II*. London: Norton, 2000.

———. *Empire and Aftermath: Yoshida Shigeru and the Japanese Experience, 1878–1954*. (Harvard East Asian Monographs 84). London: Harvard University Press, 1988.

Drifte, D. *The Security Factor in Japan's Foreign Policy, 1945–52*. Brighton: Saltire Press, 1983.

Finn, R. B. *Winner in Peace: MacArthur, Yoshida, and Postwar Japan*. London: University of California Press, 1995.

Green, M. J. *Arming Japan: Defense Production, Alliance Policies and the Postwar Search for Autonomy*. New York: Columbia University Press, 1995.

Katzenstein, P. J. and Y. Tsujinaka. *Defending the Japanese State, Structures, Norms and the Political Responses to Terrorism and Violent Social Protest in the 1970s and 1980s*. Ithaca: Cornell University Press, 1991.

Keddell, J. P. *The Politics of Defense in Japan: Managing Internal and External Pressures*. New York: Armonk, 1993.

Kowalski, Jr., F. *An Inoffensive Rearmament: The Making of the Postwar Japanese Army*. Annapolis: Naval Institute Press, 2014.

Pyle, K. B. *Japan Rising: The Resurgence of Japanese Power and Purpose*. New York: Public Affairs, 2007.

Samuels, R. J. *Securing Japan: Tokyo's Grand Strategy and the Future of East Asia*. Ithaca: Cornell University Press, 2008.

Swenson-Wright, J. *Unequal Allies?: United States Security and Alliance Policy Toward Japan, 1945–1960*. Stanford: Stanford University Press, 2005.

Takemae, E. *Inside GHQ: The Allied Occupation of Japan and Its Legacy*. London: Continuum, 2002.

Weinstein, M. E. *Japan's Postwar Defense Policy, 1947–1968*. New York: Columbia University Press, 1971.

Wooley, P. J. *Japan's Navy: Politics and Paradox, 1971–2000.* Colorado: Lynne Rienner Publishers, 2000.

Note: Treatises and articles are excluded from the above list. Interested readers should consult with the quite comprehensive list of references in the appendix of *Securing Japan: Tokyo's Grand Strategy and the Future of East Asia*, written by Richard Samuels.

APPENDICES

Appendix A

National Defense Program Outline

1. Objectives

Japan's possession of a defense capability within the scope permitted by the Constitution is not only a concrete expression of the people's will to safeguard the nation's peace and independence, but also aims - together with the Japan-United States security arrangement - directly at forestalling any aggression against Japan and repelling such aggression should it occur. Concurrently, the very fact that Japan firmly maintains such a defense posture contributes as well to the international political stability of Japan's neighboring region.

A major consideration in this regard is the nature of the defense capability which Japan should possess. Assuming that the international political structure in this region - along with continuing efforts for global stabilization - will not undergo any major changes for some time to come, and that Japan's domestic conditions will also remain fundamentally stable, the most appropriate defense goal would seem to be the maintenance of a full surveillance posture in peacetime and the ability to cope effectively with situations up to the point of limited and small-scale aggression. The emphasis is on the possession of the assorted functions required for national defense, while retaining balanced organization and deployment, including logistical support. At the same time, it is felt that consideration should be given to enabling this defense posture to contribute to the domestic welfare through disaster-relief operations and other such programs.

Japan has steadily improved its defense capability through the drafting and implementation of a series of four defense buildup plans. At this time, the present scale of defense capability seems to closely approach the target goals of the above-mentioned concept.

This outline is meant to serve as a guideline for Japan's future defense posture in the light of that concept. Based on the information given below, efforts will be made to qualitatively maintain and improve defense capability, and fulfill the purpose of that capability, in specific upgrading, maintenance and operation of defense functions.

2. International Situation

An analysis of the current international situation, at the time of drafting this outline, was made as follows:

During recent years, the world community has witnessed a pronounced trend toward more diversified international relations. While nationalistic movements have become more active in some countries, simultaneously there has been marked intensification of interdependence among nations.

Against this background, the major geopolitical blocs of East and West - which center on the relationship between the United States and the Soviet Union and their continued overwhelming military strengths - have continued a dialogue aimed at avoiding nuclear war and improving mutual relations, allowing for certain twists and turns along the path. In many individual regions as well, various efforts are being made to avoid conflict and stabilize international relations.

Deeply-rooted factors for assorted confrontations remain within the East-West relationship revolving around the United States and the Soviet Union, however, and intra-regional situations as well are fluid in many aspects with various elements of instability observable.

Within the general neighborhood of Japan, an equilibrium exists, involving the three major powers of the United States, the Soviet Union and China. Tension still persists on the Korean Peninsula, however, and military buildups continue in several countries nearby Japan.

Under present circumstances, though, there seems little possibility of a full-scale military clash between East and West or of a major conflict possibly leading to such a clash, due to the military balance - including mutual nuclear deterrence - and the various efforts being made to stabilize international relations.

Furthermore, while the possibility of limited military conflict breaking out in Japan's neighborhood cannot be dismissed, this equilibrium between the super-powers and the existence of the Japan-U.S. security arrangement seems to play a major role in maintaining international stability, and in preventing full-scale aggression against Japan.

3. Basic Defense Concept

(1) Prevention of Armed Invasion

Japan's basic defense policy is to possess an adequate defense capability of its own while establishing a posture for the most effective operation of that capability to prevent aggression. In addition, a defense posture capable of dealing with any aggression should be constructed, through maintaining the credibility of the Japan-U.S. security arrangement and insuring the smooth functioning of that system.

Against nuclear threat Japan will rely on the nuclear deterrent capability of the United States.

(2) Countering Aggression

Should indirect aggression - or any unlawful military activity which might lead to aggression against this nation - occur, Japan will take immediate responsive action in order to settle the situation at an early stage.

Should direct aggression occur, Japan will repel such aggression at the earliest possible stage by taking immediate responsive action and trying to conduct an integrated, systematic operation of its defense capability. Japan will repel limited and small-scale aggression, in principle, without external assistance. In cases where the unassisted repelling of aggression is not feasible, due to scale, type or other factors of such aggression, Japan will continue an unyielding resistance by mobilizing all available forces until such time as cooperation from the United States is introduced, thus rebuffing such aggression.

4. Posture of National Defense

In accordance with the above defense concepts, Japan will maintain a defense capability of the postures spelled out below and the systems described in Section V. This defense capability will meet the functional and postural requirements outlined in Section I as to what Japan should possess. At the same time, it will be standardized so that, when serious changes in situations so demand, the defense structure can be smoothly adapted to meet such changes:

(1) Setup of Warning and Surveillance
Japan's defense structure must possess continuous capability to conduct warning and surveillance missions within Japan's territory and neighboring sea and airspace as well as to collect required intelligence.
(2) Setup for Countering Indirect Aggression and Unlawful Actions by Means of Use of Military Power
　(i) Japan's defense structure must possess the capability to act and take the required steps to respond to such cases as intense domestic insurgency with external support, organized personnel infiltration and arms smuggling, or the covert use of force in Japan's nearby sea and airspace.
　(ii) Japan's defense structure must be capable of immediate and pertinent action to cope with aircraft invading or threatening to invade Japan's territorial airspace.
(3) Setup for Countering Direct Military Aggression
Japan's defense structure must be capable of taking immediate responsive action against any direct military aggression, in accordance with the type and scale of such aggression. It should be capable of repelling limited and small-scale aggression, in principle without external assistance. In cases where unassisted repelling of aggression is not feasible, it should be capable of continuing effective resistance until such time as cooperation from the United States can be introduced, thus rebuffing such aggression.
(4) Setup of Command Communications, Transportation and Rear Support Services
Japan's defense structure must be able to function in such fields as command communications, transportation, rescue, supply and maintenance, for swift, effective and adequate operations.
(5) Setup of Education and Training of Personnel
Japan's defense structure must be capable of carrying out intensive education and training of personnel at all times for the reinforcement of the personnel foundation of defense capability.
(6) Setup of Disaster-Relief Operations
Japan's defense structure must possess the capability to carry out disaster-relief operations in any areas of the country when required.

Realization of the structuring outlined below for the Ground, Maritime and Air Self-Defense Forces is a basic requirement for maintenance of the defense postures related in Section IV.

5. Posture of the Ground, Maritime and Air Self-Defense Forces

In addition, special consideration must be given to promoting systematic cooperation among the three branches of the SDF, and to securing maximum efficiency in integrated operations.

(1) Ground Self-Defense Force
(i) The Ground Self-Defense Force, in order to be capable of swift and effective systematic defense operations from the outset of aggression in any part of Japan, must deploy its divisions and other units with a balance conforming to Japan's natural features.
(ii) The GSDF must possess at least one tactical unit of each of the various types of forces used mainly for mobile operations.
(iii) The GSDF must possess ground-to-air missile units capable of undertaking low-altitude air defense of vital areas.

(2) Maritime Self-Defense Force
(i) The MSDF must possess one fleet escort force as a mobile operating ship unit in order to quickly respond to aggressive action and such situations at sea. The fleet escort force must be able to maintain at least one escort flotilla on alert at all times.
(ii) The MSDF must possess, as ship units assigned to coastal surveillance and defense, surface anti-submarine capability of at least one ship division in operational readiness at all times in each assigned sea district.
(iii) The MSDF must maintain submarine units, anti-submarine helicopter units and minesweeping units, providing the capability for surveillance and defense missions as well as minesweeping at important harbors and major straits when such necessity arises.
(iv) The MSDF must maintain fixed-wing anti-submarine aircraft units in order to provide the capability of carrying out such missions as surveillance and patrol of the nearby seas and surface ship protection.

(3) Air Self-Defense Force
(i) The Air Self-Defense Force must possess aircraft control and warning units capable of vigilance and surveillance throughout Japanese airspace on a continuous basis.
(ii) The ASDF must possess fighter units and high-altitude ground-to-air missile units for air defense, to provide the capability of maintaining continuous alert to take immediate and appropriate steps against violations of Japan's territorial airspace and air incursions.
(iii) The ASDF must possess units capable of engaging in such missions as interdicting airborne or amphibious landing invasion, air support, aerial reconnaissance, early warning against low-altitude intrusion and air transportation as the necessity arises.

Descriptions of the actual scales of organizations and primary equipment under the foregoing concepts are given in the attachment.

6. Basic Policy and Matters to Be Taken Into Consideration in Building Up Defense Capabilities

The basic goal in improving Japan's defense capability must be the maintenance of the postures outlined in Sections IV and V, with due consideration to qualitative improvements aimed at parity with the technical standards of other nations. In addition to carefully adapting to changing economic and fiscal conditions in harmony with government policies in other fields, the points below should be borne in mind when defense improvements are actually implemented.

Decisions on major projections in fiscal yearly defense improvement programs will be submitted to the National Defense Council for consultation. The actual scope of such major projections will be decided by the Cabinet, after consultation with the National Defense Council.

(1) Establishment of reasonable standards for personnel recruitment and consideration of measures aimed at securing quality personnel and enhancing morale.

(2) Effective maintenance and improvement of defense facilities and attempts to harmonize such facilities with the surrounding communities through consideration of environmental protection, such as anti-noise measures.

(3) Effective implementation of equipment acquisition programs, with overall consideration of such factors as swift emergency resupply, acceptable education and training ease and cost efficiency. Attention should also be given to the possibility for adequate domestic production of the equipment in question.

(4) Improvement of the technical research and development system for the maintenance and improvement of qualitative levels of defense capability.

Source: Institute of Oriental Culture, University of Tokyo, "National Defense Program Outline." www.ioc.u-tokyo.ac.jp/~worldjpn/documents/texts/docs/19761029.O1E.html (accessed December 20, 2016).

Attachment

GSDF	Authorized personnel Regular Ready reserve		180,000
	Major units	Regionally deployed units in peacetime	12 divisions 2 combined brigades
		Mobile operation units	1 armored division 1 artillery brigade 1 airborne brigade 1 combined training brigade 1 helicopter brigade
		Ground-to-air guided missile units	8 anti-aircraft artillery groups
	Main equipment	Tanks Artillery (Main artillery)[1]	(About 1,200)[2] (About 1,000/vehicle)[2]
MSDF	Major units	Destroyer units for mobile operations regional district units Submarine units Minesweeping units Patrol aircraft units	4 escort flotillas (Regional units) 10 units 6 divisions 2 minesweeper flotillas (Land-based) 16 squadrons
	Main equipment	Destroyers Submarines Combat aircraft	About 60 ships 16 ships About 220 aircraft
ASDF	Major units	Aircraft control & warning units	28 warning groups 1 squadron
		Fighter units Fighter-interceptor units Support fighter units	10 squadrons 3 squadrons
		Air reconnaissance units	1 squadron
		Air transport units Air refueling/transport units	3 squadrons —
		Surface-to-air guided missile units	6 groups
	Main equipment	Combat aircraft (Fighter aircraft)	About 430 aircraft (About 360 aircraft)[2]
Main equipment & major units which can also be used in ballistic missile defense[3]		Aegis-equipped destroyers	—
		Aircraft control & warning units Surface-to-air guided missile units	— —

Notes: 1. Categorized as main artillery up till 2004 NDPG, but categorized in the 2010 NDPG as artillery except for surface-to-air guided missile units.
2. Although not stated in the 1976 NDPG, it is listed here for comparison with the NDPG table after 1995.
3. "Main equipment and major units that can also be used in defense against ballistic missiles" refers to the number of main equipment in the MSDF or number of major units in the ASDF.

Source: Ministry of Defense, "Defense of Japan 2013." www.mod.go.jp/e/publ/w_paper/pdf/2013/25_Part2_Chapter2_Sec1.pdf, p. 4 (accessed December 20, 2016).

Appendix B

Report by the Subcommittee for Defense Cooperation, Submitted to and Approved by the Japan-U.S. Security Consultative Committee

November 27, 1978

The Japan-U.S. Security Consultative Committee held on July 8, 1976 decided to establish the Subcommittee for Defense Cooperation. The Subcommittee for Defense Cooperation which was held 8 times, agreed on the following premises and subjects of studies and consultations in assuming the mission committed by the Japan-U.S. Security Consultative Committee

1. Premises of Studies and Consultations

(1) Matters concerning "Prior Consultation," matters concerning the Japanese constitutional limitations and the Three Non-Nuclear principles will not be the subjects of the SDC's studies and consultations.

(2) The conclusions of the SDC's studies and consultations will be reported to the Security Consultative Committee and the disposition of those conclusions will be left to the judgement of the respective Governments of Japan and the United States. Those conclusions will not be such as would place either government under obligation to take legislative, budgetary or administrative measures.

2. Subjects of Studies and Consultations

(1) Matters relating to the case of an armed attack against Japan or to the case in which such an attack is imminent.

(2) Matters relating to situations in the Far East other than those mentioned in (1) above, which will have an important influence on the security of Japan.

(3) Others (joint exercise and training, etc.)

At the outset of conducting its studies and consultations, the SDC heard the Japanese side's basic concept concerning the scope and modalities of defense cooperation between Japan and the United States under the Japan-U.S. Security Treaty in the case of an armed attack against Japan, and decided to proceed with its work using this concept as a basis for its studies and consultations. The SDC established, with a view to facilitating its studies and consultations, three subsidiary panels, namely the Operations, Intelligence and Logistics Panels. These Panels have conducted studies and consultations from a professional standpoint. The SDC has also conducted studies and consultations on other matters concerning cooperation between Japan and the United States which come within its purview.

The SDC hereby submits for approval to the Security Consultative Committee "The Draft Guidelines for Japan-United States Defense Cooperation" representing the result of the SDC's activities described above.

Source: Institute of Oriental Culture, University of Tokyo, "Report by the Subcommittee for Defense Cooperation, Submitted to and Approved by the Japan-U.S. Security Consultative Committee." www. ioc.u-tokyo.ac.jp/~worldjpn/documents/texts/docs/19781127.O1E.html (accessed December 20, 2016).

Appendix C
The Guidelines for Japan-U.S. Defense Cooperation
November 27, 1978

These draft guidelines shall not be construed as affecting the rights and obligations of Japan and the United States under the Japan-U.S. Security Treaty and its related arrangements. It is understood that the extension of facilitative assistance and support by Japan to the United States, which is described in the draft guidelines, is subject to the relevant laws and regulations of Japan.

I. Posture for deterring aggression

1. Japan, as its defense policy, will possess defense capability on an appropriate scale within the scope necessary for self-defense, and consolidate and maintain a posture to ensure the most efficient operations ; and assure, in accordance with the SOFA, the stable and effective utilization of facilities and areas in Japan by U.S. Forces. The United States will maintain a nuclear deterrent capability and the forward deployments of combat-ready forces and other forces capable of reinforcing them.

2. In order to be able to take coordinated joint action smoothly in the event of an armed attack against Japan, Japan and the United States will endeavor to achieve a posture for cooperation between the Self-Defense Forces and U.S. Forces in such areas as operations, intelligence and logistics.
    Accordingly,

(1) In order jointly to conduct coordinated operations for the defense of Japan smoothly and effectively, the JSDF and U.S. Forces will conduct studies on joint defense planning.
    They will also undertake necessary joint exercises and training when appropriate. in addition, the JSDF and U.S. Forces will study and prepare beforehand common procedures deemed necessary for operational needs in order jointly to undertake operations smoothly. Such procedures include matters related to operations, intelligence and logistics. As communications/electronics are absolutely essential to effecting command and liaison, the JSDF and U.S. Forces will also determine in advance their mutual communications/electronics requirements.
(2) The JSDF and U.S. Forces will develop and exchange intelligence necessary for the defense of Japan. The JSDF and U.S. Forces will, in order to ensure smooth intelligence exchange, determine in coordination the nature of the intelligence to be exchanged and the specific JSDF/USF units to be assigned responsibility for the exchange. In addition, the JSDF and U.S. Forces will promote close intelligence cooperation by taking such required actions as establishing systems for mutual communications.
(3) The JSDF and U.S. Forces, acting from the basic principle that each nation is responsible for the logistics of its own forces, will closely coordinate with each other or conduct studies in advance in regard to such functions as supply, trans-

portation, maintenance, facilities, etc., so that mutual support can be arranged appropriately when needed. Detailed requirements for this mutual support will be developed through joint studies and planning in particular, coordination will be made in advance in regard to foreseeable supply deficiencies, quantities, priorities for satisfying deficiencies, emergency acquisition procedures, etc., and studies will be undertaken relating to the economical and efficient utilization of the bases and facilities of the two forces.

II. Actions in response to an armed attack against Japan

1. When an armed attack against Japan is imminent:
Japan and the United States will conduct closer liaison and will take necessary measures respectively and, as deemed necessary due to changes in the situation, will make necessary preparations in order to ensure coordinated joint action, including the establishment of a coordination center between the JSDF and U.S. Forces.

The JSDF and U.S. Forces will establish in advance a common standard as regards preparations which will be respectively conducted by the two forces so that the two nations may select coordinated common readiness stages, and ensure that effective preparations for operations can be cooperatively undertaken by the JSDF and U.S. Forces respectively.

This common standard will indicate readiness stages from an increase of unit alert posture to a maximization of combat readiness posture concerning intelligence activities, unit readiness, movements, logistics, and other matters relating to defense preparations. The JSDF and U.S. Forces will respectively conduct defense preparations considered necessary according to the readiness stage selected by mutual agreement between the two governments.

2. When an armed attack against Japan takes place:

(1) In principle, Japan by itself will repel limited, small-scale aggression. When it is difficult to repel aggression alone due to the scale, type and other factors of aggression, Japan will repel it with the cooperation of the United States.

(2) When the JSDF and U.S. Forces jointly conduct operations for the defense of Japan, they will strive to achieve close mutual coordination to employ the defense capacity of each force in a timely and effective manner.
    (i) Concept of Operations:
    The JSDF will primarily conduct defensive operations in Japanese territory and its surrounding waters and airspace. U.S. Forces will support JSDF operations. U.S. Forces will also conduct operations to supplement functional areas which exceed the capacity of the JSDF.
    The JSDF and U.S. Forces will jointly conduct ground, maritime and air operations as follows:
        (a) Ground Operations:
        The Ground Self-Defense Force (GSDF) and U.S. Ground Forces will jointly conduct g round operations for the defense of Japan.
        The GSDF will conduct checking, holding and repelling operations.

U.S. Ground Forces will deploy as necessary and jointly conduct operations with the GSDF, mainly those for repelling enemy forces.

(b) Maritime Operations:

The Maritime Self-Defense Force (MSDF) and U.S. Navy will jointly conduct maritime operations for the defense of surrounding waters and the protection of sea lines of communication.

The MSDF will primarily conduct operations for the protection of major ports and straits in Japan; and anti-submarine operations, operations for the protection of ships and other operations in the surrounding waters.

U.S. Naval Forces will support MSDF operations and conduct operations, including those which may involve the use of task forces providing additional mobility and strike power, with the objective of repelling enemy forces.

(c) Air Operations:

The Air Self-Defense Force (ASDF) and U.S. Air Force will jointly conduct air operations for the defense of Japan.

The ASDF will conduct air-defense, anti-airborne and anti-amphibious invasion, close air support, air reconnaissance, airlift operations, etc.

U.S. Air Force will support ASDF operations and conduct operations, including those which may involve the use of air units providing additional strike power, with the objective of repelling enemy forces.

(d) When carrying out ground, maritime, and air operations, the JSDF and U.S. Forces will provide necessary support for each other's forces in various activities related to operations, such as intelligence, Logistics, etc.

(ii) Command and Coordination:

The JSDF and U.S. Forces, in close cooperation, will take action through their respective command-and-control channels. In order to be able jointly to conduct coordinated operations effectively, the JSDF and U.S. Forces will take action in accordance with operational processes which will be coordinated in advance.

(iii) Coordination Center:

In order jointly to conduct effective operations, the JSDF and U.S. Forces will maintain close mutual coordination on operations, intelligence and logistic support through a coordination center.

(iv) Intelligence Activities:

The JSDF and U.S. Forces will, through operations of their respective intelligence systems, conduct intelligence activities in close cooperation in order to contribute to the joint implementation of effective operations. To support this, the JSDF and U.S. Forces will coordinate intelligence activities closely at each stage of requirements, collection, production, and dissemination. The JSDF and U.S. Forces will each have responsibility for their security.

(v) Logistic Activities:

The JSDF and U.S. Forces will conduct efficient and appropriate logistic support activities in close cooperation in accordance with relevant agreements between Japan and the United States.

Toward this end, Japan and the United States will undertake mutual support activities to improve the effectiveness of logistic functions and to alleviate functional shortfalls as follows:
(a) Supply
The United States will support the acquisition of supplies for systems of U.S. origin while Japan will support acquisition of supplies in Japan.
(b) Transportation
Japan and the United States will, in close cooperation, carry out transportation operations, including airlift and sealift of supplies from the United States to Japan.
(c) Maintenance
The United States will support the maintenance of items of U.S. origin, which are beyond Japanese maintenance capabilities. and Japan will support the maintenance of U.S. Forces' equipment in Japan. Maintenance support will include the technical training of maintenance personnel as required. As a related activity, Japan will also support U.S. Forces requirement for salvage and recovery in Japan.
(d) Facilities
The U.S. Forces will, in case of need, be provided additional facilities and areas in accordance with the Japan-U.S. Security Treaty and its related arrangements. If it becomes necessary to consider joint use of bases and facilities/are as to improve effective and economical utilization, the JSDF and U.S. Forces will conduct joint use in accordance with the above Treaty and arrangements.

III. Japan-U.S. cooperation in the case of situations in the Far East outside of Japan which will have an important influence on the security of Japan

The Governments of Japan and the United States will consult together from time to whenever changes in the circumstances so require.
The scope and modalities of facilitative assistance to be extended by Japan to the U.S. Forces in the case of situations in the Far East outside of Japan which will have an important influence' on the security of Japan will be governed by the Japan-U.S. Security Treaty, its related arrangements, other relevant agreements between Japan and the United States, and the relevant laws and regulations of Japan.
The Governments of Japan and the United States will conduct studies in advance on the scope and modalities of facilitative assistance to be extended to the U.S. Forces by Japan with in the above-mentioned legal framework. Such studies will include the scope and modalities of joint use of the Self-Defense Forces bases by the U.S. Forces and of other facilitative assistance to be extended.

Source: Ministry of Defense, "The Guidelines for Japan-U.S. Defense Cooperation (November 27, 1978)." www.mod.go.jp/e/d_act/anpo/19781127.html (accessed December 20, 2016).

Appendix D

National Defense Program Outline In and After FY1996

December, 1995

I. Purpose

1. In order to preserve its independence and peace, Japan, under its Constitution, has been making efforts to secure stability in the international community through diplomatic activities including efforts to prevent and settle conflicts, to establish a sound basis for security through domestic political stability, to maintain firmly the Japan-U.S. security arrangements and to build up appropriate defense capabilities.

2. In 1976, under those policies, Japan formulated the National Defense Program Outline (adopted by the National Defense Council and by the Cabinet on October 29, 1976, hereinafter cited as "the Outline"). The Outline was drafted on the premise that the international situation, in which efforts for stabilization were being continued, the international political structure of the surrounding regions and Japan's own domestic situation would not undergo any major changes for some time and judging that the existence of the Japan-U.S. security arrangements would continue to play a major role in maintaining the stability of international relations. Since then, Japan has developed its defense capability according to "the Outline", and the steady defense efforts, in conjunction with the existence of the Japan-U.S. security arrangements and the efforts made to ensure the smooth and effective implementation of these arrangements, have both prevented any aggressions against Japan and contributed to the maintenance of peace and stability in the surrounding region.

3. Herein, a new set of guidelines for Japan's defense capability is laid forth, taking into consideration that almost two decades have passed since the adoption of "the Outline," that during this time the international situation has undergone significant changes, including the demise of the structure of the military confrontation between East and West, led respectively by the Soviet Union and the United States, brought on by the end of the Cold War, and that expectations for the role of the Self-Defense Forces have been increased in such function as providing aid in cases of large-scale disasters and contributing to building a more stable security environment through participation in international peace cooperation activities, in addition to their principal mission of defending Japan.

4. Japan, abiding by its Constitution, following the guidelines set forth herein and paying due attention to enhancing the credibility of the Japan-U.S. security arrangements, will strive to ensure its own national defense and contribute to the peace and stability of the international community by appropriately upgrading, maintaining and operating its capability.

II. International Situation

The following trends in the international situation were considered in the drafting of these new guidelines.

1. With the end of the Cold War, which led to the demise of the structure of military confrontation between East and West, backed by overwhelming military capabilities, the possibility of a global armed conflict has become remote in today's international community. At the same time, various unresolved territorial issues remain, and confrontations rooted in religious and ethnic differences have emerged more prominently. Complicated and diverse regional conflicts have been taking place. Furthermore, new kinds of dangers, such as the proliferation of weapons of mass destruction including nuclear arms, and of missiles, are on the increase. Thus, unpredictability and uncertainty persist in the international community.

2. On the other hand, as interdependence among nations intensifies, efforts are underway in various areas, such as political and economic spheres, to promote international cooperation and to further stabilize international relations. An emphasis has been placed on preventing destabilizing factors from escalating into serious international problems. In the area of security, continued progress is being made in arms control and disarmament, based on agreements between the United States and Russia and within Europe. Efforts are also being made toward enhancing regional security frameworks, expanding multilateral and bilateral dialogues and promoting the role of the United Nations.

Major countries are making active efforts to reorganize and stream-line their military capabilities, which used to be aimed at countering large-scale aggression, and taking account of their respective strategic environments, to secure adequate capability to properly respond to regional conflicts and other various situations. These efforts constitute important factors toward the establishment of a more stable security environment, in combination with the initiatives based on international cooperation, including those launched by the United Nations. In this context, the United States, with its great power, continues to play a significant role for world peace and stability.

3. In the surrounding regions of Japan, the end of the Cold War and the collapse of the Soviet Union have brought about a reduction of the military force level and changes in the military posture in Far East Russia. At the same time, there still remain large-scale military capabilities including nuclear arsenals and many countries in the region are expanding or modernizing their military capabilities mainly against the background of their economic development. There remain uncertainty and unpredictability, such as continued tensions on the Korean Peninsula, and a stable security environment has not been fully established. Under these circumstances, the possibility of a situation in this region, which could seriously affect the security of Japan, cannot be excluded. At the same time, various activities are being pursued to deepen cooperative relations among nations and to achieve regional stability, such as promotion of bilateral dialogues and search for a regional security framework.

The close cooperative relationship between Japan and the United States, based on the Japan-U.S. security arrangements, will help to create a stable security environment, provide the foundation for securing the engagement of the United States and the U.S. military presence which are necessary for peace and stability in this region, and thus will continue to play a key role for the security of Japan, as well as the stability of the international community.

III. Security of Japan and Roles of Defense Capabilities

(Security of Japan and the basic defense policy)
1. Japan, under its Constitution, while promoting diplomatic efforts and establishing a sound basis for security through domestic political stability, has moderately built up its defense capability on its own initiative, in accordance with the fundamental principles of maintaining an exclusively defense-oriented policy, not becoming a military power that might pose a threat to other countries, upholding civilian control, adhering to the three non-nuclear principles, and maintaining firmly the Japan-U.S. security arrangements. Japan is determined to maintain those basic defense policies.

(Defense capability as it ought to be)
2. Japan has built its defense capability in accordance with "the Outline," which incorporates the concept of a basic and standard defense capability, defined as possessing the minimum necessary defense capability for an independent nation so that it would not become a source of instability in the surrounding regions by creating a vacuum of power rather than building a capability directly linked to a military threat to Japan. The defense capability defined in "the Outline" aims to possess the assorted functions required for national defense, while retaining a balanced posture in terms of organization and deployment, including logistical support. This capability was derived from relevant factors such as the strategic environment, geographical characteristics, and other aspects of Japan's position.

It is considered appropriate that Japan continue to adhere fundamentally to this concept of a basic and standard defense capability based on a recognition that various efforts for the stabilization of international relations will continue to be pursued, while there remain uncertainty and unpredictability in the international situation, and that the Japan-U.S. security arrangements will continue to play a key role for the security of Japan and for the peace and stability in the surrounding regions of Japan.

At the same time, in terms of the defense capability which Japan should maintain, it is necessary to review the specific content so as to seek the most efficient and appropriate capability, taking into account the reduction of military force level and changes in military posture of some of Japan's neighboring countries following the end of the Cold War, as well as the diversification of situations that should be addressed from the security point of view, including the outbreak of regional conflicts and the proliferation of weapons of mass destruction. This review also needs to reflect such factors as recent advances in science and technology, a decreasing population of young people and increasingly severe economic and fiscal conditions.

Furthermore, while the principal mission of the Self-Defense Forces continues to be the defense of Japan, the Self-Defense Forces, taking into account changes in domestic and international circumstances and Japan's position in the international society, will also have to be prepared for various situations such as large-scale disasters which can have a significant impact on our highly developed and diversified society, and play an appropriate role in a timely manner in the Government's active efforts to establish a more stable security environment.

From this perspective, it is appropriate that Japan's defense capability be restricted, both in scale and functions, by streamlining, making it more efficient and compact, as well as enhancing necessary functions and making qualitative improvements to be able to effectively respond to a variety of situations and simultaneously ensure the appropriate flexibility to smoothly deal with the development of the changing situations.

(Japan-U.S. security arrangements)
3. The security arrangements with the United States are indispensable to Japan's security and will also continue to play a key role in achieving peace and stability in the surrounding regions of Japan and establishing a more stable security environment.

From this perspective, in order to enhance the credibility of the Japan-U.S. security arrangements and ensure their effective implementation, it is necessary to make efforts (1) to promote exchange of information and policy consultation, (2) to establish an effective posture for cooperation in operational areas including joint studies, exercises and training, as well as enhancement of mutual support in those areas, (3) to enhance broad mutual exchange in the areas of equipment and technology, and (4) to implement various measures to facilitate smooth and effective stationing of U.S. forces in Japan.

Additionally, this close cooperative bilateral relationship based on the Japan-U.S. security arrangements, facilitates Japanese efforts for peace and stability of the international community, including promotion of regional multilateral security dialogues and cooperation, as well as support for various United Nations activities.

(Role of defense capability)
4. It is necessary that the roles of Japan's defense capability be appropriately fulfilled in the respective areas described below in accordance with the aforementioned concepts.

(1) National defense
a. Prevent aggressions against Japan, together with the Japan-U.S. security arrangements, by possessing a defense capability of an appropriate scale which includes the functions required for defense, consistent with Japan's geographical characteristics, taking account of the military capabilities of neighboring countries, by ensuring a posture to fully utilize the capability and by clearly showing the nation's will to defend their own country.
Against the threat of nuclear weapons, rely on the U.S. nuclear deterrent, while working actively on international efforts for realistic and steady nuclear disarmament aiming at a world free from the nuclear weapons.
b. Should indirect aggression - or any unlawful military activity which might lead to aggression against this nation - occur, take immediate responsive action in order to settle the situation at a nearly stage.
Should direct aggression occur, take immediate responsive action by conducting an integrated and systematic operation of its defense capabilities, in appropriate cooperation with the United States, in order to repel such aggression at the earliest possible stage.

(2) Response to large-scale disasters and various other situations

a. In case of large-scale disasters, disasters caused by acts of terrorism or other events which require the protection of lives or assets, and, for example, upon request for assistance from related organizations, take necessary measures in an appropriate and timely manner, including provision of disaster relief, in close cooperation with the related organizations, thereby contributing to public welfare.

b. Should a situation arise in the areas surrounding Japan, which will have an important influence on national peace and security, take appropriate response in accordance with the Constitution and relevant laws and regulations, for example, by properly supporting the United Nations activities when needed, and by ensuring the smooth and effective implementation of the Japan-U.S. security arrangements.

(3) Contribution to creation of a more stable security environment

a. Contribute to efforts for international peace through participation in international peace cooperation activities, and contribute to the promotion of international cooperation through participation in international disaster relief activities.

b. Continue to promote security dialogues and exchanges among defense authorities to enhance mutual confidence with countries, including neighboring countries.

c. Cooperate with efforts of the United Nations and other international organizations in the areas of arms control and disarmament for the purpose of preventing the proliferation of weapons of mass destruction and missiles, as well as controlling and regulating conventional weapons, including land-mines.

IV. Contents of Japan's Defense Capability

As the basis for fulfilling the roles for defense capability outlined in section III, the Ground, Maritime and Air Self-Defense Forces will maintain structures as described in paragraph 1, and assume the postures suggested in paragraphs 2 and 3.

1. Ground, Maritime and Air Self-Defense Force structures

(1) The Ground Self-Defense Force (GSDF)

a. The GSDF, in order to be capable of rapid and effective systematic defense operations from the outset of aggression in any part of Japan, must deploy its divisions and brigades in a balanced manner that conforms to Japan's geographical and other characteristics.

b. The GSDF must possess at least functional one unit of each of the various types of forces used mainly for mobile operations.

c. The GSDF must possess ground-to-air missile units capable of undertaking the air defense of divisions and other units, as well as vital areas.

d. The GSDF, in order to maintain a high level of proficiency and to rapidly counter aggressions and other situations, must, in principle, staff its units with regular Self-Defense Personnel, while, when organizing, some units may be staffed by Self-Defense Force Reserves personnel capable of being quickly mobilized.

(2) Maritime Self-Defense Forces (MSDF)

a. The MSDF must possess one fleet escort force as a mobile operating ship unit in order to quickly respond to aggressive action and such situations at sea. The fleet escort force must be able to maintain at least one escort flotilla on alert at all times.

b. The MSDF must possess, as ship units assigned to coastal surveillance and defense, at least one escort ship division in each specified sea district.

c. The MSDF must maintain submarine units, patrol helicopter and mine-sweeping units, providing the capability for surveillance and defense missions as well as minesweeping at important harbors and straits as necessary.

d. The MSDF must maintain fixed-wing patrol aircraft units to provide a capability for surveillance, patrol and other operations in nearby seas.

(3) Air Self-Defense Force (ASDF)

a. The ASDF must possess aircraft control and warning units capable of vigilance and surveillance throughout Japanese airspace on a continuous basis, as well as performing warning and control functions as necessary.

b. The ASDF must possess fighter units and ground-to-air missile units for air defense to provide the capability of maintaining continuous alert, to take immediate and appropriate steps against violations of Japan's territorial airspace and air incursions.

c. The ASDF must possess units capable of engaging in the inter-diction of airborne or amphibious landing invasions and air support for land forces as necessary.

d. The ASDF must possess units capable of effective operational supports, including air reconnaissance, air transportation and other operations as necessary.

2. Necessary postures to be maintained

In maintaining the following postures, special attention must be paid to achieving joint and integrated operations among each Self-Defense Force through enhancement of the Joint Staff Council's function and promoting integrated cooperative relationships with related organizations so that the Self-Defense Forces can quickly and effectively carry out their missions.

(1) Setup for countering aggressions or similar situations

a. In the case of direct aggression, the Japan's defense structure must be able to respond immediately in accordance with the type and scale of the aggression, and exert its capability effectively by integrating its assorted defense functions and by maintaining and enhancing the credibility of the Japan-U.S. security arrangements through various bilateral studies, joint exercises and training.

b. Japan's defense structure must be capable of responding immediately and taking appropriate actions, should an indirect act of aggression or unlawful military action occur.

c. Japan's defense structure must be capable of taking immediate and appropriate actions to cope with aircraft invading or threatening to invade its territorial airspace.

(2) Setup of disaster-relief operations
Japan's defense structure must be capable of taking timely and appropriate disaster relief activities in any area of Japan in response to large-scale disasters or other situations which require protection of lives and assets.

(3) Setup of international peace cooperation activities and others
The Self-Defense Forces must be capable of participating in inter-national peace cooperation activities and international disaster relief activities in a timely and appropriate manner to contribute to the maintenance of peace and stability in the international community.

(4) Setup of warning, intelligence, and command and communication
Japan's defense structure must be capable of conducting warning and surveillance on a continuous basis to detect any changes in circumstances as soon as possible, so as to utilize this information for quick decision-making. It must be capable of high-level intelligence gathering and analysis, including strategic intelligence, through possession of diversified intelligence-gathering means and mechanisms, and highly able intelligence specialists.

Additionally, it must possess a sophisticated command and communication capability and be able to quickly and effectively conduct integrated defense operations from a joint perspective.

(5) Setup of logistic support
Japan's defense structure must be capable of carrying out necessary functions in each area of logistic support, such as transportation, search and rescue, supply, maintenance and medical and sanitary affairs, so that responses to various situations can be effectively conducted.

(6) Setup of personnel affairs, and education and training
Japan's defense structure must be capable of exerting its full potential as an organization by forming an appropriate personnel structure, maintaining strict discipline, and being composed of individuals with high morale and capability and broad perspective. For training personnel, it is necessary to promote personnel exchange programs within the Self-Defense Forces, as well as with other ministries and the private sector. It must be capable of recruiting, treating, educating and training its personnel in appropriate ways, while paying attention to the smooth execution of international peace cooperation activities.

3. Maintenance of flexible defense capability
As a result of the revision of the scale and functions of Japan's defense capability, Japan's defense structure must possess adequate flexibility, so that smooth response can be

made to changing situations by maintaining in education and training sections, personnel and equipment which require long training or acquisition time periods and by retaining high readiness Self-Defense Force Reservists.

The specific scales of key organizations and equipment are given in the attachment.

V. Points of Note in Upgrading, Maintaining and Operating the Defense Capability

1. The following points should be noted in upgrading, maintaining and operating the defense capabilities in accordance with the outlines described in section IV including the structure of each of the Self Defense Forces. Decisions on major items in annual defense improvement programs will be submitted to the Security Council.

(1) The upgrading, maintenance and operation of Japan's defense capability will be conducted in harmony with other national policies, taking into account, economic, fiscal and other situations. In light of the increasingly tight fiscal situation, special attention will be given to making appropriate budgetary allocations from a medium-and long-term perspective, so that Japan's defense capability can smoothly and thoroughly carry out its functions as a whole.

(2) Necessary steps will be taken to promote the effective maintenance and improvement, as well as the smooth consolidation and reduction of defense facilities, with the close cooperation of relevant local governments, and to facilitate further harmonization with surrounding areas.

(3) Equipment acquisition programs will be effectively implemented with overall consideration of such factors as speedy emergency resupply, easier education and training requirement and cost effectiveness, including future obligatory expenditures accompanying the introduction of equipment, and with special attention on developing a procurement and supply mechanism which helps reduce procurement costs.

Attention will also be given to maintaining defense production and technology foundations through appropriate promotion of domestic productions.

(4) Efforts will be made to enhance technical research and development that contributes to maintaining and improving the qualitative level of Japan's defense capability to keep up with technological advances.

2. If such an important change of situations occurs in the future that it is considered necessary to reexamine Japan's defense capability, another review will be initiated based on the circumstances at that time.

Source: Ministry of Defense,"National Defense Program Outline in and after FY1996." www.mofa. go.jp/policy/security/defense96/index.html (accessed December 20, 2016).

Attachment

GSDF	Authorized personnel		160,000
	Regular		145,000
	Ready reserve		15,000
	Major units	Regionally deployed units in peacetime	8 divisions 6 brigades
		Mobile operation units	1 armored division 1 airborne brigade 1 helicopter brigade
		Ground-to-air guided missile units	8 anti-aircraft artillery groups
	Main equipment	Tanks artillery (Main artillery)[1]	About 900 (About 900/vehicle)
MSDF	Major units	Destroyer units for mobile operations regional district units	4 escort flotillas (Regional units) 7units
		Submarine units	6 divisions
		Minesweeping units	1 minesweeper flotilla
		Patrol aircraft units	(Land-based) 13 squadrons
	Main equipment	Destroyers	About 50 ships
		Submarines	16 ships
		Combat aircraft	About 170 aircraft
ASDF	Major units	Aircraft control & warning units	8 warning groups 20 warning squadrons 1 squadron
		Fighter units Fighter-interceptor units Support fighter units	9 squadrons 3 squadrons
		Air reconnaissance units	1 squadron
		Air transport units	3 squadrons
		Air refueling/transport units	—
		Surface-to-air guided missile units	6 groups
	Main equipment	Combat aircraft (Fighter aircraft)	About 400 aircraft About 300 aircraft
Main equipment & major units which can also be used in ballistic missile defense[2]		Aegis-equipped destroyers	—
		Aircraft control & warning units	—
		Surface-to-air guided missile units	—

Notes: 1. Categorized as main artillery up till 2004 NDPG, but categorized in the 2010 NDPG as artillery except for surface-to-air guided missile units.

2. "Main equipment and major units that can also be used in defense against ballistic missiles" refers to the number of main equipment in the MSDF or number of major units in the ASDF.

Source: Ministry of Defense, "Defense of Japan 2013." www.mod.go.jp/e/publ/w_paper/pdf/2013/25_Part2_Chapter2_Sec1.pdf, p. 4 (accessed December 20, 2016).

Appendix E

The Guidelines for Japan-U.S. Defense Cooperation

September 23, 1997

I. The aim of the guidelines

The aim of these Guidelines is to create a solid basis for more effective and credible U.S.-Japan cooperation under normal circumstances, in case of an armed attack against Japan, and in situations in areas surrounding Japan. The Guidelines also provided a general framework and policy direction for the roles and missions of the two countries and ways of cooperation and coordination, both under normal circumstances and during contingencies.

II. Basic premises and principles

The Guidelines and programs under the Guidelines are consistent with the following basic premises and principles.

> 1. The rights and obligations under the Treaty of Mutual Cooperation and Security between the United States of America and Japan (the U.S.-Japan Security Treaty) and its related arrangements, as well as the fundamental framework of the U.S.-Japan alliance, will remain unchanged.

> 2. Japan will conduct all its actions within the limitations of its Constitution and in accordance with such basic positions as the maintenance of its exclusively defense-oriented policy and its three non-nuclear principles.

> 3. All actions taken by the United States and Japan will be consistent with basic principles of international law, including the peaceful settlement of disputes and sovereign equality, and relevant international agreements such as the Charter of the United Nations.

> 4. The Guidelines and programs under the Guidelines will not obligate either Government to take legislative, budgetary or administrative measures. However, since the objective of the Guidelines and programs under the Guidelines is to establish an effective framework for bilateral cooperation, the two Governments are expected to reflect in an appropriate way the results of these efforts, based on their own judgments, in their specific policies and measures. All actions taken by Japan will be consistent with its laws and regulations then in effect.

III. Cooperation under normal circumstances

Both Governments will firmly maintain existing U.S.-Japan security arrangements. Each Government will make efforts to maintain required defense postures. Japan will possess defense capability within the scope necessary for self-defense on the basis of the "National Defense Program Outline." In order to meet its commitments, the United States will maintain its nuclear deterrent capability, its forward deployed forces in the Asia-Pacific region, and other forces capable of reinforcing those forward deployed forces.

Both Governments, based on their respective policies, under normal circumstances will maintain close cooperation for the defense of Japan as well as for the creation of a more stable international security environment.

Both Governments will under normal circumstances enhance cooperation in a variety of areas. Examples include mutual support activities under the Agreement between the Government of Japan and the Government of the United States of America concerning Reciprocal Provision of Logistic Support, Supplies and Services between the Self-Defense Forces of Japan and the Armed Forces of the United States of America; the Mutual Defense Assistance Agreement between the United States of America and Japan; and their related arrangements.

1. Information sharing and policy consultations
Recognizing that accurate information and sound analysis are at the foundation of security, the two Governments will increase information and intelligence sharing, and the exchange of views on international situations of mutual interest, especially in the Asia-Pacific region. They will also continue close consultations on defense policies and military postures.

Such information sharing and policy consultations will be conducted at as many levels as possible and on the broadest range of subjects. This will be accomplished by taking advantage of all available opportunities, such as SCC and Security Sub-Committee (SSC) meetings.

2. Various types of security cooperation
Bilateral cooperation to promote regional and global activities in the field of security contributes to the creation of a more stable international security environment.

Recognizing the importance and significance of security dialogues and defense exchanges in the region, as well as international arms control and disarmament, the two Governments will promote such activities and cooperate as necessary.

When either or both Governments participate in United Nations peacekeeping operations or international humanitarian relief operations, the two sides will cooperate closely for mutual support as necessary. They will prepare procedures for cooperation in such areas as transportation, medical services, information sharing, and education and training.

When either or both Governments conduct emergency relief operations in response to requests from governments concerned or international organizations in the wake of large-scale disasters, they will cooperate closely with each other as necessary.

3. Bilateral programs
Both Governments will conduct bilateral work, including bilateral defense planning in case of an armed attack against Japan, and mutual cooperation planning in situations in areas surrounding Japan. Such efforts will be made in a compre-

hensive mechanism involving relevant agencies of the respective Governments, and establish the foundation for bilateral cooperation.

Bilateral exercises and training will be enhanced in order not only to validate such bilateral work but also to enable smooth and effective responses by public and private entities of both countries, starting with U.S. Forces and the Self-Defense Forces. The two Governments will under normal circumstances establish a bilateral coordination mechanism involving relevant agencies to be operated during contingencies.

IV. Actions in response to an armed attack against Japan

Bilateral actions in response to an armed attack against Japan remain a core aspect of U.S.-Japan defense cooperation. When an armed attack against Japan is imminent, the two Governments will take steps to prevent further deterioration of the situation and make preparations necessary for the defense of Japan. When an armed attack against Japan takes place, the two Governments will conduct appropriate bilateral actions to repel it at the earliest possible stage.

1. When an armed attack against Japan is imminent
The two Governments will intensify information and intelligence sharing and policy consultations, and initiate at an early stage the operation of a bilateral coordination mechanism. Cooperating as appropriate, they will make preparations necessary for ensuring coordinated responses according to the readiness stage selected by mutual agreement. Japan will establish and maintain the basis for U.S. reinforcements. As circumstances change, the two Governments will also increase intelligence gathering and surveillance, and will prepare to respond to activities which could develop into an armed attack against Japan.

The two Governments will make every effort, including diplomatic efforts, to prevent further deterioration of the situation.

Recognizing that a situation in areas surrounding Japan may develop into an armed attack against Japan, the two Governments will be mindful of the close interrelationship of the two requirements: preparations for the defense of Japan and responses to or preparations for situations in areas surrounding Japan.

2. When an armed attack against Japan takes place

(1) Principles for coordinated bilateral actions
a. Japan will have primary responsibility immediately to take action and to repel an armed attack against Japan as soon as possible. The United States will provide appropriate support to Japan. Such bilateral cooperation may vary according to the scale, type, phase, and other factors of the armed attack. This cooperation may include preparations for and execution of coordinated bilateral operations, steps to prevent further deterioration of the situation, surveillance, and intelligence sharing.
b. In conducting bilateral operations, U.S. Forces and the Self-Defense Forces will employ their respective defense capabilities in a coordinat-

ed, timely, and effective manner. In doing this, they will conduct effective joint operations of their respective Forces' ground, maritime and air services. The Self-Defense Forces will primarily conduct defensive operations in Japanese territory and its surrounding waters and airspace, while U.S. Forces support Self-Defense Forces' operations. U.S. Forces will also conduct operations to supplement the capabilities of the Self-Defense Forces.

c. The United States will introduce reinforcements in a timely manner, and Japan will establish and maintain the basis to facilitate these deployments.

(2) Concept of operations

a. Operations to Counter Air Attack against Japan

U.S. Forces and the Self-Defense Forces will bilaterally conduct operations to counter air attack against Japan. The Self-Defense Forces will have primary responsibility for conducting operations for air defense. U.S. Forces will support Self-Defense Forces' operations and conduct operations, including those which may involve the use of strike power, to supplement the capabilities of the Self-Defense Forces.

b. Operations to Defend Surrounding Waters and to Protect Sea Lines of Communication

U.S. Forces and the Self-Defense Forces will bilaterally conduct operations for the defense of surrounding waters and for the protection of sea lines of communication.

The Self-Defense Forces will have primary responsibility for the protection of major ports and straits in Japan, for the protection of ships in surrounding waters, and for other operations.

U.S. Forces will support Self-Defense Forces' operations and conduct operations, including those which may provide additional mobility and strike power, to supplement the capabilities of the Self-Defense Forces.

c. Operations to Counter Airborne and Seaborne Invasions of Japan

U.S. Forces and the Self-Defense Forces will bilaterally conduct operations to counter airborne and seaborne invasions of Japan.

The Self-Defense Forces will have primary responsibility for conducting operations to check and repel such invasions.

U.S. Forces will primarily conduct operations to supplement the capabilities of the Self-Defense Forces. The United States will introduce reinforcements at the earliest possible stage, according to the scale, type, and other factors of the invasion, and will support Self-Defense Forces' operations.

d. Responses to other threats

i. The Self-Defense Forces will have primary responsibility to check and repel guerrilla-commando type attacks or any other unconventional attacks involving military infiltration in Japanese territory at the earliest possible stage. They will cooperate and coordinate closely with relevant agencies, and will be supported

271

in appropriate ways by U.S. Forces depending on the situation.
ii. U.S. Forces and the Self-Defense Forces will cooperate and co-ordinate closely to respond to a ballistic missile attack. U.S. Forces will provide Japan with necessary intelligence, and consider, as necessary, the use of forces providing additional strike power.

(3) Activities and requirements for operations
  a. Command and coordination
U.S. Forces and the Self-Defense Forces, in close cooperation, will take action through their respective command-and-control channels. To conduct effective bilateral operations, the two Forces will establish, in advance, procedures which include those to determine the division of roles and missions and to synchronize their operations.
  b. Bilateral coordination mechanism
Necessary coordination among the relevant agencies of the two countries will be conducted through a bilateral coordination mechanism. In order to conduct effective bilateral operations, U.S. Forces and the Self-Defense Forces will closely coordinate operations, intelligence activities, and logistics support through this coordination mechanism including use of a bilateral coordination center.
  c. Communications and electronics
The two Governments will provide mutual support to ensure effective use of communications and electronics capabilities.
  d. Intelligence activities
The two Governments will cooperate in intelligence activities in order to ensure effective bilateral operations. This will include coordination of requirements, collection, production, and dissemination of intelligence products. Each Government will be responsible for the security of shared intelligence.
  e. Logistics support activities U.S. Forces and the Self-Defense Forces will conduct logistics support activities efficiently and properly in accordance with appropriate bilateral arrangements. To improve the effectiveness of logistics and to alleviate functional shortfalls, the two Governments will undertake mutual support activities, making appropriate use of authorities and assets of central and local government agencies, as well as private sector assets. Particular attention will be paid to the following points in conducting such activities:
    i. Supply
The United States will support the acquisition of supplies for systems of U.S. origin while Japan will support the acquisition of supplies in Japan.
    ii. Transportation
The two Governments will closely cooperate in transportation operations, including airlift and sealift of supplies from the United States to Japan.
    iii. Maintenance
Japan will support the maintenance of U.S. Forces' equipment in

Japan; the United States will support the maintenance of items of U.S. origin which are beyond Japanese maintenance capabilities. Maintenance support will include the technical training of maintenance personnel as required. Japan will also support U.S. Forces' requirement for salvage and recovery.
iv. Facilities
Japan will, in case of need, provide additional facilities and areas in accordance with the U.S.-Japan Security Treaty and its related arrangements. If necessary for effective and efficient operations, U.S. Forces and the Self-Defense Forces will make joint use of Self-Defense Forces facilities and U.S. facilities and areas in accordance with the Treaty and its related arrangements.
v. Medical services
The two Governments will support each other in the area of medical services such as medical treatment and transportation of casualties.

V. Cooperation in situations in areas surrounding Japan that will have an important influence on Japan's peace and security (situations in areas surrounding Japan)

Situations in areas surrounding Japan will have an important influence on Japan's peace and security. The concept, situations in areas surrounding Japan, is not geographic but situational. The two Governments will make every effort, including diplomatic efforts, to prevent such situations from occurring. When the two Governments reach a common assessment of the state of each situation, they will effectively coordinate their activities. In responding to such situations, measures taken may differ depending on circumstances.

1. When a situation in areas surrounding Japan is anticipated
When a situation in areas surrounding Japan is anticipated, the two Governments will intensify information and intelligence sharing and policy consultations, including efforts to reach a common assessment of the situation.
    At the same time, they will make every effort, including diplomatic efforts, to prevent further deterioration of the situation, while initiating at an early stage the operation of a bilateral coordination mechanism, including use of a bilateral coordination center. Cooperating as appropriate, they will make preparations necessary for ensuring coordinated responses according to the readiness stage selected by mutual agreement. As circumstances change, they will also increase intelligence gathering and surveillance, and enhance their readiness to respond to the circumstances.

2. Responses to situations in areas surrounding Japan
The two Governments will take appropriate measures, to include preventing further deterioration of situations, in response to situations in areas surrounding Japan. This will be done in accordance with the basic premises and principles listed in Section II above and based on their respective decisions. They will support each other as necessary in accordance with appropriate arrangements.
    Functions and fields of cooperation and examples of items of cooperation

are outlined below, and listed in the Annex.

(1) Cooperation in activities initiated by either government
Although either Government may conduct the following activities at its own discretion, bilateral cooperation will enhance their effectiveness.
    a. Relief activities and measures to deal with refugees
Each Government will conduct relief activities with the consent and cooperation of the authorities in the affected area. The two Governments will cooperate as necessary, taking into account their respective capabilities.
    The two Governments will cooperate in dealing with refugees as necessary. When there is a flow of refugees into Japanese territory, Japan will decide how to respond and will have primary responsibility for dealing with the flow; the United States will provide appropriate support.
    b. Search and rescue
The two Governments will cooperate in search and rescue operations. Japan will conduct search and rescue operations in Japanese territory; and at sea around Japan, as distinguished from areas where combat operations are being conducted. When U.S. Forces are conducting operations, the United States will conduct search and rescue operations in and near the operational areas.
    c. Noncombatant evacuation operations
When the need arises for U.S. and Japanese noncombatants to be evacuated from a third country to a safe haven, each Government is responsible for evacuating its own nationals as well as for dealing with the authorities of the affected area. In instances in which each decides it is appropriate, the two Governments will coordinate in planning and cooperate in carrying out their evacuations, including for the securing of transportation means, transportation and the use of facilities, using their respective capabilities in a mutually supplementary manner. If similar need arises for noncombatants other than of U.S. or Japanese nationality, the respective countries may consider extending, on their respective terms, evacuation assistance to third country nationals.
    d. Activities for ensuring the effectiveness of economic sanctions for the maintenance of international peace and stability
Each Government will contribute to activities for ensuring the effectiveness of economic sanctions for the maintenance of international peace and stability. Such contributions will be made in accordance with each Government's own criteria.
    Additionally, the two Governments will cooperate with each other as appropriate, taking into account their respective capabilities. Such cooperation includes information sharing, and cooperation in inspection of ships based on United Nations Security Council resolutions.

(2) Japan's support for U.S. Forces activities
    a. Use of facilities

Based on the U.S.-Japan Security Treaty and its related arrangements, Japan will, in case of need, provide additional facilities and areas in a timely and appropriate manner, and ensure the temporary use by U.S. Forces of Self-Defense Forces facilities and civilian airports and ports.

b. Rear area support

Japan will provide rear area support to those U.S. Forces that are conducting operations for the purpose of achieving the objectives of the U.S.-Japan Security Treaty. The primary aim of this rear area support is to enable U.S. Forces to use facilities and conduct operations in an effective manner. By its very nature, Japan's rear area support will be provided primarily in Japanese territory. It may also be provided on the high seas and international airspace around Japan which are distinguished from areas where combat operations are being conducted.

In providing rear area support, Japan will make appropriate use of authorities and assets of central and local government agencies, as well as private sector assets. The Self-Defense Forces, as appropriate, will provide such support consistent with their mission for the defense of Japan and the maintenance of public order.

(3) U.S.-Japan operational cooperation

As situations in areas surrounding Japan have an important influence on Japan's peace and security, the Self-Defense Forces will conduct such activities as intelligence gathering, surveillance and minesweeping, to protect lives and property and to ensure navigational safety. U.S. Forces will conduct operations to restore the peace and security affected by situations in areas surrounding Japan.

With the involvement of relevant agencies, cooperation and coordination will significantly enhance the effectiveness of both Forces' activities.

VI. Bilateral programs for effective defense cooperation under the guidelines

Effective bilateral cooperation under the Guidelines will require the United States and Japan to conduct consultative dialogue throughout the spectrum of security conditions: normal circumstances, an armed attack against Japan, and situations in areas surrounding Japan. Both sides must be well informed and coordinate at multiple levels to ensure successful bilateral defense cooperation. To accomplish this, the two Governments will strengthen their information and intelligence sharing and policy consultations by taking advantage of all available opportunities, including SCC and SSC meetings, and they will establish the following two mechanisms to facilitate consultations, coordinate policies, and coordinate operational functions.

First, the two Governments will develop a comprehensive mechanism for bilateral planning and the establishment of common standards and procedures, involving not only U.S. Forces and the Self-Defense Forces but also other relevant agencies of their respective Governments.

The two Governments will, as necessary, improve this comprehensive mechanism. The SCC will continue to play an important role for presenting policy direction to the work to be conducted by this mechanism. The SCC will be responsible for presenting directions, validating the progress of work, and issuing directives as necessary. The SDC will assist the SCC in bilateral work.

Second, the two Governments will also establish, under normal circumstances, a bilateral coordination mechanism that will include relevant agencies of the two countries for coordinating respective activities during contingencies.

1. Bilateral work for planning and the establishment of common standards and procedures
Bilateral work listed below will be conducted in a comprehensive mechanism involving relevant agencies of the respective Governments in a deliberate and efficient manner. Progress and results of such work will be reported at significant milestones to the SCC and the SDC.

(1) Bilateral defense planning and mutual cooperation planning
U.S. Forces and the Self-Defense Forces will conduct bilateral defense planning under normal circumstances to take coordinated actions smoothly and effectively in case of an armed attack against Japan. The two Governments will conduct mutual cooperation planning under normal circumstances to be able to respond smoothly and effectively to situations in areas surrounding Japan.

Bilateral defense planning and mutual cooperation planning will assume various possible situations, with the expectation that results of these efforts will be appropriately reflected in the plans of the two Governments. The two Governments will coordinate and adjust their plans in light of actual circumstances. The two Governments will be mindful that bilateral defense planning and mutual cooperation planning must be consistent so that appropriate responses will be ensured when a situation in areas surrounding Japan threatens to develop into an armed attack against Japan or when such a situation and an armed attack against Japan occur simultaneously.

(2) Establishment of common standards for preparations
The two Governments will establish under normal circumstances common standards for preparations for the defense of Japan. These standards will address such matters as intelligence activities, unit activities, movements and logistics support in each readiness stage. When an armed attack against Japan is imminent, both Governments will agree to select a common readiness stage that will be reflected in the level of preparations for the defense of Japan by U.S. Forces, the Self-Defense Forces and other relevant agencies.

The two Governments will similarly establish common standards for preparations of cooperative measures in situations in areas surrounding Japan so that they may select a common readiness stage by mutual agreement.

(3) Establishment of common procedures
The two Governments will prepare in advance common procedures to ensure smooth and effective execution of coordinated U.S. Forces and Self-Defense Forces operations for the defense of Japan. These will include procedures for communications, transmission of target information, intelligence activi-

ties and logistics support, and prevention of fratricide. Common procedures will also include criteria for properly controlling respective unit operations. The two Forces will take into account the importance of communications and electronics interoperability, and will determine in advance their mutual requirements.

2. Bilateral coordination mechanism

The two Governments will establish under normal circumstances a bilateral coordination mechanism involving relevant agencies of the two countries to coordinate respective activities in case of an armed attack against Japan and in situations in areas surrounding Japan.

Procedures for coordination will vary depending upon items to be coordinated and agencies to be involved. They may include coordination committee meetings, mutual dispatch of liaison officers, and designation of points of contacts. As part of such a bilateral coordination mechanism, U.S. Forces and the Self-Defense Forces will prepare under normal circumstances a bilateral coordination center with the necessary hardware and software in order to coordinate their respective activities.

VII. Timely and appropriate review of the guidelines

The two Governments will review the Guidelines in a timely and appropriate manner when changes in situations relevant to the U.S.-Japan security relationship occur and if deemed necessary in view of the circumstances at that time.

Annex

Functions and fields and examples of items of cooperation in situations in areas surrounding Japan

Functions and Fields		Examples of Items of Cooperation
Cooperation in activities initiated by either Government	Relief activities and measures to deal with refugees	- Transportation of personnel and supplies to the affected area - Medical services, communications and transportation in the affected area - Relief and transfer operations for refugees, and provision of emergency materials to refugees
	Search and rescue	- Search and rescue operations in Japanese territory and at sea around Japan and information sharing related to such operations
	Noncombatant evacuation operations	- Information sharing, and communication with and assembly and transportation of noncombatants - Use of Self-Defense Forces facilities and civilian airports and ports by U.S. aircraft and vessels for transportation of noncombatants - Customs, immigration and quarantine of noncombatants upon entry into Japan - Assistance to noncombatants in such matters as temporary accommodations, transportation and medical services in Japan
	Activities for ensuring the effectiveness of economic sanctions for the maintenance of international peace and stability	- Inspection of ships based on United Nations Security Council resolutions for ensuring the effectiveness of economic sanctions and activities related to such inspections - Information sharing

Source: Ministry of Defense, "The Guidelines for Japan-U.S. Defense Cooperation (September 23, 1997)." www.mod.go.jp/e/d_act/anpo/19970923.html (accessed December 20, 2016).

Functions and Fields			Examples of Items of Cooperation
Japan's support for U.S. Forces activities	Use of facilities		- Use of Self-Defense Forces facilities and civilian airports and ports for supplies and other purposes by U.S. aircraft and vessels - Reservation of spaces for loading/unloading of personnel and materials by the United States and of storage areas at Self-Defense Forces facilities and civilian airports and ports - Extension of operating hours for Self-Defense Forces facilities and civilian airports and ports for the use by U.S. aircraft and vessels - Use of Self-Defense Forces airfields by U.S. aircraft - Provision of training and exercise areas - Construction of offices, accommodations, etc., inside U.S. facilities and areas
	Rear area support	Supply	- Provision of materials (except weapons and ammunition) and POL (petroleum, oil and lubricants) to U.S. aircraft and vessels at Self-Defense Forces facilities and civilian airports and ports
			- Provision of materials (except weapons and ammunition) and POL to U.S. facilities and areas
		Transportation	- Land, sea and air transportation inside Japan of personnel, materials and POL
			- Sea transportation to U.S. vessels on the high seas of personnel, materials and POL
			- Use of vehicles and cranes for transportation of personnel, materials and POL
		Maintenance	- Repair and maintenance of U.S. aircraft, vessels and vehicles
			- Provision of repair parts
			- Temporary provision of tools and materials for maintenance
		Medical services	- Medical treatment of casualties inside Japan - Transportation of casualties inside Japan - Provision of medical supply
		Security	- Security of U.S. facilities and areas - Seas surveillance around U.S. facilities and areas - Security of transportation routes inside Japan - Information and intelligence sharing
		Communications	- Provision of frequencies (including for satellite communications) and equipment for communications among relevant U.S. and Japanese agencies
		Others	- Support for port entry/exit by U.S. vessels - Loading/unloading of materials at Self-Defense Forces facilities and civilian airports and ports - Sewage disposal, water supply, and electricity inside U.S. facilities and areas - Temporary increase of workers at U.S. facilities and areas
U.S.-Japan operational cooperation	Surveillance		- Intelligence sharing
	Minesweeping		- Minesweeping operations in Japanese territory and on the high seas around Japan, and information and intelligence sharing on mines
	Sea and airspace management		- Maritime traffic coordination in and around Japan in response to increased sea traffic - Air traffic control and airspace management in and around Japan

Appendix F

National Defense Program Guidelines, FY2005–

Approved by the Security Council and
the Cabinet on December 10, 2004

I. Purpose

In order to ensure the peace and safety of Japan and peace and stability of the international community, given the current security environment surrounding our country, the Security Council and Cabinet of the Government of Japan approved the "National Defense Program Guidelines, FY2005–." The Guidelines build on the December 19, 2003 Security Council and Cabinet decision, "On Introduction of Ballistic Missile Defense System and Other Measures."

II. Security Environment Surrounding Japan

1. The 9-11 terrorist attacks on the United States demonstrated that, in addition to such traditional problems as inter-state military confrontations, non-state actors such as international terrorist organizations have emerged as a dire threat in today's security environment.

    Against a backdrop of increased interdependence and growing globalization, the international community is facing urgent new threats and diverse situations to peace and security, including the proliferation of weapons of mass destruction and ballistic missiles, as well as international terrorist activities (hereinafter "new threats and diverse situations"). We need to bear in mind that conventional forms of deterrence may no longer work effectively against international terrorist organizations, which have neither states nor citizens to protect.

    Ten years have passed since the end of the Cold War. Mutual cooperation and interdependence among major countries have deepened, as exemplified by the growing trust between the United States and the Russian Federation. Since a stable international environment serves the interests of all nations, greater efforts at international coordination and cooperation on security issues have taken root in the international community, including those within the framework of international organizations such as the United Nations.

    In this context, the United States, as the sole superpower, continues to contribute significantly to international peace and stability by taking active measures to combat terrorism and to prevent proliferation of weapons of mass destruction.

    In the meantime, the use of military force now plays a broader role in the international community than simply deterring or responding to armed conflict: Military force is also used for a variety of purposes, including the prevention of conflict and the reconstruction assistance.

2. As a result of the further expansion and deepening of interdependence among the nations in recent years, greater efforts are also being made to promote and strengthen bilateral and multilateral coordination and cooperation in the Asia-Pacific region. How-

ever, although Russia has drastically reduced its armed forces in the Far East since the end of the Cold War, massive military might, including nuclear arsenals, continue to exist in the region, and a number of countries are pouring in efforts to modernize their military forces. The situation on the Korean Peninsula is unpredictable and cross-Taiwan Strait relations remain uncertain.

North Korea is engaged in the development, deployment and proliferation of weapons of mass destruction and ballistic missiles, and it maintains a large number of special operations forces. Such military activities by North Korea constitute a major destabilizing factor to regional and international security, and are a serious challenge to international non-proliferation efforts.

China, which has a major impact on regional security, continues to modernize its nuclear forces and missile capabilities as well as its naval and air forces. China is also expanding its area of operation at sea. We will have to remain attentive to its future actions.

The close and cooperative relationship between Japan and the United States, based on the Japan-U.S. Security Arrangements, continues to play an important role for the security of Japan as well as for peace and stability in the Asia-Pacific region.

3. In light of the security environment surrounding our country, as outlined above, even though a full-scale invasion against Japan is increasingly unlikely, Japan must now deal with new threats and diverse situations in addition to regional security issues.

4. In considering Japan's security, we have to take into account vulnerabilities resulting from: limited strategic depth; long coast lines and numerous small islands; a high population density; the concentration of population and industry in urban areas; and a large number of important facilities in coastal areas, in addition to frequent natural disasters due to Japan's geological and climatic conditions, and the security of sea lines of communication which are indispensable to the country's prosperity and growth.

III. Basic Principles of Japan's Security Policy

1. Basic Principles
The first objective of Japan's security policy is to prevent any threat from reaching Japan and, in the event that it does, repel it and minimize any damage. The second objective is to improve the international security environment so as to reduce the chances that any threat will reach Japan in the first place. Japan will achieve these objectives by both its own efforts as well as cooperative efforts with the United States, Japan's alliance partner, and with the international community.

To this end, Japan will: support United Nations activities for international peace and security; make diplomatic efforts to promote cooperative relationships with other countries; further develop its close cooperative relationship with the United States, based on the Japan-U.S. Security Arrangements; establish a basis for national security by preserving domestic political stability; and, develop efficient defense forces.

Based on the Constitution of Japan, and the ideas of maintaining the exclusively defensive defense policy by not becoming a military power that might pose a threat to other countries, Japan will continue to uphold the fundamental principles of developing modest defense forces of its own under civilian control and will continue to adhere to the three non-nuclear principles.

To protect its territory and people against the threat of nuclear weapons, Japan will continue to rely on the U.S. nuclear deterrent. At the same time, Japan will play an active role in creating a world free of nuclear weapons by taking realistic step-by-step measures for nuclear disarmament and non-proliferation. Japan also will play an active role in international disarmament and non-proliferation efforts regarding other types of weapons of mass destruction and their delivery means, such as missiles.

2. Japan's Own Efforts

(1) Basic Ideas

Based on the premise that any country's security depends first and foremost on its own efforts, Japan will utilize all appropriate means to prevent any threat from reaching the country. In addition, based on the principle of acting closely with the international community and its alliance partner—the United States—Japan will engage in diplomatic and other activities to improve the international security environment so as to prevent the emergence of any new threats.

(2) Japan's Integrated Response

In the event that these efforts fail to prevent a threat from reaching Japan, the Government of Japan will take an integrated response by swiftly making appropriate decisions through mechanisms such as the Security Council, and bringing together all relevant organizations. To this end, the Government will improve its ability to collect and analyze information which serves as the basis of the Government's decision-making. The Self-Defense Forces, police, Japan Coast Guard and other relevant organizations will improve their close cooperation through increased intelligence sharing, joint exercises, and other activities, while appropriately sharing their roles, and improve their overall performances. In addition, the Government will establish national protection systems including those for responding to different types of disasters, by quickly issuing warning signals and promoting mutual cooperation between the central and local governments.

(3) Japan's Defense Forces

Japan's defense forces are the ultimate guarantee of its national security, representing Japan's will and ability to repel any threat that might reach its shores.

Japan has developed its defense forces in accordance with the "National Defense Program Guidelines, FY 1996-" (The Security Council and Cabinet decision on November 28, 1995) which incorporated the key elements of the Basic Defense Force Concept. The Basic Defense Force Concept espouses the idea that, rather than preparing to directly counter a military threat, Japan, as an independent state, should maintain the minimum necessary basic defense forces lest it becomes a destabilizing factor in the region by creating a power vacuum. Combined with the Japan-U.S. Security Arrangements, this concept has been successful in preventing an armed invasion from occurring.

Given the new security environment, however, future defense forces should be capable of effectively responding to new threats and diverse situations while maintaining those elements of the Basic Defense Force Concept that remain valid.

Because the peace and stability of Japan is inextricably linked to that of the international community, Japan should voluntarily and actively participate in activities that nations of the world cooperatively undertake to enhance the international security environment (hereinafter "international peace cooperation activities").

In developing Japan's defense forces, we have to take into account the fact that while the roles that our defense forces have to play are multiplying, the number of young people in Japan is declining as a result of the low birth rate, and fiscal conditions continue to deteriorate.

From this standpoint, Japan will develop multi-functional, flexible, and effective defense forces that are highly ready, mobile, adaptable and multi-purpose, and are equipped with state-of-the-art technologies and intelligence capabilities measuring up to the military-technological level of other major countries.

In building such a defense force, without expanding its size, the Government of Japan will rationalize and streamline personnel, equipment, and operations so as to attain greater results with the limited resources that are available.

3. Japan-U.S. Security Arrangements

The Japan-U.S. Security Arrangements are indispensable in ensuring Japan's security. In addition, the U.S. military presence is critically important to peace and stability in the Asia-Pacific region, where unpredictability and uncertainty continue to persist.

Close cooperative relations between Japan and the United States, based on the Japan-U.S. Security Arrangements, play an important role in facilitating international efforts to prevent or to respond to new threats and diverse situations, such as terrorism and ballistic missiles attacks.

Japan will proactively engage in strategic dialogue with the United States on wide-ranging security issues such as role-sharing between the two countries and U.S. military posture, including the structure of U.S. forces in Japan, while working to harmonize our perceptions of the new security environment and appropriate strategic objectives.

In doing so, the Government of Japan will bear in mind the need to reduce the excessive burden that the existence of U.S. military bases and facilities places on local communities, while maintaining the deterrent that the U.S. military presence in Japan provides.

In addition, Japan will continue to strengthen the Japan-U.S. Security Arrangements by actively promoting such measures as: intelligence exchange; operational cooperation, including in "situations in areas surrounding Japan"; cooperation on ballistic missile defense; equipment and technology exchange; and, efforts to make the stationing of U.S. forces in Japan smoother and more efficient.

4. Cooperation with the International Community

In order to improve the international security environment and help maintain security and prosperity of Japan, the Government of Japan will actively engage in diplomatic efforts, including the strategic use of Official Development Assistance (ODA).

Based on the recognition that the destabilization of the international community by events such as regional conflicts, proliferation of weapons of mass destruction, and international terrorist attacks would directly affect its own peace and security, Japan will, on its own initiative, actively participate in international peace cooperation activities as an integral part of its diplomatic efforts.

In particular, stability in the region spreading from the Middle East to East Asia is critical to Japan. Japan traditionally has close economic ties with this region, its sea lines of communication run through the region, and Japan depends almost entirely on energy and natural resources from overseas. In this context, Japan will strive to stabilize the region by promoting various cooperative efforts in conjunction with other countries sharing common security challenges.

In order to enable the international community to effectively address the range of new issues in the twenty-first century, measures must be taken to reform the world's only global and comprehensive international organization—the United Nations—to make it more effective and reliable. Japan will actively pursue this goal.

In the Asia-Pacific region, multilateral frameworks for regional security, such as the ASEAN Regional Forum (ARF), as well as multilateral efforts to deal with common agendas such as counter-terrorism and counter-piracy are taking root. By continuing to support these positive developments, Japan will continue to play an appropriate role, together with the cooperation with the United States, to promote a stable security environment in the region.

IV. Future Defense Forces

1. Role of the Defense Forces
Based on the recognition described above, Japan will develop and maintain, in an efficient manner, the necessary Self-Defense Forces posture to effectively carry out missions in the following areas:

(1) Effective Response to the New Threats and Diverse Situations
Japan will deal effectively with the new threats and diverse situations by developing highly responsive and mobile defense force units capable of responding properly to various different situations and by deploying them appropriately in accordance with Japan's geographical characteristics. Should such a situation emerges, the defense forces will respond quickly and appropriately in smooth and close collaboration with the police and other relevant organizations, thereby providing a seamless response to the situation in accordance with circumstances and designated roles.

Japan's Self-Defense Forces posture to address the key elements of the new threats and diverse situations will be as follows:

a. Response to ballistic missile attacks
We will respond to ballistic missile attacks by establishing necessary defense force structure, including the introduction of ballistic missile defense systems, to deal effectively with ballistic missile attacks. We will adequately respond to the threat of nuclear weapons by doing so, in addition to relying on U.S. nuclear deterrence.

b. Response to guerrillas and special operations forces attacks
We will maintain necessary defense force structure to respond effectively to attacks carried out by guerrillas and special operations forces. We will also enhance readiness and mobility of the defense force units, and deal with such attacks in a flexible manner.

c. Response to the invasion of Japan's offshore islands
We will maintain necessary defense force structure to respond effectively to the invasion of Japan's offshore islands, improve and strengthen capabilities to transport and deploy forces, and deal with the invasion in a flexible manner.
d. Patrol and surveillance in the sea and airspace surrounding Japan, and response to the violation of Japan's airspace and the intrusion of armed special-purpose ships and other similar vessels
We will maintain necessary defense force structure, including ships, aircraft and other assets, to carry out around-the-clock patrol and surveillance in the sea and airspace surrounding Japan. We will also maintain fighter aircraft units to respond instantly to the violation of our territorial airspace, as well as combatant ships and other assets in order to respond to armed special-purpose ships operating in waters surrounding Japan, submerged foreign submarines operating in Japan's territorial waters, and other similar vessels.
e. Response to large-scale and/or special-type (nuclear, biological, chemical, and radiological) disasters
To deal effectively with large-scale and/or special-type (nuclear, biological, chemical, and radiological) disasters, where protection of life and property is desperately needed, we will maintain an adequate force structure with defense force units, as well as specialized capabilities and expertise to conduct disaster relief operations in any part of Japan.

(2) Preparations to Deal with Full-Scale Invasion
Since in our judgment, the likelihood of full-scale invasion of Japan has declined and is expected to remain modest in the foreseeable future, we will modify our current defense force building concept that emphasized Cold War-type anti-tank warfare, anti-submarine warfare and anti-air warfare, and will significantly reduce the personnel and equipment earmarked for a full-scale invasion. However, because the original role of our defense forces is to cope with full-scale invasion and reconstructing these forces cannot be accomplished in a short period of time, Japan will continue to maintain the most basic capabilities of its defense forces, while also taking into account developments in neighboring countries and making use of technological progress.

(3) Proactive Efforts to Improve the International Security Environment
In order to engage actively in international peace cooperation activities, we will take the following measures: develop education and training systems, highly responsive force posture for relevant units, and transport and other required capabilities; establish necessary infrastructure to quickly dispatch defense force units overseas and to carry out missions continuously; and, make necessary arrangements to include the promotion of international peace cooperation activities in the Self-Defense Forces mission priorities.
We will strongly promote activities for international peace and stability, including security dialogue and defense exchanges, bilateral and multilateral training and exercises, and arms control and disarmament efforts carried out by

international organizations such as the United Nations.

2. Critical Elements of Our Defense Capabilities
Following are the critical elements for developing defense forces capable of carrying out the missions described above.

(1) Enhancing Joint Operation Capabilities
In order to have three services of the Self-Defense Forces work integrally and to enable them to execute their missions swiftly and effectively, we will employ them jointly whenever possible. We will create a central organization to facilitate joint operations, and establish infrastructure for training and education as well as intelligence and communications. In doing so, we will reexamine existing organizations so as to enhance their efficiency.

(2) Strengthening Intelligence Capabilities
In order to employ our defense forces successfully to respond effectively to the new threats and diverse situations, it is imperative for the Government to be able to identify events at the earliest possible time and to collect, analyze, and share intelligence promptly and accurately. For this purpose, we will strengthen our diversified intelligence collection capability and enhance our comprehensive analysis and assessment capability, keeping in mind the changes in the security environment and technological trends. We will also strengthen the Self-Defense Forces' intelligence structure, including the Defense Intelligence Headquarters, that supports our capabilities. In this way, we will build a sophisticated intelligence capability.

(3) Incorporating the Progress in Science and Technology into Our Defense Forces
We will incorporate the outcome of science and technological progress, in such areas as information and communications technologies, into our defense forces. In particular, we will develop the command and control systems and agile intelligence sharing systems that are indispensable for joint operations, in tune with information and communication technologies available at home and overseas. In addition, we will create advanced systems for command and communications and a network for information and communications, with sufficient protection against possible cyberattacks, to enhance operational and organizational efficiency.

(4) Utilizing Human Resources More Efficiently
We will take various measures to maintain high morale and firm discipline within the Self-Defense Forces. We will recruit, cultivate, train and educate high quality personnel to meet the challenge of the diversification and internationalization of Self-Defense Forces missions, and the need to properly operate rapidly advancing high-tech equipment. In addition, we will promote activities related to research and education on security issue, and develop human resources.
　　The defense force level required to fulfill missions described above is indicated in the attached table.

V. Additional Elements for Consideration

1. In developing, maintaining, and operating the defense forces as described in section IV, the following elements will be taken into consideration.

(1) Mindful of increasingly severe fiscal conditions, we will restrict defense expenditures by further rationalizing and streamlining defense forces. We will also work to make our defense forces successful in carrying out their missions by harmonizing their operations with other measures taken by the Government.

(2) We will make procurement and research and development (R&D) more effective and efficient by taking the following measures: curbing life-cycle cost, including purchase price, of defense equipment; actively using cutting-edge technologies developed by private enterprises, universities, and governmental organizations in carrying out R&D as well as by allocating R&D resource in a more focused manner; and, appropriately and timely reviewing various R&D projects. At the same time, we will work to establish defense production and technological base, especially in core technological areas indispensable for our national security.

(3) In order to efficiently develop and maintain defense-related facilities, the Government of Japan will, in close cooperation with relevant local authorities, take various measures to make those facilities coexist more harmoniously with local communities.

2. These National Defense Program Guidelines provide the vision for our defense forces for the next decade. However, five years from now or in case there is a significant change in the international situation, we will review and, if necessary, revise the Guidelines in light of the security environment, technological progress, and other relevant factors at the time.

Attached Table

The following posture will be established in order to make Japan's new defense forces multi-functional, flexible and effective, and able to undertake diverse roles as discussed above (IV).

	Personnel		155,000
	Regular		148,000
	Reserve (Ready reserve personnel)		7,000
Ground Self-Defense Force	Major units	Regionally deployed units	8 divisions
			6 brigades
		Mobile operation units	1 armored division
			Central Readiness Group
		Surface-to-air guided missile units	8 anti-aircraft artillery groups
	Major equipment	Tanks	approx. 600
		Main artillery	approx. 600
Maritime Self-Defense Force	Major units	Destroyer units (for mobile operations)	4 flotillas (8 divisions)
		Destroyer units (regional district units)	5 divisions
		Submarine units	4 divisions
		Minesweeper unit	1 flotilla
		Patrol aircraft units	9 squadrons
	Major equipment	Destroyers	47
		Submarines	16
		Combat aircraft	approx. 150
Air Self-Defense Force	Major units	Air warning and control units	8 warning groups
			20 warning squadrons
			1 airborne early-warning group (2 squadrons)
		Fighter aircraft units	12 squadrons
		Air reconnaissance unit	1 squadron
		Air transport units	3 squadrons
		Aerial refueling/transport unit	1 squadron
		Surface-to-air guided missile units	6 groups
	Major equipment	Combat aircraft	approx. 350
		Fighters	approx. 260*
Assets for ballistic missile defense**	Major equipment	Aegis-equipped destroyers	4
	Major units	Air warning and control units	7 warning groups
			4 warning squadrons
		Surface-to-air guided missile units	3 groups

*The number already included in total figure for combat aircraft, above.
**The numbers of units and equipment below are already included in the Maritime and Air Self-Defense Forces sections above.

Source: Ministry of Defense,"National Defense Program Guidelines, FY2005–." www.mod.go.jp/e/d_act/d_policy/pdf/national_guidelines.pdf (accessed December 20, 2016).

Appendix G

National Defense Program Guidelines for FY2011 and Beyond

Approved by the Security Council and the Cabinet on December 17, 2010

I. NDPG's Objective

In light of the current security environment surrounding our country, and according to the 'Defense Program of Fiscal Year 2010' (approved by the Security Council and the Cabinet on December 17, 2009), the Government of Japan sets out the "National Defense Program Guidelines for FY2011 and beyond" as a new guideline for Japan's security policy and defense forces.

II. Basic Principles of Japan's Security

The first objective of Japan's security policy is to prevent any threat from directly reaching Japan and to eliminate external threats that have reached it so as to minimize the ensuing damage, and thereby secure the peace and security of Japan and its people. The second objective is to prevent threats from emerging by further stabilizing the security environment in the Asia-Pacific region and by improving the global security environment, so as to maintain and strengthen a free and open international order and ensure Japan's security and prosperity. The third objective is to contribute to creating global peace and stability and to secure human security.

In order to achieve these objectives, Japan will promote its own efforts, facilitate cooperation with its ally and countries in the Asia-Pacific, and pursue multi-layered security cooperation with the international community in a consolidated manner. Measures for this include more active utilization of Japan's diplomatic and defense capability, support for the United Nations' activities related to international peace and security, and promotion of diplomatic efforts such as establishing cooperative relationships with other countries.

Under the Constitution, and in line with basic principles such as maintaining an exclusively defense-oriented policy and not becoming a military power that poses a threat to other countries, Japan will continue to uphold its basic defense policies, such as securing civilian control, maintaining the three non-nuclear principles, and building a modest defense force. At the same time, Japan will participate more actively in activities in which the international community cooperates to improve the international security environment (hereinafter referred to as "international peace cooperation activities"), including United Nations peace-keeping activities and activities to deal with non-traditional security issues, such as humanitarian assistance, disaster relief and counter-piracy initiatives.

To address the threat of nuclear weapons, Japan will play a constructive and active role in international nuclear disarmament and non-proliferation efforts, so as to achieve the long-term goal of creating a world without nuclear weapons. At the same time, as long as nuclear weapons exist, the extended deterrence provided by the United States, with nuclear deterrent as a vital element, will be indispensable. In order to maintain and improve the credibility of the extended deterrence, Japan will closely cooperate with the United States, and will also appropriately implement its own efforts, including ballistic missile defense and civil protection.

III. Security Environment Surrounding Japan

1. Looking at trends of the global security environment, the probability of large-scale war between major countries has declined due to increasing interdependence among countries, but there is now a growing risk that the impact of unrest or a security problem in a single country will immediately spread worldwide. Moreover, in addition to regional conflicts arising from ethnic and religious disputes, there are a growing number of so-called "gray-zone" disputes—confrontations over territory, sovereignty and economic interests that are not to escalate into wars.

In such an environment, we are witnessing a global shift in the balance of power with the rise of powers such as China, India and Russia, along with the relative change of influence of the United States. On the other hand, the United States continues to play the most significant role in securing global peace and stability.

Proliferation of weapons of mass destruction and ballistic missiles, international terrorist organizations and piracy remain imminent security challenges for the international community, including Japan. Regional conflicts and the countries whose governance has weakened or collapsed also pose a challenge that could affect the global security environment. Moreover, risks concerning sustained access to the seas, outer space and cyberspace have emerged as a new challenge. From a long-term perspective, we should also be aware of the impact which climate change may have on the security environment.

It is extremely difficult for countries to individually deal with these global security challenges, and thus, it is important that countries that share common interests to regularly cooperate with each other.

The role of military forces in the international community is becoming increasingly diverse. In addition to deterring or responding to armed conflicts and building confidence and promoting friendship among countries, military forces, in cooperation with the non-military sector, are playing an important role in a growing number of cases, in conflict prevention, peace building such as reconstruction assistance, and in the non-traditional security field.

2. In the Asia-Pacific region, as interdependence expands and deepens, countries are strengthening their cooperation with each other to resolve security challenges. In particular, specific cooperative measures are being undertaken to resolve challenges in the non-traditional security field.

The global shift in the balance of power is apparent in the Asia-Pacific region. Large-scale military forces, including nuclear forces, continue to be concentrated in the areas surrounding Japan, and many countries are modernizing their military forces and increasing their military activities. In addition, there remain unclear and uncertain elements in the region, such as disputes over territories and the maritime domain, and issues over the Korean Peninsula and the Taiwan Strait.

North Korea is continuing its development, deployment and proliferation of weapons of mass destruction and ballistic missiles, and maintains a large-scale special operations force. It has also repeatedly conducted provocative military actions on the Korean Peninsula. North Korea's military activities constitute an immediate and grave destabilizing factor to regional security. They also pose a serious challenge to international non-proliferation efforts.

China, a growing major power, is beginning to play an important role for regional and global security. On the other hand, China is steadily increasing its defense expenditure. China is widely and rapidly modernizing its military force, mainly its nuclear and missile force as well as navy and air force, and is strengthening its capability for extended-range power projection. In addition, China has been expanding and intensifying its maritime activities in the surrounding waters. These trends, together with insufficient transparency over China's military forces and its security policy, are of concern for the regional and global community.

Russia has significantly reduced the size of its military forces in the Far East since the end of the Cold War, but its military activities are increasingly robust.

In such an environment, the United States is strengthening its engagement in this region. It attaches increasing importance to cooperation with its allies and partners, including Japan, the Republic of Korea and Australia, and is striving to enhance security ties through bilateral and multilateral frameworks. These efforts are important contributions to the peace and stability of the Asia-Pacific region and lay the foundation for the United States in tackling global security challenges.

3. Japan, with its vast territorial waters, is a trading nation which heavily depends on imports for the supply of foods and resources and on foreign markets. Thus, securing maritime security and international order is essential for the country's prosperity. Moreover, Japan is geographically surrounded by water and has a long coastline and numerous islands. In addition to frequent natural disasters, Japan faces security vulnerabilities resulting from the concentration of industry, population and information infrastructure in urban areas and from the presence of a large number of key facilities in coastal areas.

4. In considering the above, a full-scale invasion against Japan that will threaten its existence, such as a large-scale landing invasion, is unlikely to occur, but the security challenges and destabilizing factors Japan faces are diverse, complex and intertwined. Japan needs to appropriately deal with various contingencies arising from such challenges and factors (hereinafter referred to as "various contingencies"). It is also important that Japan actively tackle both regional and global security challenges in cooperation with its ally, partners and other countries concerned.

IV. Basic Policies to Ensure Japan's Security

1. Japan's Own Efforts

(1) Basic ideas
Recognizing that a country's security depends first and foremost on its own efforts, Japan will constantly utilize all means to ensure its security under the basic

defense policies, and in cooperation with its ally, partners and other countries concerned. In the event of various contingencies, it will seamlessly deal with the situation as it unfolds.

(2) Integrated and strategic activities
Japan will conduct integrated and strategic activities as follows.
a. Japan will improve its capability to collect and analyze information in the relevant government ministries and agencies. It will also strengthen its information security system that extends across ministries and agencies so as to facilitate information sharing among them. In doing so, Japan will promote its efforts to develop and use outer space, from the perspective of, strengthening information gathering and communications functions, among others. In order to enable stable use of cyberspace, Japan will also expand its posture and strengthen its capability in dealing with cyberattacks in a comprehensive manner.
b. The Cabinet Secretariat, the Ministry of Defense and the Self-Defense Forces (SDF), the police forces, the Japan Coast Guard, the Ministry of Foreign Affairs, the Ministry of Justice and other government agencies will regularly cooperate with each other. In the event of various contingencies, the Cabinet, led by the Prime Minister, will make rapid and appropriate decisions and respond to such contingencies in an integrated manner in cooperation with the local governments. To this end, the Government will examine the functions and systems related to its decision-making and response, through initiatives such as regular simulation exercises of various contingencies and comprehensive training and exercises, and consider necessary policies, including legal measures.
c. After examining the current organization, functions, and structure of the Cabinet related to security issues, including the Security Council, the Government will establish a body in the Prime Minister's Office which will be responsible for national security policy coordination among relevant ministers and for providing advice to the Prime Minister.
d. Japan will continue to improve its system for responding to various disasters and for civil protection. The national government and local governments will closely cooperate with each other to ensure an appropriate response.
e. Japan will participate in activities to improve the global security environment, including international peace cooperation activities, in a more efficient and effective manner, with government ministries and agencies cooperating not only with each other but also with non-governmental organizations and other entities. Taking into consideration the actual situations of United Nations peace-keeping operations, Japan will consider how it will participate in future peace-keeping operations by examining current policies, such as the five principles for participation in peace-keeping operations.
f. Japan will strive to make its security and defense policies easier to understand, so as to promote an understanding of security and defense issues among its people, as well as to secure national security. It will also strengthen its information dissemination abroad in order to further deepen the inter-

national community's understanding of its security and defense policies.

(3) Japan's defense force—Dynamic Defense Force
Japan's defense force is the ultimate guarantee of its national security, representing Japan's will and ability to prevent direct threats to Japan from reaching the country and to eliminate any threat that reaches it.

Under the current trends of the security environment, building defense forces that can effectively respond to security challenges is important. In particular, comprehensive operational performance such as readiness for an immediate and seamless response to contingencies is increasingly important, considering shortening warning times of contingencies due to exponential advances in military technology. Clear demonstration of national will and strong defense capabilities through such timely and tailored military operations as regular intelligence, surveillance, and reconnaissance activities (ISR), not just maintaining a certain level of defense force, is a critical element for ensuring credible deterrence and will contribute to stability in the region surrounding Japan. To this end, Japan needs to achieve greater performance with its defense forces through raising levels of equipment use and increasing operations tempo, placing importance on dynamic deterrence, which takes into account such an operational use of the defense forces.

At the same time, the roles of the defense forces are increasing and becoming more diverse, and it is necessary to strengthen bilateral and multilateral cooperation and actively conduct international peace cooperation activities.

For these reasons, Japan's future defense forces need to acquire dynamism to effectively deter and respond to various contingencies, and to proactively engage in activities to further stabilize the security environment in the Asia-Pacific and to improve the global security environment. Japan should no longer base its defense on the traditional defense concept, "Basic Defense Force Concept," which places priority on ensuring deterrence through the existence of defense forces per se. More specifically, Japan will develop a Dynamic Defense Force that possesses readiness, mobility, flexibility, sustainability, and versatility. These characteristics will be reinforced by advanced technology based on the trends of levels of military technology and intelligence capabilities.

In order to deal with the increasingly difficult security environment, Japan needs to steadily build an appropriate-size defense force. In doing so, Japan will choose truly necessary functions on which to concentrate resources, and carry out structural reform of the defense forces, thereby producing more outcome with limited resources. To this end, Japan will drastically rationalize and streamline the SDF overall through fundamentally reviewing, in light of its difficult fiscal condition, the equipment, personnel, organization and force disposition, including the equipment and personnel that have been maintained as preparation to defend against a full-scale invasion. Moreover, by implementing a drastic review of the SDF personnel management system, Japan will seek to curb personnel costs and improve efficiency as well as increase the strength of SDF personnel by lowering its average age. These initiatives will lead to improving the structure of the defense budget, which has a high proportion of personnel cost that currently suppresses the expenditure for the SDF's activities.

2. Cooperation with its Ally
Japan and the United States, which share basic values, have maintained an alliance centering on the Japan-U.S. Security Arrangements, and the Japan-U.S. Alliance remains indispensable in ensuring the peace and security of Japan. In addition, the military presence of the U.S. armed forces in Japan allow countries in the Asia-Pacific region to have a strong sense of security by functioning as deterrence against and response to contingencies in this region. The Japan-U.S. Alliance is also important for Japan to participate in multilateral security cooperation and effectively respond to global security challenges.

In light of the significance of the Japan-U.S. Security Alliance as described above, Japan will further deepen and develop the Alliance to adapt to the evolving security environment. In doing so, Japan will continue to engage in strategic dialogue and specific policy coordination with the United States, including bilateral assessment of the security environment and bilateral consultations on common strategic objectives, and roles, missions and capabilities. Japan will also promote cooperation in existing fields, including intelligence cooperation, deepening of bilateral contingency planning, various operational cooperation including that upon situations in areas surrounding Japan, ballistic missile defense and equipment and technology cooperation, as well as consultations to improve the credibility of extended deterrence and information security. In addition, in order to strengthen the U.S. forces' deterrent and response capability to regional contingencies, Japan will study measures to enhance bilateral cooperation with the United States. Moreover, Japan will strengthen various regular cooperation, such as joint training and joint/shared usage of facilities, and promote regional and global cooperation through international peace cooperation activities, maintenance and enhancement of international public goods such as outer space, cyberspace and sea lanes, as well as in the field of climate change.

At the same time, while maintaining the deterrence provided by the U.S. forces, to reduce the burden on local communities such as Okinawa where U.S. military bases are located, Japan will steadily implement specific measures to review the posture of the U.S. forces in Japan. It will also take active measures for the smooth and effective stationing of U.S. forces in Japan, including Host Nation Support.

3. Multi-layered Security Cooperation with the International Community

(1) Cooperation in the Asia-Pacific region
In order to effectively promote measures to further stabilize the Asia-Pacific region, together with the Japan-U.S. Alliance, a security network needs to be created by combining bilateral and multilateral security cooperation in a multi-layered manner.

In particular, Japan will strengthen its cooperation with the Republic of Korea and Australia, which are allies of the United States and share basic values and many security-related interests with Japan, through bilateral initiatives and multilateral cooperation involving the United States. Japan will also maintain and enhance security cooperation with the Association of Southeast Asian Nations (ASEAN) countries, which are its traditional partners. Moreover, Japan will enhance cooperation with India and other countries that share common interests in ensuring the security of maritime navigation from Africa and the Middle East to East Asia.

Japan will promote confidence with China and Russia, which have significant influence over regional security, through security dialogues and exchanges, and establish and develop a cooperative relationship with them in areas including non-traditional security fields. In particular, with regard to China, in line with efforts to establish a "Mutually Beneficial Relationship based on Common Strategic Interests," and recognizing that it is extremely important to enhance a constructive and cooperative relationship with China in various fields, Japan, together with countries including its ally, partners and other countries concerned, will actively engage in encouraging China to take responsible actions in the international community..

Concerning multilateral security cooperation, through such frameworks as the ASEAN Regional Forum (ARF) and the ASEAN Defense Ministers' Meeting Plus (ADMM Plus), Japan will play an appropriate role in efforts toward establishing regional order, norms and practical cooperative relationships, particularly through initiatives in the non-traditional security field.

(2) Cooperation as a member of the international community

In order to improve the global security environment and help maintain the security and prosperity of Japan, Japan will actively engage in diplomatic efforts, including the strategic and effective use of Official Development Assistance (ODA), in order to resolve root causes of conflicts and terrorism.

Along with these diplomatic efforts, Japan will robustly engage in international peace cooperation activities. In doing so, Japan will strive to provide assistance which makes use of its knowledge and experience and will conduct such activities strategically, while comprehensively taking into account the various conditions surrounding it.

Moreover, regarding activities concerning the global security environment, Japan will enhance cooperation with the European Union (EU), the North Atlantic Treaty Organization (NATO) and European countries, play an active role in international activities to maintain and strengthen international public goods, including the stable use of the maritime domain, outer space and cyberspace, and actively facilitate efforts by the international community to promote disarmament and prevent proliferation of weapons of mass destruction, missiles and other means of delivery. In addition, Japan will actively participate in humanitarian assistance and disaster relief in the event of large-scale natural disasters or pandemics.

For the international community to effectively respond to new challenges of the 21st century, the organization of the United Nations, as the sole universal and comprehensive international body, needs to be reformed in a way that increases its effectiveness and credibility. Japan will continue to actively tackle this challenge.

V. Future Defense Forces

1. Roles of Defense Forces

Japan will strengthen its defense forces in order to perform its roles properly in the following fields based on the Dynamic Defense Force concept. In doing so, the SDF will ensure regular cooperation with relevant organizations.

(1) Effective deterrence and response
In order to closely follow trends in military activities of neighboring countries and detect indications of various contingencies promptly, the SDF will ensure information supremacy through continuous ISR in the country and its surrounding areas. Should various contingencies occur, the SDF will quickly and seamlessly respond as the situation unfolds. In addition, the SDF will maintain a minimum necessary level of preparations against full-scale invasion, given possible changes in uncertain future circumstances.

In pursuing the above, priority will be placed on the following areas in particular.

a. Ensuring security of sea and air space surrounding Japan
The SDF will strive to ensure the security of the surrounding sea and air space and effectively respond to acts that harm Japan's national interests through such measures as continuous ISR.

b. Response to attacks on offshore islands
The SDF will respond to attacks on Japan's offshore islands by quickly deploying mobile units to prevent and reject invasion, in cooperation with other permanently stationed units. In such circumstances, the SDF will ensure air defense readiness on those islands to respond to cruise missiles and other attacks. It will also ensure air supremacy and the security of sea lanes in the surrounding sea and air space.

c. Response to cyber attacks
The SDF will respond to cyberattacks by operating functions necessary for defending the information system of the SDF in an integrated manner. By accumulating advanced expertise and skills needed to tackle cyberattacks, the SDF will contribute to the government-wide response to cyberattacks.

d. Response to attacks by guerrillas and special operations forces
The SDF will respond to attacks by guerrillas and special operations forces quickly and flexibly by deploying units with a high level of readiness while focusing on mobility. In particular, priority will be placed on ISR to prevent guerrillas and special operations forces from infiltrating coastal areas, protecting key facilities, and searching and destroying invading units.

e. Response to ballistic missile attacks
The SDF will respond to ballistic missile attacks by maintaining a continuous ISR posture. In addition, the SDF will respond effectively to ballistic missiles capable of evading interceptors by developing a multi-layered defense posture. Should by some chance any damage were to occur, the Government will take consequence management measures to minimize it.

f. Response to complex contingencies
The SDF will effectively respond to the above-mentioned contingencies while taking into account the possibility of different and multiple contingencies occurring consecutively or simultaneously.

g. Response to large-scale and/or chemical, biological, radiological and nuclear (CBRN) disasters
The SDF will respond to large-scale and CBRN disasters by conducting di-

saster relief operations anywhere in Japan through cooperation with local governments and other organizations.

(2) Efforts to further stabilize the security environment of the Asia-Pacific region
Japan will aim to stabilize the security environment in the areas surrounding Japan by conducting various activities, including continuous ISR, training and exercises, in a timely and appropriate manner.

In order to maintain stability in the Asia-Pacific region, Japan will also promote bilateral and multilateral defense cooperation and exchanges as well as joint training and exercises in a multi-layered manner while enhancing the Japan-U.S. Alliance. Moreover, in non-traditional security fields, Japan will promote practical cooperation by utilizing SDF capabilities, including disposal of landmines and unexploded shells. Japan will also strive to establish and strengthen regional cooperation practice and support the capacity building of countries in the region.

(3) Efforts to improve the global security environment
Japan will continue to actively participate in international peace cooperation activities, including peace building such as humanitarian and reconstruction assistance and ceasefire monitoring. Japan will also actively engage in various activities conducted by the United Nations and other organizations such as arms control and disarmament, nonproliferation and support for capacity building. Moreover, Japan will cooperate with its ally, partners and other countries concerned to actively promote efforts to tackle international terrorism, secure the safety of maritime traffic and maintain maritime order.

2. Self-Defense Forces: Force Posture
The SDF will maintain the following postures in addition to capabilities necessary for responding to various contingencies so as to effectively perform the roles prescribed for the defense forces in section 1.

(1) Readiness
The SDF will raise the readiness of units by maintaining a readiness posture, enhancing mobility, and sustaining and improving skills and operations tempo. It will appropriately and efficiently station units so they can operate quickly and effectively enough. Japan will also secure durable base functions, fuel and ammunition supplies (including training ammunition) and ensure the maintenance of equipment so that the SDF, as a Dynamic Defense Force, will be able to effectively perform its roles in deterrence and response.

(2) Joint operations
The SDF will facilitate smooth joint operations by maintaining command and control functions and an information-sharing system, utilizing advanced information and communications networks including satellite communications, as well as maintaining a posture to deal with cyberattacks, in addition to an information-collecting posture to collect information necessary for quick and effective responses.

(3) International peace cooperation activities
The SDF will strive to enhance capabilities and posture applicable to diverse missions, rapid deployment and long-term operations so it can actively participate in international peace cooperation activities.

3. Self-Defense Forces: Organization, Equipment and Force Disposition

(1) Basic concept
Japan will maintain an efficient organization, equipment and force disposition that will enable the SDF to effectively perform its roles described in section 1 while maintaining the posture described in section 2.

In this respect, in order to effectively and efficiently build up its defense forces, Japan will prioritize strengthening functions applicable to a wide variety of operations, functions that have asymmetrical capability, and functions which cannot be substituted. Specifically, Cold War-style equipment and organizations will be reduced, and the geographical location of forces and operational modalities of each service of the SDF will be appropriately reviewed. In addition, the SDF will enhance its defense posture by placing priority on strengthening such functions as ISR, maritime patrol, air defense, response to ballistic missile attacks, transportation, and command communications, including in the southwestern region.

To respond to changes in the security environment, budget allocation among each service of the SDF will be subject to drastic review by excluding sectionalism and from a comprehensive perspective regardless of precedent.

To promote joint operations of the SDF and strengthen the posture for co-operation between the SDF and the U.S. Forces, Japan will comprehensively review the modality of basic operational units (divisions and brigades) and the five Regional Armies of the Ground Self-Defense Force while giving consideration to improving the efficiency of command and control functions.

As regards preparations against full-scale invasion, the SDF will maintain relevant knowledge and expertise at a minimum necessary level in order to respond to possible changes in uncertain future circumstances.

(2) Priorities in strengthening SDF organization, equipment and force disposition
To strengthen the organization, equipment and force disposition, the SDF will place priority on the following matters.
a. Strengthening of joint operations
In order to facilitate joint operations, the SDF will enhance the basis for joint operations, including the functions of the Joint Staff, command and control system, information-collecting capability and education and training. The SDF will also develop effective and efficient systems applicable to joint operations by reorganizing, merging, centralizing and creating hubs for functions that extend across all three services of the SDF, such as transportation, medical service, anti-aircraft artillery, search and rescue, procurement, supply and maintenance of equipment, and management of camps and bases.
b. Response to attacks on off-shore islands
The SDF will permanently station the minimum necessary units on off-shore islands where the SDF is not currently stationed. Also, the SDF will

enhance its capability to respond to attacks on those islands and ensure the security of the surrounding sea and air space by securing bases, mobility, transport capacity and effective countermeasures necessary for conducting operations against such attacks.

c. Strengthening capabilities for international peace cooperation activities
The SDF will enhance its capabilities for international peace cooperation activities by upgrading equipment, strengthening maritime and air transport capability, enhancing its logistical support posture, enhancing its engineering and medical functions, and reinforcing its education and training systems.

d. Enhancement of intelligence functions
In order to detect indications of various contingencies promptly and collect, analyze and share information appropriately, the SDF will strengthen its diverse information-collecting capabilities utilizing advanced technology, including space technology, and the all-source analysis and assessment capabilities of the Defense Intelligence Headquarters and other organizations. Additionally, the SDF will strengthen the information sharing system among sections responsible for information collection, operations and policy making. Furthermore, the SDF will improve the system for providing appropriate intelligence support for activities conducted in remote areas through such measures as strengthening capabilities to collect geospatial information, so as to enable SDF units dispatched abroad to perform missions smoothly and safely. In addition, the SDF will make efforts to expand and enhance intelligence cooperation and exchanges with countries concerned.

e. Incorporating progress in science and technology into defense forces
In order to develop defense forces underpinned by advanced technology and information capabilities, the SDF will appropriately exploit the achievements of technological innovation. In particular, the SDF will ensure reliable command and control and quick information sharing by developing an advanced command communications system and information and communications network, as well as develop a system for responding to cyberattacks in an integrated manner.

f. Efficient and effective buildup of defense forces
Mindful of increasingly severe fiscal conditions, Japan will control defense expenditures by further rationalizing and streamlining its defense forces. At the same time, Japan will make sure its defense forces smoothly and successfully perform their missions while harmonizing other measures taken by the Government. To that end, Japan will clearly prioritize among its defense projects, concentrate resources on selected projects and promote efforts described in chapter VI.

(3) Organization, equipment and disposition of each service of the Self-Defense Forces

    A. Ground Self-Defense Force (GSDF)
        (a) The GSDF will achieve appropriate force disposition of highly mobile units with ISR capabilities according to geographical characteris-

tics in order to integrally intertwine various functions and effectively respond to various contingencies. These units can be rapidly deployed to various locations, and are capable of performing diverse missions, including international peace cooperation activities. In so doing, priority will be placed on the defense of off-shore islands where SDF units are not currently stationed, and the organization and personnel structure of units will be reviewed so as to ensure thorough rationalization and streamlining of the defense forces.

(b) The GSDF will maintain mobile operating units sustaining specialized functions so that it can effectively perform such operations as air transportation, airborne operations, defense against NBC (nuclear, biological, and chemical) weapons, special operations and international peace cooperation activities.

(c) The GSDF will maintain surface-to-air guided missile units so that it can effectively provide air defense to protect operational units and key areas.

B. Maritime Self-Defense Force (MSDF)

(a) The MSDF will maintain destroyer units and ship-based patrol helicopter units that can be operated flexibly so as to ensure the defense of the seas surrounding Japan, the security of sea lanes, and conduct of international peace cooperation activities, by regularly conducting such operations as ISR and anti-submarine operations. In addition, the destroyer units will maintain Aegis-equipped destroyers capable of providing multi-layered defense for the whole of Japan against ballistic missile attacks, together with the surface-to-air guided missile (SAM) units mentioned in paragraph C(c).

(b) The MSDF will maintain augmented submarine units so that it can effectively conduct regular underwater ISR on a broad scale in the seas surrounding Japan as well as patrolling activity in those seas.

(c) The MSDF will maintain fixed-wing patrol aircraft units so that it can effectively conduct regular sea-surface ISR on a broad scale in the seas surrounding Japan as well as patrol in those seas.

(d) The MSDF will maintain minesweeper units so that it can effectively conduct minesweeping in the seas surrounding Japan.

C. Air Self-Defense Force (ASDF)

(a) The ASDF will maintain air warning and control units so that it can conduct continuous ISR in most air space over Japan and the surrounding areas, detect and track any ballistic missiles flying into Japanese air space, and effectively conduct warning and control when necessary.

(b) In addition to the air warning and control units mentioned in paragraph (a), the ASDF will maintain fighter aircraft units comprised of highly capable new fighter aircraft, an air reconnaissance unit, as well as air transport units and aerial refueling/transport units which enable effective international peace cooperation activities, so that fighter aircrafts and support functions can conduct national air defense in an integrated manner.

(c) The ASDF will maintain surface-to-air guided missile units which will provide air defense to protect key areas and multi-layered defense for the whole of Japan against ballistic missile attacks, together with the Aegis-equipped destroyers mentioned in paragraph B(a).

The specifics of major organizations and equipment are as shown in the Annex Table.

VI. Basic Foundations to Maximize Defense Capability

In order to prepare, maintain, and operate the defense forces in an efficient and effective manner, Japan will place priority on the following matters.

(1) Effective utilization of human resources

Japan will take various measures to maintain high morale and rigorous discipline among SDF personnel. In order to appropriately adapt to the declining birth rate, the increasing ratio of people receiving higher education and the diversification of SDF missions, it will strive to recruit, retain and develop high-quality human resources and provide necessary education and training. The SDF will also enhance a medical service infrastructure to maintain the health and strength of personnel. Moreover, Japan will enhance the intellectual foundations for national security issues by promoting research and education in that field. In order to ensure appropriate treatment of personnel involved in the execution of arduous or dangerous missions, Japan will review the overall institutional framework of the SDF personnel treatment system.

At the same time, the SDF will appropriately manage the total number and structure of SDF personnel so as to maintain the vigor of the forces. In this respect, the SDF will review the rank and age structure so as to reduce the proportion of officers, warrant officers and sergeants and increase the number of privates while giving consideration to the balance among the missions of the SDF and the physical strength, experiences and skills of personnel. In addition, the SDF will also carry out reform of its personnel management system by reviewing the duties of SDF personnel from the perspective of optimization of assignments, so as to give precedence to younger personnel in assignment to front-line units while applying an optimum level of salaries and other terms to personnel engaged in other duties. This reform will include review of personnel management policy in line with the direction toward personnel cost reduction for national civil servants as a whole. Moreover, the SDF will secure effective defense capability amid severe fiscal conditions by further rationalizing personnel and curbing personnel costs while streamlining logistical operations through effective utilization of private-sector resources and capabilities. In this respect, Japan will promote effective use of retired SDF personnel in society, implement measures to support their re-employment including in the public sector, and ensure they receive adequate post-retirement treatment. The SDF will also seek to introduce an early retirement system to be implemented together with the above measures. In addition, Japan will actively promote public-private cooperation and personnel exchanges.

(2) Enhancement of the basis for operating equipment
The SDF will enhance the operational basis of equipment essential to the exercise of defense capability through such measures as efficiently and effectively maintaining equipment and by maintaining a high level of operations tempo.

(3) Improvement in the efficiency of equipment procurement
The SDF will improve the cost-efficiency of equipment procurement by making thorough efforts to curb the lifecycle costs of equipment, including the acquisition cost, and through improving the overall contract system and further adopting efficient procurement systems such as short-term lump-sum purchases. The SDF will also enhance transparency over procurement by strengthening the external audit system.

(4) Development and maintenance of defense production capability and technological bases
From the perspective of the importance of national security, Japan will set forth a strategy for defense production capability and technological bases. With this strategy, Japan will identify critical defense production capabilities and technologies that should be kept in the country and, through selection and concentration, develop and maintain defense forces in a stable manner from the medium- to long-term perspective by concentrating resources on the development and maintenance of those capabilities and technologies.

(5) Consideration of measures in response to changes in the international environment regarding defense equipment
In contributing to peace and promoting cooperation in international community, there are increasing opportunities to conduct effective cooperation activities through measures such as the utilization of heavy machinery and other defense equipment carried to the site by the SDF and providing equipment to disaster-stricken countries. Moreover, it has become the mainstream among developed countries to improve the performance of defense equipment and to deal with rising costs of equipment by participating in international joint development and production projects. Japan will study measures to respond to such major changes.

(6) Relationship between defense facilities and local communities
In order to promote efficient maintenance and improvement of defense facilities, Japan will implement various measures to reconcile interests between such facilities and the surrounding local communities in close cooperation with relevant local governments.

VII. Additional Elements for Consideration

1. These Guidelines provide the vision for our defense forces for approximately the next decade, to promote innovation of the defense forces. In case there are significant changes in circumstances, Japan will review and, if necessary, revise the Guidelines in light of the security environment and technological trends at that time, among other things.

2. Japan will conduct systematic transition management and ex-post verification so as to ensure smooth, swift and appropriate transition to the defense forces outlined in these Guidelines. Japan will also conduct constant study on the future of its defense forces so as to contribute to the review and revision process mentioned in paragraph 1.

Attached Table

		Personnel	154,000
		Regular personnel	147,000
		Ready reserve personnel	7,000
Ground Self-Defense Force	Major units	Regionally deployed units	8 divisions 6 brigades
		Mobile operation units	Central Readiness Force 1 armored division
		Surface-to-air guided missile units	7 anti-aircraft artillery groups/regiments
	Major equipment	Tanks	Approx. 400
		Howitzers and rockets	Approx. 400
Maritime Self-Defense Force	Major units	Destroyer units	4 flotillas (8 divisions) 4 divisions
		Submarines units	6 divisions
		Minesweeper unit	1 flotilla
		Patrol aircraft units	9 squadrons
	Major equipment	Destroyers	48
		Submarines	22
		Combat aircraft	Approx. 150
Air Self-Defense Force	Major units	Air warning & control units	4 warning groups 24 warning squadrons 1 AEW group (2 squadrons)
		Fighter aircraft units	12 squadrons
		Air reconnaissance unit	1 squadron
		Air transport units	3 squadrons
		Aerial refueling/transport unit	1 squadron
		Surface-to-air guided missile units	6 groups
	Major equipment	Combat aircraft	Approx. 340
		Fighters	Approx. 260
Assets capable of ballistic missile defense (BMD)*		Aegis-equipped destroyers	**6
		Air warning & control units	11 warning groups/squadrons
		Surface-to-air guided missile units	6 groups

*The numbers of units and equipment in this row are and Air Self-Defense Forces' major units sections above.already included in the Maritime.
**Additional acquisition of BMD-capable, Aegis-equipped destroyers, if to be provided separately, will be allowed within the number of destroyers set above after consideration of development of BMD-related technologies and fiscal conditions in the future, among other factors.

Source: Ministry of Defense,"National Defense Program Guidelines for FY2011 and Beyond." www. mod.go.jp/e/d_act/d_policy/pdf/guidelinesFY2011.pdf (accessed December 20, 2016).

Appendix H

National Security Strategy

December 17, 2013

I. Purpose

Maintaining the peace and security of Japan and ensuring its survival are the primary responsibilities of the Government of Japan. As Japan's security environment becomes ever more severe, Japan needs to identify its national interests from a long-term perspective, determine the course it should pursue in the international community, and adopt a whole-government approach for national security policies and measures in order to continue developing a prosperous and peaceful society.

Japan has contributed to peace, stability and prosperity of the region and the world. In a world where globalization continues, Japan should play an even more proactive role as a major global player in the international community.

Based on such a recognition, the Government of Japan hereby sets forth this National Security Strategy (hereinafter referred to as "the Strategy") in order to set out Japan's fundamental policies pertaining to national security.

The Strategy first elaborates on Japan's peaceful orientation to date and the policy of "Proactive Contribution to Peace" based on the principle of international cooperation, examines its national interests and identifies its national security objectives. Furthermore, the Strategy identifies national security challenges Japan faces, taking into account the trends of the security environment surrounding Japan. Finally, the Strategy presents strategic approaches to be taken for national security, with diplomatic and defense policies at their core, based on the recognition that in order to overcome the challenges and achieve its objectives, Japan needs to effectively utilize its diverse resources and promote comprehensive measures, strengthen the domestic foundation for national security and seek deeper understanding both at home and abroad, and advance efforts at various levels in a multifaceted and coordinated manner.

The Strategy, as fundamental policies pertaining to national security, presents guidelines for policies in areas related to national security, including sea, outer space, cyberspace, official development assistance (ODA) and energy.

Pursuant to the Strategy, and with the National Security Council (NSC) serving as the control tower, as well as with strong political leadership, the Government of Japan will implement national security policies in a more strategic and structured manner through a whole-government approach.

In addition, when implementing policies in other areas, the Government of Japan will give due consideration to national security so that Japan can utilize its strengths, such as its diplomatic ability and defense capability, in a smooth and fully-functional way as a whole, based on the Strategy.

The Strategy will guide Japan's national security policy over the next decade. Through the implementation of concrete policies, the NSC will regularly carry out systematic evaluation and upgrade the Strategy in a timely and appropriate manner. Should any major changes in the situation occur, the NSC will review this Strategy in consideration of the security environment at the time, and make necessary revisions.

II. Fundamental Principle of National Security

1. Principles Japan Upholds

Japan is a country with rich culture and tradition, and upholds universal values, such as freedom, democracy, respect for fundamental human rights and the rule of law. Japan has a wealth of highly educated human capital and high cultural standards, and is an economic power with strong economic capacity and high technological capabilities. Japan has achieved its development benefiting from an open international economic system.

Surrounded by the sea on all sides and blessed with an immense exclusive economic zone and an extensive coastline, Japan as a maritime state has achieved economic growth through maritime trade and development of marine resources, and has pursued "Open and Stable Seas."

Japan has consistently followed the path of a peace-loving nation since the end of World War II. Japan has adhered to a basic policy of maintaining an exclusively national defense-oriented policy, not becoming a military power that poses a threat to other countries, and observing the Three Non-Nuclear Principles.

In addition, Japan has maintained its security, and contributed to peace and stability in the Asia-Pacific region, by enhancing its alliance with the United States (U.S.) with which it shares universal values and strategic interests, as well as by deepening cooperative relationships with other countries.

Moreover, Japan has contributed to the realization of stability and prosperity in the international community through initiatives for supporting the economic growth of developing countries and for addressing global issues based on the principle of human security, as well as through trade and investment relations with other countries. In particular, Japan's cooperation contributed to realizing stability, economic growth and democratization in many countries, especially those in Asia, including the member states of the Association of Southeast Asian Nations (ASEAN).

Furthermore, as a peace-loving nation, complying with the United Nations (U.N.) Charter, Japan has been cooperating with the U.N. and other international organizations, and has actively contributed to their activities. In particular, Japan has continuously participated in U.N. peacekeeping operations (PKO), as the role of military forces diversified after the end of the Cold War. In addition, as the only country to have ever suffered atomic bombings in war, Japan has consistently engaged in disarmament and non-proliferation efforts, playing a leading role in international initiatives to realize "a world free of nuclear weapons."

The course that Japan has taken as a peace-loving nation has garnered significant praise and respect from the international community, and Japan must continue these steps to further consolidate such a position.

At the same time, surrounded by an increasingly severe security environment and confronted by complex and grave national security challenges, it has become indispensable for Japan to make more proactive efforts in line with the principle of international cooperation. Japan cannot secure its own peace and security by itself, and the international community expects Japan to play a more proactive role for peace and stability in the world, in a way commensurate with its national capabilities.

Against this backdrop, under the evolving security environment, Japan will continue to adhere to the course that it has taken to date as a peace-loving nation, and as a major player in world politics and economy, contribute even more proactively in securing peace, stability, and prosperity of the international community, while achieving its own security as well as peace and stability in the Asia-Pacific region, as a "Proactive Contributor to Peace" based on the principle of international cooperation. This is the fundamental principle of national security that Japan should stand to hold.

2. Japan's National Interests and National Security Objectives

In order to achieve the fundamental principle of national security by implementation of concrete policies, the Government of Japan needs to define our national interests and national security objectives, examine them in the context of the constantly evolving security environment, and mobilize all possible means.

Japan's national interests are, first of all, to maintain its sovereignty and independence; to defend its territorial integrity; to ensure the safety of life, person, and properties of its nationals, and to ensure its survival while maintaining its own peace and security grounded on freedom and democracy and preserving its rich culture and tradition.

In addition, Japan's national interests are to achieve the prosperity of Japan and its nationals through economic development, thereby consolidating its peace and security. To this end, especially in the Asia-Pacific region, it is essential that Japan, as a maritime state, strengthens the free trade regime for accomplishing economic development through free trade and competition, and realizes an international environment that offers stability, transparency and predictability.

Similarly, the maintenance and protection of international order based on rules and universal values, such as freedom, democracy, respect for fundamental human rights, and the rule of law, are likewise in Japan's national interests.

In order to safeguard these national interests and to fulfill our responsibility in the international community, Japan, adopting the policy of "Proactive Contribution to Peace" based on the principle of international cooperation as a fundamental principle, will seek to achieve the following national security objectives.

The first objective is to strengthen the deterrence necessary for maintaining its peace and security and for ensuring its survival, thus deterring threats from directly reaching Japan; at the same time, if by any chance a threat should reach Japan, to defeat such threat and to minimize the damage.

The second objective is to improve the security environment of the Asia-Pacific region, and prevent the emergence of and reduce direct threats to Japan, through strengthening the Japan-U.S. Alliance, enhancing the trust and cooperative relationships between Japan and its partners within and outside the Asia-Pacific region, and promoting practical security cooperation.

The third objective is to improve the global security environment and build a peaceful, stable, and prosperous international community by strengthening the international order based on universal values and rules, and by playing a leading role in the settlement of disputes, through consistent diplomatic efforts and further personnel contributions.

III. Security Environment Surrounding Japan and National Security Challenges

1. Global Security Environment and Challenges

(1) Shift in the Balance of Power and Rapid Progress of Technological Innovation

Since the beginning of the twenty first century, the balance of power in the international community has been changing on an unprecedented scale, and this has substantially influenced the dynamics of international politics.

The primary drivers of this change in the balance of power are the emerging countries, including China and India. In particular, China is further increasing its presence in the international community. On the other hand, though its relative influence in the international community is changing, the U.S. remains the country that has the world's largest power as a whole, composed of its soft power originating from its values and culture, on top of its military and economic power. Furthermore, the U.S. has manifested its policy to shift its emphasis of national security and economic policy towards the Asia-Pacific region (the "rebalance" policy).

While the change in the balance of power has encouraged the shift of the center of gravity of world politics and economy from the Atlantic to the Pacific, it has also been a reason for a weakening leadership in global governance, as exemplified by the stalled negotiations in the World Trade Organization (WTO) and of the United Nations Framework Convention on Climate Change (UNFCCC). In addition, while the rapid advancement of globalization and technological innovation has deepened interdependence among states, it has also invited a change in the relative influence between states and non-state actors, and brought about a complex impact on the global security environment.

Sovereign states remain the principal actors in the international community, and conflict and coordination between states continue to be the most significant factors affecting global stability. However, as cross-border flow of people, goods, capital, information and other items have been facilitated more easily by the advancement of globalization, non-state actors are beginning to play a more important role in decision-making in the international community.

In addition, the advancement of globalization and technological innovation bears negative impact. Terrorism and crimes committed by non-state actors are posing serious threats to the security of any country. Today, these threats, irrespective of where they originate in the world, could instantly have a direct influence on the security of Japan.

(2) Threat of the Proliferation of Weapons of Mass Destruction and Other Related Materials

As the only country to have ever suffered atomic bombings in war, Japan best understands the tragedy of the use of nuclear weapons and shoulders the responsibility to realize "a world free of nuclear weapons." The issue of the transfer, proliferation, and performance improvement of weapons of mass destruction (WMD), including nuclear, biological, and chemical weapons (NBC), and their means of delivery, such as ballistic missiles, remain major threats to Japan and the international community. In particular, the issue of nuclear and missile development by

North Korea and the nuclear issue of Iran continue to pose grave threats to peace and stability, not only in each region but also in the entire international community. Moreover, there remain concerns over the acquisition and the use of WMD and related items by non-state actors, including international terrorist organizations, against which traditional deterrence may not function effectively.

(3) Threat of International Terrorism
Terrorist attacks continue to occur around the world, and the threat of terrorism by international terrorist organizations remains serious. The advancement of globalization has made it easier for those organizations to share information and conspire within their own organizations and with other groups, and to secure geographical access and acquire arms.

International terrorism has spread and become diverse in its forms. International terrorist organizations are utilizing politically unstable and weakly governed countries and regions as bases for operation and training for terror activities. The ideologies of such terrorist organizations are also motivating other groups and individuals to commit terrorist acts.

Some international terrorist organizations designate Japan as their target. Terrorist attacks against Japanese nationals and interests have actually taken place overseas. Japan and its people face the threat of international terrorism both at home and abroad. Diversity of nationality of the perpetrators and victims in recent international terrorism cases has underscored the increasing importance of combating terrorism through international cooperation.

(4) Risks to Global Commons
In recent years, risks that can impede the utilization of and free access to global commons, such as the sea, outer space, and cyberspace, have been spreading and become more serious. While the seas are governed by international maritime law, in particular the United Nations Convention on the Law of the Sea (UNCLOS), there have been an increasing number of cases of unilateral actions in an attempt to change the status quo by coercion without paying respect to existing international law. With regard to outer space and cyberspace, applicable norms remain to be developed due to the different positions among relevant countries.

Against such a backdrop, not only for economic development but also for the national security of each country, it has therefore become even more important to promote appropriate international rule-making over global commons and to make concerted efforts by the international community while respecting such rules.

"Open and Stable Seas" constitute the basis for peace and prosperity of the international community as a whole. In this regard, each state has been tackling on its own or with others various issues including piracy, unidentified vessels, illegal dumping, contraband, human smuggling, maritime disasters, and the removal of hazardous substances, for maintaining the stability of sea lanes of communication.

However, in recent years, the number of cases of conflict of interests between or among states over natural resources and the security of respective states is increasing. As a result, there is a growing risk of incidents at sea, and of possible escalation into unexpected situations.

In the South China Sea in particular, disputes that have arisen over sovereignty between coastal states and China cause concerns over the maintenance of the rule of law at sea, freedom of navigation, and stability in the Southeast Asian region. In addition, vulnerability is also increasing in sea lanes of communication, spanning between Japan and the Middle East, on which Japan is largely dependent for its natural and energy resources, due to various problems including regional conflicts and international terrorism in and around the coastal states, as well as piracy. Therefore, advancing efforts to address these issues is also important for securing the sea lanes.

Furthermore, the Arctic Sea is deemed to have enormous potential for developing new shipping routes and exploration of natural resources. While it is expected that states concerned work together under relevant international rules, such potential could provide new causes of friction among them.

While outer space has been utilized for civil purposes, from security perspective, the importance of outer space has dramatically increased in recent years, given its use for the reinforcement of capabilities for information gathering and surveillance, as well as for securing communication means for military purposes.

On the other hand, the congestion of outer space has heightened as more countries utilize outer space. There exist risks that could impede the continuous and stable use of outer space with an increasing amount of space debris caused by anti-satellite tests and satellite collisions amongst others, as well as with the development of counter-space weapons.

Cyberspace, a global domain comprised of information systems, telecommunications networks and others, provides a foundation for social, economic, military and other activities. Meanwhile, risks of cyber-attacks with the intent to steal classified information, disrupt critical infrastructure and obstruct military systems, are becoming more serious.

In Japan, with an increasing level of connecting networks of social systems and various other elements, cyberspace is necessary for promoting both economic growth and innovation through the free flow of information in cyberspace. Protecting cyberspace from the above-mentioned risks is vital to secure national security.

(5) Challenges to Human Security

Globalization has enabled people, goods, capital, and information to instantaneously move across borders in large quantities. As a result, international economic activities have expanded, thereby bringing prosperity to the international community.

In contrast, global issues that cannot be dealt with by a single country—namely, poverty, widening inequality, global health challenges including infectious diseases, climate change and other environmental issues, food security, and humanitarian crises caused by civil wars and natural disasters—are emerging as critical and urgent issues of human security, threatening the very survival and dignity of individuals. The Millennium Development Goals (MDGs), common goals in the development field to be achieved by the international community, are not likely to be achieved in some regions and sectors. In addition, the increasing demand for energy, food, and water resources due to the population growth in developing countries and the expansion of economic scale could cause new conflicts.

These challenges could have repercussions on peace and stability of the international community; therefore, Japan needs to promote necessary measures based on the principle of human security.

(6) The Global Economy and Its Risks

In today's global economy, no economy is self-sufficient and isolated from the world economy; thus the risk of the expansion of an economic crisis from one country to the entire global economy is growing. While this trend is conspicuous in the financial economy, today, it is also witnessed in the real economy, as value chains and supply chains are established across borders with increasing international specialization.

Under these circumstances, there are concerns over fiscal problems and the slowdown in the growth of emerging economies. In some emerging economies and developing countries, visible signs of protectionism as well as reluctance towards the creation of new trade rules have been observed.

Furthermore, in recent years, with the advancement of technological innovation in energy sector, one has seen the rise of resource nationalism in resource rich countries and growing global demand, especially in emerging economies, for energy and mineral resources, followed by the intensified competition for the acquisition of such resources. In addition, given the aggravating environmental problems arising from climate change, there are risks of crunches in global supply and demand as well as temporary shortages of supply in food and water.

2. Security Environment and Challenges in the Asia-Pacific Region

(1) Characteristics of the Strategic Environment of the Asia-Pacific Region

The shift in the global power balance has elevated the importance of the Asia-Pacific region in the international community. While this shift provides opportunities for security cooperation, it has also given rise to regional issues and tensions. In particular, the region of Northeast Asia is home to a host of actors, such as countries with large-scale military forces, or those possessing nuclear weapons or continuing with nuclear development. Yet a regional cooperation framework in the security realm has not been sufficiently institutionalized. Countries in the region have contrasting political, economic, and social systems, and thus their security views are diverse, which constitutes another characteristic of the strategic environment of this region.

In this context, in addition to the issues and tensions arising from the shift in the balance of power, the Asia-Pacific region has become more prone to so-called "gray-zone" situations, situations that are neither pure peacetime nor contingencies over territorial sovereignty and interests. There is a risk that these "gray-zone" situations could further develop into grave situations.

On the other hand, the Asia-Pacific region is also witnessing a rise in opportunities for bilateral exchanges and cooperation among countries in the region. In addition, there have been multilateral security dialogues, including the ASEAN Regional Forum (ARF), and bilateral and multilateral joint exercises. These initiatives are contributing to the development of mutual understanding and enhancement of joint response capabilities. Therefore, it is important to further promote and develop these multilayered initiatives for regional stability.

(2) North Korea's Military Buildup and Provocative Actions
In the Korean Peninsula, the large-scale military forces of the Republic of Korea (ROK) and North Korea confront each other. While North Korea continues to face serious economic difficulties without any improvement in its human rights situation, North Korea heavily allocates its resources on military affairs today.
In addition, North Korea has enhanced the capability of WMDs including nuclear weapons and that of ballistic missiles. At the same time, North Korea has repeatedly taken provocative military actions in the Korean Peninsula including the use of provocative rhetoric, some of which are directed at Japan, thereby increasing the tension in the region.

In particular, North Korea's ballistic missiles development, including those with ranges covering the mainland of the U.S., along with its continued attempts to miniaturize nuclear weapons for warheads and equipping them to ballistic missiles, substantially aggravate the threat to the security of the region, including Japan. These concerns pose a serious challenge to the entire international community from the viewpoint of the non-proliferation of WMD and related materials.
As Kim Jong-un, First Chairman of the National Defense Commission, has been making efforts to consolidate his regime, the domestic situation in North Korea needs to be closely monitored.

Furthermore, North Korea's abduction is a grave issue affecting Japan's sovereignty as well as the lives and safety of Japanese nationals. It is an urgent issue for the Government of Japan to resolve under its responsibility and a universal issue for the international community to address as a violation of fundamental human rights.

(3) China's Rapid Rise and Intensified Activities in Various Areas
There is an expectation for China to share and comply with international norms, and play a more active and cooperative role for regional and global issues. On the other hand, China has been rapidly advancing its military capabilities in a wide range of areas through its continued increase in its military budget without sufficient transparency. In addition, China has taken actions that can be regarded as attempts to change the status quo by coercion based on their own assertions, which are incompatible with the existing order of international law, in the maritime and aerial domains, including the East China Sea and the South China Sea. In particular, China has rapidly expanded and intensified its activities in the seas and airspace around Japan, including intrusion into Japan's territorial waters and airspace around the Senkaku Islands. Moreover, China has shown the move that appears to unduly infringe the freedom of overflight above the high seas by establishing its own "Air Defense Identification Zone" over the East China Sea.

Such an external stance and military activities by China, coupled with a lack of transparency in its military affairs and security policy, have become an issue of concern to the international community including Japan; therefore, the Government of Japan needs to pay careful attention to this situation.

The relationship between the two sides of the Taiwan Strait has deepened in recent years, primarily in economic areas. Meanwhile, the military balance between the two sides has been changing. Thus, the cross-strait relationship contains both orientations towards stability and potential instability.

IV. Japan's Strategic Approaches to National Security

To ensure national security, Japan needs to first and foremost strengthen its own capabilities and the foundation for exercising those capabilities. Japan must also steadily fulfill the role it should play and adapt its capabilities to respond to future developments.

Enhancing Japan's resilience in national security, through reinforcing its diplomatic power and defense force, as well as bolstering its economic strengths and technological capabilities, contributes to peace and stability in the Asia-Pacific region and the international community at large. This belief forms the core of the strategic approaches in the Strategy.

Moreover, in order to overcome national security challenges and achieve national security objectives, as well as to proactively contribute to peace in cooperation with the international community, Japan needs to expand and deepen cooperative relationships with other countries, with the Japan-U.S. Alliance as the cornerstone. At the same time, Japan needs to make effective use of its diverse resources and promote comprehensive policies.

In light of this, Japan will take the following concrete strategic approaches, centering on diplomatic policy and defense policy.

1. Strengthening and Expanding Japan's Capabilities and Roles

(1) Strengthening Diplomacy for Creating a Stable International Environment
The key of national security is to create a stable and predictable international environment, and prevent the emergence of threats. It is thus necessary for Japan to realize an international order and security environment that are desirable for Japan, by playing an even more proactive role in achieving peace, stability and prosperity of the international community as a "Proactive Contributor to Peace" based on the principle of international cooperation.

This strategic approach first requires the capability to analyze the constantly changing security environment and the course that the international community is taking. On top of this, Japan must have the power to take the lead in setting the international agenda and to proactively advance its national interests, without being confined to a reactionary position to events and incidents after they have already occurred. In doing so, it is necessary to enhance diplomatic creativity and negotiating power to deepen the understanding of and garner support for Japan's position in the international community, through effectively utilizing all strengths and features of the nation. In addition, by highlighting Japan's attractiveness, Japan needs to strengthen its soft power that would benefit the international community. Japan also needs to strengthen its capacity to promptly and accurately identify the needs of Japanese nationals and firms to support their overseas activities. Furthermore, it is the responsibility of Japan as a "Proactive Contributor to Peace" to make even more proactive contributions to international organizations such as the U.N., including through increasing the number of Japanese staff in such institutions. In order to advance such vibrant diplomacy, Japan will strengthen the institutional capabilities through which it undertakes diplomacy. Such overall strengthening of diplomatic capability is critical to ensure the security of Japan.

(2) Building a Comprehensive Defense Architecture to Firmly Defend Japan

Japan's defense force is the final guarantee of its national security which deters direct threats from reaching Japan and defeats any threat that reaches it. Japan will steadily develop its defense force.

To ensure peace and security in Japan amid the severe security environment surrounding the country, Japan will efficiently develop a highly effective and joint defense force, adapting to the change in strategic environment with consideration of its national power and the political, economic, and social situations; and strive to ensure operations with flexibility and readiness based on joint operations.

Japan will also advance not only the coordination within the government, but also coordination with local governments and the private sector. In doing so, even in peacetime, Japan will maintain and improve a comprehensive architecture for responding seamlessly to an array of situations, ranging from armed attacks to large-scale natural disasters.

In developing the structure of the Japan Self-Defense Forces (SDF), which plays a central role in the above-mentioned efforts, Japan will develop a streamlined planning and programming process, which includes the National Defense Program Guidelines and the Medium Term Defense Program, based on the Strategy to enhance its defense structure for deterrence and response to various situations, prioritizing important functions from a joint and comprehensive perspective.

In addition, with regard to the threat of nuclear weapons, the extended deterrence of the U.S. with nuclear deterrence at its core is indispensable. In order to maintain and enhance the credibility of the extended deterrence, Japan will work closely with the U.S., and take appropriate measures through its own efforts, including ballistic missile defense (BMD) and protection of the people.

(3) Strengthening Efforts for the Protection of Japan's Territorial Integrity

To fully protect its territories, in addition to building a comprehensive defense architecture, Japan will enhance the capabilities of the law enforcement agencies responsible for territorial patrol activities and reinforce its maritime surveillance capabilities. Furthermore, Japan will strengthen coordination among relevant ministries and agencies to be able to respond seamlessly to a variety of unexpected situations.

Japan will also make a constant review on issues that are relevant to ensuring the security of its territories, and take effective measures.

In addition, Japan will proactively engage in the protection, management, and development of remote islands near national borders. Furthermore, from a national security viewpoint, Japan will study the situation of land ownership in areas such as remote islands near national borders and areas surrounding defense facilities, and review issues related to the use of such land.

(4) Ensuring Maritime Security

As a maritime state, Japan will play a leading role, through close cooperation with other countries, in maintaining and developing "Open and Stable Seas," which are upheld by maritime order based upon such fundamental principles as the rule of law, ensuring the freedom and safety of navigation and overflight, and peaceful settlement of disputes in accordance with relevant international law. More concretely, Japan will take necessary measures to address various threats in sea lanes of communication, including anti-piracy operations to ensure safe maritime transport and promote maritime security cooperation with other countries.

Japan will strengthen its maritime domain awareness capabilities that are necessary for the above-mentioned measures, in a comprehensive manner that involves the use of outer space, while paying attention to the establishment of international networks. At the same time, Japan will strive to enhance the frequency and the quality of bilateral and multilateral cooperation on maritime security such as joint exercises.

In particular, sea lanes of communication, stretching from the Persian Gulf, the Strait of Hormuz, the Red Sea and the Gulf of Aden to the surrounding waters of Japan, passing through the Indian Ocean, the Straits of Malacca, and the South China Sea, are critical to Japan due to its dependence on the maritime transport of natural and energy resources from the Middle East. In this regard, Japan will provide assistance to those coastal states alongside the sea lanes of communication and other states in enhancing their maritime law enforcement capabilities, and strengthen cooperation with partners on the sea lanes who share strategic interests with Japan.

(5) Strengthening Cyber Security

Japan as a whole will make concerted efforts in comprehensively promoting cross-cutting measures to defend cyberspace and strengthen the response capability against cyber-attacks, so as to protect cyberspace from malicious activities threatening cyber security; to ensure the free and safe use of cyberspace; and to guard its critical infrastructure against cyber-attacks, including those in which state involvement is suspected.

To this end, Japan will strengthen public-private partnership in the areas of system design, development and operations based on risk assessment, as well as identifying incidents, minimizing damages and their expansion, and analyzing the causes of and preventing similar incidents. In addition, Japan will comprehensively consider and take necessary measures with regard to expanding the pool of human resources in the security field, protection of control systems, and response to the issues of supply chain risk.

Furthermore, Japan will strengthen inter-agency cooperation and define the roles of relevant agencies so that it can reinforce its capability to protect cyberspace and respond to incidents as a nation at large. At the same time, Japan will promote a range of measures, including enhancing the ability and function to oversee, assess, apprehend, analyze, and internationally coordinate on cyber incidents, as well as reinforcing relevant agencies in charge of those tasks.

In promoting these measures, strengthening international partnership in a wide range of areas is essential. For this, Japan will take measures at technical and operational levels to enhance international cooperation. Japan will also strengthen information sharing and promote cyber defense cooperation with relevant countries.

(6) Strengthening Measures against International Terrorism
Japan will first and foremost strengthen its domestic measures against international terrorism such as ensuring the security of nuclear facilities in Japan. Moreover, in order to ensure the safety of Japanese nationals living abroad, Japan will strengthen such measures as building a network where risk information held by private sectors can be shared more effectively and efficiently; and reinforcing the structure for analyzing the situation of international terrorism and overseas information-collecting capabilities.

(7) Enhancing Intelligence Capabilities
In order to appropriately support decision-making on national security policies, Japan will fundamentally strengthen its information-collecting capabilities from a diverse range of sources, including human intelligence, open source intelligence, signals intelligence, and imagery intelligence. In addition, Japan will promote the utilization of geospatial intelligence with which various types of intelligence are combined.

Moreover, Japan will enhance its intelligence analysis, consolidation, and sharing capabilities by bolstering its human resources, including developing highly-skilled intelligence experts. Japan will thereby promote all-source analysis that makes use of the array of information-collecting means at the Government's disposal.

Furthermore, Japan will operate the intelligence cycle more effectively through the timely provision of materials and intelligence to the NSC, which serves as the control tower of foreign and security policy, and through the appropriate utilization of intelligence in policy formulation. In addition, under the Act on the Protection of Specially Designated Secrets (*provisional English translation), Japan will strengthen its counter intelligence functions by developing such intelligence protection system in order to facilitate intelligence functions throughout the Government.

(8) Defense Equipment and Technology Cooperation
In cases that contribute to peace and international cooperation, there are increasing opportunities to cooperate in a more effective manner, including through the utilization and provision of heavy machinery and other defense equipment carried to disaster-stricken countries and sites by the SDF. Moreover, internationally, it has become mainstream to participate in international joint development and production projects in order to improve the performance of defense equipment, while dealing with the rising costs of defense equipment. In this context, from the perspective of "Proactive Contribution to Peace" based on the principle of international cooperation, Japan is required to contribute more proactively to peace and international cooperation including through utilizing defense equipment, and to participate in joint development and production of defense equipment and other related items.

Against this backdrop, while giving due consideration to the roles that the Three Principles on Arms Exports and their related policy guidelines have played so far, the Government of Japan will set out clear principles on the overseas transfer of arms and military technology, which fit the new security environment. In this context, considerations will be made with regard to defining cases where transfers are prohibited; limiting cases where transfers could be allowed with strict examination; and ensuring appropriate control over transfers in terms of unauthorized use and third party transfer.

(9) Ensuring the Stable Use of Outer Space and Promoting Its Use for Security Purposes
The stable use of outer space is not only fundamental to the lives of the people and the economy, but is also crucial for national security. Japan will therefore maintain and improve the foundation of science, technology and industry that supports the development and utilization of outer space, and promote the utilization of outer space from a security perspective.

In particular, Japan will engage itself in enhancing the functions of information-gathering satellites and in making effective use of satellites, including ones Japan possesses for the operation of the SDF units, information-gathering and analysis, maritime domain awareness, telecommunication, positioning, navigation and timing. In addition, Japan will enhance a system for space situational awareness.

Furthermore, Japan will promote the development and utilization of outer space in a manner that contributes to national security in the medium- to long-term, including the development of technologies such as satellite manufacturing.

(10) Strengthening Technological Capabilities
The advanced technology of Japan constitutes the foundation of its economic strength and defense forces, and is also a valuable resource that the international community strongly seeks from Japan. Therefore, Japan should encourage the further promotion of technologies, including dual use technologies, thereby strengthening Japan's technological capabilities.

In promoting measures for strengthening its technological capabilities from a national security viewpoint, Japan will constantly grasp science and technology trends, including information on technology development. Japan will also make effective use of technology in the area of security, by combining the efforts of industries, academia, and the Government.

Furthermore, Japan's outstanding energy-saving and other environment-related technologies play an important role in Japan's efforts to tackle global issues together with the international community. Therefore, Japan will proactively utilize these technologies in diplomacy as well.

2. Strengthening the Japan-U.S. Alliance
For more than 60 years, the Japan-U.S. Alliance, with the Japan-U.S. security arrangements at its core, has played an indispensable role for peace and security in Japan as well as peace and stability in the Asia-Pacific region. In recent years, the Alliance has also played a more critical role for peace, stability, and prosperity in the international

community.

The Japan-U.S. Alliance is the cornerstone of Japan's security. Likewise, for the U.S., the Alliance has served as the core of its alliance network with countries in the region, including the Republic of Korea (ROK), Australia, Thailand, and the Philippines. In this context, the Japan-U.S. Alliance has been serving as a foundation for the U.S. strategy in the Asia-Pacific region. Such close alliance between Japan and the U.S. is underpinned by various factors, including that the two countries share common strategic interests and universal values, such as freedom, democracy, respect for fundamental human rights, and the rule of law. Furthermore, Japan's geostrategic importance in supporting the U.S. engagement in the Asia-Pacific region underlies the close alliance of the two countries.

With the above-mentioned Japan-U.S. Alliance serving as the foundation, the two countries have been working closely at various levels, including at the summit and ministerial levels. The two countries address not only bilateral issues, but also the situation in the Asia-Pacific region, including North Korea, as well as global security issues, including counterterrorism measures and non-proliferation of WMD.

In the area of economy, Japan and the U.S. aim to achieve economic prosperity in the Asia-Pacific region in a rules-based and transparent manner, including through the Trans-Pacific Partnership (TPP) negotiations, which will be mentioned later in this document.

Thus, Japan and the U.S. have persistently strengthened and expanded their cooperation on a wide range of areas for peace, stability, and prosperity of not only the two countries themselves, but also the Asia-Pacific region and the broader international community.

As Japan strengthens its efforts in security as elaborated above, the U.S., based on its Defense Strategic Guidance emphasizing a rebalancing towards the Asia-Pacific region, aspires to enhance its presence in the region and strengthen cooperation with its allies, including Japan and its partners.

In order to ensure the security of Japan and to maintain and enhance peace, stability, and prosperity in the Asia-Pacific region and the international community, Japan must further elevate the effectiveness of the Japan-U.S. security arrangements and realize a more multifaceted Japan-U.S. Alliance. Based on this recognition, Japan will undertake the following initiatives:

(1) Further Strengthening of Japan-U.S. Security and Defense Cooperation in a Wide Range of Areas
Japan ensures its national security by enhancing deterrence through the strengthening of its own defense capability, as well as by the deterrence of the Japan-U.S. Alliance, including the extended deterrence provided by the U.S.

Japan will work with the U.S. to revise the Guidelines for Japan-U.S. Defense Cooperation, through discussions on a variety of issues such as the concrete manner of defense cooperation and basic concepts of bilateral roles, missions, and capabilities (RMC), while ensuring consistency with various policies in line with the Strategy.

In addition, Japan will strive to enhance the deterrence and response capability of the Japan-U.S. Alliance through the following efforts: advancing joint training, joint intelligence, surveillance, and reconnaissance (ISR) activities, and joint/shared use of facilities by the SDF and the U.S. forces; working closely with the U.S. on operational cooperation and policy coordination on issues such as response to contingencies and the medium- to long-term strategy; strengthening its security cooperation with the U.S. in such broad areas as BMD, maritime affairs, outer space, cyberspace and large-scale disaster response operations.

Moreover, in order to strengthen the foundation of the Alliance, including enhanced interoperability, Japan will advance multilayered initiatives with the U.S. such as defense equipment and technology cooperation and personnel exchanges.

(2) Ensuring a Stable Presence of the U.S. Forces
To maintain and enhance the Japan-U.S. security arrangements, it is important for Japan to cooperate proactively with the U.S. to realize the optimal force posture of the U.S. forces in the Asia-Pacific region. At the same time, it is also important for Japan to reduce the impact of the U.S. forces in Japan on local communities, including Okinawa, while maintaining and enhancing the deterrence of the Japan-U.S. Alliance.

As part of this effort, while firmly supporting the smooth and effective stationing of the U.S. forces in Japan through various measures, including Host Nation Support, Japan will steadily implement the realignment of the U.S. forces in Japan including the relocation of the U.S. Marine Corps in Okinawa to Guam in accordance with the existing bilateral agreements. In addition, Japan will further promote the joint/shared use of facilities by the SDF and the U.S. forces, while taking into consideration relations with local communities.

Furthermore, Japan will steadily implement measures to reduce the impact on people living near the facilities and areas of the U.S. forces in Japan. In particular, Okinawa Prefecture is situated in a critically important location in terms of national security, and the stationing of the U.S. forces there significantly contributes to the deterrence of the Japan-U.S. Alliance. In the meantime, as a large part of the facilities and areas for the exclusive use of the U.S. forces in Japan are concentrated in the prefecture, Japan will make utmost efforts to reduce the impact on Okinawa, including through the relocation of Marine Corps Air Station Futenma.

3. Strengthening Diplomacy and Security Cooperation with Japan's Partners for Peace and Stability in the International Community
As elaborated above, strengthening the Japan-U.S. alliance in all its aspects, including in political, economic and security areas is indispensable to improve the security environment surrounding Japan. On top of that, Japan will engage itself in building trust and cooperative relations with other partners both within and outside the Asia-Pacific region through the following approaches, as it plays an important role in enhancing Japan's security environment.

(1) Japan will strengthen cooperative relations with countries with which it shares universal values and strategic interests, such as the ROK, Australia, the countries of ASEAN, and India:
• The ROK is a neighboring country of the utmost geopolitical importance for the security of Japan. Close cooperation with the ROK is of great significance for

peace and stability of the region, including in addressing North Korean nuclear and missile issues. For this reason, Japan will construct future-oriented and multi-layered relations and strengthen the foundation for security cooperation with the ROK. In particular, trilateral cooperation among Japan, the U.S. and the ROK is a key framework in realizing peace and stability in East Asia. Japan will strengthen this trilateral framework, including in cooperation on North Korean nuclear and missile issues. With regard to the issue over the sovereignty of Takeshima, Japan will make persevering diplomatic efforts, based on the principle of peaceful resolution of conflicts in accordance with international law.

• Australia is an important regional partner that shares not only universal values but also strategic interests with Japan. In addition to strengthening the mutually complementary economic relations between the two countries, Japan will also strengthen its strategic partnership by steadily sharing strategic recognition and advancing security cooperation. Japan will also promote a wide range of cooperation with Australia in its efforts to shape a regional order in the Asia-Pacific and to maintain and reinforce peace and stability in the international community. In so doing, Japan will utilize the trilateral framework among Japan, the U.S. and Australia, as necessary.

• The countries of ASEAN, where economic growth and democratization have been progressing and which embraces great cultural diversity, are located in the critical areas of sea lanes of communication of Japan. Japan will further deepen and develop cooperative relations with the ASEAN countries in all sectors, including politics and security based on the traditional partnership lasting more than 40 years. Given the influence ASEAN has on peace, stability and prosperity of the Asia-Pacific region as a whole, Japan will provide further assistance to their efforts towards maintaining and strengthening the unity of ASEAN. Furthermore, Japan appreciates the efforts by the countries concerned to settle disputes in the South China Sea not by force, but in accordance with the law and rules, as shown in their efforts towards the formulation of a Code of Conduct (COC) with China. Japan will support these efforts so that an effective and legally binding code of conduct is formulated.

• India is becoming increasingly influential, due to what is projected to become the world's largest population, and to high economic growth and potential. India is also geopolitically important for Japan, as it is positioned in the center of sea lanes of communication. Japan will strengthen bilateral relations in a broad range of areas, including maritime security, based on the bilateral Strategic and Global Partnership.

(2) Stable relations between Japan and China are an essential factor for peace and stability of the Asia-Pacific region. From a broad, as well as a medium- to long-term perspective, Japan will strive to construct and enhance a Mutually Beneficial Relationship Based on Common Strategic Interests with China in all areas, including politics, economy, finance, security, culture and personal exchanges. In particular, Japan will continue to encourage China to play a responsible and constructive role for the sake of regional peace, stability and prosperity, to adhere to international norms of behavior, as well as to improve openness and transparency in its advancing military capabilities through its rapidly increasing military budget. As a part of

such efforts, through continuing and promoting defense cooperation, Japan will seek to urge improvement in transparency of China's military and security policies, and promote measures such as establishing a framework to avert or prevent unexpected situations. Furthermore, with regard to China's recent attempts to change the status quo by coercion based on its unique assertion in its relations with neighboring countries, including Japan, Japan will urge China to exercise self-restraint and will continue to respond firmly but in a calm manner without escalating the situation.

(3) With regard to the issues of North Korea, Japan will cooperate closely with relevant countries to urge North Korea to take concrete actions towards its denuclearization and other goals, based on the Joint Statement of the Six-Party Talks and relevant U.N. Security Council (UNSC) Resolutions. Concerning Japan-North Korea relations, Japan will endeavor to achieve a comprehensive resolution of outstanding issues of concern, such as the abduction, nuclear and missile issues, in accordance with the Japan-North Korea Pyongyang Declaration. In particular, it is the basic recognition of Japan that normalization of relations with North Korea will not be possible without resolving the abduction issue. Japan will make every effort to realize the safety and prompt return of all abductees at the earliest possible date, investigate the truth regarding the abductions, and transfer those who executed the abductions.

(4) Under the increasingly severe security environment in East Asia, it is critical for Japan to advance cooperation with Russia in all areas, including security and energy, thereby enhancing bilateral relations as a whole, in order to ensure its security. Based on this recognition, Japan will cooperate with Russia in securing peace and stability of the Asia-Pacific region. With regard to the issue of the Northern Territories, the most important pending issue between the two countries, Japan will vigorously negotiate with Russia under a consistent policy of resolving the issue of the attribution of the four islands and concluding a peace treaty.

(5) In promoting the efforts mentioned above, Japan will actively utilize and engage in the further development of functional and multilayered frameworks for regional cooperation, starting from Asia-Pacific Economic Cooperation (APEC), the East Asia Summit (EAS), ASEAN+3, ARF, the ASEAN Defense Ministers' Meeting-Plus (ADMM-Plus), to the Trans-Pacific Partnership (TPP) and trilateral frameworks, such as Japan-U.S.-ROK, Japan-U.S.-Australia and Japan-U.S.-India, as well as Japan-China-ROK, a grouping of three large neighboring economic powers. In addition, Japan will appropriately contribute to the creation of a more institutional security framework in East Asia in the future.

(6) Japan will also cooperate with other partners of the Asia-Pacific region towards ensuring the stability of the region. These partners include Mongolia, Central Asian countries, Southwest Asian nations, the Pacific Island Countries (PICs), New Zealand, Canada, Mexico, Colombia, Peru and Chile. In particular, Japan will deepen its cooperation with the PICs, which possess vast exclusive economic zones and abundant maritime resources in the Pacific Ocean, in many areas including

maritime cooperation, through such fora as the Pacific Islands Leaders' Meeting (PALM).

(7) Furthermore, Japan will strengthen cooperative relations with countries outside the Asia-Pacific region that play an important role in ensuring the peace and stability of the international community.
• Europe has the influence to formulate international public opinions, the capacity to develop norms in major international frameworks and a large economy. Japan and European countries, especially the United Kingdom, France, Germany, Italy, Spain and Poland, share universal values of freedom, democracy, respect for fundamental human rights and the rule of law, and principles such as market economy. They are partners for Japan which together take a leading role in ensuring the peace, stability and prosperity of the international community. At a time when the power balance of the international community is changing, in order to establish an international order based on universal values and rules, to effectively address global challenges, and to accomplish Japan's initiatives for a peaceful and prosperous international community, Japan will further strengthen its relations with Europe, including cooperation with the European Union (EU), the North Atlantic Treaty Organization (NATO), and the Organization for Security and Co-operation in Europe (OSCE). Japan has contributed to the democratization of East European countries and Baltic countries, and will engage in strengthening relations with them, as well as the Caucasus countries.
• Emerging countries such as Brazil, Mexico, Turkey, Argentina and South Africa have been increasing their presence not only in the international economy, but also in international politics. Japan will therefore endeavor to further develop relations with such countries, not merely on a bilateral basis, but in cooperative efforts in tackling global challenges.
• Stability in the Middle East is an issue that is inseparably linked to the stable supply of energy, and therefore Japan's very survival and prosperity. Given that the Gulf States are the largest source of crude oil for Japan, in order to ensure the stability of the Middle East, Japan will engage in constructing multilayered cooperative relations with these countries, encompassing wide-raging economic cooperation beyond resources and energy, as well as politics and security. In this context, Japan will play a proactive role in the resolution of major issues affecting the stability of the Middle East, including the issue of democratization in Arab countries that stems from the "Arab Spring," the situation in Syria, Iran's nuclear issue, the Middle East peace process and peacebuilding in Afghanistan. In the same vein, Japan will also collaborate with other countries that play important roles in the Middle East, such as the U.S., European countries, Saudi Arabia and Turkey.
• Africa is a prospective economic frontier with abundant strategic natural resources and sustained economic growth. In addition, Africa has been increasing its influence in the international community. Japan will continue to contribute to the development and the consolidation of peace in Africa through various avenues, especially through the Tokyo International Conference on African Development (TICAD) process, and promote cooperation in international fora.

4. Proactive Contribution to International Efforts for Peace and Stability of the International Community
As a "Proactive Contributor to Peace" based on the principle of international cooperation, Japan will play an active role for the peace and stability of the international community.

(1) Strengthening Diplomacy at the United Nations
The U.N. was established with the UNSC as the core of a collective security system for maintaining international peace and security. However, the system has not fully functioned as originally anticipated. Nevertheless, the U.N. has taken the lead on various efforts for peace and security of the world, backed by its legitimacy through universal participation by the Member States and its expertise. In particular, since the end of the Cold War, the role played by the U.N. in maintaining international peace and security has continued to grow.

Building on the invaluable experiences of having served on numerous occasions as a non-permanent member of the UNSC, Japan will further engage in active efforts by the U.N. for the maintenance and restoration of international peace and security.

Moreover, Japan will actively contribute to diverse U.N.-led efforts, including U.N. peacekeeping operations (PKO) and collective security measures; diplomatic efforts such as preventive diplomacy and mediation; seamless assistance efforts from the phase of post-conflict emergency humanitarian relief to recovery and reconstruction, as well as assistance through the U.N. Peacebuilding Commission.

At the same time, one must be mindful that realizing the enhancement of the effectiveness and legitimacy of the U.N., including the strengthening of collective security functions, is an urgent challenge. Therefore, Japan will continue to strive to achieve the UNSC reform, including through an expansion of both permanent and non-permanent categories, with Japan becoming a permanent member of the Council.

(2) Strengthening the Rule of Law
Japan will continue to faithfully comply with international law as a guardian of the rule of law. In addition, in order to establish the rule of law in the international community, Japan will participate proactively in international rule-making from the planning stage, so that Japan's principles and positions based on fairness, transparency and reciprocity are duly reflected. Furthermore, Japan will actively support international judicial organs in terms of both human capital and finance. In addition, Japan will actively engage in assistance for the development of legal systems in other countries.

In particular, Japan will involve itself in realizing and strengthening the rule of law relating to the sea, outer space and cyberspace. While advancing policy coordination with countries with shared interests, Japan will contribute proactively to the development of international rules in the above-mentioned areas, and to the promotion of confidence building measures among countries of mutual interest. In addition, Japan will further strengthen capacity building efforts for developing countries in these fields. More concretely:

• With regard to the sea, Japan will promote regional efforts and play a leading role in creating a shared recognition that reinforcement of the maritime order governed by law and rules and not by coercion is indispensable for peace and prosperity of the international community as a whole.

• With regard to outer space, emphasizing the concept of ensuring freedom of access and utilization of space, Japan will participate proactively in the efforts to formulate an international code of conduct that aims to prevent experiments of anti-satellite weapons (ASAT) and avoid collision of satellites, and consequently strive to ensure safe and stable use of outer space.

• With regard to cyberspace, based on the recognition of ensuring the free flow of information in cyberspace, Japan will actively cooperate with like-minded countries in the development of international rules on the premise that existing international law applies to cyberspace. Japan will also vigorously support the capacity building efforts of developing countries in this area.

(3) Leading International Efforts on Disarmament and Non-Proliferation

Japan, as the only country in the world to have suffered atomic bombings in war, will continue its vigorous efforts to seek "a world free of nuclear weapons."

In view of the threat posed by progress in nuclear and missile development by North Korea, and being mindful of future trends in the balance of nuclear forces in the Asia-Pacific region together with the rapid advancement of military technologies, Japan will lead international efforts on disarmament and non-proliferation, including those towards the resolution of North Korea's nuclear and missile development issues and Iran's nuclear issues, in a manner consistent with the maintenance of the credibility of extended deterrence under the Japan-U.S. alliance.

Furthermore, Japan will steadily implement export control measures from a security perspective, including active participation in the discussions in the international export control regime, in coordination with other relevant countries, to prevent the proliferation of arms, as well as dual use items or technologies to countries of proliferation concern. In addition, Japan will engage in international efforts on conventional weapons, such as small arms and light weapons, and anti-personnel mines.

(4) Promoting International Peace Cooperation

Over the course of more than 20 years, Japan has dispatched SDF units and other personnel to various regions on international peace cooperation assignments, including in Cambodia, the Golan Heights, Timor-Leste, Nepal, and South Sudan. These contributions have been deeply appreciated both in Japan and by the international community.

Japan will further step up its cooperation with U.N. PKO and other international peace cooperation activities with its determination to contribute even more proactively to peace based on the principle of international cooperation, taking into account the appreciation and expectation Japan receives from the international community. In addition, when participating in PKO, Japan will endeavor to ensure effective implementation of its operations, through coordination with other activities, including ODA projects.

Moreover, in order to implement seamless assistance in security-related areas, including through further strategic utilization of ODA and capacity building assistance, as well as coordination with non-governmental organizations (NGOs), Japan will develop a system that enables assistance to potential recipient organizations that cannot receive Japan's assistance under the current schemes.

Furthermore, Japan as a whole will proactively engage in training for peace-building experts and PKO personnel in various countries. When engaging in such efforts, Japan will consult closely with countries or organizations that have experience in the same fields, including the U.S., Australia and European countries.

(5) Promoting International Cooperation against International Terrorism

Acts of terrorism are unjustifiable regardless of their motivation and must be firmly condemned. It is important for the international community as a whole to take a firm position against them.

Japan will promote international counter-terrorism efforts with the international community for national security. Japan will promote consultations and exchanges of views with other countries on the situation on international terrorism and international counter-terrorism cooperation; reinforcement of the international legal framework to stringently punish terrorists; and assistance to developing countries which do not have sufficient capacity for counter-terrorism and other measures.

Furthermore, Japan must be aware that terrorism and transnational organized crime are closely linked in light of the situation whereby the proceeds of organized crime, such as illicit trafficking, the trade of arms and drugs, and kidnapping, form an important source of funding for terrorists. Therefore, Japan will enhance international cooperation and assistance for developing countries to prevent and combat transnational organized crime.

5. Strengthening Cooperation Based on Universal Values to Resolve Global Issues

Japan will endeavor to share universal values and reinforce an open international economic system, which form the basis of peace, stability and prosperity of the international community. At the same time, Japan will advance the following measures towards the resolution of development issues and global issues that could hinder peace and stability of the international community, such as poverty, energy issues, widening disparity, climate change, natural disasters, and food-related issues, through the active and strategic utilization of ODA, as necessary.

(1) Sharing Universal Values

Through a partnership with countries with which Japan shares universal values, such as freedom, democracy, respect for fundamental human rights including women's rights, and the rule of law, Japan will conduct diplomacy that contributes to addressing global issues.

The wave of democratization that began in the countries of Eastern Europe and ASEAN in the 1990s and spread to the countries of the Arab world at the beginning of the 2010s has become an irreversible tide, coupled with the rapid development of globalization and market-oriented economic reforms.

On the other hand, as was observed in the "Arab Spring," the process of democratization does not always proceed smoothly. As an advanced, liberal and democratic nation, based on the principle of human security, Japan will actively utilize its ODA in supporting democratization, the development of legal systems, and human rights, and contribute to the enhancement of the growing international trend towards the protection of human rights, including through dialogues in the area of human rights.

Japan will also engage proactively in diplomatic issues on women, cooperating with the international community to implement measures to empower women in conflict prevention and peacebuilding, and promote their social advancement.

(2) Responding to Global Development and Global Issues and Realizing Human Security

Japan has garnered high recognition by the international community, by its proactive contribution to global development in the world through utilizing ODA. Addressing development issues contributes to the enhancement of the global security environment, and it is necessary for Japan to strengthen its efforts as part of "Proactive Contribution to Peace" based on the principle of international cooperation.

Against this backdrop, in order to contribute to the realization of human security, Japan will utilize its ODA in a strategic and effective manner. Japan will also strengthen efforts towards the achievement of the MDGs, in areas such as poverty eradication, global health, education and water, in cooperation with diverse stakeholders, including international organizations and NGOs.

In addition, Japan will play a leading role in the formulation of new international development goals, namely the post-2015 development agenda. In this context, Japan will engage in further efforts in mainstreaming the concept of human security in the international community, building on our initiatives on this agenda to date.

Moreover, Japan will share the lessons learned and experiences from the many natural disasters that it has experienced, including the Great Hanshin-Awaji Earthquake, the Great East Japan Earthquake and Tsunami. Given the expanding scale, impact and frequency of disasters globally, Japan will take the lead in international cooperation on disaster management and ensure that communities around the world have a high degree of resilience to disasters.

(3) Cooperating with Human Resource Development Efforts in Developing Countries

Japan will invite a broad range of personnel from developing countries, including eminent students and administrative officials who are expected to become future leaders. Japan will make use of such opportunities to learn from their knowledge and experience, as well as providing them with opportunities to be familiarized with Japanese systems, technologies and expertise. Japan will further promote human resource development in order to enhance mutual understanding with Japan, and ensure that these personnel can contribute to sustainable economic and social development in their home countries.

Japan will engage in efforts to maintain and develop such human networks to expand and reinforce the foundations of cooperation.

(4) Maintaining and Strengthening the Free Trade System
The expansion of the open and rule-based international economic system, where Japan continues to be a major player, is essential for the world economy and Japan's economic prosperity. In this regard, Japan will promote economic partnership, including through the Trans-Pacific Partnership (TPP), the Japan-EU Economic Partnership Agreement (EPA), a Free Trade Agreement (FTA) among Japan, China and the ROK, and the Regional Comprehensive Economic Partnership (RCEP), so as to achieve comprehensive and high-level trade agreements. Through these efforts, Japan will contribute to the growth of the global economy, which in turn, will also bring economic growth to Japan.

In addition, rule-making for trade and investment in the Asia-Pacific region through the above-mentioned efforts strengthens the vigor and prosperity in the region, and has a strategic importance of strengthening the foundation for a stable security environment in the region.

It is expected that the conclusion of such 21st- century economic partnership agreements will set new and attractive precedents of trade liberalization, and promote global-scale trade liberalization in the multilateral trade regime based on the WTO.

(5) Responding to Energy and Environmental Issues
The stable supply of energy and other resources is essential for a vibrant Japanese economy and thus constitutes a challenge to national security. Promoting measures such as the diversification of supply sources is necessary for securing stable and low-cost resource supply. Japan will actively utilize diplomatic tools to gain the understanding of countries concerned in this course.

In the area of climate change, Japan will increase its engagements towards emission reduction. Japan will implement a proactive strategy for countering global warming (the Actions for Cool Earth (ACE)) that utilizes its strengths in outstanding technologies on environment and energy, and its assistance to developing countries. At the same time, Japan will engage in establishing a fair and effective international framework with participation by all countries. Through these efforts, Japan will contribute to the achievement of emission reduction by the international community as a whole and to the resolution of climate change issues.

(6) Enhancing People-to-people Exchanges
People-to-people exchanges are significant as they enhance mutual understanding and friendship between countries and solidify national ties, while also helping to develop a stable and friendly security environment by deepening an appropriate understanding towards Japan in the international community.

In particular, Japan will implement measures to expand two-way youth exchanges and will seek to strengthen relations with various countries into the future. For example, Japan has recently marked 40 years of friendship and cooperation with ASEAN, where regional integration is advancing while maintaining cultural diversity. By further vitalizing exchange programs with ASEAN, Japan will further promote mutual understanding.

Moreover, through events of interest for the world, such as the 2020 Olympic and Paralympic Games in Tokyo, Japan will promote people-to-people exchanges through sport and culture, and will work to construct and deepen friendly relations at the individual level.

6. Strengthening the Domestic Foundation that Supports National Security and Promoting Domestic and Global Understanding
In order to fully ensure national security, in addition to strengthening key capabilities with diplomatic power and defense force at their core, it is vital to reinforce the domestic foundation for these capabilities to be effectively demonstrated.

Furthermore, considering the importance of seeking a deeper understanding for Japan's security policies both at home and abroad to ensure national security, Japan will advance the following measures.

(1) Maintaining and Enhancing Defense Production and Technological Bases
Defense production and technological bases are one of the important factors that support defense forces through research, development, production, operation and maintenance of defense equipment. In order to develop, maintain and operate defense capability steadily with limited resources in the medium- to long-term, Japan will endeavor to engage in effective and efficient acquisition of defense equipment, and will maintain and enhance its defense production and technological bases, including through strengthening international competitiveness.

(2) Boosting Communication Capabilities
In order to promote its security policy from a medium- to long-term perspective, it is imperative that Japan proactively and effectively communicate its policy to the world and its people, and increase transparency. In this regard, it is necessary to deepen the understanding among the people of Japan regarding security policy and build cooperative relations and trust with other countries.

To this end, with the Prime Minister's office serving as the control tower, Japan will enhance its public relations in an integrated and strategic manner through a government-wide approach. Fully utilizing various information technologies and diverse media, Japan will also strengthen its information dissemination in foreign languages. In addition, the Government as a whole will cooperate with educational institutions, key figures, and think tanks. In doing so, Japan will promote Japanese language education overseas, and train personnel who are capable of contributing to strategic public relations efforts and other areas.

At a time when the global security environment is becoming more complex and diverse, it becomes increasingly likely for countries to have conflicting interests. However, by precisely and effectively communicating information on Japan's position based on objective facts, Japan will be able to gain accurate understanding in the forum of international opinion, and contribute to the stability of the international community.

(3) Reinforcing the Social Base
In order to support national security policy from a medium- to long-term perspective, it is essential that each and every Japanese national hopes to contribute to peace and stability in the region and the world, and to the improvement of the welfare of humanity. In addition, it is also essential that they perceive national se-

curity as a familiar and immediate issue for them, and have deep understanding of its importance and complexity.

To that end, the Government of Japan will promote the following measures: foster respect for other countries and their people as well as love for the country and region; raise awareness with regard to security on such issues as territory and sovereignty; and ensure the understanding and cooperation of residents around defense facilities, which serve as the foundation for the activities of the SDF and the U.S. forces in Japan, through advancing measures that widen the understanding of the general public about the current status of such activities.

(4) Enhancing the Intellectual Base
In order to invigorate a national discussion and debate and contribute to high-quality policymaking on national security, Japan will seek to enhance and strengthen education on security-related subjects at institutions of higher education, including through the dispatch of officials of relevant ministries. In addition, Japan will promote practical research on national security, and engage in deepening exchanges among the Government, higher education institutions and think tanks, thereby promoting the sharing of insight and knowledge.

Furthermore, Japan will promote the creation of experts and government officials that can make practical and constructive contributions to national security policy, thus broadening the pool of experts on national security.

Source: Cabinet Secretariat, "National Security Strategy." www.cas.go.jp/jp/siryou/131217anzenho-shou/nss-e.pdf (accessed December 20, 2016).

Appendix I

National Defense Program Guidelines for FY2014 and Beyond

December 17, 2013

I. NDPG's Objective

In light of the current security environment surrounding Japan, the Government of Japan sets out the "National Defense Program Guidelines for FY2014 and beyond" as new guidelines for Japan's national defense, based on "Defense Capability Build-up in FY2013" (approved by the Security Council and the Cabinet on January 25, 2013) and the "National Security Strategy" (approved by the National Security Council and the Cabinet on December 17, 2013).

II. Security Environment Surrounding Japan

1. As interdependence among countries expands and deepens, there is a growing risk that unrest in the global security environment or a security problem in a single country or region could immediately develop into a security challenge or destabilizing factor for the entire international community. The multi-polarization of the world continues as a result of shifts in the balance of power due to the further development of countries such as China and India and the relative change of influence of the United States (U.S.). At the same time, the U.S. is expected to continue to play the role in maintaining world peace and stability as it retains the largest national power.

There are ongoing regional conflicts involving various countries as well as an increase in the number of so-called "gray-zone" situations, that is, neither pure peacetime nor contingencies over territory, sovereignty and maritime economic interests.

The proliferation of weapons of mass destruction (WMD) and ballistic missiles continues to be a deep concern despite non-proliferation efforts by the international community. The presence of countries with weak governance and failed states feeds the expansion and spread of international terrorism. These problems continue to pose imminent security challenges.

In the maritime domain, piracy acts have taken place in various parts of the world, and there have been cases where coastal states unilaterally asserted their rights and took action based on their own assertion concerning international maritime law, thereby unduly infringing the freedom of the high seas.

Securing the stable use of outer space and cyberspace as global commons is becoming a significant security challenge for the international community including Japan against the backdrop of rapid technology innovation. In addition, military strategies and military balance in the future are anticipated to be significantly affected by the progress and proliferation of technologies such as those related to precision guided munitions, unmanned vehicles, stealth capability and nanotechnology.

2. In the Asia-Pacific region, including areas surrounding Japan, countries are enhancing and strengthening their cooperative relationships to resolve security challenges. Specific and practical cooperation and collaboration have progressed to settle challenges particularly in non-traditional security fields. In the meantime, gray-zone situations over territory, sovereignty and maritime economic interests tend to linger, raising concerns that they may develop into more serious situations.

North Korea is military-focused and deploys a massive military force. It is also proceeding with the development, deployment and proliferation of WMDs including nuclear weapons and ballistic missiles which may be used to deliver such weapons, and it maintains a large-scale special operations force. Through these activities, North Korea is maintaining and strengthening its asymmetrical military capabilities.

North Korea has also repeatedly heightened tension in the region by conducting military provocations in the Korean Peninsula and by escalating its provocative rhetoric and behavior against Japan and other countries. Such North Korean military trend constitutes a serious destabilizing factor to the security not only of Japan but of the entire region and the international community. Therefore, Japan needs to pay utmost attention to such activities.

In particular, North Korea's ballistic missile development has presumably entered a new stage, as technological improvements have been made to extend the range and increase the accuracy of its missiles through a series of missile launches. Also, North Korea has conducted nuclear tests in defiance of calls for restraint from the international community, so the possibility cannot be ruled out that it has successfully miniaturized nuclear weapons for warheads and equipped them on ballistic missiles. North Korea's nuclear and missile development, coupled with its provocative rhetoric and behavior, such as suggesting a missile attack on Japan, pose a serious and imminent threat to Japan's security.

As for China, while it is greatly expected to play an active role in a more cooperative manner in the region and the world, it has been continuously increasing its defense expenditures and has been rapidly reinforcing its military in a wide range of areas. As part of such effort, China is believed to be making efforts to strengthen its asymmetrical military capabilities to prevent military activity by other countries in the region by denying access and deployment of foreign militaries to its surrounding areas. However, China has not clearly stated the purposes and goals of the military buildup and therefore, transparency concerning its military and security is not fully achieved.

In addition, China is rapidly expanding and intensifying its activities in the maritime and aerial domains in the region including in the East China Sea and the South China Sea. In particular, China has taken assertive actions with regard to issues of conflicts of interest in the maritime domain, as exemplified by its attempts to change the status quo by coercion. As for the seas and airspace around Japan, China has intruded into Japanese territorial waters frequently and violated Japan's airspace, and has engaged in dangerous activities that could cause unexpected situations, such as its announcement of establishing an "Air Defense Identification Zone" based on its own assertion thereby infringing the freedom of overflight above the high seas.

China is also expanding and intensifying its activities in the maritime and aerial domains farther offshore than before. For example, Chinese military vessels and aircraft routinely enter the Pacific Ocean, and are expanding their operational areas which include areas north of Japan.

As Japan has great concern about these Chinese activities, it will need to pay utmost attention to them, as these activities also raise concerns over regional and global security.

As for Russia, it is observed that the country is proceeding to reform and modernize its military forces mainly by strengthening their readiness and introducing new equipment. The activities of Russian armed forces have been active.

The U.S. has clearly manifested its strategic decision to put greater emphasis on the Asia-Pacific region (the rebalance to the Asia-Pacific region) and is maintaining and strengthening its engagement and presence in the region despite fiscal and various other constraints in order to maintain the stability and growth of the region while enhancing its relationships with its allies and expanding cooperation with partner countries. In addition, the U.S. has made its stance clear to prevent coercive actions that aim at changing the status quo in the region in cooperation with allies and partners.

3. Japan is surrounded by the sea, and has a long coastline, numerous remote islands and a vast Exclusive Economic Zone. Japan is a maritime state and dependent largely on international trade for its supply of food and natural resources. Therefore, securing the safety of maritime and air traffic, through strengthening an "Open and Stable Seas" order based upon such fundamental principles as the rule of law and the freedom of navigation, constitutes the basis of peace and prosperity.

Japan also faces security vulnerabilities resulting from concentration of industry, population and information infrastructure in urban areas and from the presence of a large number of key facilities, such as nuclear power plants, in coastal areas.

In the event of another massive earthquake like the Great East Japan Earthquake, Japan may suffer enormous damage and the impact may spread not only nationwide but also to other countries. The possibility of future huge earthquakes such as a Nankai Trough earthquake or a Tokyo inland earthquake makes it increasingly necessary to take every possible measure to prepare for large-scale disasters.

4. In light of the above, while the probability of a large-scale military conflict between major countries, which was a concern during the Cold War era, presumably remains low, various security challenges and destabilizing factors are emerging and becoming more tangible and acute. As a result, the security environment surrounding Japan has become increasingly severe, since the formulation of "National Defense Program Guidelines, FY2011 and beyond" (approved by the Security Council and the Cabinet on December 17, 2010). As the security challenges and destabilizing factors are diverse and wide-ranging, it is difficult for a single country to deal with them on its own. Under these circumstances, it is increasingly necessary not only that the military sector cooperate with the non-military sector but also that countries which share interests in responding to shared security challenges cooperate and actively respond to maintain regional and global stability.

III. Japan's Basic Defense Policy

1. Basic Policy
In light of the National Security Strategy, Japan will strengthen its diplomatic and defense capabilities along the policy of "Proactive Contribution to Peace" based on the

principle of international cooperation, thereby expanding the role it can play. At the same time, Japan will contribute even more proactively in securing peace, stability and prosperity of the international community while achieving its own security as well as peace and stability in the Asia-Pacific region by expanding and deepening cooperative relationships with other countries, with the Japan-U.S. Alliance as its cornerstone.

Under this basic principle, Japan will build a comprehensive defense architecture and strengthen its posture for preventing and responding to various situations. In addition, Japan will strengthen the Japan-U.S. Alliance and actively promote bilateral and multilateral security cooperation with other countries while closely coordinating defense and diplomatic policies. Japan will also seek to establish an infrastructure necessary for its defense forces to fully exercise their capabilities.

When implementing these measures, under the Constitution, Japan will efficiently build a highly effective and joint defense force in line with the basic principles of maintaining an exclusively defense-oriented policy, not becoming a military power that poses a threat to other countries, while adhering to the principle of civilian control of the military and observing the Three Non-Nuclear Principles.

With regard to the threat of nuclear weapons, the extended deterrence provided by the U.S. with nuclear deterrence at its core, is indispensable. In order to maintain and enhance the credibility of the extended deterrence, Japan will closely cooperate with the U.S. In addition, Japan will take appropriate responses through its own efforts, including ballistic missile defense (BMD) and protection of the people. At the same time, Japan will play a constructive and active role in international nuclear disarmament and non-proliferation efforts so as to achieve the long-term goal of creating a world free of nuclear weapons.

2. Japan's Own Efforts
Recognizing that a country's security depends first and foremost on its independent efforts, Japan will make full-scale efforts on its own initiative to prevent various situations and will seamlessly respond to them as the situation evolves with the National Security Council as the control tower, while maintaining cooperation with its ally, partners and other countries concerned.

(1) Building a comprehensive defense architecture
Given the increasingly severe security environment, Japan will efficiently develop a highly effective joint defense force and make efforts to employ it with a high level of flexibility and readiness based on joint operations. Japan will also ensure close regular interagency cooperation in normal times. In the event of various situations, the Government, under strong political leadership, will appropriately and promptly make decisions. Japan will seamlessly respond to situations as they unfold, in a whole-of-the-government approach, to ensure the protection of the lives and property of its people and the sovereignty of Japan's territorial land, waters and airspace, in coordination with local governments, private sectors, and others.

Japan will also continue to develop various systems to respond to a variety of disasters and protect its people and will enhance the capability to quickly evacuate Japanese nationals from foreign countries in an emergency situation and ensure their safety.

In order to take such approaches appropriately, Japan will increase the effectiveness of its situation and disaster response posture by systemizing various related plans and formulating and reviewing them as well as expanding the use of simulations, comprehensive training and exercises.

(2) Japan's defense forces – building a Dynamic Joint Defense Force
Japan's defense forces are the ultimate guarantee of national security, and represent Japan's will and ability to deter threats from directly reaching Japan and defeat them if threats should reach Japan.

In the times of an ever-changing security environment surrounding Japan, defense forces need to be constantly reviewed to adapt to the environment. To this aim, Japan needs to allocate limited resources in a focused and flexible way to prioritize the functions and capabilities from a comprehensive perspective, identified through joint operation-based capability assessments of the Self-Defense Force's (SDF's) total functions and capabilities against various situations.

Amid the increasingly severe security environment surrounding Japan, the SDF, in addition to its regular activities, needs to respond to various situations, including "gray zone" situations which require SDF commitment. The frequency of such situations and the duration of responses are both increasing. Therefore, Japan will regularly conduct persistent intelligence, surveillance and reconnaissance (hereinafter "ISR") activities. Moreover, the SDF will conduct strategic training and exercises in accordance with the development of the situation and swiftly build a response posture including advance deployment of units in response to the security environment and rapid deployment of adequate units. Thus Japan will demonstrate its will and highly developed capability to prevent further escalation. In dealing with situations, depending on their development, minimizing damage by effective response through achieving maritime supremacy and air superiority is essential in safeguarding the lives and property of the Japanese people, and the sovereignty of Japan's territorial land, waters and airspace.

Therefore, Japan will enhance its deterrence and response capability by improving the mission-capable rate of equipment and its employment to conduct tailored activities swiftly and sustainably based on joint operations, as well as by developing defense capabilities adequate both in quantity and quality that underpin various activities to realize a more robust defense force.

At the same time, from the perspective of "Proactive Contribution to Peace" based on the principle of international cooperation, Japan will strengthen its bilateral and multilateral cooperative relationships in order to ensure the stability of the Asia-Pacific region, which is closely related to its own security. Japan will also engage in international peacekeeping and other similar activities (peacekeeping operations by the United Nations, non-traditional security initiatives including Humanitarian Assistance/Disaster Relief (HA/DR), and other internationally collaborative activities to improve the international security environment) and other efforts more proactively than before as efforts to address the global security challenges, in light of the diversified roles and increased opportunities of the defense force.

From these viewpoints, given the changes in the security environment, the defense force based on this NDPG should prioritize particularly important functions and capabilities through optimal resource allocation as a whole. The defense force also must be an effective one which enables conducting a diverse range of activities to be seamless as well as dynamic and adapting to situations as they demand. To that end, Japan will build a Dynamic Joint Defense Force, which emphasizes both soft and hard aspects of readiness, sustainability, resiliency and connectivity, reinforced by advanced technology and capability for C3I, with a consideration to establish a wide range of infrastructure to support the SDF's operation.

3. Strengthening of the Japan-U.S. Alliance
The Japan-U.S. Security Arrangements based on the Japan-U.S. Security Treaty, together with Japan's own efforts, constitute the cornerstone for Japan's national security. The Japan-U.S. Alliance centered on bilateral security arrangements functions as public goods that contribute to the stability and prosperity not only of Japan but also of the Asia-Pacific region and the world at large.

Under its policy of strategic rebalancing towards the Asia-Pacific region, the U.S. is maintaining and strengthening its engagement and presence in the region while enhancing its partnerships and cooperation with its allies, including Japan, and partner countries. As the security environment surrounding Japan becomes increasingly severer, it has become more important than ever for Japan's security to strengthen the Japan-U.S. Alliance and make it more balanced and effective.

(1) Strengthening deterrence and response capabilities of the Japan-U.S. Alliance
In order to ensure Japan's national security by maintaining and strengthening the commitment of the U.S. towards Japan and the Asia-Pacific region, Japan will revise the Guidelines for Japan-U.S. Defense Cooperation, further enhance Japan-U.S. defense cooperation and reinforce the deterrence provided by the Japan-U.S. Alliance and the alliance's contingency response capabilities, while strengthening Japan's own capabilities as a premise for these efforts.

At the same time, in response to the increasingly severe security environment, while increasing the presence of Japan and the U.S. in the western Pacific region, Japan will build seamless cooperation with the U.S. ranging from situations on a day-to-day basis to various situations, including cooperation in responding to "gray-zone" situations.

To that end, Japan will continue to expand joint training and exercises, joint ISR activities and the joint/shared use of facilities and areas with the U.S. It will also tighten the Japan-U.S. operational cooperation and policy coordination including contingency response and medium-to long-term strategies, such as BMD, bilateral planning, and Extended Deterrence Dialogue.

(2) Strengthening and expanding cooperation in a broad range of fields
The Japan-U.S. Alliance will contribute to the peace and stability of the world, including the Asia-Pacific region, by strengthening cooperation not only in the fields of anti-piracy efforts, capacity building assistance, HA/DR, peacekeeping and counter terrorism but also in maritime affairs, outer space and cyberspace.

As for disaster response, Japan will further strengthen its cooperation between the SDF and the U.S. forces within and outside Japan in light of the fact that the U.S. forces, including its USFJ facilities and areas, greatly contributed to the safety of the Japanese people during the Great East Japan Earthquake.

In addition, Japan will constantly strengthen and expand the Japan-U.S. cooperative relationship over a broad range of fields, including efforts for intelligence cooperation and information security, and cooperation in the field of defense equipment and technology, to build a firmer and effective alliance.

(3) Steady implementation of measures relating to the stationing of U.S. Forces in Japan

Japan will provide stable support for the smooth and effective stationing of U.S. forces in Japan through various measures, including Host Nation Support (HNS). At the same time, efforts will be made to steadily implement the realignment of U.S. forces in Japan and mitigate the impact on local communities while maintaining the deterrence provided by U.S. forces. In particular, Japan will seek to mitigate the impact on Okinawa, located in a critically important location in terms of national security and where the stationing of U.S. forces significantly contributes to the deterrence of the Japan-U.S. Alliance, by realignment, consolidation and reduction of USFJ facilities and areas including through the relocation of Marine Corps Air Station Futenma as well as the dispersion of the impact and other measures, in light of the heavy concentration of such facilities and areas there.

4. Active Promotion of Security Cooperation

(1) Cooperation in the Asia-Pacific region

In the Asia-Pacific region, specific cooperative measures have been taken mainly in non-traditional security fields, including disaster relief. Multilateral frameworks such as the ASEAN Regional Forum (ARF), the ASEAN Defense Ministers' Meeting-Plus (ADMM-Plus) and the East Asia Summit (EAS) have been developed and the regional integration initiative led by ASEAN has been making progress. However, security challenges are becoming more serious than ever in North East Asia. Japan will promote a variety of further cooperative initiatives in a multi-layered manner to ease the atmosphere of confrontation and the sense of curiosity toward one another in the region.

Japan will promote close cooperation with the Republic of Korea (ROK), which is in a position to support the U.S. presence in North East Asia together with Japan, and will make efforts to establish a foundation for further cooperation with the ROK, for example by concluding an agreement on security information protection and an acquisition and cross-servicing agreement.

Japan will further deepen its relationship with Australia, with which Japan shares security interests and security cooperation has been advancing, and strengthen cooperation in fields such as international peacekeeping activities. Japan will also actively conduct joint training and other activities so as to improve interoperability with Australia.

Moreover, efforts will be made to promote the partnerships among U.S. allies in the Asia-Pacific region by strengthening cooperative relationships under trilateral frameworks among Japan, the U.S. and ROK and among Japan, the U.S. and Australia.

As Chinese activities have a significant impact on regional security, Japan will promote security dialogue and exchanges with China in order to enhance mutual understanding and will develop confidence-building measures to prevent unexpected situations. Japan will maintain a calm and firm stance in dealing with the rapid expansion and intensification of Chinese activities on the sea and in the air surrounding Japan.

Japan will promote security dialogues with Russia, including the Foreign and Defense Ministerial Consultations ("2+2"), high-level exchanges, and unit-to-unit exchanges in order to deepen understanding about the intention of Russian military activities and develop mutual trust with Russia. In addition, Japan will enhance bilateral training and exercises with Russia to promote regional stability.

Japan will also further strengthen its relationships with partner countries in the region, including Southeast Asian countries, and will actively promote joint training and exercises and capacity building assistance. In addition, Japan will strengthen its cooperation with these countries in the field of disaster management in light of the increasing frequency and growing scale of disasters in the region. Japan will strengthen its relationship with India in a broad range of fields, including maritime security, through joint training and exercises as well as joint implementation of international peacekeeping activities.

As capacity building assistance is effective in stabilizing the security environment and strengthening bilateral defense cooperation, Japan will promote it in full coordination with diplomatic policy initiatives, including the Official Development Assistance, and aligning it with joint training and exercises and international peacekeeping activities. Japan will also strengthen cooperation with relevant countries which actively provide such support, thereby expanding the range of countries receiving support as well as its scope.

Under ongoing multilateral security cooperation and dialogue in the Asia-Pacific region, Japan in cooperation with the United States and Australia will proactively contribute to building cooperative relationships in the region. Moreover, Japan will actively participate in multilateral joint training and exercises and play a major role in enhancing confidence-building measures among countries in the region, attaching importance to multilateral frameworks such as the ARF and the ADMM-Plus.

(2) Cooperation with the international community

It is very difficult for a single country to respond to global security challenges on its own. Moreover, as the roles of military forces have diversified, there are increasing opportunities for such forces to play an important role not only in preventing and responding to conflicts and maintaining peace but also in supporting post-conflict reconstruction, building peace and promoting confidence-building and friendly relationships.

Therefore, Japan will promote various initiatives to improve the global security environment on a regular basis in cooperation with the international community.

Japan will continue and strengthen various initiatives concerning arms control, disarmament, nonproliferation and capacity building assistance in order to respond to global security challenges, including regional conflicts, expansion and spread of international terrorism, failed states, proliferation of weapons of mass destruction and problems related to the sea, outer space and cyberspace, while regularly cooperating with its ally and relevant countries with which it shares security interests and with international organizations and other relevant bodies. In this respect, Japan will further strengthen its cooperation with the European Union (EU), North Atlantic Treaty Organization (NATO), the Organization for Security and Co-operation in Europe (OSCE) and with the United Kingdom, France and other European countries and will work with them in responding to these challenges. Japan will also promote cooperation and exchanges with regard to equipment and technology with these countries and organizations.

In order to stabilize the security environment in the Asia-Pacific region and improve the global security environment based on the policy of "Proactive Contribution to Peace" based on the principle of international cooperation, Japan will actively promote various international peace cooperation activities, including international peace cooperation assignments and emergency relief activities, in a multi-layered manner. To this end, Japan will ensure close cooperation between the defense and foreign affairs authorities, with comprehensive consideration given to the significance of the dispatch of SDF units, the situation of countries accepting SDF units and Japan's political and economic relationships with recipient countries.

With regard to international peace cooperation activities and other similar activities in particular, Japan will continue to actively conduct activities utilizing the SDF's capabilities and will increase the number of SDF personnel it dispatches to assume positions of responsibility at organizations such as the local mission headquarters and the United Nations Department of Peacekeeping Operations. In addition, Japan will conduct a study on various challenges it has to overcome to enable the dispatch of SDF personnel in a broad range of fields, and take necessary measures. Japan will also contribute to the training of domestic and foreign personnel engaging in peacebuilding by making use of the SDF's experience and knowledge.

IV. Future Defense Forces

1. The Role of the Defense Force
Japan's future defense forces will be developed as described in III. 2 (2) above, and will be capable of effectively fulfilling the expected roles in the following fields, and will maintain the necessary posture.

(1) Effective deterrence of and response to various situations
In order to respond to various situations in a timely and appropriate manner, and certainly protect the lives and property of its people and the sovereignty of its land, sea and airspace, Japan will achieve intelligence superiority through persistent ISR activities in an extensive surrounding area to constantly gain an understanding of military developments in other countries and to detect any signs of development at an early stage.

Through such activities, Japan will clearly express its resolve not to tolerate the change of the status quo by force, thereby preventing various situations from occurring.

At the same time, Japan will swiftly and seamlessly respond to situations including gray zone situations, and will establish the necessary posture to continuously address a protracted situation.

Moreover, Japan will implement an effective response tailored to each situation, even in cases when multiple events occur in a consecutive or concurrent manner.

When implementing the initiatives above, the following points are emphasized in particular:

a. Ensuring security of the sea and airspace surrounding Japan

In addition to persistent ISR in an extensive area around Japan, Japan will immediately take appropriate measures to deal with any incursions into its territorial airspace. Japan will respond effectively and promptly to gray-zone situations or any other acts that may violate its sovereignty. Furthermore, should the acts in question become protracted or escalate, Japan will respond seamlessly as the situation evolves, taking all possible measures for the defense and security of the sea and airspace surrounding Japan.

b. Response to an attack on remote islands

In responding to an attack on remote islands, Japan will intercept and defeat any invasion, by securing maritime supremacy and air superiority, with the necessary SDF units swiftly deployed to interdict, in addition to the units deployed in advance in accordance with the security environment. Moreover, should any remote islands be invaded, Japan will recapture them. In doing so, any ballistic missile or cruise missile attacks will be dealt with appropriately.

c. Response to ballistic missile attacks

Japan will promptly detect any signs of a ballistic missile launch and facilitate a swift, sustained response by establishing a multi-layered defense posture. Should any damage result, Japan will take steps to minimize it. Moreover, in the event of an attack by guerrillas or special operations forces concurrent with a ballistic missile attack, Japan will protect key facilities including nuclear power plants and search and destroy the infiltrating units.

d. Responses in outer space and cyberspace

In regard with outer space and cyberspace, Japan will build up persistent ISR capabilities to prevent any acts that could impede efficient action by the SDF. Furthermore, should any situation arise, Japan will identify the event without delay and swiftly repair any damage, while taking necessary steps to contain it. Moreover, in light of society's growing dependence on outer space and cyberspace, Japan will make effective use of the SDF's capabilities when endeavoring to strengthen collaboration with relevant organizations and clarify the division of roles, thereby contributing to comprehensive, government-wide initiatives.

e. Responses to major disasters

Should a major disaster occur, Japan will swiftly transport and deploy the requisite units and take all possible measures as part of its initial response, and maintain its presence in the longer term, when required. Moreover, as well as providing a meticulous response to the needs of disaster-stricken citizens and local government bodies, Japan will engage in appropriate part-nerships and cooperation with local governments and the private sector, in order to save lives, carry out emergency repairs, and provide livelihood support.

(2) Stabilization of the Asia-Pacific and improvement of global security environments
Through persistent ISR in the area surrounding Japan and the timely and appro-priate implementation of training, exercises, and various other activities, Japan will ensure the stability of the security environment in the Asia-Pacific region as a whole including the vicinity of Japan.

Moreover, working in partnership with its ally and partners, Japan will pro-mote multi-tiered initiatives, including bilateral and multilateral defense coopera-tion and exchange, joint training and exercises, and capacity building assistance, effectively fulfilling its key role in initiatives focused on the stabilization of the se-curity environment, including the building and strengthening of intra-regional cooperative frameworks in the Asia-Pacific region.

As the roles played by military capacity diversify, in order to respond appro-priately to global security issues including regional conflicts, the expansion and spread of international terrorism, failed states, and the proliferation of weapons of mass destruction, Japan will strengthen various initiatives focused on arms con-trol, disarmament and non-proliferation, as well as actively promote international peace cooperation activities, anti-piracy initiatives and capacity building assistance, thereby working on improvement of the global security environment.

Japan will attach importance to the following in particular, when engaging in the aforementioned initiatives.
a. Holding training and exercises
As well as the timely and appropriate implementation of SDF training and exercises, Japan will promote bilateral and multilateral joint training and exercises in the Asia-Pacific region, proactively and visibly demonstrating our nation's resolve and advanced capabilities focused on regional stabiliza-tion. In addition, it will build and strengthen cooperative relationships with relevant countries.
b. Promoting defense cooperation and exchange
Enhancing mutual understanding and relationships of trust with other countries and international organizations is the cornerstone of efforts to sta-bilize the security environment. Japan will take further steps to promote multi-layered defense cooperation and exchange, such as building and strengthening cooperative relationships focused on wide-ranging security issues of common interest including HADR and ensuring the stable use of the seas, outer space and cyberspace.
c. Promoting capacity building assistance
Utilizing the capabilities of the SDF, Japan will continuously engage in capac-ity building assistance such as human resource development and technical support on a regular basis in order to enhance the ability of developing countries themselves, thereby improving the security environment with par-ticular focus on active creation of stability in the Asia-Pacific region.

d. Ensuring maritime security

As it is particularly vital for Japan as a maritime state to maintain an "Open and Stable Seas" order which serves as the cornerstone of peace and prosperity, Japan will take all possible measures to secure the safety of maritime traffic. Japan will also conduct anti-piracy activities in cooperation with countries concerned, and will promote various efforts including capacity building assistance of coastal states in this field and enhancement of joint training and exercises by taking various opportunities in waters other than those surrounding our country.

e. Implementing international peace cooperation activities

Working in partnership with non-governmental organizations and other relevant organizations, Japan will actively engage in international peace cooperation assignments and emergency relief activities to meet diverse needs, from peacekeeping to peacebuilding, placing greater emphasis on playing more of a leading role. In doing so, as well as enhancing its readiness posture to facilitate rapid overseas dispatch according to the situation, Japan will strengthen its sustainable preparedness for a protracted overseas deployment.

f. Cooperating with efforts to promote arms control, disarmament, and nonproliferation

Japan will be actively involved in arms control and disarmament activities undertaken by the United Nations and other bodies. In doing so, Japan will make active, effective use of the SDF's knowledge, including through personnel contribution. Moreover, the proliferation of weapons of mass destruction and missiles that can serve as their means of delivery, as well as the proliferation of arms and goods and technology which could be diverted to military use pose severe threats to the peace and stability not only of Japan but also of the international community as a whole. Thus, Japan will cooperate with relevant countries and international organizations and other relevant bodies in promoting nonproliferation initiatives.

2. Priorities in strengthening architecture of the Self Defense Forces

(1) Basic approach

The SDF will maintain an appropriate structure to effectively fulfill the abovementioned roles of defense forces. As such, Japan has conducted capability assessments based on joint operations in relation to various potential contingencies to identify the functions and capabilities that should be prioritized in order to pursue more effective build-up of the defense force.

Based on the results of the capability assessments, in the defense capability buildup, the SDF will prioritize the development of capacities to ensure maritime supremacy and air superiority, which is the prerequisite for effective deterrence and response in various situations, including defense posture buildup in the southwestern region. Furthermore, the SDF will emphasize the establishment of rapid deployment capabilities with a consideration to establishing a wide-ranging logistical support foundation.

At the same time, in terms of preparation for a Cold-War era style invasion such as the landing of large-scale ground forces, the SDF will possess the minimum necessary level of expertise and skills required to respond to unforeseen changes in the situation in the future and to maintain and inherit them, and thereby further promote efforts to achieve even greater efficiency and rationalization.

(2) Functions and capabilities to be emphasized

From the perspective of efficiently developing an effective defense force, the SDF will selectively strengthen the following functions and capabilities in particular, paying attention to enhance joint functions with interoperability with the U.S. forces.

a. ISR capabilities

In order to ensure effective deterrence and response to various situations, while utilizing unmanned equipment, Japan will implement extensive persistent ISR on objectives such as aircraft and vessels in the seas and airspace surrounding it, and the SDF will adopt a flexible approach to boosting its ISR posture according to the developments of situations.

b. Intelligence capabilities

Japan will strengthen its system for intelligence collection, processing information, and analyzing and sharing the collected information, so that the SDF can promptly detect and swiftly respond to signs of various situations and take necessary measures based on medium-to long-term military trends mainly in its vicinity.

In doing so, the SDF will seek to augment its various information collection capabilities, including HUMINT, OSINT, SIGINT, and IMINT, as well as persistent ISR capabilities using unmanned aerial vehicles. Also, the SDF will engage in integrated efforts to strengthen its geospatial intelligence capabilities to combine various types of intelligence on images and maps to exploit them in a sophisticated manner, while establishing a framework for the integrated and systematic nurturing of highly capable personnel in information gathering analysis.

c. Transport capability

In order to secure swift and large-scale transport and deployment capability, and to swiftly deploy and move necessary units, the SDF will strengthen integrated transport capacity including maritime and airborne transport capacity, with collaboration with the civilian transport sector. In doing so, the SDF will avoid redundancy in functions by clarifying roles and assignments among various means of transport, considering their respective characteristics.

d. Command and control, and information and communications capabilities

In order to establish a command and control system that can manage units nationwide in a mobile, joint integrated manner, the SDF will take steps to deploy the Ground Self-Defense Force (GSDF), Maritime Self-Defense Force (MSDF) and Air Self-Defense Force (ASDF) personnel in the main headquarters of each service, making effective use of the knowledge and experience held by each respective service. Furthermore, the SDF will facilitate swift, resilient nationwide operation of the GSDF's units such as basic operational units (divisions and brigades) through the establishment of a new central headquarters to control all of the regional armies, as well as greater efficiency and streamlining of the command and control function in each regional army headquarters, and other measures.

Moreover, the SDF will strive to enhance and strengthen its information and communications capabilities that are prerequisites for supporting nationwide operation, starting with the communications infrastructure on remote islands and data link functions among the three services.

e. Response to an attack on remote islands

In order to ensure maritime supremacy and air superiority which is a prerequisite for effective response to an attack on remote islands, the SDF will strengthen its ability to deal with attacks by aircraft, naval vessels, and missiles, etc.

Moreover, while strengthening the integrated capabilities to seek to interdict any attack on Japan's remote islands at sea, the SDF will newly develop sufficient amphibious operations capability, which enables the SDF to land, recapture and secure without delay in the case of an invasion of any remote islands.

Furthermore, the SDF will enhance its logistical support capabilities, so that SDF units can swiftly and continuously respond in the event of a situation in the southwestern region.

In addition, the SDF will also examine the desirable air defense posture in remote islands in the Pacific.

f. Response to ballistic missile attacks

To counter North Korea's improved ballistic missile capability, Japan will pursue comprehensive improvement of its response capability against the threat of ballistic missiles.

With regard to the BMD system, Japan will enhance readiness, simultaneous engagement capability and sustainable response capability to strengthen the capability to protect the entire territory.

Based on appropriate role and mission sharing between Japan and the U.S., in order to strengthen the deterrent of the Japan-U.S. Alliance as a whole through enhancement of Japan's own deterrent and response capability, Japan will study a potential form of response capability to address the means of ballistic missile launches and related facilities, and take means as necessary.

g. Responses in outer space and cyberspace

While strengthening information collection capability using satellites equipped with a variety of sensors, and reinforcing command, control and telecommunications capabilities, the SDF will secure effective, stable use of outer space so that satellites can continuously exercise their capabilities even in contingencies by enhancing the survivability of satellites through such initiatives as space situational awareness. In implementing such initiatives, the SDF will form organic partnerships with research and development institutions in Japan, as well as with the U.S.

As for cyberspace, Japan will enhance integrated persistent surveillance and response capabilities and expertise and latest equipment will be continuously developed and secured in order to prevent actions that hinder efficient SDF activities.

h. Responses to major disasters, etc.

In the event of a large-scale natural disaster such as a Nankai Trough earthquake, or an atypical disaster such as a nuclear emergency, it is of vital importance to respond swiftly from the initial stages of the impact and carry out such tasks as information gathering on the extent and nature of the damage from the air by aircrafts, rescue operations and emergency repairs. In this regard, the SDF will develop a response posture sustainable for longterm operation, through swift transportation and deployment of appropriately size units, and by establishing a rotating staffing posture based on a joint operational approach.

i. Responses focused on international peace cooperation activities and other similar activities

In international peace cooperation activities and other similar activities, the SDF will strengthen the necessary protective capabilities to carry out its operations, ensuring the safety of personnel and units. Moreover, the SDF will work on enhancing transport and deployment capability, information communication capability with a view to long term activities in Africa and other remote locations, and strengthening logistic and medical service structure for smooth and continuous operation.

From the standpoint of carrying out international peace cooperation activities more effectively, Japan will consider measures for making more effective use of the SDF Operational Facility for Deployed Air Force for Anti-Piracy Operation in Djibouti. Furthermore, while strengthening intelligence gathering capability required for operations, the SDF will enhance its education, training and personnel management systems in order to facilitate the continuous dispatch of adequate personnel for overseas cooperation activities.

3. Architecture of each service of the Self-Defense Forces

The organization, equipment and disposition in each service of the SDF are outlined in (1) to (3) below. The specifics of major organizations and equipment in the future are as shown in the Annex table.

(1) Ground Self-Defense Force (GSDF)

a. In order to be able to respond swiftly and deal effectively and nimbly with an attack on offshore islands and various other situations, the GSDF will maintain rapidly deployable basic operational units (rapid deployment divisions, rapid deployment brigades and an armored division) furnished with advanced mobility and ISR capabilities. In addition, the GSDF will maintain mobile operating units sustaining specialized functions in order to effectively perform such operations as airborne operations, amphibious operations, special operations, air transportation, defense against NBC (nuclear, biological, and chemical) weapons, and international peace cooperation activities.

Keeping in mind that the role of these highly-proficient rapidly deployable basic operational units is to swiftly deploy and move via the integrated transport capacity referred to in 2. (2) c. above, the GSDF will maintain half of these in Hokkaido, given the excellent training environment there.

The defense posture in the remote islands of the southwestern region will be enhanced and strengthened via the permanent stationing of the units where the SDF is not currently stationed, the deployability of the aforementioned units, and the establishment of organic partnerships and networks with the MSDF and ASDF.

b. The GSDF will maintain surface-to-ship guided missile units in order to prevent invasion of Japan's remote islands while still at sea, as far as possible.

c. The GSDF will maintain surface-to-air guided missile units in order to effectively provide air defense to protect operational units and key areas, working in tandem with the surface-to-air guided missile units referred to in (3) d. below.

d. The GSDF will review the organization and equipment of the basic operational units (divisions and brigades) other than the rapidly deployable ones referred to in a. above, with a particular focus on tanks/howitzers and rockets. Following thorough rationalization and streamlining, these units will be deployed appropriately, according to geographical characteristics.

(2) Maritime Self Defense Force (MSDF)

a. The MSDF will maintain destroyer units and ship-based patrol helicopter units strengthened by increased numbers of equipment, including the new destroyers, with additional multifunctional capability and with a compact-type hull, in order to effectively conduct persistent ISR and antisubmarine operations etc., thereby facilitating agile response in such areas as the defense of the seas surrounding Japan, the security of maritime traffic, and international peace cooperation activities etc.

Along with the surface-to-air guided missile units referred to in (3) d. below, the destroyer units will maintain Aegis-equipped destroyers capable of providing Japan with multi-layered defense against ballistic missile attacks.

b. The MSDF will maintain submarine units strengthened by increased numbers of them, in order to effectively conduct patrol and defense of the seas surrounding Japan, as well as regularly engage in broad underwater intelligence gathering and warning and surveillance in those seas.

c. The MSDF will maintain fixed-wing patrol aircraft units in order to effectively conduct patrol and defense of the seas surrounding Japan, as well as regularly engage in broad maritime intelligence gathering and warning and surveillance in those seas.

d. The MSDF will maintain minesweeper units in order to effectively conduct minesweeping operations in the seas surrounding Japan in collaboration with the new destroyers with additional multifunctional capability and with the compact-type hull referred to in a. above.

(3) Air Self-Defense Force (ASDF)

a. The ASDF will maintain air warning and control units consisting of warning and control units and air warning units. Warning and control units will be equipped with ground-based warning and control radar that can detect and track any ballistic missiles flying into Japanese air space, as well as providing persistent ISR in most air space over Japan and the surrounding areas. Air warning units will be enhanced in order to conduct effective warning, surveillance and control in the air over long periods in the event of "gray zone" situations.

b. The ASDF will maintain fighter aircraft units reinforced by highly capable fighter aircrafts in order to provide aerial defense for Japan based on a comprehensive posture that brings together fighter aircrafts and relevant support functions. In addition, the ASDF will maintain enhanced aerial refueling and transport units that will enable fighter aircraft units and air warning units, etc. to carry out various operations sustainably in the air space surrounding Japan.

c. The ASDF will maintain air transport units in order to effectively carry out the mobile deployment of ground-based units etc., and international peace cooperation activities etc.

d. The ASDF will maintain surface-to-air guided missile units providing multi-layered defense for Japan against ballistic missile attacks, together with the Aegis destroyers referred to in (2) a. above, as well as protecting key areas in tandem with the surface-to-air guided missile units referred to in (1) c. above.

V. Basic Foundations for SDF

To ensure that the diverse activities required of the SDF are carried out in a timely and appropriate manner, it is not sufficient simply to upgrade the main elements of the organization and its equipment; it is also imperative to strengthen the various foundations underpinning the defense force, in order to ensure that it can function as effectively as possible. The key aspects of this are as follows.

1. Training and Exercises

Through routine training and exercises, the SDF will ceaselessly review and examine various plans for dealing with situations, as well as strive to enhance and strengthen its training and exercises in order to improve the tactical skills in each of its branches. In doing so, as well as making more effective use of the excellent training environment in Hokkaido, the SDF will work in partnership with relevant organizations and the civilian sector, in order to ensure systematic implementation of more practical training and exercises.

In the southwestern region, where there are limitations on the exercise areas, etc. of the SDF, the SDF will secure a favorable training environment through the joint use of U.S. military facilities and areas, while remaining sensitive to relationships with the local community, so that timely and appropriate training and exercises can be carried out, including Japan-U.S. bilateral training and exercises.

2. Operational Infrastructure

The SDF will improve survivability, including the recovery capabilities of military camps and bases, etc., in order to maintain the support functions that serve as the operational infrastructure for units, so that units can be deployed swiftly and respond to various situations effectively.

Moreover, in light of the fact that some SDF facilities are currently dilapidated, the SDF will implement a steady repair and maintenance program, as well as expansion of the necessary quarters in order to ensure an emergency call-up of personnel in the event of various situations, thereby enhancing readiness.

The SDF will undertake necessary deliberations concerning civilian airports and ports, including approaches to the various systems on a day-to-day basis, in order to ensure that such facilities can be used as part of the operational infrastructure for the SDF, etc. from an early stage, depending on the situation. Furthermore, it will implement various family support measures, in order to alleviate the anxieties both of troops serving away from home and of their families while they are away.

The SDF will enhance and strengthen the operational infrastructure in terms of equipment and materials, such as improving the operational availability of equipment, by taking all possible measures to maintain and upgrade SDF equipment, as well as securing and stockpiling the necessary ammunition.

3. Personnel and Education

Given that equipment has become more advanced and complex, and missions more diverse and internationalized in recent years, the SDF will implement measures to reform the personnel management system, in order to ensure the edge of its troops and the effective use of human resources amid a severe fiscal situation, taking into consideration a variety of elements, including skills, experience, physical strength and morale.

Accordingly, the SDF will implement measures to ensure an appropriate composition of ranks and age distribution, taking into account the various missions and characteristics of each branch of the SDF.

The SDF will implement measures to make effective use of human resources, such as more effective use of female SDF personnel and expansion of reappointment, and measures related to honors and privileges. In order to strengthen the joint operations structure, the SDF will enhance education and training, and, through secondments to the Joint Staff and relevant ministries and agencies, retain adequate personnel who have a broad outlook and ideas, as well as wide-ranging experience in Japan's security-affairs, and who can respond flexibly and rapidly to various situations as part of the government.

In light of the deterioration of the recruiting environment resulting from social factors such as the declining birthrate and popularization of higher education, the SDF will promote a diverse range of recruitment measures to spread the perception that the SDF is an attractive job option.

Furthermore, as it is the responsibility of the Government of Japan to secure the livelihoods of the SDF personnel, who are compelled to resign at a younger age than ordinary civil servants, the SDF will promote support for re-employment by strengthening collaboration with local governments and relevant organizations.

In order to support sustainable operation of units in situations that are becoming increasingly diversified and protracted, the SDF will promote utilization of reserve personnel in broad areas, including those with professional skills such as aviators, and will take measures to improve the sufficiency of reserve personnel.

4. Medical
In order to keep SDF personnel in good health and enhance their ability to engage in a diverse range of missions, such as various situation responses and international peace cooperation activities, the SDF will establish an efficient and high-quality medical care structure, through endeavors including upgrading of SDF hospitals into hubs with enhanced functions, and improvements in the management of the National Defense Medical College Hospital. The SDF will also attach greater importance to securing and training of such medical staff as medical officers, nurses and emergency medical technicians.

The SDF will consider such matters as revisions of regulations of emergency medical treatment on situation responses, and improve first aid capabilities on the frontline, and will put in place a posture for rapid medical evacuation that takes into account the viewpoints of enhanced joint capabilities.

5. Defense Production and Technological Bases
Retaining an adequate level of defense production and technological bases is essential not only for the production, operation, maintenance and upkeep of equipment, but also for research and development of equipment that fits the operational environment, and for the expected potential to contribute to enhancing deterrence.

At the same time, against the backdrop of the severe fiscal situation and rises in the equipment unit price as it becomes increasingly sophisticated and complex, the numbers of units of procured equipment are on the decline. Moreover, the environment surrounding Japan's defense production and technological bases is becoming more severe. For instance, the competitiveness of foreign companies is growing, as a result of the advance of large-scale and cross-border restructuring and consolidation of the defense industry.

In this kind of environment, the Ministry of Defense will formulate a strategy that sets forth its future vision for Japan's defense production and technological bases as a whole and will promote participation in international joint development and production and adapting defense equipment to civilian use, in order to maintain and reinforce such bases without delay.

With regard to contribution to peace and international cooperation, there are increasing opportunities to cooperate in a more effective manner through, for example, the utilization and provision to disaster-stricken countries and others of heavy machinery and other defense equipment carried to sites by the SDF. Moreover, internationally, it has become the mainstream to participate in international joint development and production projects in order to improve the performance of defense equipment while dealing with the rising costs of the equipment. In this context, from the perspective of "Proactive Contribution to Peace" based on the principle of international cooperation, Japan is required to engage more proactively in peacebuilding efforts and international cooperation by utilizing defense equipment in various ways, and to participate in joint development and production of defense equipment and other related items.

Against this backdrop, while giving due consideration to the roles that the Three Principles on Arms Exports and their related policy guidelines have played so far, the Government of Japan will set out clear principles on the overseas transfer of arms and military technology, which fit the new security environment. In this context, considerations will be made with regard to defining cases where transfers are prohibited; limiting cases where transfers could be allowed with strict examination; and ensuring appropriate control over transfers in terms of unauthorized use and third party transfer.

6. Efficient Acquisition of Equipment

In order to achieve effective and efficient acquisition of equipment, including in research and development activities, the Ministry of Defense will strengthen project management throughout the life-cycle of equipment through introducing a project manager system, as well as through considering the possibility of further introducing long-term contracts and further upgrading the contract system to provide cost reduction incentives to companies, aiming to improve cost-effectiveness throughout the life-cycle of equipment.

Moreover, the Ministry of Defense will try to improve readiness and response capabilities through reforms of the logistics posture through effective use of capacity in the private sector. Furthermore, it will ceaselessly pursue greater transparency in the acquisition process and increased rationalization of the contract system, and strive to achieve more rigorous procedures for the acquisition of equipment.

7. Research and Development

The Ministry of Defense will ensure consistency with the priorities for upgrading defense capability when commencing research and development, in order to guarantee that research and development that meets the operational needs of the SDF is prioritized in view of the severe fiscal situation.

In conjunction with this, the Ministry of Defense will promote research and development based on a medium- to long-term perspective, taking into account the latest trends in science and technology, changes in combat modality, cost-effectiveness and the potential for international joint research and development, with a view to implementing research and development that can ensure Japan's technological superiority against new threats in strategically important areas.

From the aspect of security, it is necessary to utilize civilian technology effectively also in the field of security through regularly assessing the trend in science and technology including information related to technological development as well as consolidating the capabilities of the government, industry and academia. Under such recognition, the Ministry of Defense will strive to make effective use of civilian technology that can also be applied to defense (dual-use technologies), by enhancing partnerships with universities and research institutes, while strengthening technology control functions to prevent the outflow of advanced technologies.

The Ministry of Defense will examine its research and development initiative for achieving the aforementioned objectives.

8. Collaboration with Local Communities

The Ministry of Defense and the SDF will further strengthen collaboration with relevant organizations, including local governments, the police and the fire service, in order to enable the SDF to provide accurate response to various situations. Such close partnerships with local governments, etc. are exceedingly important from the perspective not only of the effective improvement and smooth operation of defense facilities, but also of the recruitment of SDF personnel, as well as the provision of re-employment support for them.

Accordingly, as well as continuing to advance measures targeting the areas around defense facilities, with a view to their improvement and operation, the Ministry of Defense and SDF will routinely engage in various measures such as intensive public relations activities focused on their policies and activities, in order to secure the understanding and cooperation of local governments and communities.

Given that the presence of SDF units makes a substantial contribution to the maintenance and revitalization of local communities in some areas, and supports community medicine through emergency patient transport using SDF search and rescue aircraft in others, the Ministry of Defense and the SDF will give consideration to the attributes of each area in the reorganization of units and deployment of military camps and bases, etc., in order to secure the understanding of local governments and residents. At the same time, in operating the military camps and bases, etc., the Ministry of Defense will pay attention to the contribution of the operation to the local economy.

9. Boosting Communication Capabilities
The Ministry of Defense and SDF will strengthen strategic public relations and communication to enhance the dissemination of information via a diverse range of media, in order to secure domestic and overseas understanding which is vital to effectively conduct SDF duties.

10. Enhancing the Intellectual Base
The Ministry of Defense will promote education on security-related matters at educational institutions, in order to enhance understanding of security and crisis management among the populace. Moreover, in addition to strengthening the Ministry of Defense and SDF research systems, with a particular focus on the National Institute for Defense Studies, the Ministry of Defense will promote various partnerships, including education and research exchange with other research and educational institutions within the government, as well as universities and think-tanks both within Japan and overseas.

11. Promoting Reform of the Ministry of Defense
The Ministry of Defense will further promote reforms by constantly reviewing its work methods and organization in order to foster a sense of unity among civilian officials and uniformed personnel, total optimization in building up defense capability, strengthening SDF's joint operation functions and enhancing policy-making and communication functions.

VI. Additional Points

1. These Guidelines set out the form of Japan's defense force over the next decade or so. The National Security Council will conduct regular, systematic review over the course of implementation of the various measures and programs. Smooth, swift and accurate transition to the future defense force will be facilitated through validations based on joint operational capability assessment while advancing such initiatives in a timely and appropriate manner.

2. When major changes in the situation are anticipated during the review and verifica-

tion process, necessary examination of the security environment at that time will be taken into account and these guidelines will be revised adequately.

3. In light of the increasingly tough fiscal conditions, Japan will strive to achieve greater efficiency and streamlining in the defense capability buildup to curb costs, and harmonize with other initiatives in other fields to ensure that Japan's defense force as a whole can smoothly fulfill its expected function.

Source: Ministry of Defense,"National Defense Program Guidelines for FY2014 and Beyond." www. mod.go.jp/j/approach/agenda/guideline/2014/pdf/20131217_e2.pdf (accessed December 20, 2016).

Annex Table

Category			Present (as of the end of FY2013)	Future
Authorized number of personnel			approx. 159,000	159,000
Active-duty personnel			approx. 151,000	151,000
Reserve-ready personnel			approx. 8,000	8,000
Ground Self-Defense Force	Major units	Rapid deployment units	Central Readiness Force 1 armored division	3 rapid deployment divisions 4 rapid deployment brigades 1 armored division 1 airborne brigade 1 amphibious rapid deployment brigade 1 helicopter brigade
		Regional deployment units	8 divisions 6 brigades	5 divisions 2 brigades
		Surface-to-ship guided missile units	5 surface-to-ship guided missile regiments	5 surface-to-ship guided missile regiments
		Surface-to-air guided missile units	8 anti-aircraft artillery groups/regiments	7 anti-aircraft artillery groups/regiments
Maritime Self-Defense Force	Major units	Destroyer units	4 flotillas (8 divisions) 5 divisions	4 flotillas (8 divisions) 6 divisions
		Submarine units	5 divisions	6 divisions
		Minesweeper unit	1 flotilla	1 flotilla
		Patrol aircraft units	9 squadrons	9 squadrons
	Major equipment	Destroyers	47	54
		(Aegis-equipped destroyers)	(6)	(8)
		Submarines	16	22
		Combat aircraft	approx. 170	approx. 170
Air Self-Defense Force	Major units	Air warning & control units	8 warning groups 20 warning squadrons 1 AEW group (2 squadrons)	28 warning squadrons 1 AEW group (3 squadrons)
		Fighter aircraft units	12 squadrons	13 squadrons
		Air reconnaissance units	1 squadron	—
		Aerial refueling/transport units	1 squadron	2 squadrons
		Air transport units	3 squadrons	3 squadrons
		Surface-to-air guided missile units	6 groups	6 groups
	Major equipment	Combat aircraft	approx. 340	approx. 360
		Fighters	approx. 260	approx. 280

Notes: 1. The current numbers of tanks and howitzers/rockets (authorized number as of the end of FY2013) are respectively approx. 700 and approx. 600, which will be reduced respectively to approx. 300 and approx. 300 in the future.

2. Regarding major equipment/units that may also serve for BMD missions, their acquisition/ formation will be allowed within the number of Destroyers (Aegis-equipped destroyers), Air warning & control units and Surface-to-air guided missile units specified above.

Appendix J

The Guidelines for Japan-U.S. Defense Cooperation

April 27, 2015

I. Defense Cooperation and the Aim of the Guidelines

In order to ensure Japan's peace and security under any circumstances, from peacetime to contingencies, and to promote a stable, peaceful, and prosperous Asia-Pacific region and beyond, bilateral security and defense cooperation will emphasize:
- seamless, robust, flexible, and effective bilateral responses;
- synergy across the two governments' national security policies;
- a whole-of-government Alliance approach;
- cooperation with regional and other partners, as well as international organizations; and
- the global nature of the Japan-U.S. Alliance.

The two governments will continuously enhance the Japan-U.S. Alliance. Each government will maintain its individual defense posture based on its national security policy. Japan will possess defense capability on the basis of the "National Security Strategy" and the "National Defense Program Guidelines." The United States will continue to extend deterrence to Japan through the full range of capabilities, including U.S. nuclear forces. The United States also will continue to forward deploy combat-ready forces in the Asia-Pacific region and maintain the ability to reinforce those forces rapidly.

The Guidelines for Japan-U.S. Defense Cooperation ("the Guidelines") provide the general framework and policy direction for the roles and missions of Japan and the United States, as well as ways of cooperation and coordination, with a view to improving the effectiveness of bilateral security and defense cooperation. In this way, the Guidelines advance peace and security, deter conflict, secure the basis for economic prosperity, and promote domestic and international understanding of the significance of the Japan-U.S. Alliance.

II. Basic Premises and Principles

The Guidelines, as well as actions and activities under the Guidelines, are and will be consistent with the following basic premises and principles.

A. The rights and obligations under the Treaty of Mutual Cooperation and Security between Japan and the United States of America (the Japan-U.S. Security Treaty) and its related arrangements, as well as the fundamental framework of the Japan-U.S. Alliance, will remain unchanged.

B. All actions and activities undertaken by Japan and the United States under the Guidelines will be consistent with international law, including the Charter of the United Nations and its provisions regarding the peaceful settlement of disputes and sovereign equality of States, as well as other relevant international agreements.

C. All actions and activities undertaken by Japan and the United States will be in accordance with their respective constitutions, laws, and regulations then in effect, and basic positions on national security policy. Japan will conduct actions and activities in accordance with its basic positions, such as the maintenance of its exclusively national defense-oriented policy and its three non-nuclear principles.

D. The Guidelines do not obligate either government to take legislative, budgetary, administrative, or other measures, nor do the Guidelines create legal rights or obligations for either government. Since the objective of the Guidelines, however, is to establish an effective framework for bilateral cooperation, the two governments are expected to reflect in an appropriate way the results of these efforts, based on their own judgment, in their specific policies and measures.

III. Strengthened Alliance Coordination

Effective bilateral cooperation under the Guidelines will require the two governments to conduct close, consultative dialogue and sound policy and operational coordination from peacetime to contingencies.

The two governments must be well informed and coordinate at multiple levels to ensure successful bilateral security and defense cooperation. To that end, the two governments will take advantage of all available channels to enhance information sharing and to ensure seamless and effective whole-of-government Alliance coordination that includes all relevant agencies. For this purpose, the two governments will establish a new, standing Alliance Coordination Mechanism, enhance operational coordination, and strengthen bilateral planning.

A. Alliance Coordination Mechanism

Persistent and emerging threats can have a serious and immediate impact on the peace and security of Japan and the United States. In order to address seamlessly and effectively any situation that affects Japan's peace and security or any other situation that may require an Alliance response, the two governments will utilize the Alliance Coordination Mechanism. This mechanism will strengthen policy and operational coordination related to activities conducted by the Self-Defense Forces and the United States Armed Forces in all phases from peacetime to contingencies. This mechanism also will contribute to timely information sharing as well as the development and maintenance of common situational awareness. To ensure effective coordination, the two governments will establish necessary procedures and infrastructure (including facilities as well as information and communication systems) and conduct regular training and exercises.

The two governments will tailor to the situation the procedures for coordination as well as the exact composition of participating agencies within the Alliance Coordination Mechanism structure. As part of these procedures, contact information will be shared and maintained from peacetime.

B. Enhanced Operational Coordination

Enhanced bilateral operational coordination for flexible and responsive command and control is a core capability of critical importance to Japan and the United

States. In this context, the two governments recognize the continued importance of collocating operational coordination functions to strengthen cooperation between the Self-Defense Forces and the United States Armed Forces.

The Self-Defense Forces and the United States Armed Forces will exchange personnel to ensure robust information sharing, to facilitate coordination from peacetime to contingencies, and to support international activities. The Self-Defense Forces and the United States Armed Forces, in close cooperation and coordination, will take action through their respective chains-of-command.

C. Bilateral Planning

The two governments will continue to develop and update bilateral plans to ensure smooth and effective execution of coordinated operations by the Self-Defense Forces and the United States Armed Forces. To ensure the effectiveness of the plans and the ability to make flexible, timely, and appropriate responses, the two governments will exchange relevant information, including identifying operational and logistic support requirements and sources in advance, as appropriate.

The two governments will conduct bilateral planning in peacetime for contingencies relevant to Japan's peace and security through an upgraded Bilateral Planning Mechanism, which includes relevant agencies of the respective governments. Bilateral plans will be developed with input from relevant agencies, as appropriate. The Security Consultative Committee (SCC) will continue to be responsible for presenting directions, validating the progress of the planning under the mechanism, and issuing directives as necessary. The SCC will be assisted by an appropriate subordinate body.

Bilateral plans are to be reflected appropriately in the plans of both governments.

IV. Seamlessly Ensuring Japan's Peace and Security

Persistent and emerging threats can have a serious and immediate impact on Japan's peace and security. In this increasingly complex security environment, the two governments will take measures to ensure Japan's peace and security in all phases, seamlessly, from peacetime to contingencies, including situations when an armed attack against Japan is not involved. In this context, the two governments also will promote further cooperation with partners.

The two governments recognize that these measures need to be taken based on flexible, timely, and effective bilateral coordination tailored to each situation and that interagency coordination is essential for appropriate Alliance responses. Therefore, the two governments will utilize the whole-of-government Alliance Coordination Mechanism, as appropriate, to:
- assess the situation;
- share information; and
- develop ways to implement the appropriate Alliance response, including flexible deterrent options, as well as actions aimed at de-escalation.

To support these bilateral efforts, the two governments also will coordinate strategic messaging through appropriate channels on issues that could potentially affect Japan's peace and security.

A. Cooperative Measures from Peacetime
In order to ensure the maintenance of Japan's peace and security, the two governments will promote cooperation across a wide range of areas, including through diplomatic efforts, to strengthen the deterrence and capabilities of the Japan-U.S. Alliance.

The Self-Defense Forces and the United States Armed Forces will enhance interoperability, readiness, and vigilance to prepare for all possible situations. To these ends, the two governments will take measures, including, but not limited to, the following:

1. Intelligence, Surveillance, and Reconnaissance
In order to identify at the earliest possible stage any indications of threats to Japan's peace and security and to ensure a decisive advantage in intelligence gathering and analysis, the two governments will share and protect information and intelligence, while developing and maintaining common situational awareness. This will include enhancing coordination and cooperation among relevant agencies.

The Self-Defense Forces and the United States Armed Forces will conduct intelligence, surveillance, and reconnaissance (ISR) activities based on the capabilities and availability of their respective assets. This will include conducting bilateral ISR activities in a mutually supportive manner to ensure persistent coverage of developments that could affect Japan's peace and security.

2. Air and Missile Defense
The Self-Defense Forces and the United States Armed Forces will maintain and strengthen deterrence and their defense postures against ballistic missile launches and aerial incursions. The two governments will cooperate to expand early warning capabilities, interoperability, network coverage, and real-time information exchange and to pursue the comprehensive improvement of capabilities to respond to the threat of ballistic missiles. Moreover, the two governments will continue to coordinate closely in responding to provocative missile launches and other aerial activities.

3. Maritime Security
The two governments will cooperate closely with each other on measures to maintain maritime order based upon international law, including freedom of navigation. The Self-Defense Forces and the United States Armed Forces will cooperate, as appropriate, on various efforts such as maintaining and enhancing bilateral presence in the maritime domain through ISR and training and exercises, while further developing and enhancing shared maritime domain awareness including by coordinating with relevant agencies, as necessary.

4. Asset Protection
The Self-Defense Forces and the United States Armed Forces will provide mutual protection of each other's assets, as appropriate, if engaged in activities that contribute to the defense of Japan in a cooperative manner, includ-

ing during training and exercises.

5. Training and Exercises
The Self-Defense Forces and the United States Armed Forces will conduct effective bilateral and multilateral training and exercises both inside and outside of Japan in order to strengthen interoperability, sustainability, and readiness. Timely and realistic training and exercises will enhance deterrence. To support these activities, the two governments will cooperate to ensure that training areas, facilities, and associated equipment are available, accessible, and modern.

6. Logistic Support
Japan and the United States are primarily responsible for providing logistic support for their respective forces in all phases. The Self-Defense Forces and the United States Armed Forces will provide mutual logistic support where appropriate, including, but not limited to, supply, maintenance, transportation, engineering, and medical services, for such activities as set forth in the Agreement between the Government of Japan and the Government of the United States of America Concerning Reciprocal Provision of Logistic Support, Supplies and Services between the Self-Defense Forces of Japan and the Armed Forces of the United States of America (the Acquisition and Cross-Servicing Agreement) and its related arrangements.

7. Use of Facilities
In order to expand interoperability and improve flexibility and resiliency of the Self-Defense Forces and the United States Armed Forces, the two governments will enhance joint/shared use and cooperate in ensuring the security of facilities and areas. Recognizing the importance of being prepared for contingencies, the two governments also will cooperate in conducting site surveys on facilities including civilian airports and seaports, as appropriate.

B. Responses to Emerging Threats to Japan's Peace and Security
The Alliance will respond to situations that will have an important influence on Japan's peace and security. Such situations cannot be defined geographically. The measures described in this section include those that may be taken, in accordance with the two countries' respective laws and regulations, in circumstances that have not yet amounted to such a situation. Early recognition and adaptable, resolute decision-making on bilateral actions will contribute to deterrence and de-escalation of such situations.

In addition to continuing cooperative measures from peacetime, the two governments will pursue all avenues, including diplomatic efforts, to ensure the peace and security of Japan. Utilizing the Alliance Coordination Mechanism, the two governments will take additional measures, based on their own decisions, including, but not limited to, those listed below.

1. Noncombatant Evacuation Operations
When Japanese and U.S. noncombatants need to be evacuated from a third country to a safe haven, each government is responsible for evacuating its own nationals, as well as dealing with the authorities of the affected area. As

appropriate, the two governments will coordinate in planning and cooperate in carrying out evacuations of Japanese or U.S. noncombatants. These evacuations will be carried out using each country's capabilities such as transportation means and facilities in a mutually supplementary manner. The two governments may each consider extending evacuation assistance to third-country noncombatants.

The two governments will conduct early-stage coordination through the Alliance Coordination Mechanism, as appropriate, to carry out cooperation in fields such as the safety of evacuees, transportation means and facilities, customs, immigration and quarantine processing, safe havens, and medical services. The two governments will enhance coordination in noncombatant evacuation operations from peacetime, as appropriate, including by conducting training and exercises.

2. Maritime Security

Taking into account their respective capabilities, the two governments will cooperate closely to enhance maritime security. Cooperative measures may include, but are not limited to, information sharing and inspection of ships based on a United Nations Security Council resolution or other basis under international law.

3. Measures to Deal with Refugees

If a situation develops such that a flow of refugees into Japan becomes likely or actually begins, the two governments will cooperate to maintain Japan's peace and security while handling refugees in a humane manner consistent with applicable obligations under international law. Primary responsibility for such refugee response lies with Japan. The United States will provide appropriate support upon a request from Japan.

4. Search and Rescue

The two governments will cooperate and provide mutual support, as appropriate, in search and rescue operations. The Self-Defense Forces, in cooperation with relevant agencies, will provide support to combat search and rescue operations by the United States, where appropriate, subject to Japanese laws and regulations.

5. Protection of Facilities and Areas

The Self-Defense Forces and the United States Armed Forces are responsible for protecting their own facilities and areas in cooperation with relevant authorities. Upon request from the United States, Japan will provide additional protection for facilities and areas in Japan in close cooperation and coordination with the United States Armed Forces.

6. Logistic Support

The two governments will enhance mutual logistic support (which includes, but is not limited to, supply, maintenance, transportation, engineering, and medical services), as appropriate, to enable effective and efficient operations. This includes rapid validation and resourcing of operational and logistic support requirements. The Government of Japan will make appropriate use of the authorities and assets of central and local government agencies as well as private sector assets. The Government of Japan will provide logistic or other associated support where appropriate, subject to Japanese laws and regulations.

7. Use of Facilities
The Government of Japan will provide, as needed, temporary use of facilities, including civilian airports and seaports, in accordance with the Japan-U.S. Security Treaty and its related arrangements. The two governments will enhance cooperation in joint/shared use of facilities and areas.

C. Actions in Response to an Armed Attack against Japan
Bilateral actions in response to an armed attack against Japan remain a core aspect of Japan-U.S. security and defense cooperation.

When an armed attack against Japan is anticipated, the two governments will take steps to deter the armed attack and to de-escalate the situation, while making preparations necessary for the defense of Japan.

When an armed attack against Japan occurs, the two governments will conduct appropriate bilateral actions to repel it at the earliest possible stage and to deter any further attacks. The two governments also will take necessary measures including those listed earlier in Chapter IV.

1. When an Armed Attack against Japan is Anticipated
When an armed attack against Japan is anticipated, the two governments will intensify, through a comprehensive and robust whole-of-government approach, information and intelligence sharing and policy consultations, and will pursue all avenues, including diplomatic efforts, to deter the attack and to de-escalate the situation.

The Self-Defense Forces and the United States Armed Forces will assume appropriate postures for bilateral operations, including the execution of necessary deployments. Japan will establish and maintain the basis for its support of U.S. deployments. The preparations by the two governments may include, but would not be limited to: joint/shared use of facilities and areas; mutual logistic support, including, but not limited to, supply, maintenance, transportation, engineering, and medical services; and reinforced protection of U.S. facilities and areas in Japan.

2. When an Armed Attack against Japan Occurs
a. Principles for Coordinated Actions
If an armed attack against Japan occurs despite diplomatic efforts and deterrence, Japan and the United States will cooperate to repel promptly the attack and deter any further attacks to return peace and security to Japan. Such coordinated actions will contribute to the reestablishment of peace and security in the region.

Japan will maintain primary responsibility for defending the citizens and territory of Japan and will take actions immediately to repel an armed attack against Japan as expeditiously as possible. The Self-Defense Forces will have the primary responsibility to conduct defensive operations in Japan and its surrounding waters and airspace, as well as its air and maritime approaches. The United States will coordinate closely with Japan and provide appropriate support. The United

States Armed Forces will support and supplement the Self-Defense Forces to defend Japan. The United States will take actions to shape the regional environment in a way that supports the defense of Japan and reestablishes peace and security.

Recognizing that all instruments of national power will be required to defend Japan, the two governments respectively will employ a whole-of-government approach, utilizing their respective chains-of-command, to coordinate actions through the Alliance Coordination Mechanism.

The United States will employ forward-deployed forces, including those stationed in Japan, and introduce reinforcements from elsewhere, as required. Japan will establish and maintain the basis required to facilitate these deployments.

The two governments will take actions as appropriate to provide defense of each other's forces and facilities in response to an armed attack against Japan.

b. Concept of Operations

　　i. Operations to Defend Airspace

The Self-Defense Forces and the United States Armed Forces will conduct bilateral operations to defend airspace above and surrounding Japan.

　　The Self-Defense Forces will have primary responsibility for conducting air defense operations while ensuring air superiority. For this purpose, the Self-Defense Forces will take necessary actions, including, but not limited to, defense against attacks by aircraft and cruise missiles.

　　The United States Armed Forces will conduct operations to support and supplement the Self-Defense Forces' operations.

　　ii. Operations to Counter Ballistic Missile Attacks

The Self-Defense Forces and the United States Armed Forces will conduct bilateral operations to counter ballistic missile attacks against Japan.

　　The Self-Defense Forces and the United States Armed Forces will exchange real-time information for early detection of ballistic missile launches. When there is an indication of a ballistic missile attack, the Self-Defense Forces and the United States Armed Forces will maintain an effective posture to defend against ballistic missile attacks heading for Japan and to protect forces participating in ballistic missile defense operations.

　　The Self-Defense Forces will have primary responsibility for conducting ballistic missile defense operations to defend Japan.

　　The United States Armed Forces will conduct operations to support and supplement the Self-Defense Forces' operations.

　　iii. Operations to Defend Maritime Areas

The Self-Defense Forces and the United States Armed Forces will conduct bilateral operations to defend waters surrounding Japan and to secure the safety of sea lines of communication.

The Self-Defense Forces will have primary responsibility for the protection of major ports and straits in Japan and of ships and vessels in waters surrounding Japan and for other associated operations. For this purpose, the Self-Defense Forces will take necessary actions, including, but not limited to, coastal defense, anti-surface warfare, anti-submarine warfare, mine warfare, anti-air warfare, and air interdiction.

The United States Armed Forces will conduct operations to support and supplement the Self-Defense Forces' operations.

The Self-Defense Forces and the United States Armed Forces will cooperate in the interdiction of shipping activities providing support to adversaries involved in the armed attack.

The effectiveness of these activities will be enhanced through information sharing and other forms of cooperation among relevant agencies.

iv. Operations to Counter Ground Attacks

The Self-Defense Forces and the United States Armed Forces will conduct bilateral operations to counter ground attacks against Japan by ground, air, maritime, or amphibious forces.

The Self-Defense Forces will have primary responsibility for conducting operations to prevent and repel ground attacks, including those against islands. If the need arises, the Self-Defense Forces will conduct operations to retake an island. For this purpose, the Self-Defense Forces will take necessary actions, including, but not limited to, operations to prevent and repel airborne and seaborne invasions, amphibious operations, and rapid deployment.

The Self-Defense Forces, in cooperation with relevant agencies, also will have primary responsibility for defeating attacks by special operations forces or any other unconventional attacks in Japan, including those that involve infiltration.

The United States Armed Forces will conduct operations to support and supplement the Self-Defense Forces' operations.

v. Cross-Domain Operations

The Self-Defense Forces and the United States Armed Forces will conduct bilateral operations across domains to repel an armed attack against Japan and to deter further attacks. These operations will be designed to achieve effects across multiple domains simultaneously.

Examples of cooperation across domains include the actions described below.

The Self-Defense Forces and the United States Armed Forces, in cooperation with relevant agencies, as appropriate, will strengthen their respective ISR postures, enhance the sharing of intelligence, and provide protection for each other's ISR assets.

The United States Armed Forces may conduct operations

involving the use of strike power, to support and supplement the Self-Defense Forces. When the United States Armed Forces conduct such operations, the Self-Defense Forces may provide support, as necessary. These operations will be based on close bilateral coordination, as appropriate.

The two governments will cooperate to address threats in the space and cyberspace domains in accordance with bilateral cooperation set out in Chapter VI.

The Self-Defense Forces and the United States Armed Forces' special operations forces will cooperate during operations, as appropriate.

c. Operational Support Activities

The two governments will cooperate in the following activities in support of bilateral operations.

i. Communications and Electronics

The two governments will provide mutual support to ensure effective use of communications and electronics capabilities, as appropriate.

The Self-Defense Forces and the United States Armed Forces will ensure effective communication between the two forces and maintain a common operational picture for bilateral operations under common situational awareness.

ii. Search and Rescue

The Self-Defense Forces and the United States Armed Forces, in cooperation with relevant agencies, will cooperate and provide mutual support in search and rescue operations, including combat search and rescue, as appropriate.

iii. Logistic Support

When operations require supplementing their respective logistics resources, the Self-Defense Forces and the United States Armed Forces will provide flexible and timely mutual logistic support, based on their respective capabilities and availability.

The two governments will make appropriate use of the authorities and assets of central and local government agencies, as well as private sector assets, to provide support.

iv. Use of Facilities

The Government of Japan will provide, as needed, additional facilities in accordance with the Japan-U.S. Security Treaty and its related arrangements. The two governments will enhance cooperation in joint/shared use of facilities and areas.

v. Chemical, Biological, Radiological, and Nuclear Protection

The Government of Japan will maintain primary responsibility for emergency responses to chemical, biological, radiological, and nuclear (CBRN) incidents or attacks in Japan. The United States retains primary responsibility for maintaining and restoring the mission capability of the United States Armed Forces in Japan. At Japan's request, the United States will support Japan in CBRN incident or attack prevention and response-related activities in an effort to ensure the protection of Japan, as appropriate.

D. Actions in Response to an Armed Attack against a Country other than Japan
When Japan and the United States each decides to take actions involving the use of force in accordance with international law, including full respect for sovereignty, and with their respective Constitutions and laws to respond to an armed attack against the United States or a third country, and Japan has not come under armed attack, they will cooperate closely to respond to the armed attack and to deter further attacks. Bilateral responses will be coordinated through the whole-of-government Alliance Coordination Mechanism.

Japan and the United States will cooperate as appropriate with other countries taking action in response to the armed attack.

The Self-Defense Forces will conduct appropriate operations involving the use of force to respond to situations where an armed attack against a foreign country that is in a close relationship with Japan occurs and as a result, threatens Japan's survival and poses a clear danger to overturn fundamentally its people's right to life, liberty, and pursuit of happiness, to ensure Japan's survival, and to protect its people.

Examples of cooperative operations are outlined below:

1. Asset Protection
The Self-Defense Forces and the United States Armed Forces will cooperate in asset protection, as appropriate. Such cooperation will include, but not be limited to, protection of assets that are engaged in operations such as Noncombatant Evacuation Operations or Ballistic Missile Defense.
2. Search and Rescue
The Self-Defense Forces and the United States Armed Forces, in cooperation with relevant agencies, will cooperate and provide support in search and rescue operations, including combat search and rescue, as appropriate.
3. Maritime Operations
The Self-Defense Forces and the United States Armed Forces will cooperate in minesweeping, as appropriate, including to secure the safety of sea lines of communication.

The Self-Defense Forces and the United States Armed Forces, in cooperation with relevant agencies, will cooperate in escort operations to protect ships and vessels, as appropriate.

The Self-Defense Forces and the United States Armed Forces, in cooperation with relevant agencies, will cooperate in the interdiction of shipping activities providing support to adversaries involved in the armed attack, as appropriate.
4. Operations to Counter Ballistic Missile Attacks
The Self-Defense Forces and the United States Armed Forces will cooperate in intercepting ballistic missiles, as appropriate, in accordance with their respective capabilities. The two governments will exchange information to ensure early detection of ballistic missile launches.

5. Logistics Support
When operations require supplementing their respective logistics resources, the Self-Defense Forces and the United States Armed Forces will provide flexible and timely mutual logistic support, based on their respective capabilities and availability.

The two governments will make appropriate use of the authorities and assets of central and local government agencies, as well as private sector assets, to provide support.

E. Cooperation in Response to a Large-scale Disaster in Japan
When a large-scale disaster takes place in Japan, Japan will have primary responsibility for responding to the disaster. The Self-Defense Forces, in cooperation with relevant agencies, local governments, and private actors, will conduct disaster relief operations. Recognizing that immediate recovery from a large-scale disaster in Japan is essential for Japan's peace and security and that such a disaster could affect the activities of the United States Armed Forces in Japan, the United States, in accordance with its own criteria, will provide appropriate support for Japan's activities. Such support may include search and rescue, transportation, supply, medical services, incident awareness and assessment, and other specialized capabilities. The two governments will coordinate activities through the Alliance Coordination Mechanism, as appropriate.

To improve the effectiveness of the United States Armed Forces' cooperation in humanitarian assistance and disaster relief activities in Japan, the two governments will work together closely, including through information sharing. In addition, the United States Armed Forces also may participate in disaster-related drills, which will increase mutual understanding in responding to large-scale disasters.

V. Cooperation for Regional and Global Peace and Security

In an increasingly interconnected world, Japan and the United States will take a leading role in cooperation with partners to provide a foundation for peace, security, stability, and economic prosperity in the Asia-Pacific region and beyond. For well over half a century, both countries have worked together to deliver effective solutions to challenges in diverse regions of the world.

When each of the two governments decides to participate in international activities for the peace and security of the region and beyond, the two governments, including the Self-Defense Forces and the United States Armed Forces, will cooperate closely with each other and with partners, as appropriate, such as in the activities described below. This cooperation also will contribute to the peace and security of both countries.

A. Cooperation in International Activities
The two governments will participate in international activities, based on their own judgment. When working together, the Self-Defense Forces and the United States Armed Forces will cooperate to the maximum extent practicable.

The two governments may coordinate the activities through the Alliance Coordination Mechanism, as appropriate, and also will pursue trilateral and multilateral cooperation in these activities. The Self-Defense Forces and the United States

Armed Forces will share procedures and best practices, as appropriate, for smooth and effective cooperation. While the two governments will continue to cooperate on a broad array of issues that may not be explicitly included in the Guidelines, common areas for cooperation by the two governments in regional and international activities will include:

1. Peacekeeping Operations
When the two governments participate in peacekeeping operations authorized by the United Nations (UN) in accordance with the Charter of the United Nations, the two governments will cooperate closely, as appropriate, to maximize interoperability between the Self-Defense Forces and the United States Armed Forces. The two governments also may cooperate in providing logistic support for and protecting UN and other personnel who participate in the same mission, as appropriate.

2. International Humanitarian Assistance/Disaster Relief
When the two governments conduct international humanitarian assistance/ disaster relief (HA/DR) operations in response to requests from governments concerned or international organizations in the wake of large-scale humanitarian and natural disasters, the two governments will cooperate closely to provide mutual support, as appropriate, maximizing interoperability between participating Self-Defense Forces and United States Armed Forces. Examples of cooperative activities may include mutual logistic support and operational coordination, planning, and execution.

3. Maritime Security
When the two governments conduct activities for maritime security, the two governments will cooperate closely, as appropriate. Examples of cooperative activities may include efforts for: safe and secure sea lines of communication such as counter-piracy and minesweeping; non-proliferation of weapons of mass destruction; and counterterrorism activities.

4. Partner Capacity Building
Proactive cooperation with partners will contribute to maintaining and enhancing regional and international peace and security. The two governments will cooperate in capacity building activities, as appropriate, by making the best use of their capabilities and experience, with the objective of strengthening the capability of partners to respond to dynamic security challenges. Examples of cooperative activities may include maritime security, military medicine, defense institution building, and improved force readiness for HA/DR or peacekeeping operations.

5. Noncombatant Evacuation Operations
In circumstances when international action is required for the evacuation of noncombatants, the two governments will utilize, as appropriate, all possible avenues including diplomatic efforts to ensure the safety of noncombatants, including those who are Japanese or U.S. nationals.

6. Intelligence, Surveillance, and Reconnaissance
When the two governments participate in international activities, the Self-Defense Forces and the United States Armed Forces will cooperate in ISR activities, as appropriate, based on the respective capabilities and avail-

ability of their assets.

7. Training and Exercises

In order to enhance the effectiveness of international activities, the Self-Defense Forces and the United States Armed Forces will conduct and participate in joint training and exercises, as appropriate, to strengthen interoperability, sustainability, and readiness. The two governments also will continue to pursue opportunities to work with partners in training and exercises to contribute to enhancing interoperability with the Alliance and the development of common tactics, techniques, and procedures.

8. Logistic support

When participating in international activities, the two governments will cooperate to provide mutual logistic support. The Government of Japan will provide logistic support where appropriate, subject to Japanese laws and regulations.

B. Trilateral and Multilateral Cooperation

The two governments will promote and improve trilateral and multilateral security and defense cooperation. In particular, the two governments will reinforce efforts and seek additional opportunities to cooperate with regional and other partners, as well as international organizations. The two governments also will work together to strengthen regional and international institutions with a view to promoting cooperation based upon international law and standards.

VI. Space and Cyberspace Cooperation

A. Cooperation on Space

Recognizing the security aspects of the space domain, the two governments will maintain and strengthen their partnership to secure the responsible, peaceful, and safe use of space.

As part of such efforts, the two governments will ensure the resiliency of their space systems and enhance space situational awareness cooperation. The two governments will provide mutual support, as appropriate, to establish and improve capabilities and will share information about actions and events that might affect the safety and stability of the space domain and impede its use. The two governments also will share information to address emerging threats against space systems and will pursue opportunities for cooperation in maritime domain awareness and in space-related equipment and technology that will strengthen capabilities and resiliency of the space systems, including hosted payloads.

To accomplish their missions effectively and efficiently, the Self-Defense Forces and the United States Armed Forces will continue to cooperate and to contribute to whole-of-government efforts in utilizing space in such areas as: early-warning; ISR; positioning, navigation, and timing; space situational awareness; meteorological observation; command, control, and communications; and ensuring the resiliency of relevant space systems that are critical for mission assurance. In cases where their space systems are threatened, the Self-Defense Forces and the United States Armed Forces will cooperate, as appropriate, in mitigating risk and preventing damage. If damage occurs, they will cooperate, as appropriate, in reconstituting relevant capabilities.

B. Cooperation on Cyberspace

To help ensure the safe and stable use of cyberspace, the two governments will share information on threats and vulnerabilities in cyberspace in a timely and routine manner, as appropriate. The two governments also will share, as appropriate, information on the development of various capabilities in cyberspace, including the exchange of best practices on training and education. The two governments will cooperate to protect critical infrastructure and the services upon which the Self-Defense Forces and the United States Armed Forces depend to accomplish their missions, including through information sharing with the private sector, as appropriate.

The Self-Defense Forces and the United States Armed Forces will:
- maintain a posture to monitor their respective networks and systems;
- share expertise and conduct educational exchanges in cybersecurity;
- ensure resiliency of their respective networks and systems to achieve mission assurance;
- contribute to whole-of-government efforts to improve cybersecurity; and
- conduct bilateral exercises to ensure effective cooperation for cybersecurity in all situations from peacetime to contingencies.

In the event of cyber incidents against Japan, including those against critical infrastructure and services utilized by the Self-Defense Forces and the United States Armed Forces in Japan, Japan will have primary responsibility to respond, and based on close bilateral coordination, the United States will provide appropriate support to Japan. The two governments also will share relevant information expeditiously and appropriately. In the event of serious cyber incidents that affect the security of Japan, including those that take place when Japan is under an armed attack, the two governments will consult closely and take appropriate cooperative actions to respond.

VII. Bilateral Enterprise

The two governments will develop and enhance the following areas as a foundation of security and defense cooperation, in order to improve further the effectiveness of bilateral cooperation:

A. Defense Equipment and Technology Cooperation

In order to enhance interoperability and to promote efficient acquisition and maintenance, the two governments will:
- cooperate in joint research, development, production, and test and evaluation of equipment and in mutual provision of components of common equipment and services;
- strengthen the basis to repair and maintain common equipment for mutual efficiency and readiness;
- facilitate reciprocal defense procurement to enhance efficient acquisition, interoperability, and defense equipment and technology cooperation; and
- explore opportunities for cooperation with partners on defense equipment

and technology.

B. Intelligence Cooperation and Information Security
  • Recognizing that common situational awareness is essential, the two governments will enhance intelligence cooperation and information sharing at all levels, including the national strategic level.
  • In order to enable robust intelligence cooperation and information sharing, the two governments will continue to promote cooperation in strengthening policies, practices, and procedures related to the protection of classified information.
  • The two governments also will explore opportunities for cooperation with partners on information sharing.

C. Educational and Research Exchanges
Recognizing the importance of intellectual cooperation concerning security and defense, the two governments will deepen exchanges of members of relevant organizations and strengthen communication between each side's research and educational institutions. Such efforts will serve as the enduring foundation for security and defense officials to share their knowledge and reinforce cooperation.

VIII. Processes for Review

The SCC, assisted by an appropriate subordinate body, will regularly evaluate whether the Guidelines remain adequate in light of the evolving circumstances. The two governments will update the Guidelines in a timely and appropriate manner when changes in situations relevant to the Japan-U.S. Alliance relationship occur and if deemed necessary in view of the circumstances at that time.

Source: Ministry of Defense, "The Guidelines for Japan-U.S. Defense Cooperation." www.mod.go.jp/e/d_act/anpo/shishin_20150427e.html (accessed December 20, 2016).

Index

Sado Akihiro

Born in Fukuoka prefecture in 1958, Sado Akihiro graduated from the Faculty of Law, Gakushuin University in 1983 and the Graduate School of Social Sciences, Tokyo Metropolitan University in 1989 and earned his Ph.D. in political science at Gakushuin University. Presently, Sado is a professor at the School of Business and Public Policies of Chukyo University. His recent publications include: *Jieitai-shi: Boei seisaku no 70-nen* [History of the Japan Self-Defense Forces: 70 years of defense policy] (2015); *Jieitai-shi ron: Sei-kan-gun-min no 60-nen* [Historiography of the Japan Self-Defense Forces: 60 years of government-bureaucracy-military-civilian relations] (2015); *Okinawa gendai seijishi* [Contemporary political history of Okinawa] (2014); *Gendai Nippon seiji-shi (5): Kaikaku seiji no konmei* [Contemporary political history of Japan (5): Reform politics in a confusion] (2012); and *Sengo Nippon no boei to seiji* [National defense and politics in postwar Japan] (2003).

（英文版）戦後政治と自衛隊
The Self-Defense Forces and Postwar Politics in Japan

2017年3月27日　第1刷発行

著　者　佐道明広
訳　者　野田牧人
発行所　一般財団法人 出版文化産業振興財団
　　　　〒101-0051 東京都千代田区神田神保町3-12-3
　　　　電話　03-5211-7282（代）
　　　　ホームページ　http://www.jpic.or.jp/

印刷・製本所　大日本印刷株式会社